Applications of Nonlinear Dynamics to Developmental Process Modeling

Applications of Nonlinear Dynamics to Developmental Process Modeling

Edited by

Karl M. Newell
Pennsylvania State University

Peter C. M. Molenaar
University of Amsterdam
Pennsylvania State University

LEA LAWRENCE ERLBAUM ASSOCIATES, PUBLISHERS
1998   Mahwah, New Jersey   London

Lawrence Erlbaum Associates, Inc., Publishers
10 Industrial Avenue
Mahwah, New Jersey 07430

Library of Congress Cataloging-in-Publication Data

Applications of nonlinear dynamics to developmental process modeling /
edited by Karl M. Newell, Peter C. M. Molenaar.
  p.   cm.
Includes bibliographical references and indexes.
ISBN 0-8058-2115-5 (alk. paper).
1. Human growth—Mathematical models—Congresses. 2. Nonlinear
systems—Congresses. 3. Dynamics—Congresses. 4. Developmental
biology—Mathematical models—Congresses. 5. Cognition—
Mathematical models—Congresses. I. Newell, Karl M.
II. Molenaar, Peter C. M.
QP84.A65 1997
612.6′01′51—dc21   97-3672
                                                           CIP

Books published by Lawrence Erlbaum Associates are printed on acid-free paper,
and their bindings are chosen for strength and durability.

Printed in the United States of America
10 9 8 7 6 5 4 3 2 1

CONTENTS

PREFACE

This book is a product of a conference on dynamical systems and development held at University Park in October 1994. Penn State has a long and strong tradition in the study of development; there are many people currently on campus who have interest in the potential application of dynamical systems to development, an interest that ranges over a number of subdomains of development.

Our motivation for organizing the conference was driven to a large degree by the idea of bringing together people in various subdomains of development who were currently applying models of dynamical systems to their developmental data. There has been an explosion of interest in this field recently but the modeling of empirical work is lagging behind the claims of the potential of dynamical systems as a metaphor for development. This progression of theory leading data is a natural one, but it seemed a good time to take a harder look at the promise, progress, and problems of linking dynamical systems to developmental issues.

There appeared to be three major subdomain areas of development with ongoing use of the application of the techniques of nonlinear dynamics: cognition, physical growth and movement, and communication. Accordingly, we structured the conference and book around these three areas, plus a general methodological section as it pertained to nonlinear dynamics and development. Our major goal was to invite people who were actively modeling a particular developmental issue with the techniques of nonlinear dynamics. A subsidiary goal was to achieve diversity in the model applications of nonlinear dynamics, as well as breadth in the developmental phenomena being studied. These goals were achieved and the organization and content of the book reflect this.

One of the emergent advantages in the application of nonlinear dynamics to development is that it inherently provides a vehicle for the unification of ideas and thinking about the process of development, even across subdomains that are rarely brought together or seen to provide any prospect of the same. This is because the ideas of nonlinear dynamics are abstract and inherently concerned with time evolutionary processes, the hallmark of development. Thus, individuals within this orientation to development have common methodological ground, and this excitement about methods generalizes to the ideas per se about the dynamical processes of development.

It is our belief, however, that the future of dynamical systems as an approach to development will depend very much on the success of formally modeling developmental data from experiments. If the operational enterprise fails either to get off the ground in any significant way, or to sustain its momentum once obtained, it will soon die as a metaphor for development. The interactions at the conference and the products in this book confirm the promise of the metaphor and provide a rich array of examples of modeling work. It is clear, however, that the problems inherent in the successful application of nonlinear dynamics to development do not rest entirely on the appropriate technical use of dynamical models and equations, although this in itself holds difficulties, particularly for those not versed in the formalities of the approach. An integral part of the success of this approach is and will be the identification of relevant developmental control parameters to enter into model equations. Thus, the act of modeling forces a sharpening of thinking about developmental processes per se and points up the significance of linking theory to data through models.

ACKNOWLEDGMENTS

Gerald E. McClearn, then Dean of the College of Health and Human Development at Penn State, was very enthusiastic about the possibilities of this endeavor and provided significant financial support for the conference. Many individuals at University Park contributed to the organization of the conference, particularly members of the motor behavior group. A special thanks to Sue Eberly and Kelly Williams for their superb organizational skills and efforts on behalf of the conference and the resulting book.

—Karl M. Newell
—Peter C. M. Molenaar

1

INTRODUCTION:
MODELING DEVELOPMENT
AS DYNAMICAL SYSTEMS

Karl M. Newell
Pennsylvania State University

Peter C. M. Molenaar
University of Amsterdam
Pennsylvania State University

Over the last decade there has been growing interest in the application of dynamical systems to the study of development. Indeed, the explosion of the dynamical systems framework in the physical and biological sciences seems to have opened the door also to a new zeitgeist for studying development. This appeal to dynamical systems by developmentalists is natural, given the intuitive links between the established fundamental problems of development and the conceptual and operational scope of nonlinear dynamical systems. This promise of a new approach and framework within which to study development has led to some progress in recent years but also to a growing appreciation of the difficulty of fully examining and realizing the potential of the new metaphor.

Certain features of a dynamical approach to development have their roots at least as early as Gesell (1929, 1952), who claimed that growth is a patterning process that simultaneously organizes the forms of body, bones, and brain—and of behavior. Gesell did not have access to formal dynamical tools (although of course Poincaré's ground breaking insights were available), but he discussed the "field-like" neuromuscular and biochemical processes of development that organize as a result of concentration differences, gradients, and asymmetries, all concepts that have a remarkably contemporary ring to them in light of dynamical systems theory. Gesell championed a maturational genetic theory of the dynamical processes of development, a theoretical stance that is in sharp contrast to current perspectives on self-organization, development, and system dynamics (Thelen & Smith, 1994), and even current attempts to integrate nonlinear dynamics and developmental behavior genetics (Molenaar, Boosma, & Dolan, 1993).

A dynamical systems approach to development is also not entirely distinct from a number of other and more recent theoretical orientations to development (Aslin, 1993). This is perhaps not surprising, given the centrality of the concepts of stability and change to both theories of development and dynamical systems. However, the uniqueness of the dynamical systems approach for theories of development is its formal links to the concepts of self-organization and nonlinear dissipative systems. These latter concepts provide the background principles for change and stability in developing open systems that are striking different from cognitive representational accounts of development (see Kugler, Kelso, & Turvey, 1982) that still dominate the general theorizing in development. Thus, the appeal of dynamical systems for development does not rest simply on the introduction of new ways to describe the changes of development, but in addition, on the potential power of the related concepts to prescribe the dynamical processes that harness the organization of the system and its change over time.

ISSUES IN DEVELOPMENT AND DYNAMICAL SYSTEMS

There have been several recent accounts outlining the general promise of a dynamical systems approach to development (Smith & Thelen, 1993; Thelen & Smith, 1994; Van Geert, 1994), so that there is no need here to reiterate this promissory note in full. Suffice it to say that development is fundamentally concerned with the *stability* and *change* in behavior over the time course of the life span. The qualitative and quantitative change in the structure and function of individuals through the life span provides the time series to which the concepts and tools of nonlinear dynamical systems can be applied. The application of dynamical systems theory to development has been appealing because it seems to provide a way to characterize many of the basic phenomena of development, including change, stability, variability, and the emergence of new forms of structure and function.

The emergence of new qualitative states is a hallmark of development, whether these states be new movement forms not previously produced by an infant, the onset of speech or cognitive strategies that were not previously exhibited by a child, or behavioral transitions that are becoming increasingly apparent in the functioning of the elderly at the upper end of the age continuum. The central developmental concepts of emergent forms, stages, and the issue of whether development is continuous or discontinuous appear to represent phenomena that are prime candidates to be modeled as a nonlinear dynamical system where complex dynamical forms can be realized from relatively simple equations (Glass & Mackey, 1988; May, 1976). Moreover, the transitions between states may be a particularly critical point of entry to understanding the dynamics of the system and the nature of the control parameters that are driving the organism through the qualitative behavioral states of the life span (Kelso, Ding, & Schöner, 1993).

A major challenge for developmentalists is to identify the relevant developmental variables that are or may be acting as control variables in the channeling of the system dynamics over time. The determination of the relevant control variables of development is not a straightforward enterprise because the emergent forms of development are products of the coalescing of many constraints to action (Newell, 1986; Thelen, 1986), each of which has its own dynamic with its own time scale. Thus, the notion that small quantitative changes in one aspect of a system can lead to large-scale qualitative changes in its dynamic organization seems very relevant to a variety of issues of development, but it is also very difficult to examine operationally in the developing organism. Indeed, at this point in time, there appear to be no examples in the developmental literature that have successfully modeled (formally) the emergence of qualitative states through the influence of developmentally relevant control variables.

A number of dynamic models of developmental phenomena encompass the dual and complementary processes of cooperation and competition as the building blocks of both the stability of emergent forms and the transitions of state over time. A common example of these complementary sources of dynamic tension is to be found in the predator–prey models (May, 1976). Again, a key challenge for developmentalists is the identification of the relevant developmental variables that may be acting in cooperation and those that may be acting in competition in the abstract dynamical workspace. Thus, a general point that emerges is that the principles of dynamical systems are principles of the dynamic relations between variables, no matter what the particulars of the context, substrate, or variables. The challenge for developmentalists, then, is the identification and examination of the relevant developmental variables in a parsimonious dynamical model. To date, there has been limited effort and hence limited success in identifying these possible developmental processes and the linking of them formally to equations that represent the dynamics.

The dual and complementary processes of competition and cooperation are also at the heart of changes in the dynamics of behavior that are usually associated with the concept of learning. This raises the question of the uniqueness of the concepts of development and learning from a dynamical systems standpoint, given that both are concerned with stability and change over time. Consistent with the theme already outlined, the answer to this question is more likely to be found in the unraveling of the variables that channel the dynamics over time than in the fundamental nature of the dynamical relations or processes themselves. The same argument can be made in the contrast of structural and functional processes of development that may well be driven by similar dynamical principles, even if the time scales of change are fundamentally different (Kugler et al., 1982). In other words, the principles of system dynamics are likely to be common to learning and the many aspects of development, even if the equation variables isolated with each concept are different. The examination of these concepts experimentally in a dynamical framework requires sufficient longitudinal data collection to create an adequate time series to examine the relevant dynamical processes.

The concepts of nonlinear dynamics and chaos theory have also provided the stimulus to consider the variability of features of development not merely as noise in the system but as a reflection of nonlinear deterministic processes. This perspective generates questions about the roles of deterministic and stochastic processes in development. The changing levels of variability can be viewed as an index of the changing degree of stability or instability of developmental processes. Furthermore, the structure of the variability of the output of a system may also not be strictly random, as assumed in many white Gaussian noise models of behavior, but may vary with a variety of features of system organization. Indeed, the structure of the variability of the output may provide an indication of the degrees of freedom being regulated, a feature that has interesting implications for models of development (Bernstein, 1967; Lipsitz & Goldberger, 1992), and the change in adaptation and complexity over the life span.

There has been some interest in the determination of whether certain developmental phenomena are reflections of chaotic systems. This interest follows the trends in other areas of application, such as electroencephalography (EEG) and electrocardiography (EKG), and arises perhaps in part to the large amount of publicity that has been given to the concept of chaos (Gleick, 1987). Although there have been some isolated claims of the determination of chaotic systems in development (e.g., Robertson & Bacher, 1995), it is our view that such claims are premature, as the relevant critical tests do not seem to have been performed with any degree of rigor and vigor. The notion of small changes in the initial conditions being critical in chaotic systems, however, holds intuitive appeal as a contributing factor to the change in the emergent forms of development.

CHALLENGES TO MODELING DEVELOPMENT

The metaphors of self-organization and dynamical systems are global ones, and there is not one unified perspective to which developmentalists can turn. Indeed, there are a number of related approaches that have emerged, including nonequilibrium thermodynamics (Nicolis & Prigogine, 1977), castastrophe theory (Thom, 1975), synergetics (Haken, 1983), neural networks (Grossberg, 1982), and chaos theory (Ott, 1993). The breadth and incompatibility of certain elements of these related concepts can make it difficult for the potential user to apply dynamical systems to the developmental domain of interest. In short, there is not one approach to dynamical systems and development. At this stage of the application of dynamical systems to development this lack of coherence should not be viewed as a serious problem, for indeed, the richness of the approaches may well hold some advantages. A difficulty, however, is that it is requires considerable background in the various concepts to distill what that advantage may be, and to isolate a tractable operational dynamical approach to a theoretical issue of development.

There are also a number of other more local methodological difficulties that have arisen in the application of dynamical systems to development. The processes of change over the life span, whether interpreted as either learning or development, inevitably imply nonstationarity of the behavioral phenomena. In short, and by definition, both learning and development are nonstationary. The nonstationarity of development can occur over a wide range of time scales from cycles of years to months, weeks, days, and even within a few minutes or seconds of a single trial of a given action. Nonstationarity is, therefore, both a phenomenon to be modeled in equations of change and a source of an operational problem, for many dynamical and statistical models assume implicitly or explicitly stationarity. The degree to which nonstationarity interferes with the assumptions and veracity of models of nonlinear dynamics is an area that is not well developed or understood.

Another problem faced by developmentalists is that the experimental data collected may not meet strictly the assumptions of the models of nonlinear dynamics. The impact of relatively short, noisy data sets with the additional likelihood of missing data can present severe challenges to the assumptions of existing dynamical models. It seems likely that there will be continued efforts to unravel the impact of these departures from the mathematical assumptions of different dynamical theorems, but that the tension will continue to exist between theory and applications of dynamical systems, as it has in the field of statistics. A key factor here will be the aspirations of the scientist in terms of whether discrimination between groups or conditions is the major motive or whether it is the veridical modeling of the system. The former experimental approach can probably function effectively with the limits of relative estimates of features of system dynamics, but in theory development there is a greater need for the veridical determination of absolute values.

A final limitation to current efforts in dynamical systems and development is that even where model equations have been applied to developmental data, the application has been indirect. That is, the model is used more as a metaphor and guide to the interpretation of data trends, rather than the data being fitted directly to the equation for parameter estimation and determination of residuals. This is an issue that is taken up more fully by Molenaar and Raymakers in the closing chapter. The important point to note is that there can be significant differences in the interpretation of the fit of the model between direct and indirect approaches to modeling.

Because the degree of modeling work that has been undertaken with developmental issues has been very limited, the full impact of some of these potential problems to the application of dynamical systems to development is difficult to assess. As we remarked earlier, the metaphor of dynamical systems for development has outstripped the actual formal use of the approach in experimental work (Van der Maas, 1996). One goal of the conference was to bring together people who were actually modeling various types of developmental data to discuss progress and common problems.

ABOUT THE BOOK

The book is structured in four parts. The first three parts reflect the content domains of development that have given most theoretical and empirical attention to the potential applications of dynamical systems. These subareas of development are physical growth and movement, cognition, and communication. The fourth and final section of the book emphasizes two particular methodological issues that hold important implications for the modeling of developmental phenomena with dynamical systems techniques.

It seems fitting that the opening chapter for a book on development is on the dynamics of physical growth in infants. It has long been established that there is rapid change in many of the parameters of physical growth during infancy, and the traditional and still prevailing growth models for these phenomena are all continuous (see, e.g., Tanner, 1990). Lampl's recent work challenged these long-held assumptions of continuity by showing through careful longitudinal data collection that the length changes in infants are in fact discontinuous or saltatory. In the chapter presented here, Lampl and Johnson outline a nonlinear modeling approach to the discontinuous growth data that is also consistent with current pulsatile models of hormone development.

The area of motor development is the subarea of development in which researchers have most vigorously pursued a dynamical systems approach. There are several reasons for this emphasis beyond the more general points outlined already in the promise of dynamical systems and development. First, the introduction of the metaphor of self-organization to the theory of movement coordination and control provided a natural impetus to seek operational methods that were compatible with the concept (Kugler, Kelso, & Turvey, 1980; Kugler et al., 1982; Kugler, 1986). Second, the movement domain provides readily available measures of space–time observables that intuitively lend themselves to a dynamical systems approach. These conceptual and operational forces have coalesced to make the dynamical systems approach to motor development the prevailing theory of the day (see *Child Development*, 1993; Thelen, Kelso, & Fogel, 1987; Thelen & Smith, 1994). The extant empirical and modeling work has been largely descriptive to date (Turvey & Fitzpatrick, 1994; Van der Maas, 1996), however, leaving the potential of the dynamical systems approach in this domain, as of others in development, still a promissory note.

The two motor development chapters in this book examine different theoretical issues of the development of movement coordination and control and emphasize different aspects and tools of nonlinear dynamics in the empirical and modeling work. Fitzpatrick investigates the development of interlimb coordination in 4-, 5-, and 7-year-old children clapping using the Haken, Kelso, and Bunz (1985) model and its extensions. She shows that a stable oscillatory dynamic was not exhibited in clapping until 7 years of age and that parameters of the model are sensitive to age change and environmental manipulations, such as adding mass to the limbs. Newell examines the structure of variability in postural control over a range of different age groups. Understanding the nature of variability provides some clues as to the type of dynamic model that is yielding the observed movement dynamics. The changing structure of movement variability with skill and age level changes also ties in nicely with the degrees of freedom problem in the learning and development of movement coordination and control (Bernstein, 1967). Furthermore, Lipsitz and Goldberger (1992) proposed that aging is associated with the "loss of complexity."

The many facets of cognitive development have long been characterized by the qualitative and quantitative changes that occur with development over the life span. For example, the notion of stages is central in many approaches to cognitive development and development in general (e.g., Piaget, 1929). One attraction of pursuing a dynamical systems approach to development is that it provides the promise of describing and predicting the observed qualitative and quantitative changes over time. Several investigators in cognitive development have begun to investigate this promise (Van Geert, 1991; Van der Maas & Molenaar, 1992; Thelen & Smith, 1994).

The chapter by Thatcher examines linkages between qualitative changes in neural events and cognitive performance in children. A particular interest is the qualitative and in some cases cyclical change in synaptic organization that occurs over the early years of life. Thatcher models these phenomena at different levels of analysis using a predator–prey model of human cerebral development. These types of predator–prey models have been shown to have wide application in biological systems (May, 1976) and rest on understanding the competitive coupling between parameters of the model.

Van Geert develops further his growth modeling approach to cognitive development (Van Geert, 1991, 1994) using language acquisition as the phenomena of focus. He shows that empirical growth phenomena such as the growth of linguistic variables (e.g., words, sentences) in spontaneous speech recordings of children can be modeled with the aid of a connected growers model. The model rests on the cooperation and competition of particular linguistic variables and their changing relations over time. This approach is consistent with the perspective that relatively simple equations can handle a considerable degree of the variance in the development of cognitive phenomena.

Finally, in this cognitive section, Van der Maas examines more directly qualitative changes (transitions) in cognitive development using the tools of catastrophe theory. Catastrophe theory provides explicit dynamic criteria for determining transitions of state (Thom, 1975), a feature that heretofore has been approached only intuitively or informally in much of the study of cognitive development. Van der Maas proposes that the cognitive variable of strategy can be linked to the dynamical concept of attractors.

The third section of the book has contributions on different aspects of communication and development. There are many facets of communication that could be modeled as a dynamical system, including speech production of an individual, verbal and nonverbal communication among people, and the coordination of individuals engaged in a common action. There has probably been less direct application of dynamical systems in these areas than in those of cognitive and movement development.

The chapter by Been reports on his studies of a nonlinear dynamic model of neural networks and its application to cognitive tasks in normal and abnormal speech development. He selected the parieto-occipital region of the brain for study because it can be modeled at the neural network level and it shows clear maturational changes. The model has linear equations that capture the excitatory and inhibitory neurons with a coupling term that is nonlinear. The nature of the input term varies according to the nature of the task being studied, and the processes of learning and development can be incorporated by varying the parameter that reflects the number of synaptic relays. The model has the growth spurts in the maturation cycle of cortical regions as an indicator of an increasing eigen frequency, due to an increase in the number of intracortical synaptic relays. The central concept of eigen frequency in Been's modeling affords differential predictions concerning the execution of different tasks in relation to learning and development.

Newtson tackles the very difficult problem of considering the verbal communication between people as a dynamical system. A key element in this approach is adopting the appropriate unit of analysis for examining ongoing behavior as a dynamical system. Newtson discusses several key criteria that need to be considered in determining these criteria and subsequently the potential of several model systems of interaction and relationships are explored.

Schmidt applies the Haken et al. model (1985), which has been used so successfully in interlimb coordination, to the issue of interperson coordination and communication. His experimental work shows that the same model fits well the dynamics arising in between-person limb coordination. The interesting theoretical point to emerge from this experimental work is that information must be driving the change of coordinative relations between people because, unlike the within-person interlimb coordination protocol, there is no direct physical link present between the nervous systems of the independent oscillators. Schmidt outlines how this approach can be generalized to a range of developmental interactions, with a focus on child–parent communication.

The full impact of a dynamical systems approach to development will only be understood with the further application of formal models (equations) to empirical data. To date, it would be fair to say that the actual modeling of developmental data has lagged behind the invocation of dynamical systems as a guiding theoretical metaphor. Part of the challenge for scholars is the selection and use of appropriate techniques of nonlinear dynamics to developmental phenomena. The two chapters on methodological issues each pick up on an important aspect to modeling developmental phenomena with nonlinear dynamics—approaches that also hold importance to modeling beyond the developmental domain.

A considerable number of developmental phenomena are linked to the notion of the change in complexity that accompanies development (Lipsitz & Goldberger, 1992). A major problem operationally has been the measurement of complexity in the developmental subdomain at hand. Pincus introduced the metric ApEn, which quantifies the continuum from perfectly orderly to completely random in a time series. A major benefit of this metric is that it can be used on relatively short and noisy data sets. Pincus shows the conceptual development of the ApEn measure together with examples of its use in discriminating between conditions in biological time-series.

Finally, Molenaar and Raumakers propose that essentially all of the modeling of nonlinear dynamical processes in development has been indirect to date. That is, even though a number of papers in dynamical systems and development have a model equation to guide the analysis of the data in the link of experiment to theory, there is actually no direct fit of the data to the model. The direct fit of data to model is important because most developmental time series are noisy, and estimates of the emergence of residuals over time can be very revealing about the veracity of the model. Molenaar and Raymakers use a recursive estimator (a version of an extended Kalman filter) for nonlinear dynamical models to fit the data from the model of phase transitions in human interlimb coordination (Schöner, Haken, & Kelso, 1986) and a simple version of Van Geert's nonlinear growth model. In short, Molenaar and Raymakers show the important difference between having a model of the data and the *modeling* of the data.

CONCLUDING COMMENTS

The chapters presented in the content areas of physical growth and move-ment, cognition, and communcation show that a range of nonlinear models have been applied to a range of developmental phenomena. These are early days in this zeitgeist of modeling development as dynamical systems, and therefore it is too soon to arrive at any firm conclusions as to the potential success of the venture. It seems appropriate to close with the insight of Robertson, Cohen, and Mayer-Kress (1993, p. 148), who argued that the real test is not whether dynamic systems theory can account for the phenomena we study, but whether it yields any new insights, integrates previously unrelated empirical facts, or in some other way leads to deeper under-standing of those phenomena.

REFERENCES

Aslin, R. N. (1993). The strange attractiveness of dynamic systems to development. In L. B. Smith & E. Thelen (Eds.), *A dynamic systems approach to development: Applications* (pp. 385–400). Cambridge, MA: MIT Press.

Bernstein, N. (1967). *The co-ordination and regulation of movements*. Oxford: Pergamon Press.

Child Development. (1993). *64*(4). Special issue.

Gesell, A. (1929). Maturation and infant behavior pattern. *Psychological Review, 36*, 307–319.

Gesell, A. (1952). *Infant development.* Westport, CT: Greenwood.

Glass, L., & Mackey, M. C. (1988). *From clocks to chaos: The rhythms of life.* Princeton, NJ: Princeton University Press.

Gleick, J. (1987). *Chaos: Making a new science.* New York: Viking.

Grossberg, S. (1982). *Studies of mind and brain: Neural principles of learning, perception, develop-ment, cognition and motor control.* Dordrecht: Reidel.

Haken, H. (1983). *Advanced synergetics.* Berlin: Springer-Verlag.

Haken, H., Kelso, J. A. S., & Bunz, H. (1985). A theretical model of phase transitions in human hand movements. *Biological Cybernetics, 51*, 347–356.

Kelso, J. A. S., Ding, M., & Schöner, G. (1993). Dynamic pattern formation: A primer. In L. B. Smith & E. Thelen (Eds.), *A dynamic systems approach to development: Applications* (pp. 13–50). Cambridge, MA: MIT Press.

Kugler, P. N. (1986). A morphological perspective on the origin and evolution of movement patterns. In M. G. Wade & H. T. A. Whiting (Eds.), *Motor development in children: Aspects of coordination and control* (pp. 459–525). Dordrecht: Martinus Nijhoff.

Kugler, P. N., Kelso, J. A. S., & Turvey, M. T. (1980). On the concept of coordinative structures as dissipative structures: 1. Theoretical lines of convergence. In G. E. Stelmach & J. Requin (Eds.), *Tutorials in motor behavior* (pp. 3–70). Amsterdam: North-Holland.

Kugler, P. N., Kelso, J. A. S., & Turvey, M. T. (1982). On the control and co-ordination of naturally developing systems. In J. A. S. Kelso & J. E. Clark (Eds.), *The development of movement control and coordination* (pp. 1–78). New York: Wiley.

Lipsitz, L. A., & Goldberger, A. L. (1992). Loss of "complexity" and aging: Potential applications of fractals and chaos theory to senescence. *Journal of the American Medical Association, 267*, 1806–1809.

May, R. M. (1976). Simple mathematical models with very complicated dynamics. *Nature, 261*, 459–467.

Molenaar, P. C. M., Boosma, D. I., & Dolan, C. V. (1993). A third source of developmental differences. *Behavior Genetics, 23*, 519–524.

Newell, K. M. (1986). Constraints on the development of coordination. In M. G. Wade & H. T. A. Whiting (Eds.), *Motor development in children: Aspects of coordination and control* (pp. 341–360). Dordrecht: Martinus Nijhoff.

Nicolis, G., & Prigogine, I. (1977). *Self-organization in nonequilibrium systems: From dissipative structures to order through fluctuations.* New York: Wiley.

Ott, E. (1993). *Chaos in dynamical systems.* Cambridge: Cambridge University Press.

Piaget, J. (1929). *The child's conception of the world.* New York: Harcourt.

Robertson, S. S., & Bacher, L. F. (1995). Oscillation and chaos in fetal motor activity. In J.-P. Lecanuet, W. P. Fifer, N. A. Krasnegor, & W. P. Smotherman (Eds.), *Fetal development: A psychobiological perspective* (pp. 169–190). Hillsdale, NJ: Lawrence Erlbaum Associates.

Robertson, S. S., Cohen, A. H., & Mayer-Kress, G. (1993). Behavioral chaos: Beyond the metaphor. In L. B. Smith & E. Thelen (Eds.), *A dynamic systems approach to development: Applications* (pp. 119–150). Cambridge, MA: MIT Press.

Schöner, G., Haken, H., & Kelso, J. A. S. (1986). A stochastic theory of phase transitions in human hand movement. *Biological Cybernetics, 53*, 247–257.

Smith, L. B., & Thelen, E. (Eds.). (1993). *A dynamic systsms approach to development: Applications.* Cambridge, MA: MIT Press.

Tanner, J. M. (1990). *Fetus into man: Physical growth from conception to maturity.* Cambridge, MA: Harvard University Press.

Thelen, E. (1986). Development of coordinated movement: Implications for early human development. In M. G. Wade & H. T. A. Whiting (Eds.), *Motor development in children: Aspects of coordination and control* (pp. 107–124). Dordrecht: Martinus Nijhoff.

Thelen, E., & Smith, L. B. (1994). *A dynamic systems approach to the development of cognition and action.* Cambridge, MA: MIT Press.

Thelen, E., Kelso, J. A. S., & Fogel, A. (1987). Self-organizing systems and infant motor development. *Developmental Review, 7*, 39–65.

Thom, R. (1975). *Structural stability and morphogenesis.* Reading: Benjamin.

Turvey, M. T., & Fitzpatrick, P. (1994). Commentary: Development of perception-action systems and general principles of pattern formation. *Child Development, 64*, 1175–1190.

Van der Maas, H. L. J. (1996). Beyond the metaphor? *Cognitive Development, 10*, 621–642.

Van der Maas, H. L. J., & Molenaar, P. C. M. (1992). Stagewise cognitive development: An application of catastrophe theory. *Psychological Review, 99*, 395–417.

Van Geert, P. (1991). A dynamic systems model of cognitive and language growth. *Psychological Review, 98*, 3–53.

Van Geert, P. (1994). *Dynamic systems of development: Change between complexity and chaos.* London: Harvester Wheatsheaf.

Waddington, C. H. (1957). *The strategy of the genes: A discussion of some aspects of theoretical biology.* London: Allen & Unwin.

PHYSICAL GROWTH AND MOTOR DEVELOPMENT

2

NORMAL HUMAN GROWTH AS SALTATORY: ADAPTATION THROUGH IRREGULARITY

Michelle Lampl
Emory University

Michael L. Johnson
University of Virginia Health Sciences Center

The biological process that takes a single cell to adult form takes some 20 years in modern humans. It is a process characterized by remarkable individual variability in the pace at which it proceeds: The acquisition of adult size, or *growth*, and the acquisition of adult-like characteristics, or *maturation*, occur by species-specific patterns that have wide potential ranges of variability, depending on both genetics and environmental context (Eveleth & Tanner, 1976, 1990).

In spite of many reports of oscillations in children's growth patterns from data collected at the turn of the century, it has been the scientific view for most of the present century that children grow slowly and continuously each day in the absence of environmental insult or pathology. These views derive from a number of international longitudinal studies that have provided data taken on individuals at annual or biannual intervals, intervals suggested for protocols to eliminate the fluctuations observed during shorter time periods (Marshall, 1971). Analyses of these data most commonly employ descriptive statistics and consist of graphic representations of percentile distributions of children by chronological age. These smoothly rising percentile distribution curves serve quite effectively as reference standards for clinicians to assess clinical normality of the size of individual children in the context of a sample of children with similar genetic and environmental backgrounds.

Many pediatricians and health care workers have been trained to think of an individual child's growth process in terms of the pattern that unfolds as discrete measurements are taken and plotted on these percentile growth curves during routine well-child visits. Biannual measurements describe an individual's growth as a relatively smooth curve after an initial adjustment period during infancy, as infants recover from *in utero* growth, a time when an interplay between infant and maternal variables controls growth patterns (Smith et al., 1976). Beyond infancy, it was proposed that there is a target-seeking biological function that sets each individual onto a trajectory of growth along a smooth percentile channel that is followed until adolescence (Tanner, 1986).

Growth charts of velocity by age have been devised to represent the rate at which growth occurs, as this is a variable more representative of the underlying growth process itself. The human growth curve is said to be characterized by three sequential developmental phases: (a) infancy, a period of rapid growth lasting from birth until approximately 3 years of age during which the rate of growth is continuously decreasing, (b) childhood, a time of relatively constant growth rate lasting until adolescence, and (c) adolescence, when the pubertal growth spurt commences with a surge in growth rate and subsequent decline associated with the acquisition of adult morphology.

Certainly, these descriptions represent the broad outlines of human growth. However, it is now recognized that growth curves do not represent the biological process of growth itself, which is characterized by nonlinearities that were both obscured by traditional data acquisition protocols and formally eliminated by traditional mathematical modeling procedures (Togo & Togo, 1982). When longitudinal measurements are taken with care for measurement accuracy and precision at high-frequency intervals (e.g., daily), and analytic methods designed to identify noise from signal are applied to these data, it is clear that growth itself is neither a smooth nor a continuous process. Instead, human growth as measured by traditional auxological methods is a pulsatile biological process.

Measurements taken at daily to weekly intervals illustrate that growth in body dimensions occurs as rapid bursts in increments that can be reliably documented. These bursts in growth are separated by times of no measurable growth and thus identify a pattern of pulsatility as the basic process of human growth. In 1992, we termed this pattern of discontinuous growth by bursts *saltatory growth* (Lampl, Veldhuis, & Johnson, 1992). Saltatory growth is the normal pattern of human growth throughout development: from fetal life until the end of adolescence. The acquisition of adult size and dimensions is achieved in humans by distinct incremental pulses that punctuate a stable growth-free background during which most of development occurs.

SALTATORY GROWTH:
A DEVELOPMENTAL PERSPECTIVE

Beginning in fetal life, growth pulses punctuate periods during which no change in dimensions are documented by serial ultrasound assessments of long bones, the skull, and abdominal dimensions during measurements taken less than 1 week apart. The durations of the stasis intervals during which no growth occurs are variable and, in general, increase with gestational age with up to 25 days of no detectable body growth late in gestation (Lampl, Jeanty, & Johnson, 1997; Bernstein, Blake, & Badger, 1995).

Postnatal growth during infancy continues in this pulsatile pattern. Our original postnatal studies of infants aged between 2 days and 21 months documented that growth in total body length, as assessed by traditional techniques of maximal body length measurement, occurs during episodic pulses of between 0.5 and 1.6 cm during 24-hr measurement intervals. As has been reported, these pulses significantly exceed errors of measurement and are separated by 2 to 63 days of no detectable growth in normal healthy infants (Lampl, 1993; Lampl et al., 1992).

Total body height assessed in childhood and adolescence by the careful application of traditional methods documents the same saltatory pattern, with growth pulses ranging from 0.5 to 1.5 cm in 24 hr, separated by variable intervals of no growth ranging between 3 and 100 days in duration (Lampl & Johnson, 1993). Significant differences in pulse frequency are notable in these data with age, observations that correlate with the well-known differences in annual growth rates with age. For all of these individuals, normal annual rates of growth are accrued during discrete and relatively rare growth pulses.

A process of saltatory pulsations in growth have been sought in studies aiming to measure growth in individual body parts. These studies were initiated in the past decade following the renewed appreciation that non-linearities characterized the growth charts of some children. It was assumed that technology aiming to measure discrete body parts might allow the documentation of nonlinear growth patterns better than traditional total body measurements. This view reflected long-held notions that growth occurs daily in such minute increments that frequent measurements by traditional techniques are necessarily uninformative because error is indistinguishable from true incremental growth. This viewpoint is based on the assumption that growth charts are accurate reflections of the growth process, whereby children grow statistically insignificant increments each day in view of the ±2 mm traditional anthropometric measurement error (Fomon & Nelson, 1005).

We have shown that this view is erroneous: When time-intensive traditional anthropometric measurements are taken on children with attention to accuracy, the gold standard of documentable incremental growth, 90% of the measurement error (Meredith, 1955), is actually accrued during time intervals as short as 24 hr and these traditional techniques, carefully employed, can well capture growth increments as they occur.

Nevertheless, the development of alternative technology for the assessment of growth proceeded and measurements of the lower leg by a device known as the knemometer was designed to measure what has come to be called *short-term growth* (Valk et al., 1983; Michaelsen, Skov, Badsberg, & Jorgensen, 1991). These instruments were designed to measure with micrometer accuracy. However, the application of this technology to human soft tissue by a method based on pressure measurements from the heel to the flexed knee results in variability within a day that is nearly as great as lower leg pulsatile growth rates based on ultrasound measurements. Thus, while some observers have reported "mini growth spurts" in lower leg growth increments during childhood (Hermanussen, Geiger-Benoit, Burmeister, & Sippell, 1988) as well as leg length pulses during infancy (Gibson, Pearse, & Wales, 1994), other data sets are not so clear in their delineation of underlying growth patterns. The considerable noise component in the measurements may prevent knemometry from attaining the goals as the presumptive technique of choice for following short-term growth.

It is notable that the phrases *short-term growth* and *mini growth spurt* now often found in the literature reflect the unexpected nature of the initial observations of pulses in time-intensive growth data by contrast with the traditional annualized growth curve representations of how children grow. However, it must be stated that there is no short-term versus long-term version of the basic human growth process: It is only that our perceptions of what the process looks like are altered based on the window of time through which we assess it. Growth, as a process, is a discrete, time-constrained pulsatile process, not only in the recent human data, but also found in data from other species (e.g., Roush, Barbato, & Cravener, 1994), which help to clarify the temporal nature of the process. Notably, measurements taken every 3 hours in a recent study of the rat limb identify a saltation and stasis process: Significant growth is documented during only one 3-hour interval during the 24-hour day in this sample (Hermanussen, de los Angeles Rol de Lama, Burmeister, & Fernandez-Tresguerres, 1995). Clearly, the pulsatile nature of the process would have been missed if only daily measurements had been taken, and growth would have appeared to be the linear trend which it is when assessed infrequently (e.g., Oerter Klein, Munson, Bacher, Cutler, & Baron, 1994).

Taken together, the time-intensive growth data support the hypothesis of a saltatory process of sporadic, time-constrained events of growth. These observations lead to two important questions:

1. What determines the timing of growth episodes?
2. What controls concerted body growth?

Our understanding of the actual amount of time involved in a single discrete growth pulse is hampered by the limitations of when we choose to take measurements. Although much more descriptive work is still necessary, the most intensive studies suggest that growth events occur within a 24-hr time frame and thus involve highly controlled cellular activity.

What determines when these growth pulses will occur has yet to be identified, because the genetic, hormonal, and cell regulatory mechanisms to explain the pulsatile patterns of normal growth are currently unknown. However, a pattern of saltation and stasis reflects well-documented normal cell cycle controls (e.g., Sherr, 1993) at the organismic level. The interface between genetics, environment, and local cell mechanisms has been assumed to be hormonal signals. A recent study documenting previously unrecognized infradian irregularities in growth hormone patterns (Thalange et al., 1995) presented an example of an endocrine growth hormone signal that is on the same order of time as the observed saltations in growth. These observations of episodic short-term rhythms in growth hormone secretory patterns provide experimental evidence for an endocrinological connection for the observed saltatory growth patterns and support the importance of further studies employing innovative, time-intensive protocols for data collection and model-independent analytic methods. Such research may be most informative in elucidating previously unsuspected endocrine mechanisms (Hartman et al., 1994; Prank, Harms, Brabant, & Hesch, 1995). Indeed, the recent expansion of our understanding of morphogenesis in general may be most important in better understanding the mechanisms responsible for patterns of human growth.

ANALYSIS OF NONLINEAR PROCESSES IN HUMAN GROWTH

The analysis of the nonlinearities present in time-intensive growth data has been problematic as there was no traditional analytical protocols for such data prior to the studies just noted. Thus, we have been occupied by the process of developing methodological approaches appropriate for the questions these data raise. In our own studies, initial visual inspection suggested that the data may be a stepwise function and that the central tendency might not be best captured by a simple linear or nonlinear continuous function, the traditional descriptors of longitudinal human growth data (Fig. 2.1). A critical feature for such an investigation was to identify a mathematical descriptor that could accommodate the inherent statistical considerations of serial growth data while at the same time providing a statistical assessment of any pulsatility present in these data.

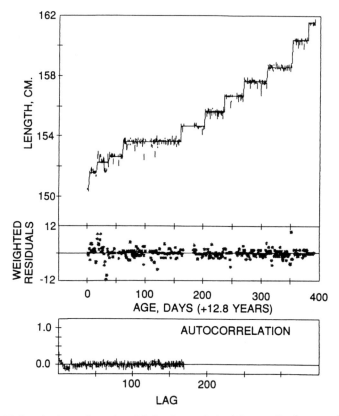

FIG. 2.1. Analysis of a series of daily observations of the growth of a normal healthy adolescent male (Lampl & Johnson, 1993) by the saltatory model. Upper panel: Experimental data with measurement uncertainties. The solid line is the least-squares fit of the data identifying 12 significant increments at the $p < .05$ level (fitted variance of 4.9). Middle panel: Weighted residuals of the fit. Lower panel: Autocorrelation function of the weighted residuals. This figure was first published in, Analysis of serial growth data, M. L. Johnson, *American Journal of Human Biology*, Vol. 5, Copyright © 1993, M. L. Johnson. Reprinted by permission of John Wiley & Sons, Inc.

Analysis of longitudinal growth data requires methods designed to model dependent, serially autocorrelated data characterized by an increasing trend. The data points themselves are also characterized by the presence of error deriving from measurement equipment, observer error, subject placement, and physiological variation. Thus, any method used to investigate the presence of statistically significant nonlinear patterns in such data must be designed to accommodate the assessment of noise from signal and must be robust to dependent, potentially non-Gaussian data.

Similar requirements for analytic models have confronted the identification of pulsatile hormonal patterns during the past decade as endocrinologists attempt to describe endogenous pulsatile patterns in the presence of noise including assay error (e.g., Veldhuis & Johnson, 1992). Methods developed for the investigation of endocrinological data are the bases of the saltatory model used here for pulse identification in serial growth data. In the presence of nontrivial noise, pulse analysis involves two steps: (a) the identification and separation of noise from the biological time series, and (b) the evaluation of the resulting time series. Thus, traditional pulse identification algorithms identify pulse occurrence and amplitude within a statistical significance set by the analyst. We have employed such a method for the analysis of the time-intensive serial growth data.

The Saltatory Model

In the analysis of serial growth data to identify the biological process of growth, it is preferable to analyze the original series of individuals' raw growth data. Repeated measures at each observation time are desirable in order to capture errors of replicate measurement. This approach contrasts with the analysis of increments, or differenced data, often the data employed in analyses in lieu of the raw data themselves. If the goal of analysis is to understand the underlying biological process, it is important to use a mathematical descriptor that makes no assumptions regarding the underlying temporal structure of the process. This provides the possibility for further hypotheses regarding the underlying growth process itself.

Our first approach to the analysis of growth data from this perspective has been to define a procedure that answers the question, "If intervals of saltations and stasis occur in a data series, where are they?" The saltatory analytic procedure is described in detail elsewhere (Johnson, 1993; Johnson & Lampl, 1995); it is a descriptor that models the original individual serial growth data as a series of discrete, intermittent pulses. The model makes the assumption that growth occurs as a series of distinct positive growth events separated by intervals of stasis. No temporal assumptions regarding the timing of pulses are made. This procedure is one of a number of mathematical descriptors of the data series, and the goodness-of-fit of this model can be judged in a relative sense by a statistical comparison of the fit of other models. Thus, we compare the results of the saltatory description with previously published mathematical descriptors of growth.

As an example of our quantitative analyses, each individual's serial growth data were initially fitted by three methods.

1. *Model-free derivative method.* As a preliminary model-independent method of examining the data, we calculated the growth rate as a function of time. This was performed by weighted linear least squares (WLS) fitting a sliding 1-week window of data to a quadratic equation. The confidence

intervals of the estimated coefficients of the quadratic equation were determined by standard linear least-squares methods. To determine the growth rate, these quadratic equations were differentiated with respect to time and the standard errors of the growth rates were determined by propagation of measurement uncertainties. This is an important adjunct to other approaches because it is a model-independent investigation of growth rate.

2. *Saltatory model method.* Growth data were modeled as a series of putative distinct stepwise (saltatory) increases or jumps separated by variable intervals of unchanging length. The amplitudes and significance of the putative step increases were evaluated by weighted nonlinear least-squares (WNLS) regression using measurement replicates and a constraint of nonnegative length increases. This method fits the actual serial growth data using a weighted nonlinear least-squares (WNLS) parameter estimation procedure. The analytical method aims to compare the actual experimental data to a series of models with increasing numbers of pulses. From an initial model consisting of no pulses, subsequent models are generated through the addition of pulses at points of greatest decrement in the variance until no statistically significant improvement of fit is gained from pulse addition. This technique makes use of the variance inherent in each of the replicate measurements, offering a statement of the probability that any one step increase is due to random variation alone. A critical value (z score) is identified at a chosen type I error level, which is experimentally defined (e.g., .05). Thus, significant jumps in length can be tested at an *a priori z* score corresponding to a desired type I statistical error.

3. *Curvilinear model method.* The data also were fitted by a weighted nonlinear least-squares procedure similar to equations previously proposed to account for human growth at the ages studied (Karlberg, 1987). The infant growth data were fitted to an equation of the form

$$Y = a_1 + b_1\{1 - e^{-(c_1 \cdot t)}\} + b_c t \qquad (1)$$

where a_1, b_1, c_1, and b_c are the parameters to be estimated. Our application of Equation 1 simultaneously estimated all four of these parameters for children over 6 months of age. For younger children the b_c term was assumed to be zero.

For the children in our samples, results for the three approaches include:

1. The sliding quadratic analysis of growth rate documented pulsatile patterns of growth.

2. The saltatory model was a better fit to the growth data than the curvilinear model in all individual cases as assessed by comparisons of WNLS

variance and autocorrelation. The latter is a measure of the randomness of the residuals (differences between observed and predicted measurements). Significant autocorrelations denote systematic variations of the model from the data. Randomness of residuals in our model was confirmed by the runs' test as well as autocorrelation.

Specifically, the serial growth data of all subjects in this study were characterized by saltatory growth increments identified at the $p < .05$ level, punctuating periods when no statistically significant growth occurred (Lampl et al., 1992). The weighted residual variance for the serial length data of individual children fitted by the saltatory model ranged from a 3- to 35-fold decrease compared to the curvilinear model (mean curvilinear model variance 32.18, standard error of the mean [SEM] 2.7; mean saltatory model variance 4.20, SEM 0.61; $p < .01$). In addition, only the saltatory hypothesis yielded randomly distributed residuals (runs' test) and the absence of significant autocorrelations of the residuals.

As an example, Figs. 2.1 and 2.2 illustrate a comparison of the saltatory analysis and the Karlberg equation as they are fitted to daily observations of a male adolescent during the 13th year. The saltatory analysis indicates that 12 statistically significant ($p < .05$) saltatory events are evident ranging in size from 0.3 to 1.4 cm. The solid line in the upper panel of Fig. 2.1 is the calculated saltatory pattern, and the solid line in the upper panel of Fig. 2.2 is the calculated Karlberg equation least-squares fit to the same data.

The performance statistics of the saltatory method were investigated by Monte Carlo simulations and the saltatory analysis protocol was found to perform very well, with an extremely low false positive rate in terms of the identification of saltatory growth pulses (Johnson & Lampl, 1995). Thus, the saltatory analysis provides a good first-order description of pulsatility in terms of the number of significant pulses and their amplitude and timing. In order to further analyze the temporal ordering of saltatory patterns, it is necessary to employ additional methods.

SALTATORY GROWTH PATTERNS

The further characterization of the growth pulse patterns is of practical importance to identify predictability in (1) the timing of saltatory growth pulses and (2) the duration of stasis intervals. The identification of saltatory pulse patterns will help to define the range of normality and pathology in the growth patterns of developing children as well as to further our understanding of the underlying hormonal and molecular mechanisms at the basis of normal organismic growth.

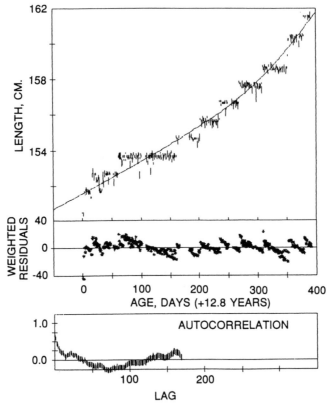

FIG. 2.2. The data shown in Fig. 2.1 fitted by Equation 2 (upper panel) with a variance of 68.3. By comparison with the saltatory model fit, systematic deviations from randomness are demonstrated in the middle panel (runs' test) and autocorrelations are not random (lower panel). The saltatory model is a better fit of these data ($p < .05$, F-test). This figure was first published in, Analysis of serial growth data, M. L. Johnson, *American Journal of Human Biology*, Vol. 5, Copyright © 1993, M. L. Johnson. Reprinted by permission of John Wiley & Sons, Inc.

Time-Series Analysis: Fourier Analysis

Serial growth data are a time-series data set. Time-series data are classified as either stationary or nonstationary, based on the presence of constancy or change in local averages between cycles. Growth is a nonstationary time series because it is characterized by a systematic increasing trend (the very essence of biological growth is increase in size). Traditionally, Fourier series methods have been used in the analysis of time-series data. In its simplest form, a Fourier series analysis applied to nonstationary time-series data consists of four steps:

1. Removal of the systematic trend, or central tendency, of the data series.
2. The experimental data, now a stationary time series, are approximated by a Fourier series.
3. The Fourier series is transformed into a power spectrum.
4. The power spectrum is interpreted in terms of one or more frequencies with significant amplitudes.

The basic goal of representing experimental data by a Fourier series is to find an equation that is the sum of sine and cosine terms that pass through every data point. Inherently, the central idea of a Fourier series method is that the mechanism that created the data is the sum of a series of sine/cosine waves. For biological data, it is commonly assumed that the molecular mechanism that created the original data must have a component that oscillates at a constant frequency; this may or may not be an appropriate assumption. Although all data sets can be mathematically approximated by such a Fourier series, it must be stated that it may or may not be appropriate to model growth as a sum of sine and cosine waves with higher harmonics. In other words, it is difficult, if not impossible, to explain the biological mechanisms of growth (cell regulation, etc.) simply in terms of multiple sine wave processes. As a mathematical model, a high-order Fourier series can describe experimental observations, but the Fourier coefficients will have little or no meaning in terms of the molecular mechanisms of growth.

We investigated the applicability of Fourier series analysis to our data set as follows: The most appropriate method for the analysis of nonstationary time series is to estimate simultaneously the Fourier coefficients and the model parameters that describe the central tendency of the data. This can be done with the modeled mathematical form of the central tendency with a finite summation of sine and cosine terms from the Fourier expansion (Johnson & Lampl, 1994). We employed the Karlberg equations (Karlberg, 1987) for modeling the central tendency of our growth data sets, equations commonly used to characterize growth during infancy, childhood, and adolescence as

$$Y_i = a_c + b_c + \frac{a_p}{1 + \exp[-b_p(t_i - t_v)]} \tag{2}$$

where a_c, b_c, a_p, b_p, and t_v are the parameters of the model and Y_i is the height at any time t_i.

Thus, to perform the Fourier series analysis of growth we fit our serial growth data to the sum of the Karlberg equation and the Fourier series expansion using a least-squares approach simultaneously estimating a_c, b_c, a_p, b_p, t_v, c_n, and ϕ_n,

$$Y_i = a_c + b_c t + \frac{a_p}{1 + \exp[-b_p(t_i - t_v)]} + \sum_{n=1}^{n_{max}} c_n \sin\left[\left(\frac{n\pi t_i}{L}\right) + \phi_n\right] \qquad (3)$$

With this approach, the corresponding joint confidence intervals of the Fourier coefficients include the uncertainties of the estimate of the central tendency. The Fourier analysis was performed by a WNLS technique not requiring equally spaced data points (Faunt & Johnson, 1992). The advantage of this method is that missing data points can be ignored, rather than inserting unmeasured artificial data points as required by standard Fourier analysis methods. In addition, this method does not require the data series to be truncated to a number of data points equal to a power of two.

We used this approach to test for significant periodicity within the observational data pertaining to the growth of the children in our infant sample, as well as our adolescent data. Although the addition of a sine wave reduced the curvilinear model variances between 10 and 30%, the resulting variances were still significantly higher than those found with the saltatory analysis (Johnson, 1993; Lampl & Johnson, 1993; Johnson & Lampl, 1994). There is no clear periodicity in the data.

For example, for the individual's growth data shown in Figs. 2.1 and 2.2, a power spectrum analysis of the residuals from Equation 3 was performed that identified significant periodicities at 28, 14, 7, and 5.6 days. From an observation of the original data series, it is not clear whether the results identified periodicity present in the data or were merely a consequence of methodological bias: The Fourier series method of analysis assumes that the biologically significant wave form is a sine wave. If the biological wave form is not a simple sine wave, the Fourier series analysis will still be able to describe the data, and will resolve the discrepancies between the sine wave function and the actual function by introducing a near infinite series of higher frequency components. This is a potential problem in our data because episodic patterns have a nearly infinite number of higher frequency Fourier components.

To investigate this problem, a simulated data series was analyzed as a control: A saltatory growth pattern was simulated with a growth event at exactly 28-day intervals, with a realistic amount of Gaussian noise (Johnson, 1993). These synthetic data were least-squares fitted to a straight line to create a stationary data set and the residuals were analyzed by Fourier series methods. The power spectrum analysis showed apparent periodicities at 14, 7, and 5.6 in addition to the control of 28 days. As we know that the simulated growth events did not exist at these additional periodicities, it is clear that the Fourier analysis found these as a consequence of fitting a non-square-wave function (the simulated growth events) with a series of sine waves of decreasing period.

Therefore, the apparent periodicities identified in the residual analysis of our original data are, likewise, an artifact of Fourier assumptions. This is similar to the artifacts that result from aliasing (Blackman & Tukey, 1958). We believe that the apparent periodicities that have been reported elsewhere in time-intensive serial growth data based on Fourier-type analytic methods (Hermanussen et al., 1988, 1995; Hermanussen & Burmeister, 1993) reflect this same artifact and that episodicity may in fact be at the basis of these time-series data. Certainly, other methods need to be employed before conclusions regarding periodicity in such data are assumed. Although it is true that any stationary time series can be mathematically described as a Fourier series of sine waves, this does not imply that the underlying biological process is indeed a sine wave, and careful interpretation is warranted (Johnson & Lampl, 1994).

In conclusion, these growth data cannot be described by a central tendency with a small number of added periodicities. These analyses clarify that the saltuses in the data from the children in our sample are nonperiodic: Growth events do not occur at consistent and regular intervals. Instead, growth is proceeding as a series of discrete, intermittent episodic saltations.

These observations led us to ask if the saltatory pulses in the data were characterized by a random process. In order to address this question, we undertook a sequence of analyses directed toward diagnosing the probability that growth pulse saltations and the accompanying durations of stases were randomly distributed.

The Binomial Theorem

As a first approach to this problem, we wanted to test the hypothesis that the probability of a saltation on any day is random, for example, independent of saltations on any of the preceding days. This is a question classically addressed by the binomial theorem. From the probability of a saltation occurring for any child or for the sample as a group, it is possible to calculate the distribution of stasis periods within the constraints of the hypothesis. The binomial theorem states that the probability of x successes in n tries is:

$$P_n = \frac{n!}{x!\,(n-x)!}\; p^x(1-p)^{n-x} \tag{4}$$

where p is the probability of the event. The mean number of events is given by:

$$\mu = np \tag{5}$$

For the present example, p is the probability of a saltation having occurred since the last measurement and can be easily evaluated as the observed number of saltations divided by one less than the total number of observations. The probability of a stasis interval of length n can then be evaluated from Equation 4 where $x = 0$ (no events) as:

$$(1 - p)^n \qquad (6)$$

The probability of a stasis interval of length n or more is given as 1 minus the probability of all of the stasis intervals from 0 to $n - 1$,

$$1 - p - \sum_{i=1}^{n-1} (1 - p)^i \qquad (7)$$

where the first subtracted p term is the probability of a stasis interval of zero length.

For the infants in our sample, the probability of a stasis of length 70 days is nearly zero. The probability of a stasis event of some length is related to the probability of a saltation event, given by Equation 7.

However, the method just described has an inherent problem: The biological stasis interval is the actual duration between saltatory growth pulses. The stasis interval as we are able to define it is that during which we measure a child and no observable growth has occurred. Our ability to identify the precise timing of pulses, and thus the precision of our assessment of stasis intervals, is constrained by the assessment protocol. As has been discussed widely for other disciplines, the importance of sampling interval vis-à-vis pulse pattern is essential. If the time during which saltations occur is very small compared to sampling, there is always a potential underestimation of stasis lengths. In general, there is the possibility that the stasis interval is underestimated by as much as two time intervals. Our studies consist of data collected according to three time-frame protocols: weekly, semiweekly, and daily, as has been previously described (Lampl, 1993; Lampl & Johnson, 1993; Lampl et al., 1992). As we have shown that a growth pulse may occur within a 24-hr time frame, the assessment protocols longer than one day are problematic for the analysis of temporal growth patterns.

One might attempt to test the randomness of saltatory events by fitting the distribution of the known stasis intervals directly to a binomial distribution. In theory, if we knew the exact time of the saltations, we could calculate the probability of a saltation within any time interval.

When the lengths of the experimental stasis intervals were fitted to the binomial approximation for random intervals, the best estimate of the probabilities of a saltation on any given day were .098 for the weekly protocol, .098 for the semiweekly protocol, and .031 for the daily protocol. All of these are less than the observed probabilities as evaluated by the number of saltation events divided by the number of observation points minus one ($n - 1$). These results lead to the suggestion that the timing of the saltatory events and thus the lengths of the stasis intervals are not strictly random. However, as the reality of the stasis intervals is perturbed by the sampling protocol and the exact timing is often unknown, we cannot directly relate the observed lengths of the stasis intervals with the probabilities predicted by the binomial theorem. Instead, it is necessary to relate the observed duration of stasis intervals to a model of theoretically based stasis intervals and to generate a model of interval duration irrespective of sampling protocol. It is possible to employ Monte Carlo simulations to address these issues. We employed these methods to further address the question, "What is the timing between saltations?"

Monte Carlo Simulations

This procedure entails simulating a series of randomly spaced saltations in a synthetic data series as well as simulating the data collection protocol intervals. This method randomly generates saltation events according to user-selected criteria of data collection protocol and error. In addition, the probabilities of the experimentally observed stasis intervals of varying lengths are calculated. This procedure is repeated approximately one thousand times using different random spacing of the saltations. The repeated calculations are required to eliminate the effects of any particular sequence of random numbers and to obtain the overall most probable values. For these simulations, we utilized a probability for the occurrence of a saltation given by the number of observed saltations divided by one less than the total number of observations for an individual child.

Direct comparison of the Monte Carlo simulations with our observed distribution of stasis interval lengths showed marked differences. We conclude that the precise timing of saltations in these data is not strictly random.These results, taken together with the results from the Fourier analysis, support the proposition that saltatory growth is neither strictly periodic, nor is it a random process, but it is characterized by episodicity. These results parallel those from a number of biological time series in recent years and fit within an emerging class of episodic, aperiodic observations (e.g., Glass & Mackey, 1988). This leads to a question: What sort of aperiodic, nonlinear process may be at the basis of normal growth?

NORMAL HUMAN GROWTH:
ADAPTABILITY THROUGH IRREGULARITY

Human growth researchers now join physiologists and clinicians confronted with the problem of comparing specific characteristics of time-series data. As observed in other biological studies, comparisons of statistical variability in pulse characteristics cannot address specific problems of describing and comparing individuals' growth patterns (Pincus & Keefe, 1992). The saltatory model does not predict either amplitude or frequency characteristics of growth saltations, but merely states that growth is a pulsatile process. Our data document a process of growth characterized by variability in pulse amplitude and frequency not captured by previous data collection protocol and analytical methods. The errors that can arise from employing simplistic descriptive statistics in the analysis of time-series growth data have been recently documented (Heinrichs, Munson, Counts, Cutler, & Baron, 1995; Lampl, Cameron, Veldhuis, & Johnson, 1995; Johnson, Veldhuis, & Lampl, 1996).

The present description of human growth fits into a body of literature discussing the relative regularity and irregularity found in human physiological systems that exhibit pulsatile characteristics. It has been suggested that, in general, healthy processes and normative physiology are characterized by greater irregularity and complexity, by comparison with sickness and aging (Kaplan et al., 1991; Pincus, Cummins, & Haddad, 1993; Pincus & Goldberger, 1994). Pincus (1994a, 1994b) argued that a number of *in vivo* physiologic signals "represent the output of complex, multinodal networks with both stochastic and deterministic components" (Pincus, 1994a, p. 162) and healthy systems have flexible interactions with multiple influences, which, when decoupled or otherwise unable to receive and transmit information, become autonomous and isolated, thus leading to pathology.

The present discussion has focused on growth pulses as they occur at a systems level in real time. They are the output of complex, interrelated underlying processes that combine both endogenous signals and the physiological effects of the organism's interaction with environmental input. Growth pulses as described derive from gross measurements of body parameters, total body length, or single limb length. Precisely what these measurements capture is unclear.

What is well known is that length of long bones accrues by endochondral apposition at growth plates by a process involving chondroblastic cell synthesis of hyaline cartilage, the subsequent action of osteoblastic cell production of osteoid, and the respective calcification phases. Adult form is accomplished through these sequential steps combined with three-dimensional remodeling.

What is not yet clear are the precise cellular controls of these processes, their timing, and the complex signaling interactions between general hormonal input (e.g., growth hormone and insulin growth factor) and local cytokines (e.g., transforming growth factor beta, among others). It is likely that there is an upper limit for individual pulse amplitude events, constrained by local biomechanical stability (Kember, 1992), but a wide range of lesser increments is possible. Soft tissue development is likewise complex.

The emerging understanding of the complexity of the endogenous factors whose intricate coupling interacts with environmental factors and results in whole body growth strongly suggests that the realities of the system cannot be accommodated within the simple models of linear growth previously described. For example, if whole body growth were continuous or simply periodic, it would be a system held within a narrow frequency range and would be quite fragile to environmental exigencies. As a daily biological signal, daily nutritional diversity and even mild disease processes that result in fever or changes in appetite would be poorly tolerated. Indeed, growth would be highly sensitive to circadian behaviors in general, including activity patterns that themselves affect metabolic output and requirements. Such a system is marked by fragility and would result in poor flexibility.

Growth is the process by which a single cell becomes a reproductively capable member of a species, and thus its regulation is under significant evolutionary selection from the viewpoint of species survival. It is unlikely that growth is itself a fragile system, but rather a robust and flexible one. It is an excellent example of a biological process in which network and external forces substantially influence component behavior. Variability in the amplitude and frequency of discrete events is a mechanism providing pathway divergence for the attainment of reproductive adulthood amidst highly variable environmental circumstances.

Indeed, one of the hallmarks of human growth is the interindividual variability of children. The remarkable size differences between children result from both genetic and environmental influences, and the size of a child at any point in time serves as a marker of past growth, reflecting both the amount of growth at all previous growth events, and the frequency of growth episodes. Within the context of human variation, the frequency and amplitude of saltuses that we observed in our sample of middle-class, well-fed Northwestern Europeans may have serendipitously provided the opportunity to elucidate the basic saltatory growth process. It is likely that genetic and environmental influences contribute to saltus amplitude and frequency, and it is probable that the saltus amplitudes in some children may be too small to capture experimentally as discrete events.

Variability in growth patterns is the outcome of numerous small differences in genetics, ranging from morphogenesis and differentiation timing to numerous molecular and chemically mediated events. These include processes involving endocrine patterns (such as secretory burst profiles, binding protein and receptor dynamics, and signal transduction events), metabolic processes (including disease processes, nutritional intake, and physiological availability of nutrients), and factors impinging on biology that derive from general ecological and environmental circumstances. Thus, many different processes simultaneously modulate an organism's growth progress. Human growth reflects nonlinear multifactorial processes, and any model aiming to describe the reality of this process must be able to accommodate this. It is interesting to note that the complexities of the interactions of these numerous processes may in some children produce saltatory pulses that follow periodic trajectories for some time. Although not found in our data, such patterns would be expected in a nonlinear dynamical system.

The preceding observations and theoretical considerations lead to the question of whether so-called "nonlinear determinism" might be a reasonable model for what is known about the human growth process at the present time. The mathematical analyses that are employed to directly address such a question cannot be applied to the data at hand: The present data are far too limited for valid application of nonlinear dynamics as presently developed.

However, theoretically, it is interesting to note that nonlinear determinism allows for optimal adaptability to fluctuating environmental parameters, particularly for interactively coupled processes. This is precisely the type of system that is a descriptor for growth. Chaotic signals have been described as those that are highly sensitive to initial conditions and in which small perturbations change subsequent dynamics (e.g., Shinbrot, Grebogi, Ott, & Yorke, 1993). Initial conditions would include genetics, cellular phenomena at conception, and intrauterine physiology, as well as cellular conditions throughout development. Small perturbations result from numerous nodal and network signals. This would be both a positive feature for a system, lending adaptive flexibility to environmental conditions, and a potentially negative feature, if responses lead to extreme pathology and high mortality. Evolution would be expressed as the compromise between these possibilities as species-specific limits in growth patterns become established. It is interesting to reflect on what evidence might be employed in a speculative discussion of the applicability of nonlinear determinism as a model of human growth.

A model of saltatory growth permits for the first time an initial understanding of the underlying mechanisms responsible for periods of decelerated and accelerated growth that have been previously described, including growth faltering, catch-up growth, and the classic growth spurts of adolescence and middle childhood. A process of saltatory growth involves discrete growth events that can be described by several characteristics: Saltations, or growth pulses, have a timing component that determines when growth occurs; and at each saltation or growth pulse, a discrete incremental amount of growth occurs. Thus, the frequency of growth pulses and the time of stases that separate growth pulse events, together with the amplitude of the growth pulses themselves, determine the growth in size of an individual. A modification of frequency and amplitude of growth pulses are responsible for relative changes in growth rate both within a single individual and between individuals.

From this perspective, developmental changes in growth rate classically described as the infant, childhood, and adolescent growth phases can be described in terms of changes in the dynamical properties of discrete saltatory events. Changes in the frequency and/or amplitude of growth pulses can be postulated to underlie annualized velocity characteristics. Moreover, the classical notion of the adolescent growth spurt as the unique dynamical aspect of human growth is dispelled. Instead, growth during adolescence is not an essentially different process than what has come before, but rather represents an intensification in the frequency and/or amplitude of discrete growth pulses, perhaps more directly reflecting the physiological character of the pubescent period (Lampl & Johnson, 1993).

Common observations in both clinical and population studies have noted that under a number of conditions, children's growth rates change. From the viewpoint of a continuous growth model, the question of what mechanisms permit and control these changes has been perplexing. It is notable that a process of pulsations can accommodate these observations parsimoniously and provides greater understanding of the underlying mechanisms. *Growth faltering* is the term given to a relative decrease and/or cessation in active growth. The data are not yet available from intensive prospective longitudinal studies, but it can be hypothesized that this results from a decrease in the amplitude and/or frequency of discrete growth events. Such a "turning down" of the proliferative process likely reflects active inhibition, as coupled processes are interrupted and the discrete intervals between growth events elongate and/or amplitudes decrease. *Catch-up growth* is the observed increase in growth rate following an intervention usually administered to correct growth faltering (Prader, Tanner, & Von Harnack, 1963). No prospective studies employing the present protocol and analyses have been conducted, but it can be hypothesized that an increase in pulse amplitude and/or frequency underlies this process.

It may be, as has been documented for cardiac pulse patterns, that growth faltering and catch-up growth are examples of the response of an interactive nonlinear system to perturbation (Garfinkel, Spano, Ditto, & Weiss, 1992). In the presence of numerous perturbing conditions (among which may be the recent history of growth events however this may be physiologically recorded), the saltatory growth pulse intervals are reset, resulting in relatively lesser or greater accretion during the time intervals that characterize clinical data collection. A process permitting bidirectional responsivity to multifactorial input is highly adaptive and may well be at the basis of the observed changes in growth rates in changing environments. The possibility of changing subsequent saltatory growth dynamics in response to both endogenous and exogenous signals by either lengthening or shortening pulse intervals permits an organism tremendous flexibility. Such dynamical processes may explain the nature of growth as a dynamic and interactive biological process. The observed worldwide variability in growth and maturation patterns supports such a view (Eveleth & Tanner, 1976, 1990).

GROWTH AND MATURATION: HUMAN MORPHOGENESIS

Theoretically, concepts developed to describe nonlinear dynamical systems are appealing in the context of what is known about the biology of human growth. Mammalian organisms are characterized by a growth process (a) of finite duration, (b) directed toward a final so-called "adult" state, and (c) that is part of a general process of aging. The process of *growth* as an increase in size and *maturation* and the process by which an organism progressively acquires adult characteristics (e.g., permanent dentition, secondary sexual characteristics, behavioral development in terms of cognitive, motoric, and socioemotional skills) have been dichotomized in traditional studies vis-à-vis their developmental roles and effects.

It is reasonable to suggest that this traditional conceptual division may be reformulated. Growth and maturation are likely to be part of a single process, involving an increase in both size and differentiation, reflecting an underlying process of morphogenesis. It is sensible that the unfolding of a species-specific morphogenetic program is responsible for the interplay between the differentiation of an organism over time and its increase in size. It is likely that the sequence of developmental events is, in general, the consequence of a morphogenetic program that encodes event sequence and relative timing. That the precise timing for the events is modifiable is well documented: For example, the development of secondary sexual characteristics is relatively similar between children although the timing is highly variable (Tanner, 1962). It is notable, furthermore, that both brain growth and behavioral development have been reported to be episodic, with behavioral developmental acquisitions co-occurring with documented physical growth saltations (Epstein, 1974a, 1974b; Lampl & Emde, 1983). This would be well explained by a morphogenetic program unfolding in an interactive system of environmental, genetic, and cellular mechanisms.

Thus, in theory, growth is a system exquisitely designed to respond to environmental variability that might well be described by formal nonlinear dynamics. The proposition that human growth reflects a morphogenetic program that is expressed by a modulation of amplitude and frequency of discrete events and the possibility that, as in simple organisms (Goldbeter & Li, 1989), differentiation and proliferation in humans reflect nonlinear determinism are intriguing notions. However, at present, a thorough scientific description of the dynamical aspects of human growth awaits much more data than are presently in hand.

In sum, recently collected data, reflecting innovative protocols and analytic techniques applied to both body measurements and hormonal activity, support growth as a process restricted to discrete temporal events that are expressed in the real-time domain as irregular pulses. It is notable that as an episodic event, growth diverts normal physiology only momentarily. From the viewpoint of ongoing organismic metabolism, growth is an inherently expensive biological process, requiring resources in terms of energy, protein and micronutrients. A number of physiological responses are likely to be involved in the biological activity of a growth episode and momentary immune compromise may co-occur with growth pulses. It is possible that evolutionarily, a process of growth by discrete events is adaptive, as a developing organism is not continuously at-risk due to the growth process itself. Pulsatile patterns of growth episodes may differ between individuals in different populations in response to local environmental exigencies. A growth process characterized by pulse amplitude and frequency flexibility provides the species with a mechanism whereby the young can reach adulthood by numerous different paths. It is notable that, according to our present data, some 90% of human developmental time may not be characterized by active proliferation in terms of size increase. Growth saltations that occur episodically, even infrequently, put an organism at-risk and require support only rarely. The actual amplitudes of discrete growth events can vary within the constraints of the environment and thus permit a synergism between an organism's genome and environment that unfolds during the growth process itself and is recorded as an outcome in adult morphology and physiology.

The observation of saltatory growth patterns places human growth within the complexity of what is presently known about biological activity. The documentation of nonlinear patterns now permits the study of human growth to be more than a mere description of size as an outcome variable. By focusing attention on the diversity of specific patterns as they reflect the culmination of numerous interrelated processes, we may come to understand for the first time individual variability in growth and the underlying mechanisms.

ACKNOWLEDGMENTS

The authors acknowledge the support of the National Science Foundation Center for Biological Timing (DIR 8920162, M. L. Johnson), the National Institutes of Health (NIH) Center for Fluorescence Spectroscopy of the University of Maryland at Baltimore (RR-08119, M. L. Johnson), and NIH grant GM35154 (M. L. Johnson).

REFERENCES

Bernstein, I. M., Blake, K., & Badger, G. (1995). Evidence that normal fetal growth is not continuous. *American Journal of Obstetrics and Gynecology, 172*, 323.

Blackman, R. B., & Tukey, J. W. (1958). *The measurement of power spectra.* New York: Dover.

Epstein, H. T. (1974a). Phrenoblysis: Special brain and mind growth periods: I. Human brain and skull development. *Developmental Psychobiology, 7*, 207–216.

Epstein, H. T. (1974b). Phrenoblysis: Special brain and mind growth periods: II. Human mental development. *Developmental Psychobiology, 7*, 217–224.

Eveleth, P. B., & Tanner, J. M. (1976). *Worldwide variation in human growth* (1st ed.). Cambridge: Cambridge University Press.

Eveleth, P. B., & Tanner, J. M. (1990). *Worldwide variation in human growth* (2nd ed.). Cambridge: Cambridge University Press.

Faunt, L. M., & Johnson, M. L. (1992). Analysis of discrete, time-sampled data using Fourier series method. *Methods in Enzymology, 210*, 340–356.

Fomon, S. J., & Nelson, S. E. (1995). Size and growth. In S. J. Fomon (Ed.), *Nutrition in normal infants* (p. 51). St. Louis, MO: Mosby.

Garfinkel, A., Spano, M. L., Ditto, W. L., & Weiss, J. N. (1992). Controlling cardiac chaos. *Science, 257*, 1230–1235.

Gibson, A. T., Pearse, R. G., & Wales, J. K. H. (1994). Episodic growth in premature infants. *Humanbiologica Budapestensis, 24*, 34.

Glass, L., & Mackey, M. C. (1988). *From clocks to chaos: The rhythms of life.* Princeton, NJ: Princeton University Press.

Goldbeter, A., & Li, Y. X. (1989). Frequency coding in intercellular communication. In A. Goldbeter (Ed.), *Cell to cell signaling: From experiments to theoretical models* (pp. 415–432). London: Academic Press.

Hartman, M. L., Pincus, S. M., Johnson, M. L., Matthews, D. H., Faunt, L. M., Vance, M. L., Thorner, M. O., & Veldhuis, J. D. (1994). Enhanced basal and disorderly growth hormone secretion distinguish acromegalic from normal pulsatile growth hormone release. *Journal of Clinical Investigation, 94*, 1277–1288.

Heinrichs, C., Munson, P. J., Counts, D. R., Cutler, G. B., Jr., & Baron, J. (1995). Human growth patterns. Technical comment. *Science, 268*, 442–445.

Hermanussen, M., & Burmeister, J. (1993). Children do not grow continuously but in spurts. *American Journal of Human Biology, 15*, 103–109.

Hermanussen, M., de los Angeles Rol de Lama, M., Burmeister, J., & Fernandez-Tresguerres, A. (1995). Mikro-knemometry: An accurate technique of growth measurement in rats. *Physiology & Behavior, 2*, 347–352.

Hermanussen, M., Geiger-Benoit, K., Burmiester, J., & Sippell, W. G. (1988). Periodical changes of short term growth velocity ("mini growth spurts") in human growth. *Annals of Human Biology, 15*, 103–109.

Johnson, M. L. (1993). Analysis of serial growth data. *American Journal of Human Biology, 5*, 633–640.

Johnson, M. L., & Lampl, M. (1994). Artifacts of Fourier series analysis. *Methods in Enzymology, 240*, 51–68.

Johnson, M. L., & Lampl, M. (1995). Methods for the evaluation of saltatory growth in infants. *Methods in Neuroscience, 28*, 364–387.

Johnson, M. L., Veldhuis, J. D., & Lampl, M. (1996). Is growth saltatory? The usefulness and limitations of frequency distributions in analyzing pulsatile data. *Endocrinology, 137*, 5197–5204.

Kaplan, D. T., Furman, M. I., Pincus, S. M., Ryan, S. M., Lipsitz, L. A., & Goldberger, A. L. (1991). Aging and the complexity of cardiovascular dynamics. *Biophysical Journal, 59*, 945–949.

Karlberg, J. (1987). On the modelling of human growth. *Statistics in Medicine, 6,* 185–192.

Kember, N. F. (1992). The physiology of the growth plate. In M. Hernandez & J. Argente (Eds.), *Human growth: Basic and clinical aspects* (pp. 81–86). Amsterdam: Excerpta Medica.

Lampl, M. (1993). Evidence of saltatory growth in infancy. *American Journal of Human Biology, 5,* 641–652.

Lampl, M., Cameron, N., Veldhuis, J. D., & Johnson, M. L. (1995). Human growth patterns. Technical comment. *Science, 268,* 445–447.

Lampl, M., & Emde, R. N. (1983). Episodic growth in infancy: A preliminary report on length, head circumference and behavior. In K. Fischer (Vol. Ed.), *New directions for child development, Vol. 21. Levels and transitions in children's development* (pp. 21–36). San Francisco: Jossey-Bass.

Lampl, M., Jeanty, P., & Johnson, M. L. (1997). *Saltatory growth patterns in fetal tibia.* Manuscript submitted for publication.

Lampl, M., & Johnson, M. L. (1993). A case study of daily growth during adolescence: A single spurt or changes in the dynamics of saltatory growth? *Annals of Human Biology, 20,* 595–602.

Lampl, M., Veldhuis, J. D., & Johnson, M. L. (1992). Saltation and stasis: A model of human growth. *Science, 258,* 801–803.

Marshall, W. A. (1971). Evaluation of growth rate in height over periods of less than one year. *Archives of Diseases in Childhood, 46,* 414–420.

Meredith, H. V. (1955). Longitudinal anthropometric data in the study of individual growth. *Annals of the New York Academy of Science, 63,* 510–527.

Michaelsen, K. F., Skov, L., Badsberg, J. H., & Jorgensen, M. (1991). Short-term measurement of linear growth in preterm infants; Validation of a hand-held knemometer. *Pediatric Research, 30,* 464–468.

Oerter Klein, K., Munson, P. J., Bacher, J. D., Cutler G. B., Jr., & Baron, J. (1994). Linear growth in the rabbit is continuous, not saltatory. *Endocrinology, 134,* 1317–1320.

Pincus, S. M. (1994a). Greater signal regularity may indicate increased system isolation. *Mathematical Biosciences, 122,* 161–181.

Pincus, S. M. (1994b). Quantification of evolution from order to randomness in practical time series analysis. *Methods in Enzymology, 240,* 69–89.

Pincus, S. M., Cummins, T. R., & Haddad, G. G. (1993). Heart rate control in normal and aborted-SIDS infants. *American Physiological Society, 264,* R638–R646.

Pincus, S. M., & Goldberger, A. L. (1994). Physiological time-series analysis: What does regularity quantify? *American Journal of Physiology, 266,* H1643–H1656.

Pincus, S. M., & Keefe, D. L. (1992). Quantification of hormone pulsatility via an approximate entropy algorithm. *American Journal of Physiology, 262,* E741–754.

Prader, A., Tanner, J. M., & Von Harnack, G. A. (1963). Catch-up growth following illness or starvation. *Journal of Paediatrics, 62,* 645–659.

Prank, K., Harms, H., Brabant, G., & Hesch, R.-D. (1995). Nonlinear dynamics in pulsatile secretion of parathyroid hormone in normal human subjects. *Chaos, 5,* 76–81.

Roush, W. B., Barbato, G. F., & Cravener, T. L. (1994). A nonlinear dynamical (chaos) approach to the analysis of broiler growth. *Poultry Science, 73,* 1183–1195.

Sherr, C. J. (1993). Mammalian G-1 cyclins. *Cell, 73,* 1059–1064.

Shinbrot, T., Grebogi, C., Ott, E., & Yorke, J. A. (1993). Using small perturbations to control chaos. *Nature, 363,* 411–417.

Smith, D. W., Truog, W., Rogers, J. E., Greitzer, L. F., Skinner, A. L., McCann, J. J., & Sedgwick Harvey, M. A. (1976). Shifting linear growth during infancy: Illustration of genetic factors in growth from fetal life through infancy. *Journal of Pediatrics, 89,* 225–230.

Tanner, J. M. (1962). *Growth at adolescence* (2nd ed.). Oxford: Blackwell.

Tanner, J. M. (1986). Growth as a target-seeking function: Catch-up and catch-down growth in man. In F. Falkner & J. M. Tanner (Eds.), *Human growth: A comprehensive treatise* (Vol. 1, 2nd ed., pp. 167–180). New York: Plenum.

Thalange, N. K. S., Gill, M. S., Gill, L., Price, D. A., Whatmore, A. J., Addison, G. M., & Clayton, P. E. (1995, June). Infradian rhythms in urinary growth hormone excretion. *Endocrine Society 77th Annual Meeting Abstracts*, Abstract P3-91.

Togo, M., & Togo, T. (1982). Time series analysis of stature and body weight in five siblings. *Annals of Human Biology, 9,* 425–440.

Valk, I. M., Langhout-Chabloz, A. M. E., Smals, A. G. H., Kloppenborg, P. W. C., Cassorla, F., & Schutte, E. A. S. T. (1983). Accurate measurement of the lower leg length and the ulnar length and its application in short term growth measurement. *Growth, 47,* 53–66.

Veldhuis, J. D., & Johnson, M. L. (1992). Deconvolution analysis of hormone data. *Methods in Enzymology, 210,* 539–575.

3

MODELING COORDINATION DYNAMICS IN DEVELOPMENT

Paula Fitzpatrick

University of Connecticut

From birth, infants can move the articulators and spend a good deal of time performing spontaneous behaviors. These initial movements can be thought of as the source of developmental change in that they allow infants to discover things about their bodies and its potential for action, as well as properties of their surroundings. The problem for the infant is how to sculpt these initial movements into useful goal-directed actions. That is, they must learn to coordinate a large number of independent variables (e.g., the very many combinations of body segments, patterns of muscle innervation, joint angles, cell firing, etc.) to work together to achieve a movement outcome or action. The challenge for developmental theory is to explain how such a process is possible. Recently, the dynamical perspective has been considered well-suited for addressing such issues regarding the emergence of complex and stable behavioral patterns due to its reliance on self-organizing principles of stability, instability, and behavioral transitions in characterizing how patterns emerge from the interaction of many components (e.g., Kugler, 1986; Kugler, Kelso & Turvey, 1982; Thelen, 1986, 1989, 1995; Thelen & Smith, 1994; Turvey & Fitzpatrick, 1993).

As Bernstein (1967) pointed out, the high dimensional, multicomponent nature of the movement system requires that the coordination solution be abstract. He proposed that to perform a goal-directed action, a temporary, functional relationship between the component parts of the system is established. That is, the components of the movement system become "linked" to form low-dimensional units in a manner that allows the parts to change relative to each other. These temporary, flexible relationships are variously referred to as coordinative structures (e.g., Easton, 1972; Turvey, 1977), synergies (e.g., Bernstein, 1967), or task-specific devices (e.g., Bingham, 1988).

Kugler, Kelso, and Turvey (1980) consider coordinative structures to be instances of self-organizing dynamic regimes, put most simply, systems that evolve over time. That is, coordinative structures are dynamical entities and as such are governed by dynamical laws. Coordinative structures are collective or attractive states that emerge given a certain set of constraints. Equations of motion can be written to characterize or model the emergence of the coordinative structures (i.e., how the system changes over time), and parameter values in the equations of motion can be estimated experimentally. Different equations of motion (dynamic regimes) have particular regions of stability associated with them. The state space, a tool for illustrating stable regions, graphically displays the manner in which collections of trajectories change over time. Portions of the state space that trajectories continuously revisit are referred to as attractors. Attractors are preferred regions of the state space that a system will eventually settle into, even if perturbed.

The claim of the dynamical perspective, thus, is that in order to produce a particular action, the subsystems of the body are functionally organized into coordinative structures to accomplish a goal. The formation of these coordinative structures is a self-organizing process based on a confluence of constraints, perceptual, motor, task, intentional, for example (Kugler et al., 1980; Newell, 1985). The coordinative structures that emerge can be thought of as attractive states in the sense that they are preferred stable configurations that are chosen most often. The stability of these coordinative modes, however, is not static. Changes in circumstances (e.g., environmental, growth) can alter the stability characteristics such that previously stable configurations become unstable and require the discovery of more optimal solutions. Importantly, these changes are related to relevant perceptual information, that is, spatiotemporal patterns in optic, haptic, or acoustic mediums that are tied to properties of the environment and organism (Gibson, 1966, 1979). For example, increasing attunement to relevant perceptual information, perceiving consequences of actions and adjusting behavior appropriately, attending more closely to task constraints, all potentially engender changes in the stability of behavioral patterns.

Attractors are particularly important for maintaining coordination patterns because they specify optimal coordination modes. Described informationally, attractors are minima or valleys in a potential landscape. Gradients or changes in the landscape provide information about where minima are located (i.e., stable coordination modes). In other words, there is an information gradient around attractors that makes them easy to detect, find on separate occasions, and return to after a perturbation. In this sense, dynamics can be thought of as information that guides behavior (Fowler & Turvey,

1978; Kugler & Turvey, 1987; Newell, Kugler, Van Emmerik, & McDonald, 1989). An infant performing a new behavior, therefore, can be thought of as exploring such a landscape or virtual layout of attractors. Through exploration, the attractors or stable configurations emerge and the infant becomes attuned to the relevant information specifying those stable configurations. On later occasions the infant needs only to follow the information gradient to the attractor in order to perform the behavior. Whereas the initial movements will appear variable and inconsistent as the potential landscape is explored, later, more skilled movements will be less variable as a result of homing in on the attractor straight-away.

Newell (1985) has described the establishment of coordinative structures as the first phase in acquiring a new movement pattern. The initial assembly of coordinative structures is an approximate movement solution that generates a general "ballpark" of movements. Selecting the actual movement to accomplish a task, however, requires fine tuning or paramaterization of the coordinative structures. This second phase in the learning process is referred to as the tuning or optimization phase and proceeds as a result of perceptual exploration. The tuning phase is characterized by high variability as the learner homes in on the optimal solution. According to a dynamic view, the assembly and tuning phases are separate processes, both of which are dynamical (e.g., Kugler et al., 1980; Schmidt, Treffner, Shaw, & Turvey, 1992; Schöner, 1989; Schöner, Zanone, & Kelso, 1992). That is, a dynamic responsible for movement production (i.e., assembly, with an associated time scale on the order of seconds and minutes) can be identified as well as a higher order learning dynamic responsible for its optimization (which proceeds on the order of hours and days).

This same framework can be used to understand the *development* of motor coordination as well. For example, both Thelen (e.g., 1995) and Goldfield (1995) propose that in acquiring a new task the infant first assembles the subsystems to produce a "ballpark" behavioral pattern and then, through perceptual exploration, discovers the optimal parameterization of the coordinative structures. In such a dynamic view, the *dynamic processes* that engender change are the same in both learning and development. What distinguishes learning from development is the time-scale over which the behavior unfolds (e.g., Kugler et al., 1982; Newell, 1985; Newell & Van Emmerik, 1990; Saltzman & Munhall, 1992; Thelen, 1989; Zanone & Kelso, 1990): Learning proceeds across hours and days whereas development unfolds over spans of months and years. Thus, in development, similar to learning, the dynamic responsible for movement production at a given developmental stage is nested within a higher order dynamic responsible for developmental progression from one stage to the next.

Importantly, the optimization process is an intentional, goal-directed activity. An actor wishes to achieve a goal state (i.e., has an intention to achieve a goal) and therefore assembles a dynamical control structure with an equilibrium (i.e., stable) state at the goal state. Initially, the equilibrium state may not be set appropriately to achieve the goal. Through exploration and attunement to relevant perceptual information, the goal state emerges—the higher order intentional control structure governs the optimization of the lower order movement dynamic. In this way, the higher order dynamic can be considered intentional in two senses—it specifies the goal of the action as well as the goal of becoming more skilled/proficient (see Schmidt & Fitzpatrick, 1996, for a discussion of the intentional aspects of a learning dynamic). Such a dynamic can proceed on a time scale of either learning or development.

DYNAMICAL RESEARCH ON THE INFANCY PERIOD

Research on the development of interlimb coordination patterns from a dynamical perspective has focused predominantly on the infancy period. For example, a growing body of research on infant kicking and stepping has revealed a number of dynamic properties in the developmental progression from spontaneous kicking to upright locomotion. Thelen (1983) found that supine kicking and upright stepping demonstrate nearly identical movement patterns, yet stepping is no longer exhibited after a few months whereas kicking persists. She found that stepping was influenced by the composition of body tissues—when tissue mass and bone length outstrip muscle strength stepping is no longer exhibited (Thelen & Fisher, 1982). Furthermore, she has demonstrated that infant stepping is context sensitive, pointing to the fact that behavior emerges through a complex interplay of many constraints. For example, Thelen and Ulrich (1991) showed that infant stepping can be elicited by providing supporting external conditions (a motorized treadmill) and adjusts appropriately to changing task conditions (e.g., changing tread-mill speed). Additionally, Thelen and Fisher (1983) have shown that early infant leg movements, although not generally goal-directed, are well coordinated: The leg joints of a single limb move in synchrony and the movements between the limbs are well coordinated, most often in an alternating pattern. Later, infants begin to decouple the whole leg synergies to allow the leg joints within a single limb to move independently to accomplish tasks such as crawling, walking, running (Jensen, Ulrich, Thelen, Schneider, & Zernicke, 1995).

In investigations of the development of walking, Clark has demonstrated that interlimb coupling is very tight soon after the onset of walking (Clark, Whitall, & Phillips, 1988). Indeed, it may be that this strong coupling is important in defining the gait pattern as walking rather than some other locomotory pattern. Clark and Phillips (1987) found that once a steady-state velocity is achieved, the step-cycle organization of new walkers is *almost* identical to adults/mature walkers (although infants take 2 to 3 steps to achieve steady state whereas adults achieve steady state after the first step).

Such research points to the dynamical, self-organizing nature of infant behavior. It suggests that babies exhibit strong interlimb and intralimb coupling in spontaneous movements and demonstrate a preference for moving the legs in an antiphase (alternating) pattern. Further, the coupling within and between the limbs appears to wax and wane throughout the first year. Modeling strategies to test for attractor dynamics in infant behavior and to model behavioral patterns with equations of motion, however, have been more difficult to come by.

GOALS OF THIS CHAPTER

I propose a dynamical model in a task appropriate for developmental study, to establish the existence of this dynamical regime in adults (to verify the appropriateness of the dynamic at the performance time scale), to test the appropriateness of this dynamic with children's movements, and to begin to capture changes at a developmental time scale. Whereas the ultimate goal is to understand the dynamics of movement in terms of the time scale of development, testing the appropriateness of the performance or movement dynamic is an important first step in being able to capture the developmental changes.

Given the inherent difficulties in working with a developmental population (limited behavioral repertoire, high variability in movement production, etc.) selecting an appropriate task is a major concern. The task reported here, clapping, was chosen for a number of reasons. First, it is a behavior that occurs naturally in the child's repertoire, remains simple and manageable, and lends itself to the sorts of manipulations that allow a test of the coordination dynamics. Additionally, it is a coordination pattern for which a dynamical model is, intuitively, readily available. Choosing a well-established dynamical model is helpful in discovering optimal strategies for applying dynamical techniques to developmental populations. Furthermore, selection of this task extends dynamical treatments beyond the infancy period to a task with (a) expressive and communicative functions, (b) percussive functions, and (c) complex spatial and timing constraints. This is a potentially important extension because, as Thelen (1995) has pointed out, the important agents of change later in infancy (e.g., practice, environmental conditions) may well be different from those early in infancy (e.g., growth, biomechanical factors).

A hallmark property of self-organizing systems abiding by attractor dynamics is that they demonstrate spatio-temporal patterns. An obvious ques-

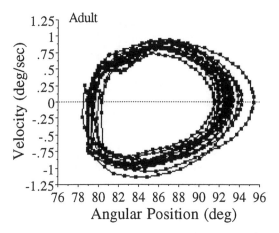

FIG. 3.1. Angular excursion of the right limb plotted against its velocity during a representative trial of adult clapping resembles a classic limit cycle attractor.

tion is whether there is evidence of spatio-temporal patterns in clapping. In particular, do trajectories of clapping movements remain within a circumscribed region of state space, demonstrating a preference for particular regions? Or, do successive movements entirely fill the space without any regions being revisited more than others?

Figure 3.1 displays a representative plot of a recording of angular excursion of the right limb during clapping plotted against its velocity for an adult clapper. The angular excursion is a measure of the oscillation of the forearm segment of the arm (finger-to-elbow) and the vertical plane of the body. The trajectory of the limb forms a closed orbit. Although an identical path is not traced in each back and forth excursion, the trajectories prefer certain regions in space and continuously revisit those regions. This closed orbit resembles a classic limit cycle or periodic attractor (Thompson & Stewart, 1986), suggesting that clapping is governed by an underlying limit cycle dynamic.

COUPLED OSCILLATOR DYNAMICS: THEORY AND EXPERIMENTATION

Limit cycle or oscillatory dynamics in the production of interlimb coordination sequences in adults have been extensively studied. For example, investigations of the oscillations of an individual's two index fingers (e.g., Kelso, 1984), an arm and a leg (Jeka, Kelso, & Kiemel, 1993; Kelso & Jeka, 1992), pendulums held in each hand (e.g., Kugler & Turvey, 1987), pendulums held by two individuals (e.g., Schmidt & Turvey, 1994), the legs of two individuals

3. DYNAMICS IN DEVELOPMENT

(Schmidt, Carello, & Turvey, 1990), juggling (Beek & Turvey, 1992), and finger tapping (Peper, Beek, & Van Wieringen, 1991) have all implicated principles of oscillatory coordination dynamics. I discuss this work and the dynamical model of interlimb coordination resulting from it and then present evidence that suggests this model can be applied to clapping.

In adults, the formation of coordinative structures underlying rhythmic movement have been shown to be constrained by the mass-spring (Kandel, Schwartz, & Jessel, 1991) and oscillatory (Kugler et al., 1980) properties of the limbs. As a result, rhythmically moved limb segments can be treated as self-sustained physical oscillators with their own preferred frequency of oscillation (ω)—each prefers to complete one cycle of its behavior at a certain rate (Kay, Kelso, Saltzman, & Schöner, 1987; Kay, Saltzman, & Kelso, 1991; Kadar, Schmidt, & Turvey, 1993).

Two important facts concerning interlimb coordination have been observed that suggest an interlimb rhythmic coordination pattern can be modeled as two such oscillators interacting across a coupling medium (Haken, Kelso, & Bunz, 1985). First, predominantly inphase and antiphase coordination patterns occur. That is, the limbs are either in the same portions of their cycles at the same time (inphase) or in opposite portions of their cycles at the same time (antiphase). Second, the antiphase coordination pattern is less stable and breaks down into inphase at higher frequencies. A noteworthy fact is that similar properties can be observed in physical coupled oscillators. In order to measure the coordination of interlimb segments, one needs an index that captures the position of the oscillators relative to one another. For this purpose, the relative phase angle (ϕ) is used. The location of an oscillator in its cycle at any point in time is represented as a phase angle θ—essentially the arctan (velocity/position). The relative phase angle ϕ of two oscillators is the difference of the two oscillators' phase angles, $\theta_1 - \theta_2$. If the two oscillators are inphase, then $\phi = 0$. If they are in antiphase, $\phi = \pi$.

A formal coupled oscillatory model of the stable modes at $\phi = 0$ and π and the breakdown of the π mode at high frequencies has been proposed by Haken et al. (1985). As a consequence, the dynamics of ϕ have been modeled by

$$\dot{\phi} = -a \sin(\phi) - 2b \sin(2\phi) + \sqrt{Q}\xi \tag{1}$$

This equation states that the rate of change of ϕ is a function of the coupling or cooperation of the two oscillators ($-a \sin(\phi) - 2b \sin(2\phi)$), and a stochastic noise process ($\sqrt{Q}\xi$) (Schöner, Haken, & Kelso, 1986). Changes in control parameters, properties that affect the dynamics indirectly, can alter the dynamical landscape. Scaling of the control parameter results in changes in behavior because coupling strengths a and b are related to the control

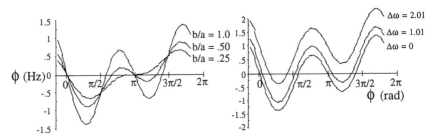

FIG. 3.2. Plot of relative phase versus its rate of change of the Haken et al. (1985) coupled oscillator equation for different values of b/a (left panel) and $\Delta\omega$ (right panel). Stable fixed points at 0 and π are represented as zero-crossings. Changes in the ratio b/a alters the concavity of the potential wells. At a critical value of b/a (here, equal to 1.0) the zero-crossing disappears, representing the annihilation of the stable fixed point. As $\Delta\omega$ deviates from 0 the function shifts over and "lifts" up until, at a critical value (here $\Delta\omega = 2.01$), the zero-crossings disappear.

parameter frequency. A plot of ϕ versus $\dot{\phi}$ (Fig. 3.2, left) demonstrates how this model is able to account for the two basic coordination facts mentioned earlier. First, places where $\dot{\phi}$ crosses the ϕ-axis with a negative slope represent stable fixed points (points of stability or attractors). In this figure, stable fixed points exist at 0 and π. Thus, this figure illustrates the 0 and π relative phases are the only stable states. Second, the slope of the line through the fixed point indicates the stability of the point. As it decreases, the variability associated with the steady state increases. Another important aspect of the plot is that as the ratio b/a decreases (which is experimentally achieved by increasing frequency), fluctuations about the stable points increase until, at a critical frequency, the stable point disappears. Thus, the model accounts for the disappearance of antiphase with increasing frequency as well.

This basic model has been modified to account for asymmetries, for example, handedness effects, hemispheric asymmetries, differential loading of the limbs (Kelso, Delcolle, & Schöner, 1990; Kelso & Jeka, 1992). A competition term ($\Delta\omega$) was added to the equation to account for the fact that the two oscillators may not prefer to oscillate at the same frequency:

$$\dot{\phi} = \Delta\omega - a\sin(\phi) - 2b\sin(2\phi) + \sqrt{Q}\xi \qquad (2)$$

Under manipulation of $\Delta\omega$, the stable fixed points drift away from the attractors at 0 and π (Fig. 3.2, right). That is, for $\Delta\omega = 0$, the zero-crossings are at 0 and π. But, as $\Delta\omega$ is increased, the whole function shifts over and lifts up. In the figure, the attractor at π disappears at a $\Delta\omega$ value of .32.

In sum, this coupled oscillator model is composed of competitive ($\Delta\omega$) and cooperative ($- a\sin(\phi) - 2b\sin(2\phi)$) terms. When the competition and cooperation balance, perfect inphase or antiphase behavior is exhibited (ϕ = 0 or π). However, as the competitive terms increase relative to the cooperative terms, fixed point drift or phase lag is exhibited. And, as the strength of the cooperative terms decrease (e.g., as frequency increases), the phase lag increases. Furthermore, a parabolic change in fluctuations (variability) is observed under manipulation of $\Delta\omega$ and this is exaggerated with increases in frequency.

Such patternings of fixed point drift and variability have been observed under experimental manipulation of $\Delta\omega$ and frequency (ω_c) in a number of laboratory tasks—oscillations of two index fingers (Kelso, 1984), an arm and a leg (Jeka, Kelso, & Kiemel, 1993; Kelso & Jeka, 1992), pendulums held in each hand (e.g., Schmidt, Shaw, & Turvey, 1993); pendulums held by two individuals (e.g., Amazeen, Schmidt, & Turvey, 1995; Schmidt & Turvey, 1994; Schmidt, Christianson, Carello, & Baron, 1994) and the legs of two individuals (e.g., Schmidt, Carello, & Turvey, 1990). Because such a variety of coordinations have been shown to adhere—in formal detail—to a coupled oscillator model, the implication is that control in such tasks is relegated to a relatively autonomous dynamical control structure that requires little attention or intervention on the part of the actor. Is clapping a self-organizing process like these that abides by coupled oscillator dynamics in Equations 1 and 2?

Modeling Adult Clapping as a Coupled Oscillator

Results from one of a set of studies testing the viability of the coupled oscillator model of interlimb phasing in adult clapping (Fitzpatrick, Schmidt, & Carello, 1996) will be summarized here. Subjects were instructed to clap in a relatively constrained palm-to-palm clap (Repp, 1987) in which the forearms were parallel to the ground plane with fingertips facing forward and palms flat together on contact. $\Delta\omega$ was manipulated by weighting the arms and frequency was manipulated by requiring subjects to clap in beat to a metronome-specified frequency. The angular excursion of the forearm segment of the arm (finger-to-elbow) and the vertical plane of the body was recorded.

Figure 3.3 displays a representative trial of clapping. The top panel displays angular position of each of the limbs along the y axis and time along the x-axis. Visual inspection of the figure reveals that the limbs are moving at a common tempo with nearly identical amplitudes—the right hand and left hand curves are on top of each other. The peaks on the plot indicate portions of the trial where the hands are apart and valleys represent portions of the trial when the hands are together. This figure suggests that each hand reaches peak extension and flexion at the same time. The bottom panel displays relative phase over the course of a trial. Inspection of this figure

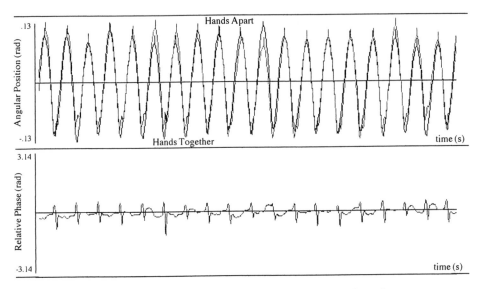

FIG. 3.3. Plots of angular position (top panel) and relative phase (bottom panel) during a representative bout of adult clapping.

indicates that a nearly constant relative phase of 0 is maintained, with slight oscillation around 0. The small spikes in the plot occur at points of hand contact.

The displacement of relative phase from perfectly in phase, an index of coordination dynamics, is displayed in Fig. 3.4 (top panel). When neither limb is weighted, relative phase is about 0 rad. However, when the limbs are asymmetrically weighted, relative phase begins to deviate slightly from 0—the larger the weighting of the limbs, the larger the deviation from 0. This patterning was evident for both weighting of the right limb and weighting of the left limb. Furthermore, increasing frequency exaggerated these effects, such that the deviation of relative phase from 0 rad is the largest for the "heavy" limb weighting at the fast frequency. The change in the steepness of these curves indicates that the effect of limb weighting is more dramatic with increasing frequency. Another index of coordination dynamics, the variability of relative phase, is displayed in the bottom panel of Fig. 3.4. Variability is the smallest when the limbs are unweighted, but increases with weighting of the limbs. And, weighting either the right limb or the left limb resulted in nearly identical increases in variability. Furthermore, the stacking of the u-shaped curves indicates increasing frequency results in an overall increase in variability. The appearance of these properties of coupled oscillator dynamics suggest this appropriately models interlimb coordination in clapping.

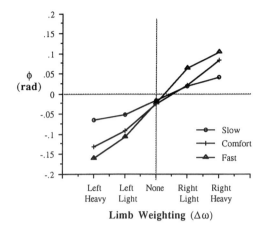

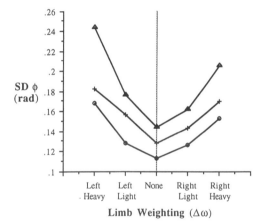

FIG. 3.4. The change in mean φ (top) and SD φ (bottom) as a function of limb weighting and frequency in adult clapping.

Modeling Clapping in Children as Coupled Oscillators

Because both quantitative and qualitative measures suggest that coupled oscillator dynamics are useful in modeling interlimb coordination in adult clapping, two important questions present themselves. First, when do children display these same coordination patterns? And, how do these patterns evolve?

One experiment investigated the clapping patterns of children 3, 4, 5, and 7 years of age (Fitzpatrick, Schmidt, & Lockman, 1996). Children were instructed to clap their hands (e.g., "Imagine you are at a birthday party or movie") and the angular excursion of the forearm was recorded. Δω and frequency were manipulated as in the previous adult studies. A portion of the data from that study are discussed here.[1]

Figure 3.5 displays mean relative phase as a function of limb weighting for the 4-, 5-, and 7-year-old groups. This reflects clapping at a self-chosen tempo (about 2.5 Hz) without metronome pacing. Inspection of the figure reveals that it is not until 7 years of age that relative phase changes as a function of limb weighting as predicted by the model. Although the plots of variability as a function of limb weighting (Fig. 3.6) appear to indicate that variability increases with limb weighting, only the patterning for the 7-year-old group is significant (Fitzpatrick, Schmidt, & Lockman, 1996). Measures of relative phase and variability of relative phase, therefore, indicate that a stable oscillatory dynamic was not exhibited before seven years.

Inspection of representative angular position and relative phase time series of a 4-year-old clapper (Fig. 3.7) further suggests that, especially for younger children, a stable oscillatory dynamic was not well established. In the top panel, the angular position curves for each of the hands are not completely overlapping—the amplitude of the right hand is much larger than the left and the peaks in each curve do not always occur at the same point. Additionally, the peaks are often a bit indistinct, in some cases looking more like plateaus than sharp peaks (especially when compared to similar adult curves, Fig. 3.3). Inspection of the bottom panel of this figure indicates that a constant phase relationship was not maintained throughout the clapping cycles—nearly all phase relations between 0 and ±3.14 rad occur. When compared to the adult time series, there is much more variability in the relative phasing in children. Comparison of mean variability scores confirms that, across subjects, movement variability in clapping is much larger in children (SD ϕ = .80, .75, and .56 for 4, 5, and 7 years of age, respectively) than in adults (SD ϕ = .16), even at 7 years. Taken together, this suggests that the coordination displayed in clapping, especially in younger children, may not be stationary.

The coupled oscillator model, as presented thus far, is based on an assumption of movement stationarity as seen in absolute coordination. Absolute coordination refers to coordination patterns in which a constant phase relation is maintained throughout the movement and phase locking is nearly perfect. As mentioned, however, the coordination patterns observed in this study (especially in the younger children) are quite variable and demonstrate rather dramatic changes in the phase relations displayed. In this sense, the clapping patterns are not necessarily stationary. Nevertheless, the coupled oscillator model is able to account for such nonstation-

---

[1]The developmental clapping data are a portion of a larger experiment presented in Fitzpatrick, Schmidt, and Lockman (1996). The analyses as presented here do not appear in the original work.

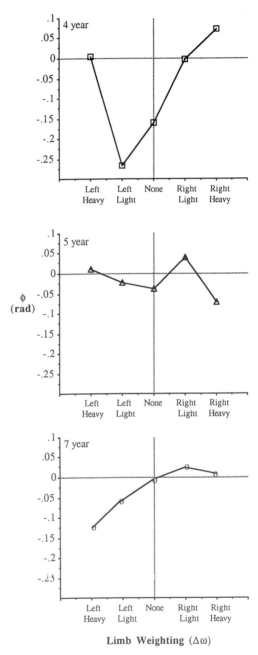

FIG. 3.5. The change in mean ϕ as a function of limb weighting for 4-year-old (top), 5-year-old (middle), and 7-year-old (bottom) participants. The patterning of results predicted by the coupled oscillator model is not demonstrated until 7 years of age.

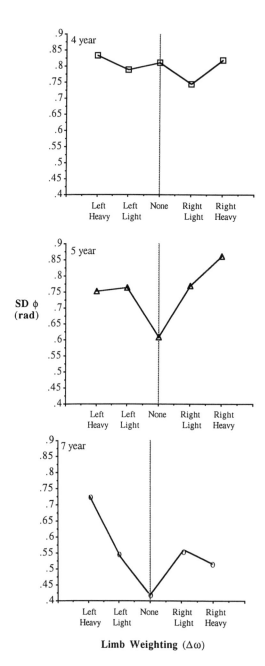

FIG. 3.6. The change in mean SD ϕ as a function of limb weighting for 4-year-old (top), 5-year-old (middle), and 7-year-old (bottom) participants.

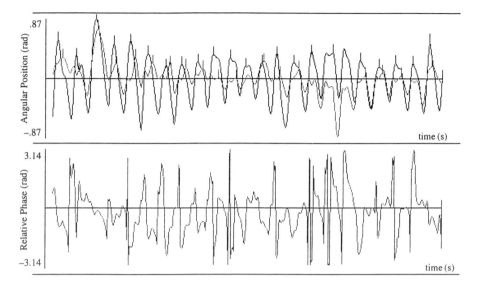

FIG. 3.7. Plots of angular position (top panel) and relative phase (bottom panel) during a representative bout of a 4-year-old clapper. The angular position of the right limb has a larger amplitude than the left. Compared to adults, relative phase is much more variable and fluctuates between $\pm\pi$, achieving all possible phase relations.

arity, as seen, for example, in relative coordination. Relative coordination refers to coordination patterns in which less phase locking is observed and every possible phase relation is exhibited, with a tendency for phase attraction to particular phase relations.

Referring back to Equations 1 and 2, the lack of stationarity is a consequence of a balancing between the competitive and cooperative terms: As the competitive term ($\Delta\omega$) overwhelms the cooperative terms ($-a \sin(\phi) - 2b \sin(2\phi)$), fixed points (attractors) become unstable and disappear. A plot of ϕ against $\dot{\phi}$ (Fig. 3.8) is instructive. In the figure, coupling terms a and b are constant. For small values of $\Delta\omega$ (equal to 1 or 2), $\dot{\phi}$ settles down to a value of 0: $\dot{\phi}$ begins with an initially high value that decreases rapidly over time and then stops at 0. The stopping of the curve at 0 indicates the existence of a fixed point. A rate of change of relative phase equal to 0 means that relative phase is constant (ϕ no longer changes). The value of ϕ at the zero-crossing indicates the relative phasing between the limbs that will be maintained. For example, if the zero-crossing occurs at $\phi = 0$, a constant relative phase of 0 rad should be maintained. For zero-crossing of $\phi = .05$, the observed relative phasing between the limbs should be .05 rad. The stability of the fixed point is indicated by where along the ϕ-axis the zero-crossing occurs: The farther out the zero-crossing is along the x-axis, the less stable the fixed point. In this figure, the fixed point at $\Delta\omega = 1$ is more

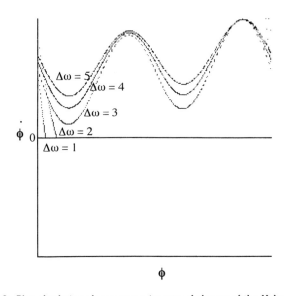

FIG. 3.8. Plot of relative phase versus its rate of change of the Haken et al. (1985) coupled oscillator equation for a range of Δω values. For small values of Δω zero-crossings are evident, with the steepness of the function indexing the stability of the fixed point. For larger values of Δω, zero-crossings are no longer evident and all possible phase values are visited. Attractive regions are represented as wells. The concavity of the well indexes the relative attractiveness of the region.

stable than the fixed point at $\Delta\omega = 2$ as indicated by the smaller ϕ-value at the zero-crossing.

At increasingly larger values of $\Delta\omega$ (e.g., $\Delta\omega = 3$, 4, or 5 in this figure), the fixed points disappear, as represented by the lack of zero-crossings in the curves: $\dot{\phi}$ approaches zero but does not come to rest at 0. This indicates that the two oscillators are no longer maintaining a constant steady phase relation. Not only is ϕ changing, but, as indicated, all possible values of ϕ between 0 and 2π result. The portions of the curves with dashed lines indicate phase relations that are less likely (around the hills, where the rate of change of relative phase is high) and the portions with solid lines (valleys, where the rate of change of relative phase is low) represent phase relations that are more likely. Thus, there is attraction to certain phase relations (i.e., around 0 and π where valleys are evident) that previously had been attractors. The depth (as represented by the minima) and concavity of the valleys indexes the attractiveness of those regions: The less deep and less shallow the valley, the more stable the region. Here, the valleys associated with $\Delta\omega$ = 3 are more attractive than the valleys associated with $\Delta\omega$ = 4 or 5, as indicated by lower minima. Additionally, the regions closer to 0 (the first valleys in the plot) are more attractive than the regions closer to 2π as represented by the higher minima. As this figure shows, as $\Delta\omega$ is continually increased and the competition outstrips cooperation, the coordination becomes increasingly weaker and more variable.

These considerations required new measures for analyzing rhythmic coordination, measures that are able to account for the fact that the movements of children are not always stable. Accordingly, the distribution of ϕ and the rate of change of relative phase—$\dot{\phi}$—were used (Kelso, 1994). The coupled oscillator model makes two important predictions regarding these measures: (a) ϕ should be distributed across all phase relationships but with a concentration around 0 and π, and (b) $\dot{\phi}$ should be smaller for stronger attractive regions.

Figure 3.9 displays frequency distributions of the mean data for 4-, 5-, and 7-year-old children as well as adults. These data reflect clapping at a comfortable self-chosen tempo (about 2.5 Hz). Inspection of this figure reveals several things. First, all possible phase relations were evident for all children, although a phase relation of ϕ less than .35 rad occurred most frequently. In adults, a phase relation greater than 1.0 rad never occurred. A comparison of the means indicates a tendency for the percent of observed ϕ less than .35 rad to increase with age and the percent of observed ϕ less than 1.0 rad to decrease with age (Table 3.1).

The rate of change of ϕ can be used to assess whether a constant phase relation is maintained. The coupled oscillator model predicts that $\dot{\phi}$ should be smaller for stronger attractive regions. Attractor stability has been shown to be affected by frequency (attractor strength decreases as frequency increases) and imbalances between the limbs (attractor strength decreases as limb imbalance increases; Schmidt et al., 1993). Figure 3.10 displays $\dot{\phi}$ as

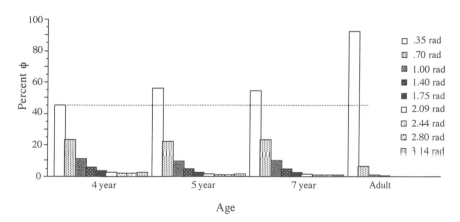

FIG. 3.9. Frequency distributions of mean ϕ for 4-year-old, 5-year-old, 7-year-old, and adult clappers. For younger clappers, all possible phase relations are demonstrated, with a phase relation close to 0 rad most prominent.

TABLE 3.1
Percent of Observed Relative Phase Across Age Groups

Age	f < .35 rad	f > 1 rad
4	45%	20%
5	56%	12%
7	54%	12%
Adult	90%	0%

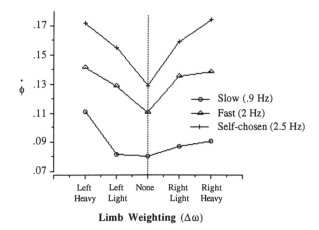

FIG. 3.10. The change in φ̇ as a function of limb weighting and frequency in children clapping. φ̇ increases with both limb weighting and frequency.

a function of limb weighting for three frequencies. As expected, φ̇ increases with frequency and with increasing difference between the limbs. There is a tendency for φ̇ to decrease with age (φ̇ = .15, .12, .11 for 4, 5, and 7 years, respectively). Interestingly, even at age 7, φ̇ does not reflect adult (φ̇ = .03) levels of stability.

These measures provide evidence for relative coordination in younger clappers, indicative of coupled oscillator attractors underlying their coordination patterns. In spite of high variability, nonstationarity, and individual differences of the children's data, coupled oscillator dynamics successfully model their interlimb coordination in clapping.

CONCLUDING REMARKS

The putatively simple act of clapping requires the specification and control of a number of parameters. For example, (a) what joint will be responsible for generating the predominant clapping movements (shoulder, elbow, wrist, or a combination thereof); (b) where will the hands contact (at midline, off to one side, above the head); (c) will the hands contact softly or with a good deal of force; (d) what type of sound will be generated (loud, soft, no sound); (e) will clapping be at a slow, moderate, or fast tempo; (f) will the hands be cupped or flat? Dynamically speaking, we assume that in order to clap, the limbs (usually the arms) must be transformed into a special-purpose, low dimensional clapping device. That is, a coordinative structure for clapping must be assembled. This presupposes an intention to clap (either internally generated or experimentally imposed) and the means for transforming the motor apparatus into a clapping device, both of which are assumed to be dynamical processes. Here, I have shown that the coordinative structure assembled for clapping abides by coupled oscillator dynamics, both for adults and children.

The movement dynamic assembled by the children is more indicative of relative coordination than absolute coordination, as seen in adults. That is, the data suggest that a constant phase relation is not maintained throughout a bout of clapping and the rate of change of relative phase is systematically related to parameters known to affect attractor strength (namely, frequency, limb imbalances). By about 7 years of age, however, the coordination in clapping demonstrates a patterning consistent with a stable oscillatory dynamic but continues to be a bit more variable than adults.

If one adopts the framework that development can be characterized as a two-step process of assembly followed by fine tuning, the persistence of high variability suggests that, even at 7 years, children are still in the fine-tuning phase of becoming proficient clappers. The assembly of a coordinative structure with underlying oscillatory dynamics appears to be accomplished early (perhaps soon after clapping onset around 8 to 12 months). The need to continue to explore the clapping dynamical landscape suggests that the parameterization of the coordination dynamic may be very different for different clapping styles, purposes, and so on. That is, it could be that because there are so many styles and functions of clapping (there are so many potential parameters to be varied), it takes a while to discover the optimal parameterization for all of them. Additionally, different varieties of clapping tasks may require different intentional resources, which probably change in tandem with developmental skill. For example, the concentration and "on-line" monitoring necessary to maintain the coordination dynamic may be high initially for very young children and children experimenting with new clapping styles. More skilled clapping patterns (presumably those of older children) most likely do not require active monitoring of the intentional dynamic in order to maintain the coordination mode.

Casual observations of babies indicates that initially they clap very rigidly and only for a limited number of successive claps. After becoming proficient at this sort of rigid clapping, the relative phasing between their limbs is probably (pending experimental verification) quite good. When they attempt to loosen the intralimb linkages, that is, clap less rigidly, it is possible that the coordination "falls apart." Such a change in the clapping task may alter the layout of the potential landscape so that the infant must attend to different information. As they perform more complex clapping games (e.g., Patacake, the clapping song B-I-N-G-O) the layout may change again, requiring yet another searching of parameter space and fine-tuning. In other words, even an apparently slight change in the clapping task (e.g., clap overhead rather than at midline, clap feet rather than hands) may alter the dynamical landscape and thus require new perceptual and motor attunement. It may well be that the form and strength of the interlimb coupling in clapping waxes and wanes throughout childhood as the child modifies the style and intent of clapping, grows, and so on.

The observed changes in the variability of clapping (as measured by standard deviation of relative phase and rate of change of relative phase) suggest that, developmentally, fixed points (attractors) are becoming more stable. In other words, the potential landscape changes such that the potential wells are deeper with steeper gradients. In terms of dynamical modeling, there are two possible routes for addressing such changes. One alternative is to treat developmental changes as a control parameter that alters the dynamical landscape thereby modifying the stability of fixed points. Perhaps other control parameters besides frequency dictate coupling strengths a and b in Equations 1 and 2. For example, scaling age (or more likely a variable associated with age—one that quantifies skill level, for instance) may result in changes in the ratio b/a and as a consequence cause fixed points to appear and disappear. A measure that quantifies the consistency of spatial location at hand contact might be another possible control parameter. Control parameters other than frequency altering the stability of relative phasing have previously been found. For example, Kelso and colleagues (Kelso, Buchanan, & Wallace, 1991) identified limb spatial orientation as an additional control parameter in single, multijoint limb movement patterns.

Another modeling alternative is to add an additional dynamical term to the Haken et al. (1985) coupled oscillator model in Equations 1 and 2, one that accounts for the developmental changes that occur in the progression from relative to absolute coordination. Such a developmental dynamic would be a process that reconfigures the initial coordinative structure for clapping (without fixed points) to have an attractor state at the to-be-acquired coordination pattern. The developmental dynamic would alter not only the concavity of the potential wells but also the location of its minima. Precedence for such a modeling strategy can be found in Schöner and colleagues' (Schöner, 1989; Schöner, Zanone, & Kelso, 1992; Zanone & Kelso, 1992) modeling of the dynamics involved in acquiring a novel bimanual phasing pattern. Their modeling entailed the learning or intentional dynamics (with an equilibrium point at the to-be-learned pattern) modifying the intrinsic dynamics such that a new attractive state emerged.

A likely scenario for understanding the developmental progression of clapping skill requires an interplay between the intentional dynamic that "sets up" the potential landscape of the movement dynamic and the coupled oscillator (movement) dynamic itself. For example, initially, the intentional dynamic may be weak (and thus require careful monitoring and concentration) and the oscillatory dynamic may have weak fixed points. This combination of dynamics could result in the types of relative coordination patterns demonstrated here. During a transitional period of perceptual exploration and attunement, the intentional dynamic may become stronger but fixed points remain weak as optimal parameterization is explored. A period of skilled absolute coordination may result from a combination of an autonomous intentional dynamic coupled with an oscillatory dynamic with strong fixed points. Such a progression from relative to transitional to absolute coordination may occur a number of times as task, environmental, and intentional constraints change.

Although additional work is necessary to determine which of these modeling strategies will be most appropriate, this research has extended understanding of the development of interlimb coordination dynamics. First, an explicit, formal model has been applied and tested in examining the development of a complex rhythmical behavior. In this case, the applicability of the Haken et al. (1985) coupled oscillator model for clapping was verified in adults and demonstrated in children. Additionally, developmental changes in the appropriateness of this model were shown. Even though this behavior manifests a good deal of nonstationarity and high variability within and across young children, quantitative dynamical modeling is possible nonetheless. The use of two measures for assessing the existence of relative coordination (the distribution of relative phase and the rate of change of relative phase) suggest that clapping goes through a period of relative coordination before absolute coordination is achieved. Finally, two ways in which this developmental progression might be handled in dynamical terms were identified. Extension of these methods to study the longitudinal development of clapping should lead to more general insights into how best to model the developmental progression.

REFERENCES

Amazeen, P., Schmidt, R. C., & Turvey, M. T. (1995). Frequency detuning of the phase entrainment dynamics of visually coupled rhythmic movements. *Biological Cybernetics, 72,* 511–518.
Beek, P. J., & Turvey, M. T. (1992). Temporal patterning in cascade juggling. *Journal of Experimental Psychology: Human Perception and Performance, 18,* 934–947.

Bernstein, N. (1967). *The coordination and regulation of movement.* London: Pergamon Press.

Bingham, G. P. (1988). Task-specific devices and the perceptual bottleneck. *Human Movement Science, 7,* 225–264.

Clark, J. E., & Phillips, S. J. (1987). The step cycle organization of infant walkers. *Journal of Motor Behavior, 19,* 421–433.

Clark, J. E., Whitall, J., & Phillips, S. J. (1988). Human interlimb coordination in the first six months of walking. *Developmental Psychology, 21,* 445–456.

Easton, T. A. (1972). On the normal use of reflexes. *American Scientist, 60,* 591–599.

Fitzpatrick, P., Schmidt, R. C., & Carello, C. (1996). Dynamical patterns in clapping behavior. *Journal of Experimental Psychology: Human Perception and Performance, 22,* 707–724.

Fitzpatrick, P., Schmidt, R. C., & Lockman, J. J. (1996). Development of clapping behavior. *Child Development, 67,* 2691–2708.

Fowler, C., & Turvey, M. T. (1978). Skill acquisition: An event approach with special reference to searching for the optimum of a function of several variables. In G. Stelmach (Ed.), *Information processing in motor control and learning* (pp. 1–39). New York: Academic Press.

Gibson, J. J. (1966). *The senses considered as perceptual systems.* Boston: Houghton Mifflin.

Gibson, J. J. (1979). *The ecological approach to visual perception.* Boston: Houghton Mifflin.

Goldfield, E. C. (1995). *Emergent forms: Origins and early development of human action and perception.* New York: Oxford University Press.

Haken, H., Kelso, J. A. S., & Bunz, H. (1985). A theoretical model of phase transitions in human hand movements. *Biological Cybernetics, 51,* 347–356.

Jeka, J. J., Kelso, J. A. S., & Kiemel, T. (1993). Pattern switching in human multilimb coordination dynamics. *Bulletin of Mathematical Biology, 55,* 829–845.

Jensen, J. L., Ulrich, B. D., Thelen, E., Schneider, K., & Zernicke, R. F. (1995). Adaptive dynamics of the leg movement patterns of human infants: III. Development. *Journal of Motor Behavior, 27,* 366–374.

Kadar, E., Schmidt, R. C., & Turvey, M. T. (1993). Constants underlying frequency changes in biological rhythmic movements. *Biological Cybernetics, 68,* 421–430.

Kandel, E. R., Schwartz, J. H., & Jessel, T. M. (1991). *Principles of neural science.* New York: Elsevier.

Kay, B. A., Kelso, J. A. S., Saltzman, E. L., & Schöner, G. (1987). Space-time behavior of single and bimanual rhythmical movements: Data and limit-cycle model. *Journal of Experimental Psychology: Human Perception and Performance, 13,* 178–192.

Kay, B. A., Saltzman, E. L., & Kelso, J. A. S. (1991). Steady-state and perturbed rhythmical movements: A dynamical analysis. *Journal of Experimental Psychology: Human Perception and Performance, 17*(1), 187–197.

Kelso, J. A. S. (1984). Phase transitions and critical behavior in human bimanual coordination. *American Journal of Physiology: Regulatory, Integrative and Comparative Physiology, 15,* R1000–R1004.

Kelso, J. A. S. (1994). Elementary coordination dynamics. In S. Swinnen, H. Heur, J. Massion, & P. Casaer (Eds.), *Interlimb coordination: Neural, dynamical, and cognitive constraints* (pp. 301–320). San Diego: Academic Press.

Kelso, J. A. S., Buchanan, J., & Wallace, S. A. (1991). Order parameters for the neural organization of single, multijoint movement patterns. *Experimental Brain Research,* 432–444.

Kelso, J. A. S., Delcolle, J. D., & Schöner, G. (1990). Action-perception as a pattern formation process. In M. Jeannerod (Ed.), *Attention and performance XIII* (pp. 139–169). Hillsdale, NJ: Lawrence Erlbaum Associates.

Kelso, J. A. S., & Jeka, J. J. (1992). Symmetry breaking dynamics of human multilimb coordination. *Journal of Experimental Psychology: Human Perception and Performance, 18,* 645–668.

Kugler, P. N. (1986). A morphological perspective on the origin and evolution of movement patterns. In M. G. Wade & H. T. A. Whiting (Eds.), *Motor development in children: Aspects of coordination and control* (pp. 459–525). The Hague: Nijhoff.

Kugler, P. N., Kelso, J. A. S., & Turvey, M. T. (1980). On the concept of coordinative structures as dissipative structures: I. Theoretical lines of convergence. In G. E. Stelmach & J. Requin (Eds.), *Tutorials in motor behavior*. Amsterdam: North-Holland.

Kugler, P. N., Kelso, J. A. S., & Turvey, M. T. (1982). On the control and coordination of naturally developing systems. In J. A. S. Kelso & J. E. Clark (Eds.), *The development of movement control and coordination* (pp. 5–78). New York: Wiley.

Kugler, P. N., & Turvey, M. T. (1987). *Information, natural law, and the self-assembly of rhythmic movement*. Hillsdale, NJ: Lawrence Erlbaum Associates.

Newell, K. M. (1985). Coordination, control and skill. In D. Goodman, R. B. Wilberg, & I. M. Franks (Eds.), *Differing perspectives in motor learning, memory, and control* (pp. 295–317). Amsterdam: North-Holland.

Newell, K. M., Kugler, P. N., Van Emmerik, R. E. A., & McDonald, P. V. (1989). Search strategies and the acquisition of coordination. In S. A. Wallace (Ed.), *Perspectives on the coordination of movement* (pp. 123–156). Amsterdam: North-Holland.

Newell, K. M., & Van Emmerik, R. E. A. (1990). Are Gesell's developmental principles general principles for the acquisition of coordination? In J. Clark & Humphrey (Eds.), *Advances in motor development research*. New York: AMS Press.

Peper, C. E., Beek, P. J., & Van Wieringen, P. C. W. (1991). Bifurcations in polyrhythmic tapping: In search of Farey principles. In J. Requin & G. E. Stelmach (Eds.), *Tutorials in motor neuroscience* (pp. 413–431). Dordrecht: Kluwer.

Repp, B. H. (1987). The sound of two hands clapping: An exploratory study. *Journal of the Acoustical Society of America, 81*(4), 1100–1109.

Saltzman, E. L., & Munhall, K. G. (1992). Skill acquisition and development: The roles of state-, parameter-, and graph-dynamics. *Journal of Motor Behavior, 24*, 58–66.

Schmidt, R. C., Carello, C., & Turvey, M. T. (1990). Phase transitions and critical fluctuations in the visual coordination of rhythmic movements between people. *Journal of Experimental Psychology: Human Perception and Performance, 16*(2), 227–247.

Schmidt, R. C., Christianson, N., Carello, C., & Baron, R. (1994). Effects of social and physical variables on between-person visual coordination. *Ecological Psychology, 6*, 159–183.

Schmidt, R. C., & Fitzpatrick, P. (1996). Advances in learning: II. Dynamical theories. In H. Zelaznik (Ed.), *Advances in motor learning and control* (pp. 195–223). Chicago: Human Kinetics.

Schmidt, R. C., Shaw, B. K, & Turvey, M. T. (1993). Coupling dynamics in interlimb coordination. *Journal of Experimental Psychology: Human Perception and Performance, 19*(2), 397–415.

Schmidt, R. C., Treffner, P. J., Shaw, B. K., & Turvey, M. T. (1992). Dynamical aspects of learning an interlimb rhythmic coordination. *Journal of Motor Behavior, 24*, 67–82.

Schmidt, R. C., & Turvey, M. T. (1994). Phase-entrainment dynamics of visually coupled rhythmic movements. *Biological Cybernetics, 70*, 369–376.

Schöner, G. (1989). Learning and recall in a dynamic theory of coordination patterns. *Biological Cybernetics, 63*, 39–54.

Schöner, G., Haken, H., & Kelso, J. A. S. (1986). A stochastic theory of phase transitions in human hand movement. *Biological Cybernetics, 53*, 442–452.

Schöner, G., Zanone, P. G., & Kelso, J. A. S. (1992). Learning as change of coordination dynamics: Theory and experiment. *Journal of Motor Behavior, 24*, 29–48.

Thelen, E. (1983). Learning to walk is still an "old" problem: A reply to Zelazo. *Journal of Motor Behavior, 15*, 139–161.

Thelen, E. (1986). Development of coordinated movement: Implications for early human development. In M. G. Wade & H. T. A. Whiting (Eds.), *Motor development in children: Aspects of coordination and control* (pp. 107–120). Boston: Martinus Nijhoff.

Thelen, E. (1989). Self-organization in developmental processes: Can systems approaches work? In M. Gunnar & E. Thelen (Eds.), *Systems in development: The Minnesota Symposia on Child Psychology*. Hillsdale, NJ: Lawrence Erlbaum Associates.

Thelen, E. (1995). Motor development: A new synthesis. *American Psychologist, 50*, 79–95.

Thelen, E., & Fisher, D. M. (1982). Newborn stepping: An explanation for a "disappearing reflex." *Developmental Psychology, 18*, 760–775.

Thelen, E., & Fisher, D. M. (1983). The organization of spontaneous leg movements in newborn infants. *Journal of Motor Behavior, 15*, 353–377.

Thelen, E., & Smith, L. B. (1994). *A dynamic systems approach to the development of cognition and action.* Cambridge, MA: MIT Press.

Thelen, E., & Ulrich, B. D. (1991). Hidden skills: A dynamic systems analysis of treadmill stepping during the first year. *Monographs of the Society for Research in Child Development, 56*(1, Serial No. 223).

Thompson, J. M. T., & Stewart, H. B. (1986). *Nonlinear dynamics and chaos.* Chichester, England: Wiley.

Turvey, M. T. (1977). Preliminaries to a theory of action with reference to vision. In R. E. Shaw & J. Bransford (Eds.), *Perceiving, acting and knowing* (pp. 211–265). Hillsdale, NJ: Lawrence Erlbaum Associates.

Turvey, M. T., & Fitzpatrick, P. (1993). Commentary: Development of perception-action systems and general principles of pattern formation. *Child Development, 64*(4), 1175–1190.

Zanone, P. G., & Kelso, J. A. S. (1990). Relative timing from the perspective of dynamic pattern theory: Stability and instability. In J. Fagard & P. H. Wolff (Eds.), *The development of timing control and temporal organization in coordinated action* (pp. 69–92). Amsterdam: Elsevier.

Zanone, P. G., & Kelso, J. A. S. (1992). Evolution of behavioral attractors with learning: Non-equilibrium phase transitions. *Journal of Experimental Psychology: Human Perception and Performance, 18*, 403–421.

4

DEGREES OF FREEDOM AND THE DEVELOPMENT OF POSTURAL CENTER OF PRESSURE PROFILES

Karl M. Newell
Pennsylvania State University

Development is fundamentally concerned with the change in behavior that occurs over the lifespan. Motor development realizes phenomena of change that are as or more obvious than many other forms of development, particularly when one observes at the extremes of the life span the periods of infancy and aging. In short, there are many qualitative and quantitative changes that are evident in movement coordination and control over the life span (McGraw, 1945; Shirley, 1931; Thelen, 1984; Woollacott, 1989). Some of these changes in motor development seem very orderly, such as the sequential structure evident in the development of the fundamental movement skills in infancy, whereas others, such as the onset of certain movement disorders in aging, seem essentially stochastic in nature. The deterministic and stochastic properties apparent in the organization of motor development provide a rich set of dynamical phenomena for the application of the concepts and tools of nonlinear dynamics and chaos theory.

It is now about 15 years or more since nonlinear dynamics was linked as an approach to the study of motor development (Garfinkel, 1983; Kugler, Kelso, & Turvey, 1980, 1982), but the ensuing period has emphasized the development of the theoretical backdrop (Hopkins, Beek, & Kalverboer, 1993; Kugler, 1986; Thelen, Kelso, & Fogel, 1987), as opposed to the pursuit of particular local applications to experimental protocols. The consequence at this point in time is that there is no established systematic operational work on the application of nonlinear dynamics to any particular developmental movement or posture issue, although efforts are beginning (see special issue of *Child Development*, 1993; Smith & Thelen, 1993). The emphasis of the operational modeling and empirical work to date on movement and nonlinear dynamics has focused on the between-limb coordination in normal healthy adults (e.g., Beek, 1989; Kelso, 1995; Turvey, 1990).

There are many developmental issues in movement coordination and control that invite the application of the techniques of nonlinear dynamics, but two classic motor development phenomena seem to stand out as candidate problems. One is the issue of the qualitative change in movement forms that occurs, particularly during certain segments of the life span. A prime example of this qualitative change is the acquisition of the fundamental movement forms of posture, locomotion, manipulation, and communication in infancy. The second is the issue of the quantitative change in movement variability that is particularly evident in the periods of early childhood and aging. The changes in the precision of movement outcome and the variation in movement trajectories are prime examples of this quantitative change over the life span. In a dynamical systems approach to motor development the issue of qualitative and quantitative change is not independent from either a theoretical or practical standpoint, but it is the case that traditionally in motor development these types of change have been approached in an isolated and even contrasting fashion. For example, throughout the twentieth century maturation perspectives have dominated accounts of the qualitative changes in movement forms (Gesell, 1929; Keogh & Sugden, 1985), whereas, and in parallel over the last 30 years, information processing perspectives have dominated accounts of the quantitative changes in movement and outcome (Connolly, 1970; Keogh & Sugden, 1985).

The focus of this chapter is the change in the structure of movement variability in posture as a function of age changes over the life-span. Postural tasks provide a useful experimental protocol to examine the variability issue because in spite of the oft-invoked task distinction between movement and posture, it is the case that there is always continuous motion in postural tasks, even if it is not evident to the eye of the observer (Massion, 1992). The postural task emphasized here is upright bipedal stance together with other associated whole-body postural tasks. Upright postural stance is a physical activity fundamental to human development and one that is essential to virtually every other action. Changes in the structure of movement variability as a function of age are important theoretically because they provide a window into the degrees of freedom problem and motor development (Bernstein, 1967; Kay, 1988; Newell & McDonald, 1994). It is also the case that the movement variability inherent in postural time series exhibits, at least to the eye, an interesting case of deterministic and stochastic processes that are "ready made" for the application of the concepts and methods of nonlinear dynamics and chaos theory.

MOTOR DEVELOPMENT AND THE DEGREES
OF FREEDOM PROBLEM

Bernstein (1967) introduced the proposition that motor skill acquisition is, in essence, the problem of learning to coordinate redundant degrees of freedom. This important viewpoint did not take hold rapidly in the Western literature (although see Greene, 1969; Turvey, 1977), but it is now increasingly interpreted as the central problem of the field of motor control (Turvey, 1990). Nowhere is this degrees of freedom problem more evident than in the period of infancy during which the child learns to harness the degrees of freedom of the system to realize the creation and production of what we now know as the fundamental movement sequence (Gesell, 1929; McGraw, 1945; Shirley, 1931). Although qualitative change in movement dynamics is more evident in certain segments of the life span than others, it almost certainly occurs throughout the life span, even if that change is not obviously apparent to the eye of an observer.

The essence of the degrees of freedom problem is reflected in the following question. How are the many degrees of freedom at different levels of analysis of the system harnessed to produce the movement form and variability associated with action? The degrees of freedom problem in motor control could, in principle, be approached from all levels of analysis of movement in action—outcome, joint space, muscles, neurons, and so on. Distinguishing the appropriate frame of reference in which to consider the coordination problem becomes, therefore, very important. Changes in joint space dynamics are, perhaps, the most obvious frame of reference in which to consider the degrees of freedom problem, and certainly this is a level of analysis that Bernstein (1967) emphasized in his writings. Moreover, the ideas of freezing and freeing the degrees of freedom has intuitive appeal in consideration of the changes in joint space dynamics that occur in the repeated performance of a particular task over the life span. There are, however, a number of limitations to Bernstein's (1967) three-stage account of the changes over time at this level of analysis that are largely driven by a failure to consider the importance of task constraints to the dynamics of action (Newell, 1986; Newell & McDonald, 1994). In short, the movement pattern that arises in action is an emergent property of the confluence of constraints in the interaction of organism and environment, together with those that are explicit or implicit with the task demands.

A more fundamental consideration to Bernstein's original proposal is that the joint space frame of reference is not a sufficient space from which to consider the development of movement coordination and control (Kots, Krinskiy, Naydin, & Shik, 1971), even if it is our most convenient entry into the problem of motor control. In other words, the degrees of freedom problem needs to be approached at the level of the control space dynamics, no matter what label or orientation one gives to this problem: abstract dynamics (Haken, Kelso, & Bunz, 1985); perceptual-motor workspace (Kugler & Turvey, 1987), or virtual dynamics (Latash, 1993). The extrapolation from Bernstein (1967) to this dynamical control space level of analysis is that, with development in childhood, there will be an attractor organization of the dynamical system that has more degrees of freedom than was evident in some earlier expression in the life span of the same movement form in action (Newell & McDonald, 1994). Similarly, at the upper end of the life span it can be postulated that there will be a reduction in the degrees of freedom regulated with advancing age in the elderly (Lipsitz & Goldberger, 1992). This change in the dimension of the attractor organization may be accompanied by a change in the degrees of freedom independently organized in joint space, but the relation between the changing degrees of freedom harnessed at each level of analysis also will be dependent on the confluence of constraints to action. The general working principle, however, is that the number of degrees of freedom of the system controlling action is much less than the number of mechanical degrees of freedom of the controlled system (Kay, 1988; Kots et al., 1971; Turvey, 1977).

The changes over time in movement form for a given action evident in children and adults seem to hold a number of parallels when described in joint space (Gesell, 1929; Newell & Van Emmerik, 1990; Newell & McDonald, 1994), but there is no substantial body of evidence available that has examined this question in terms of control space dynamics. Thus, the original degrees of freedom proposition of Bernstein with respect to motor development is still largely a guiding metaphor for current research in dynamical system approaches to motor development than an established operational framework. This is surprising because the degrees of freedom problem in motor control appears particularly suited to the techniques of nonlinear dynamics that can tease out the degrees of freedom (dimension) of attractor organization (Packard, Crutchfield, Farmer, & Shaw, 1980; Takens, 1981), together with other methods that characterize the "complexity" of the system output (e.g., Pincus, 1991).

These techniques from nonlinear dynamics also allow us to unravel the structure of a movement time series and, as it were, decompose the variability of the output to establish the deterministic and stochastic contributions. Such an approach may lead to a narrowing or even a specification of a viable dynamical model of the motor system in particular task contexts. This operational strategy is theoretically important to motor development because it also affords an examination of another long-held assumption, namely, that the noise of the perceptual-motor system in movement output changes over the life span. The information-processing approach to motor development directly proposed that the noise of the system decreases as the child develops (Connolly, 1970; Keogh & Sugden, 1985) and increases again with the advanced aging process (Welford, 1985). The noise level of the system is viewed as a direct mediator of the channel capacity to transmit information around the system. There have been no empirical attempts to examine this theoretical proposition because the analysis of variability has focused solely on the degree of variability (as measured by, e.g., a standard deviation), and this approach does not provide an index of the structure (deterministic and stochastic processes) of the movement variability. Thus, the general proposition that noise is enhanced in motor output at certain developmental periods is still without empirical verification.

In this chapter I examine recent efforts to characterize the qualitative nature of the attractor dynamics supporting posture and its link to the variability of postural control. The theoretical direction of this work is guided by the following two primary and related questions:

1. Do the degrees of freedom in the organization of the attractor dynamics supporting posture change with age—in particular, does advancing age in childhood and the advancing age of the elderly increase and decrease, respectively, the degrees of freedom?

2. Does the structure of movement variability change over the life span in postural control in a fashion consistent with the degrees of freedom proposition outlined earlier?

At this point in time the experimental data and associated modeling work are not sufficient to provide unambiguous answers to these questions. The trends from recent experimental and modeling work, however, do provide some empirical support for the changing degrees of freedom perspective to motor development across the life span and, moreover, point up the value of the operational techniques of nonlinear dynamics in investigating these theoretical problems.

THE NATURE OF POSTURAL CONTROL

Upright bipedal stance is an action that appears difficult for an infant to acquire, but once attained, its performance appears deceptively simple and straightforward to both the performer and observer. The ability to sustain a standing posture on two feet is an activity that seems to only become a problem in human development through exceptional cases of aging or movement disorder. The postural control task as studied in the laboratory is typically set up as shown in Fig. 4.1a.

The subject stands on a force platform and looks forward to a marker at eye height and is instructed to stand as still as possible. The force platform measures at the surface of support the forces and the moments in the x, y,

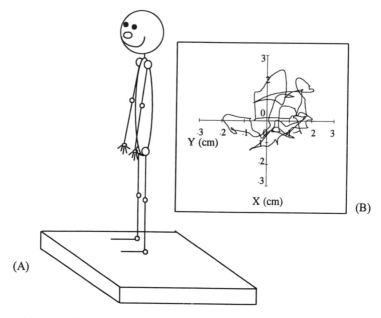

FIG. 4.1. (A) Schematic of the standard experimental set-up for posture studies; (B) typical center of pressure profile.

and z directions to create six time series of the postural activity. From these time series the position (x and y coordinates) at the surface of support of the global ground reaction force, the center of pressure, can be derived to create additional time series of the postural action. The center of pressure is a measure of the location of the macroscopic forces exerted at the base of support to accommodate the sway of the body, but technically itself is not a measure of sway. Sway of the torso is rarely measured in postural studies, and it might be usefully indexed by the motion of the center of mass or center of gravity (Massion, 1992). The organization of the center of pressure is seen as related to the motion of the center of mass, but this relationship is not well understood. Thus, the center of pressure, presumably because it is easier to measure, has been used as a primary index of the motion of the body in posture, although other variables can be derived from the force platform.

Figure 4.1b shows a typical time series of the motion of the center of pressure in the x and y dimensions. The center of pressure shows little or no structure in the horizontal dimensions, appearing essentially random to the eye, although usually there is more motion of the center of pressure in the sagittal than the lateral plane. It has been well documented that the amount of motion of the center of pressure reliably changes under a variety of experimental manipulations (Goldie, Bach, & Evans, 1989), including age changes (King, Judge, & Wolfson, 1994; Riach & Hayes, 1987). The degree of motion of the center of pressure tends to decrease as a child ages through to maturity and then, after about 50 years of age, the degree of motion of the center of pressure tends to increase with advancing age. A typical age-related trend to the degree of motion of the center of pressure is shown in Fig. 4.2, which depicts the mean and between-subject standard deviation of the center of pressure as a function of age (3 years, 5 years, young adult [18–25 years], elderly [60–80 years]) under the presence or absence of vision (Newell, Slobounov, Slobounova, & Molenaar, in press-a).

The remainder of this chapter focuses on the structure of the center of pressure time series and, in particular, the issue of whether there are qualitative changes in the center of pressure dynamics as a function of age. The theoretical proposition is that the structure of the center of pressure provides some clues to the organization of the dynamic supporting posture, the way in which the dynamical organization changes through human development, and, furthermore, ultimately narrows the range of the potential

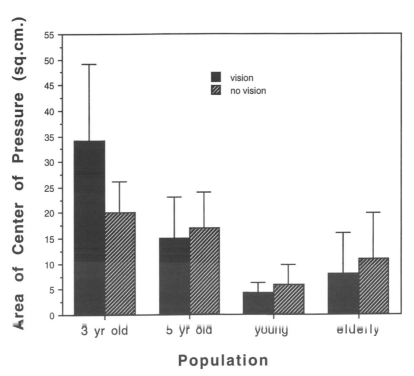

FIG. 4.2. The mean motion (cm) of the center of pressure as a function of age group: 3-year-olds, 5-year-olds, young adults (18–25 years), and elderly (60–75 years). From Newell et al., in press-a. Copyright 1997 by Elsevier. Adapted by permission.

models that produce such a dynamic(s). It is probably the case that the center of pressure is not a sufficient or the appropriate variable from which to adequately examine these issues, but it is the variable that has traditionally been considered a reflection of the macroscopic organization of posture (Massion, 1992), although a full rationale has not been developed.

The traditional approach to the analysis of force platform data has focused on the mean and standard deviation of various summary variables of the center of pressure, such as length, area, and amount of motion in a given plane (Goldie et al., 1989). These variables consistently show changes as a function of manipulations of a variety of environmental and organismic constraints but they reveal nothing directly about the time evolutionary properties of the time series of the center of pressure. In short, the dynamical properties of the center of pressure have been masked in many previous studies by averaging procedures in data analysis.

The data analysis operations have also been guided by the implicit and occasionally explicit theoretical assumption that the output of the center of pressure is a reflection of a deterministic output from the perceptual-motor system with noise superimposed. The variability in the center of pressure has been assumed then to be a reflection of noise (presumably, after Shannon, white Gaussian noise), leaving no structure in the center of pressure to be examined, a perspective that is given face validity by observation of a typical center of pressure time series from a normal healthy human adult (see Fig. 4.1b). The apparent stochastic structure in the center of pressure time series is, however, less obvious in center of pressure time series that arise from abnormal population groups (e.g., Van Emmerik, Sprague, & Newell 1993), and unusual task goals (Slobonouv & Newell, 1996). Indeed, under such conditions, structure in the form of rhythmicity is often present in the center of pressure recorded and, moreover, apparent even to the eye of the observer.

STATIONARITY OF THE CENTER OF PRESSURE

It is useful to consider the stationarity of the center of pressure time series during a postural action. Stationarity refers to the statistical similarity of successive segments of a given time series and can be assessed in both the time and frequency domains, and their interaction. This is not simply a technical prerequisite to ascertain the validity of conducting subsequent statistical and dynamic analyses that assume stationarity of the time series (which it is in part—although this strategy is rarely pursued in this or any other movement protocol!), but also because the determination of stationarity or nonstationarity is a central component to the veridical modeling of time series. Stationarity is considered an essential feature to the organization and subsequent determination of an attractor dynamic (Kaplan & Glass,

1995), but bounded nonstationarity with multiple stable attractor organizations may be an adaptive solution to the attractor dynamic of the center of pressure in posture (Newell et al., in press-a). Nonstationarity in standing posture may facilitate the change (e.g., time to switch) of the movement organization to support other actions. It is also possible that upright bipedal stance in the laboratory task is so underconstrained that a single attractor organization may not be necessary or optimal for satisfying the task constraints.

The few posture studies that have reported tests of stationarity have all provided evidence that the center of pressure time series is nonstationary. Carroll and Freedman (1993) showed that there is nonstationarity in the time domain in center of pressure profiles of adults over 60-sec trials, and that this nonstationary pattern is evident over more than 1 day of observation. The degree of nonstationarity varied over segments of the time series, but it occurred throughout the trials and the preservation of the upright bipedal stance. Harris, Reidel, Matesi and Smith (1993) also reported nonstationarity in the time domain of center of pressure profiles of children with cerebral palsy.

Newell et al. (in press-a) further pursued the stationarity of the center of pressure in bipedal stance in both the time and frequency domains over a number of age groups (3 years, 5 years, young adult, elderly). Tests of stationarity were made on trials that were 15 sec in duration where the task was to maintain upright bipedal stance with as little motion as possible under both vision and no vision conditions. Of particular interest was whether there were interactions in the time and frequency domains in determining the nonstationarity of the center of pressure, and whether the prevalence of these interactions varied over the age groups studied. Although nonstationarity in either the time or frequency domain considered separately is sufficient to invoke the determination of nonstationarity to a time series, a full perspective on stationarity requires an examination of both domains and their interaction. Newell et al. (in press-a) used the statistical test proposed by Priestley and Subba Rao (1969) to examine the prevalence of nonstationarity in the center of pressure profile as a function of age group.

The tests of stationarity in the center of pressure of the Newell et al. project were run, with a variety of low-pass filters, on the excursions in the x and y directions, radius, and angle of the center of pressure trajectory. The results showed that all trials in all age groups for all variables of the center of pressure were nonstationary in the time domain. In the interaction between the time and frequency domains only the 3-year-old group showed a small percentage of trials (about 10%) that were stationary. Thus, nonstationarity of the center of pressure also prevailed in the examination of the interaction of the time and frequency domains. This trend of an interaction of stationarity over age is in the expected direction for the degrees of freedom and development hypothesis outlined previously but the resulting trend in the data is weak. An obvious possibility is that an interaction in stationarity would be more apparent if children younger than 3 years of age and adults older than 75 years of age had been included in the testing.

The available evidence suggests, therefore, that the center of pressure time series in bipedal stance is nonstationary. It is proposed that this represents *short-term* nonstationarity of an adaptive solution to a particular task demand rather than the nonstationarity that follows from systematic and persistent change over segments of the life span of human development. The Newell et al. (in press-a) study shows that children as young as 3 years of age have a tendency to more stationary solutions in the frequency domain, which is consistent with the notion that this age group exhibits more correlated frequency structures in the center of pressure dynamic. This issue needs to be examined in children younger than 3 years and particularly around the age at which the infant first independently stands without environmental intervention other than the surface of support. Surprisingly, there have been very few studies of the acquisition of upright bipedal posture in infancy outside of the early descriptive studies of the development of the fundamental movement patterns (McGraw, 1945; Shirley, 1931).

It also needs to be mentioned in closing this section on the stationarity of the center of pressure that the exact nature of the experimental conditions surrounding the recording of the postural center of pressure are rarely (if ever) presented (including in our work!) in extant experimental reports. A major flaw of extant postural studies is that the conditions prior to the onset of recording the postural dynamic are rarely explicitly outlined in the methods sections of papers. It would seem crucial to know, for example, how long and under what conditions the subject had been standing on the platform prior to the onset of the recording of data. Furthermore, the length of the time series recorded is often not sufficient to do justice to the analysis of evolutionary properties of the postural dynamics. It might also be pertinent to distinguish the examination of the motion in posture when the minimization of postural motion is the goal of the task (as it is in most laboratory examinations of posture) from when a posture is being sustained to pursue another goal (e.g., pick up information), as it usually is in postural actions outside of the laboratory. These experimental matters require attention if we are to more fully understand the significance of the current reports of nonstationarity in the center of pressure profile and the development of posture.

THE STRUCTURE OF CENTER OF PRESSURE PROFILES

The discovery that one can reconstruct the degrees of freedom of a system from a decomposition of a given time series output (Packard et al., 1980; Takens, 1981) has been a primary application of the theory of nonlinear dynamics to specific physical and biological systems (Basar, 1990; Mayer-Kress, 1987). The determination of the dimensionality of a time series is a way to characterize the geometry of the attractor organization and the number of independent degrees of freedom in system control. Dimensionality, therefore, is a measure that can be used to directly approach Bernstein's (1967) degrees of freedom problem in motor control with respect to the attractor organization of posture and movement (Kay, 1988). Furthermore, it can be used as one index for detecting chaos in the system at hand, through the resultant determination of a fractal dimension to the attractor organization.

There are several particular requirements of a data set that need to be present if the dimensionality measure is to be appropriately applied to biological data, and a number of critiques of extant applications have been made (Mayer-Kress, 1987; Rapp, Albano, & Mees, 1988). The significance of these limitations for an interpretation of the resultant work may also reside in the goal of the experimenter in regard to whether dimensionality is being used primarily to discriminate time series between groups or conditions or to realize the veridical modeling of the system degrees of freedom. Nevertheless, it is undoubtedly the case that a number of false claims of chaos have been put forward in recent applications of dimensionality measures to biological data.

The Bernstein problem in movement control can also be approached by considering measures other than dimensionality to characterize the "complexity" of the movement dynamics in the time series at hand. One useful candidate is the Pincus (1991; see also chapter 11, this volume) measure of approximate entropy (ApEn) that directly derives an index of the regularity of the time series. This ApEn measure has fewer demands (constraints) on the features of the data set that are required when contrasted with the various techniques to determine dimension. In the main, the greater the regularity of the time series, the fewer the degrees of freedom in the system that have constructed the signal output, and, in contrast, the greater the complexity of the signal, the more the degrees of freedom in system control. Our work to date on the application of dimension measures and ApEn to movement time series suggests that these methods give relatively parallel findings over a range of experimental conditions.

The extant attempts to determine the dimension of the center of pressure in upright bipedal stance have produced inconsistent observations of the qualitative features of the dynamic. The earliest report that we are aware of documenting the application of dimensional analysis to center of pressure of adults is an abstract by Myklebust and Myklebust (1989) in which a dimension estimate of about 2.0 was advanced. Subsequently, Collins and De Luca (1991) placed a dimension estimate of 1.6 to 1.9 on the center of pressure time series for normal healthy adults, but in more recent examinations claimed that it is impossible to demonstrate saturation of the embedding dimensions, leaving the conclusion that the center of pressure time series reflects a stochastic rather than a chaotic process, despite their previous findings (Collins & De Luca, 1994). Newell, Van Emmerik, Lee, and Sprague (1993) reported a dimension estimate of about 2.2 for the center of pressure in upright bipedal stance in normal healthy adults and a lower estimate of about 1.3 for age-matched adult subjects with the movement disorder of tardive dyskinesia. Similar reports of a dimension estimate of about 2.2 for adult quiet normal stance have also been made by Yamada (1995).

Thus, there are conflicting positions of the consequence of applying the dimension measure to center of pressure data. Certainly, Collins and De Luca (1994) were the most thorough in making the appropriate surrogate data checks of the dimension tests (Theiler, Galdrikian, Longtin, Eubank, & Farmer, 1992) in their claim that the center of pressure profile is best modeled as a stochastic process. However, several laboratories independently, although without all the appropriate surrogate data checks, offered the very similar dimension estimate of about 2.1 for quiet upright bipedal stance in normal healthy young adults. This is a relatively low dimension estimate for a system, and one that is a long way from a high-dimensional determination, which might be more likely to be misread from stochastic output processes. The reason or reasons for these fundamentally different determinations of the dimension of the center of pressure dynamic are not resolved at this point in time.

The important question in the context of this chapter is whether there is any evidence for the change in dimension or regularity of the center of pressure as a function of age group that is consistent with a degrees of freedom perspective for motor development. In this view one would hypothesize a lowering of dimensionality or degrees of freedom for the younger child and the older aging adult. The nature of the constraints (at different levels of analysis) that drive these changes in the dynamics of system regulation would not be the same for young children and the elderly even if the output system dynamics in both groups happened to show considerable similarity in qualitative and quantitative properties (Newell, 1986).

In a recent set of studies we examined the structure of the center of pressure as a function of age (Newell & Slobounov, 1996). We determined the dimensionality and ApEn of the center of pressure profiles of a number of different age groups: 3 years, 5 years, young adults (18–25 years), and elderly (60–75 years), in 15-sec time series of quiet upright bipedal stance. Figure 4.3 shows the mean ApEn scores in both the x and y axes of motion as a function of age group and vision condition.

The 3-year-old group had a significantly lower ApEn mean than the 5-year-old group and young adults, and the elderly group also had a significantly lower ApEn mean than the young adults. The trend of the change in the ApEn score for the center of pressure follows the expectations of a changing

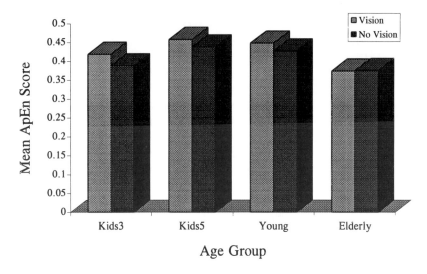

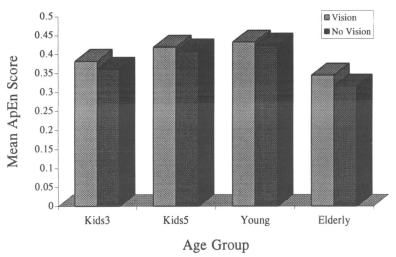

FIG. 4.3. Mean ApEn as a function of direction of motion (upper x, lower y) and age group. From Newell & Slobounov (1996).

degrees of freedom perspective to the development of posture. It is interesting to note that the structure of the 5-year-old group was essentially the
same as that of the young adults. Moreover, the pattern to the age-related ApEn
scores is the inverse of the degree of variability in the center of pressure
motion (see Fig. 4.2). This finding is consistent with the view that a reduction
in the degrees of freedom in control space is associated with an increase
in the variability exhibited in task space (Newell, 1996).

In another study we examined the same issues about the degrees of freedom of center of pressure profiles in a more stratified group of elderly subjects: 60–69 years of age, 70–79 years of age, and 80–89 years of age (Moss, Johnston, & Newell, 1996). The elderly subjects were all healthy active individuals who were not on a regimen of medication, had no clinically prevalent medical problem, and were physically active. The postural trials were of 30 sec duration and required the subjects to stand as still as possible in an upright self-determined appropriate stance. The overall level of the ApEn score was low and in the region of those reported earlier in the Newell and Slobounov study but there was no difference between the three elderly age groups. Myklebust, Prieto, Myklebust, and Lange (1990) also provided evidence that the dimensionality ($D = 1.58$) of a group of adults aged 55–65 years was lower than the dimensionality ($D = 1.97$) of a group of younger normal adults (under 40 years of age).

In summary, there is evidence that the degrees of freedom of the collective organization of the output of the center of pressure are reduced in young children and the elderly. Thus, the changes in postural control with age are consistent with the idea that development of childhood is realizing the introduction of control of more independent degrees of freedom, whereas advancing age is consistent with the reduction in the degrees of freedom (Bernstein, 1967) or a "loss of complexity" (Lipsitz & Goldberger, 1992). There is clearly more work to be done to clarify some of the inconsistencies reported here in regard to the stochastic profile of the center of pressure. It would also be very useful from a developmental perspective to examine these same issues in infants that are in the early stages of upright bipedal stance.

RANDOM WALK ANALYSES OF CENTER OF PRESSURE PROFILES

Collins and De Luca (1993, 1994, 1995a, 1995b) spearheaded an approach to examining the time evolutionary profile of the center of pressure as a random walk (Berg, 1983). In the standard and simplest single-dimensional random walk, the motion of a particle or the step of a drunk is modeled, where the displacement at time t is dependent on the displacement at time $t - 1$ plus a normal white noise process. This model is built from the classic Brownian motion of a molecule in a gas that Einstein successfully modeled in 1905. In this approach the root-mean-square displacement is proportional to the square root of time of the diffusion process. There are many variants of this simple basic random walk stochastic process model that have been applied over the years to a range of physical and biological phenomena (Berg, 1983; Gardiner, 1983).

Collins and De Luca (1993) modeled the center of pressure profiles as a two-process random walk using the square of the displacement increment as a function of increasing time intervals between data points. This calculation follows the basic Brownian motion formula of:

$$<dx^2> = \text{var}[X(t)] = 2D \; dt \qquad (1)$$

where dx^2 is the mean square of the center of pressure displacement, and D is the diffusion coefficient or an index of the rate of spreading of the stochastic process. Collins and De Luca (1993) interpreted the resulting square of the displacement trajectory as discontinuous with a short-term (approximately 1 sec) open-loop process followed by a long-term (approximately >1 sec) closed-loop process. This interpretation was based on the fitting of two regression lines to the diffusion trajectory, thus giving rise to a five-parameter model (initial diffusion [slope and intercept]; final diffusion [slope and intercept]; and critical time point where the two diffusion lines cross). The analysis revealed a correlated random walk because the exponent of the initial open-loop process is greater than ½ and the exponent of the subsequent closed-loop process is less than ½. This departure from ½ in the exponents of the square of the displacement confirms that there is structure in the time evolutionary properties of the center of pressure profile such that it is not a strict stochastic white noise model.

Collins and De Luca (1994, 1995a, 1995b, 1995c) applied their basic model to a number of other population groups and postural task conditions. In general, the two-process model fits the data of the various subject and task manipulations very well and the open- and closed-loop component processes are influenced systematically by these factors. Of particular interest here is their examination of the two-process model of posture with an elderly group (age 71–80 years) of subjects (Collins & De Luca, 1995a). They found that the initial open-loop diffusion process was a more positively correlated random walk than that of the normal healthy young adult control group (age 19–30 years), whereas the closed-loop component was a more negatively correlated random walk than that of the younger adults. Hence, in the aging group there is a greater tendency to drift away initially from the equilibrium point but in the closed-loop phase a greater tendency to provide corrective adjustments back toward the equilibrium point

The modeling of the center of pressure trajectory by Collins and De Luca, although accounting for a large percentage of the variance of the random walk in a variety of situations, can be challenged on several grounds. One is the technical point that the random walk analysis is based on the average of a group of trials (usually 10) rather than an assessment of a single trial trajectory. Determining a break point from an average trajectory generally provides a different estimate than the average of break points determined from each individual trial. Averaging trajectories also tends to smooth out critical points where they exist in individual trials and typically increases the percent of variance accounted for by curve-fitting procedures. The second concern is an inferential one and the proposal that the diffusion process of the random walk has two successive components that are driven by open- and closed-loop processes. The use of inflections or critical points in trajectories to infer the onset of error-correction processes has been used in other movement problems, such as the analysis of limb trajectories. This procedure is fraught with problems, however, not the least of which is that there are many sources of information available to the performer on varying time scales. As a consequence, recent analyses have tended to down play the use of critical points in trajectories to infer a switch of open- and closed-loop control processes (Carlton, 1992). This last challenge is more consistent with the view that the diffusion process of the random walk in center of pressure trajectories is continuous rather than discontinuous and is a reflection of multiple time-varying processes.

Finally, although the two-process model fits the center of pressure data well, it has five parameters for the curve fitting of the diffusion trajectory, and furthermore, this in and of itself is not a dynamical model. Collins and De Luca (1993) suggested that the center of pressure time series could be modeled as a dynamical system of two coupled bounded random walks and produced simulations of the diffusion trajectory from their model that matched well (to the eye) those obtained experimentally. One system is a nonlinear spring at the center of a bounded circular area. The second system is linearly imposed on the first and consists of a threshold alternating spring that is attached to the perimeter of the bounded area. Thus, in this model, the center of the bounded area is not a stable equilbrium point. It is not clear whether the stiffness term in this simulation was linear or nonlinear. If it is linear then their Equation 6 (Collins & De Luca, 1993) is in essence an Ornstein–Uhlenbeck process model. Collins and De Luca have not directly linked this model to the experimental data reported earlier and thus we are not sure, for example, which changes in the model parameters produce the change in the diffusion trajectories as a function of age and experimental conditions. More recently, Chow and Collins (1995) proposed a pinned polymer model of postural control that is clearly a dynamical system.

Newell, Slobounov, Slobounova, and Molenaar (in press-b) examined the nature of the random walk in the center of pressure profiles of several age groups: 3 years, 5 years, young adults (18–25 years), and normal healthy elderly (60–75 years). We determined the random walk of individual trials that were 15 sec duration and that were collected under vision and nonvision conditions during quiet upright bipedal stance. We used two models of the random walk process. The first was the two-process random walk approach of Collins and DeLuca (1993). The second was the application of the basic Ornstein–Uhlenbeck model that is linear and has no mass or viscosity, but simply displacement governed by a stiffness term in the random walk (Gardiner, 1983). The dynamic equation for the mean square displacement of the square of the center of pressure displacement is according to the Ornstein–Uhlenbeck stochastic process model:

$$\text{var}[X(t)] = (D/2k)[1 - \exp(-2kt)] \tag{2}$$

where D is the diffusion coefficient and k is the drift coefficient. Our results showed that both the Collins and De Luca two-process curve-fitting model and the Ornstein–Uhlenbeck dynamic model fitted the individual trials of the center of pressure data well (about 92–94% of the variance accounted for, depending on group and condition).

The Collins and De Luca model when fitted to our data generally accounted for about 96% of the variance of the diffusion trajectory, a finding that is just under the percent of variance reported in the series of papers by Collins and De Luca. The young adult group had the lowest time estimate of the critical point separating the two-component processes at about 1.25 sec, with the time lengthening in the 3-year-old group (2.04 sec), 5-year-old group (2.46 sec), and elderly group (1.97 sec). Thus, the initial phase of diffusion (open-loop process) was greater in the elderly and the two children's age groups than it was in the young adult group. In general, diffusion in all age groups was similar in the presence and absence of vision.

The application of the Ornstein–Uhlenbeck model to the same data set showed that it accounted generally for about 92–94% of the variance of the mean square of the center of pressure displacement across all age groups and conditions. There was a significant effect of age on the diffusion estimate. Diffusion increased in the 3- and 5-year-old groups in contrast to the young adult and elderly groups. The drift coefficient did not differ as a function of age and was generally very small on average over the groups and conditions. In the Ornstein–Uhlenbeck model the vision factor did not produce any significant effects in regard to either diffusion or drift.

The two parameters of the dynamic linear Ornstein–Uhlenbeck model (Newell et al., in press-b) produced almost as good a fit to the square of the center of pressure displacement data as the five-parameter two-process model of Collins and De Luca (1993). Both models are sensitive to age changes in the center of pressure profiles, and the 3- and 5-year-old children in the Ornstein–Uhlenbeck model showed greater diffusion than either the young adult or elderly age groups. In summary, these are beginning attempts to model the stochastic and deterministic properties of the center of pressure as a function age and other developmentally related variables. The products of these recent experimental and modeling efforts suggest that a dynamical approach to the center of pressure in postural control may be tractable, but that there is still considerable work to be done in this area.

DEVELOPMENT AND THE CHANGING CONTROL
OF DEGREES OF FREEDOM IN POSTURE

A prevailing perspective in dynamical approaches to motor development is that the degrees of freedom of the control space dynamics change over the course of human development. This change is assumed to be more prevalent in certain segments of the life span than others, with the degrees of freedom that can be independently regulated in movement control increasing from birth to maturity and subsequently decreasing again during advanced stages of the aging process. In this chapter we have examined experimental work related to this question using the action of upright bipedal posture as an experimental paradigm to apply the concepts and tools of nonlinear dynamics.

The measures of dimension and Ap En suggest that the qualitative properties of the attractor dynamic of the center of pressure changes as a function of age. This observation is more apparent when posture is examined under conditions of reduced base of support. The degrees of freedom that drive the organization of the center of pressure dynamic increase from 3 years to 18 years of age and decrease after about 60 years of age. This change in dimension is related to the diffusion of the random walk in that enhanced degrees of freedom in system control produce a lower level of diffusion whereas the reduced degrees of freedom produce an enhanced diffusion. The generality of this proposed relation between degrees of freedom regulated in action and development requires a fuller examination across the life span. This problem would benefit from the detailed study of similar parameters in infants who have just learned to independently stand and the period of postural development that immediately follows.

Although the data shown here provide some evidence to directional changes in the regulation of degrees of freedom in control space dynamics as a function of age, these trends may well be very task specific (Newell, 1986). That is, the pattern of change exhibited by individuals over time may be peculiar to the confluence of constraints in action, and this milieu could change with the particular task. Thus, other tasks may show a different pattern to the changes over time in the degrees of freedom regulated in action, in both control space and joint space dynamics. Thus, the notion of the change in degrees of freedom regulated in the development from birth to maturity needs to be viewed abstractly in terms what changes can occur, rather than only observing what changes actually occur in a particular task.

The changes reported here in the dynamics of posture as a function of age are clearly influenced by many variables. The nature of the primary constraints that change the course of the dynamics in movement coordination and control over the life span is poorly understood (Newell, 1986; Thelen, 1986; Woollacott, 1989). However, it also needs to be recognized that certain of the changes with age shown here could be due primarily to the experience and practice of the subject. In other words, a learning interpretation may in certain instances be a more approppriate account of the qualitative and quantitative change in postural dynamics than what is classically construed as development. This is particularly true of the observation of increasing degrees of freedom regulated over the age span of birth to maturity. Whether this argument should be invoked to capture the reduction in the degrees of freedom regulated with the aging process is, however, less obvious.

In closing, it is important to note that to demonstrate qualitatively different states in the dynamics of posture as a function of age is not synonymous with the proposal that the change of postural states is itself discontinuous. What has been provided here is simply a cross-sectional description of the dynamics of the center of pressure profiles at different ages without any analysis of the nature of the change in the dynamics over the lifespan. The introduction of the dynamical approach to the development of movement in action has opened the door to the old developmental issue of continuity and discontinuity. The idea that there are categorical states in development that can be identified should not, however, be equated or confused with the notion that the change itself from one state to another is discontinuous. In fact, the evidence of discontinuous change in the dynamics of postural and movement coordination as a function of development is very limited. The dynamics of change are an important issue that needs to be examined in the context of the degrees of freedom and postural development and that provides an extension to the work reported here.

REFERENCES

Basar, E. (Ed.). (1990). *Chaos in brain function*. Berlin: Springer Verlag.

Beek, P. J. (1989). *Juggling dynamics*. Amsterdam: Free University.

Berg, H. C. (1983). *Random walks in biology*. Princeton, NJ: Princeton University Press.

Bernstein, N. A. (1967). *Co-ordination and the regulation of movements*. London: Pergamon.

Carlton, L. G. (1992). Visual processing time and the control of movement. In L. Proteau & D. Elliott (Eds.), *Vision and motor control* (pp. 3–32). Amsterdam: North Holland.

Carroll, J. P., & Freedman, W. (1993). Nonstationarity properties of postural sway. *Journal of Biomechanics, 26*, 409–416.

Child Development. (1993). *64*(4). Special issue.

Chow, C. A., & Collins, J. J. (1995). Pinned polymer model of posture control. *Physical Review E, 52*, 907–912.

Collins, J. J., & De Luca, C. J. (1991). A non linear dynamical analysis of the human postural control system. *Annual International Conference of the IEEE Engineering in Medicine and Biology Society, 13*, 2214–2215.

Collins, J. J., & De Luca, C. J. (1993). Open-loop and closed-loop control of posture: A random-walk analysis of center-of-pressure trajectories. *Experimental Brain Research, 95*, 308–318.

Collins, J. J., & De Luca, C. J. (1994). Random walking during quiet standing. *Physical Review Letters, 73*, 764–767.

Collins, J. J., & De Luca, C. J. (1995a). Age-related changes in open-loop and closed-loop postural control mechanisms. *Experimental Brain Research, 104*, 480–492.

Collins, J. J., & De Luca, C. J. (1995b). The effects of visual input on open-loop and closed-loop postural control mechanisms. *Experimental Brain Research, 103*, 151–163.

Collins, J. J., & De Luca, C. J. (1995c). Pinned polymer model of posture control. *Physical Review E, 52*, 907–912.

Connolly, K. J. (1970). Response speed, temporal sequencing and information processing in children. In K. J. Connolly (Ed.), *Mechanisms of motor development* (pp. 161–187). New York: Academic Press.

Gardiner, C. W. (1983). *Handbook of stochastic methods*. Berlin: Springer-Verlag.

Garfinkel, A. (1983). A mathematics for physiology. *American Journal of Physiology, 245*, R455–R466.

Gesell, A. (1929). Maturation and infant behavior pattern. *Psychological Review, 36*, 307–319.

Goldie, P. A., Bach, T. M., & Evans, O. M. (1989). Force platform measures for evaluating postural control: Reliability and validity. *Archives of Physical Medicine and Rehabilitation, 70*, 510–517.

Greene, P. (1969). Seeking mathematical models for skilled actions. In D. Bootzin & H. C. Muffley (Eds.), *Biomechanics* (pp. 149–180). New York: Plenum.

Haken, H., Kelso, J. A. S., & Bunz, H. (1985). A theoretical model of phase transitions in human hand movements. *Biological Cybernetics, 51*, 347–356.

Harris, G. F., Reidel, S. A., Matesi, D., & Smith, P. (1993). Standing postural stability assessment and signal stationarity in children with cerebral palsy. *IEE Transactions on Rehabilitation Engineering, 1*, 35–42.

Hopkins, B., Beek, P. J., & Kalverboer, A. F. (1993). Theoretical issues in the longitudinal study of motor development. In A. F. Kalverboer, B. Hopkins, & R. Geuze (Eds.), *Motor development in early and later childhood: Longitudinal approaches* (pp. 343–371). Cambridge, England: Cambridge University Press.

Kaplan, D., & Glass, L. (1995). *Understanding nonlinear dynamics*. Berlin: Springer-Verlag.

Kay, B. (1988). The dimensionality of movement trajectories and the degrees of freedom problem: A tutorial. *Human Movement Science, 7*, 343–364.

Kelso, J. A. S. (1995). *Dynamic patterns: The self-organization of brain and behavior*. Cambridge, MA: MIT Press.

Keogh, J., & Sugden, D. (1985). *Movement skill development*. New York: Macmillan.

King, M. B., Judge, J. O., & Wolfson, L. (1994). Functional base of support decreases with age. *Journal of Gerontology: Medical Sciences, 49*, M258–M263.

Kots, Y. M., Krinskiy, V. I., Naydin, V. L., & Shik, M. L. (1971). The control of movements of the joints and kinesthetic afferentiation. In I. M. Gelfand, V. S. Gurfinkel, S. V. Fomin, & M. L. Tsetlin (Eds.), *Models of the structural-functional organization of certain biological systems* (pp. 373–381). Cambridge, MA: MIT Press.

Kugler, P. N. (1986). A morphological persepctive on the origin and evolution of movement patterns. In M. G. Wade & H. T. A. Whiting (Eds.), *Motor development in children: Aspects of coordination and control* (pp. 459–526). Dordrecht: Martinus Nijhoff.

Kugler, P. N., & Turvey, M. T. (1987). *Information, natural law, and the self-assembly of rhythmical movement*. Hillsdale, NJ: Lawrence Erlbaum Associates.

Kugler, P. N., Kelso, J. A. S., & Turvey, M. T. (1980). On the concept of coordinative structures as dissipative structures: I. Theoretical lines of convergence. In G. E. Stelmach & J. Requin (Eds.), *Tutorials in motor behavior* (pp. 1–48). Amsterdam: North-Holland.

Kugler, P. N., Kelso, J. A. S., & Turvey, M. T. (1982). On the control and coordination of naturally developing systems. In J. A. S. Kelso & J. E. Clark (Eds.), *The development of movement control and coordination* (pp. 5–78). New York: Wiley.

Latash, M. L. (1993). *Control of human movement.* Champaign, IL: Human Kinetics.

Lipsitz, L. A., & Goldberger, A. L. (1992). Loss of "complexity" and aging. *Journal of the American Medical Association, 267,* 1806–1809.

Massion, J. (1992). Movement, posture and equilibrium: Interaction and coordination. *Progress in Neurobiology, 38,* 35–56.

McGraw, M. B. (1945). *The neuromuscular maturation of the human infant.* New York: Hafner Press.

Mayer-Kress, G. (Ed.). (1987). *Dimensions and entropies in chaotic systems.* Berlin: Springer-Verlag.

Moss, S., Johnston, C., & Newell, K. M. (1996). *Aging and the complexity of center of pressure profiles.* Manuscript under preparation.

Myklebust, J. B., & Myklebust, B. M. (1989). Fractals in kinesiology. *Society for Neuroscience Meeting Abstract,* No. 243.2.

Myklebust, J. B., Prieto, T. E., Myklebust, B. M., & Lange, D. S. (1990). Dimensionality of postural steadiness. *Society for Neuroscience Abstract,* No. 544.2.

Newell, K. M. (1986). Constraints to the development of coordination. In M. G. Wade & H. T. A. Whiting (Eds.), *Motor development in children: Aspects of coordination and control* (pp. 341–360). Dordrecht: Martinus Nijhoff.

Newell, K. M. (1996). The dynamics of stereotypic behaviors: Movement variance and invariance in the classsification of movement disorders. In R. L. Sprague & K. M. Newell (Eds.), *Stereotyped movements: Brain and behavior relationships* (pp. 115–138). Washington, DC: American Psychological Association.

Newell, K. M., & Van Emmerik, R. E. A. (1990). Are Gesell's developmental principles general principles for the acquisition of coordination? In J. E. Clark & J. H. Humphrey (Eds.), *Advances in motor development research* (Vol. 3, pp. 143–164). New York: AMS Press.

Newell, K. M., & McDonald, P. V. (1994). Learning to coordinate redundant biomechanical degrees of freedom. In S. Swinnen, H. Heuer, J. Massion, & P. Casaer (Eds.), *Interlimb coordination: Neural, dynamical and cognitive constraints* (pp. 515–536). New York: Academic Press.

Newell, K. M., & Slobounov, S. M. (1996). *Degrees of freedom in postural control as a function of age.* Manuscript submitted for publication.

Newell, K. M., Van Emmerik, R. E. A., Lee, D., & Sprague, R. L. (1993). On postural stability and variability. *Gait & Posture, 4,* 225–230.

Newell, K. M., Slobounov, S. M., Slobounova, E., & Molenaar, P. C. M. (in press-a). Short-term nonstationarity and the development of postural control. *Gait & Posture.*

Newell, K. M., Slobounov, S. M., Slobounova, E., & Molenaar, P. C. M. (in press-b). Stochastic processes in postural center of pressure profiles. *Experimental Brain Research.*

Packard, N. H., Crutchfield, J. P., Farmer, J. D., & Shaw, R. S. (1980). Geometry from a time series. *Physical Review, A35,* 481–484.

Pincus, S. M. (1991). Approximate entropy as a measure of system complexity. *Proceedings of the National Academy of Science, 88,* 2297–2301.

Priestley, M. B., & Subba Rao, T. (1969). A test for non-stationarity of time series. *Journal of the Royal Statistical Society, Series B, 31,* 140–149.

Rapp, P. E., Albano, A. M., & Mccs, A. I. (1000). Calculation of correlation dimension from experimental data: progress and problems. In J. A. S. Kelso, A. J. Mandel, & M. Schlesinger (Eds.), *Dynamic patterns in complex systems* (pp. 191–205). Singapore: World Publishing.

Riach, C. L., & Hayes, K. C. (1987). Maturation of postural stability in young children. *Developmental Medicine and Child Neurology, 29,* 650–658.

Shirley, M. M. (1931). *The first two years: A study of twenty-five babies: Vol. 1. Postural and locomotor development.* Minneapolis: University of Minnesota Press.

Slobounov, S. M., & Newell, K. M. (1996). Postural dynamics in upright and inverted stance. *Journal of Applied Biomechanics, 12,* 185–196.

Smith, L. B., & & Thelen, E. (1993). *A dynamic systems approach to development: Applications.* Cambridge, MA: MIT Press.

Takens, F. (1981). Detecting strange attractors in turbulence. In D. Rand & L. S. Young (Eds.), *Dynamical systems and turbulence* (pp. 366–381). Berlin: Springer.

Theiler, J., Galdrikian, B., Longtin, A., Eubank, S., & Farmer, J. D. (1992). Using surrogate data to delect nonlinearity in time series. In M. Casdalgi & S. Eubank (Eds.), *Nonlinear modelling and forecasting: SFI studies in the sciences of complexity. Proc. Col. XII.* (pp. 163–188). Reading, MA: Addison-Wesley.

Thelen, E. (1984). Learning to walk: Ecological demands and phylogenetic constraints. In L. P. Lipsitt (Eds.), *Advances in infancy research* (Vol. 3, pp. 213–250). Norwood, NJ: Ablex.

Thelen, E. (1986). Development of coordinated movement: Implications for early human development. In M. G. Wade & H. T. A. Whiting (Eds.), *Motor development in children: Aspects of coordination and control* (pp. 107–124). Dordrecht: Martinus Nijhoff.

Thelen, E., Kelso, J. A. S., & Fogel, A. (1987). Self-organizing systems and infant motor development. *Developmental Review, 7,* 39–65.

Turvey, M. T. (1977). Preliminaries to a theory of action with reference to vision. In R. Shaw & J. Bransford (Eds.), *Perceiving and knowing: Toward an ecological psychology* (pp. 211–266). Hillsdale, NJ: Lawrence Erlbaum Associates.

Turvey, M. T. (1990). Coordination. *American Psychologist, 45,* 938–953.

Van Emmerik, R. E. A., Sprague, R. L., & Newell, K. M. (1993). Assessment of sway dynamics in tardive dyskinesia and developmental disability: Sway profile orientation and stereotypy. *Movement Disorders, 8,* 305–314.

Welford, A. T. (1985). Changes of performance with age: An overview. In N. Charness (Ed.), *Aging and human performance* (pp. 333–369). New York: Wiley.

Woollacott, M. H. (1989). Aging, postural control, and movement preparation. In M. H. Woollacott & A. Shumway-Cook (Eds.), *Development of posture and gait across the life span* (pp. 155–175). Columbia: University of South Carolina Press.

Yamada, N. (1995). Chaotic swaying of the upright movement patterns. *Human Movement Science, 14,* 711–726.

COGNITIVE DEVELOPMENT

5

A PREDATOR–PREY MODEL OF HUMAN CEREBRAL DEVELOPMENT

Robert W. Thatcher

VA Medical Center, Bay Pines, Florida

University of South Florida College of Medicine

Recently, Edelman and colleagues (Edelman, 1987; Finkel & Edelman, 1989; Sporns, Tononi, & Edelman, 1991, 1994) developed a neural population model of learning and memory in which competition and cooperation between populations of synapses determined the selection and survival of groups of neurons comprising neural networks. Their model primarily concerned the time domain of milliseconds to a few days of neural network interactions. Levay, Stryker, and Shatz (1978) presented a neural population model of ocular dominance column development that was confined to the lateral geniculate cortical projections and a limited time domain. Although these models are excellent in their focus on the short time domain of neural function and development, they do not address the long time domain of postnatal human cerebral development. In fact, there are currently no comprehensive neural population models of the postnatal ontogenesis of cortico-cortical connections that operate over months and years.

The size and complexity of the nervous system make it unlikely that changes in a single synapse result in significant change in the behavior of a interconnected neural network. It is more likely that significant changes in neural network behavior require changes in populations of synapses, defined as multiple synaptic modifications occurring simultaneously at multiple sites. The goal of this chapter is to develop a formal neural network model of human cerebral ontogenesis and to use the model to explain the development of human electroencephalographic (EEG) coherence over the postnatal period from 1.5 to 16 years of age. This model relies on develop-

mental cytoarchitectural findings as well as on studies of electroencephalographic development.

Two different categories of EEG analyses have been used to study life-
span human cerebral development: EEG power (Hudspeth & Pribram, 1990,
1991; Matousek & Petersen, 1973) and EEG coherence and phase (Fox & Bell,
1990; Gasser, Jennen-Steinmetz, Sroka, Verleger, & Mocks, 1988; McAlaster,
1992; Thatcher, 1991, 1992a, 1992b; Thatcher, Walker, & Guidice, 1987). Although EEG power measures differ from measures of EEG coherence, the
application of these measurements to postnatal human development reveal
two common or shared findings: (a) There is an exponential or logistic
change in EEG values from birth to approximately 6 years of age, after which
the rate of change slows and there is relative stability until late adulthood
(Hudspeth & Pribram, 1990, 1991; Matousek & Petersen, 1973; Thatcher et
al., 1987), and (b) superimposed upon the dominant exponential or logistic
developmental trajectories are oscillations in the range of 5–20% of the
mean. Further, detailed comparisons of the development of EEG power and
EEG coherence reveal common modes of oscillation and similar anatomical
discontinuities over the human life span (Thatcher, 1991). For example,
Hudspeth and Pribram (1991, 1992) and Thatcher et al. (1987) report similar
2- to 4-year periods of oscillation with similar onset times and amplitude
changes in frontal, central, temporal, and parietal-occipital regions. The
oscillations are not random "noise" because they are very ordered with
iterated anatomical sequences and dynamical phase relationships as well
as prominent power spectral peaks (Thatcher, 1991, 1992a, 1992b). An intriguing finding is that the timing of the oscillations in EEG coherence and
EEG power overlap the timing of stages in human cognitive development as
specified by Piaget (1952, 1971, 1975) and others (Case, 1985, 1987; Fischer,
1987; Fischer & Pipp, 1984).

The spatial and temporal dynamics of the postnatal oscillations in EEG
coherence exhibited highly organized features often observed in nonlinear
dynamical systems, such as phase transitions or bifurcations, frequency
doubling, in-phase and antiphase transitions, and competitive and cooperative dynamics (Gilmore, 1981; Thatcher, 1992a, 1994b; Thatcher, Krause, &
Hrybyk, 1986; Thatcher, Toro, Pfliger, & Hallett, 1994; Thom, 1975). The
oscillations in the development of EEG coherence were also anatomically
organized and involved anterior–posterior and medial–lateral gradients and
were similar to the dynamics seen in biological population growth and in
models of computational ecology. Based on these features, it was hypothesized that the postnatal EEG coherence oscillations involved synaptic competition, which was driven by a propagated wave of nerve growth factor
(i.e., a traveling wave) such that the leading edge of the wave resulted in
the local production of a surplus of synaptic connections and/or increased
synaptic strength of existing synapses and the trailing edge was followed

by a pruning of excess connections and/or decreased synaptic strength of existing synapses (Thatcher, 1992a, 1992b, 1994a). It was postulated that these dynamics, whether an increase in synaptic number or strength, were part of a process that shapes and sculpts the microanatomy of the brain over the life span of human development (Thatcher, 1992a).

The purpose of the present study is to evaluate these hypotheses of human cerebral development by formulating a nonlinear dynamical model capable of characterizing the main features of the postnatal development of EEG coherence. This will be accomplished by (a) evaluating the critical features of the EEG coherence developmental data and creating a qualitative model to explain the findings, (b) developing a formal mathematical model and then performing sensitivity analyses on the model, and (c) simulating the observed EEG coherence developmental trajectories through the appropriate selection of resource and control variables.

POSTNATAL OSCILLATIONS IN CORTICAL CYTOARCHITECTURAL DEVELOPMENT

Oscillations in Neuronal Packing Density and Cortical Thickness

By the age of 6 years there is an estimated loss (i.e., cell death) of greater than 20% of the number of neurons present at birth (Cowan, 1979; Cowan, Fawcett, O'Leary, & Stanfield, 1984; O'Leary, 1987), whereas skull volume has increased from approximately 30% at birth to approximately 90% of adult value (Blinkov & Glezer, 1968). This large loss of neurons and simultaneous increase in skull volume result in a large decrease in neuronal packing density, with neuronal packing density D_n defined as:

$$D_n = \frac{N}{V} \tag{1}$$

where N is the number of neurons per unit volume V (e.g., cubic millimeters) (Rabinowicz, 1979; Blinkov & Glezer, 1968). Decreases in neuronal packing density are heterogeneous, with different values and rates in different cortical regions (Bok, 1959; Blinkov & Glezer, 1968) as well as different onset times and rates of change in different cortical layers (Blinkov & Glezer, 1968; Huttenlocher, 1979, 1984, 1990; Huttenlocher & de Courten, 1987). For example, there are postnatal oscillations and discontinuous developments in the thickness of cortical gray matter (Rabinowicz, 1979; Conel, 1955, 1959, 1963, 1967), the packing density of cortical neurons (Blinkov & Glezer, 1968; Rabinowicz, 1979), and the cortical volume (Blinkov & Glezer, 1968; Schade & Groeningen, 1961). The latter measures of cerebral development demonstrate oscillations with specific periods and rhythmicities. An example of some of the differential changes in postnatal neuronal packing density and cortical thickness are shown in Fig. 5.1. Rhythmic increases and decreases in packing densities are evident in Fig. 5.1, with the most pronounced changes occurring in the upper cortical layers (i.e., layers II and III).

A consistent feature of Blinkov and Glezer's data and Conel's (1955, 1959, 1963, 1967) data is that the upper cortical layers (e.g., II and III) tend to exhibit larger amplitude of oscillation in neuronal packing density than the lower layers (e.g., IV, V and VI). As shown by Rabinowicz (1979), rhythmic increases and decreases in cortical thickness are also present in different cortical layers. Cyclic changes in cortical thickness may reflect cyclic

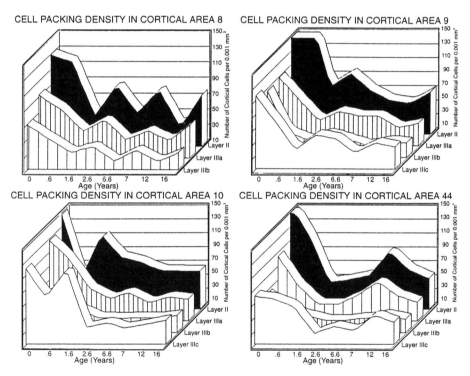

FIG. 5.1. Developmental changes in cell packing density in different layers and areas of the human frontal lobes (i.e., Broadman's areas 8, 9, 10, and 44). The x axis is age in years and the y axis is number of cortical cells per 0.001 mm^3. Although the age samples are not at regular intervals, this figure illustrates two important phenomena: (a) the presence of postnatal oscillations in neuronal packing density and (b) that there are different postnatal rhythms in different cortical regions and in different cortical layers. Numbers were obtained from Blinkov and I. Glezer (1968). From Thatcher (1991). Reprinted by permission.

changes in dendritic ramification, in the size of neurons, and/or in the numbers of glia cells and presynaptic terminals. The important point is that there is evidence indicating a dynamic and cyclical alteration in the cytoarchitecture of the human cerebral cortex during the postnatal period, which can most easily be understood as a consequence of changes in dendritic ramification and in the regional density of synapses.[1]

Relations Between Synaptogenesis, Dendrite Length and Packing Density

It seems reasonable that both axons and dendrites develop in a coordinated or interrelated manner. For example, synapse differentiation on developing dendrites is closely correlated with developing afferent axons, suggesting a preferential growth of these elements toward one another (Becker, 1991). This indicates that synaptic contacts increase the probability of dendritic differentiation, such that dendritic growth would likely extend into rich synaptic fields and retract from impoverished ones (Henrikson & Vaughn, 1974). Vaughn (1989) postulated that synapses are initially formed on dendritic filopodia and growth cones, and then as the dendrite differentiates and radially lengthens along its glial guide (Rakic, 1985) the synapses become located on the differentiated segments. It was further postulated by Vaughn (1989) that synaptotrophic processes induce dendritic branching such that the direction of dendritic growth is toward the highest concentration of axons during both prenatal and postnatal periods.

A more quantitative analysis of available dendritic surface area is based on the studies of Bok (1959), Jerison (1973), and Wright (1934), which demonstrated an inverse relationship between dendritic length L and cortical neuron packing density:

$$L = \frac{1}{D_n} \quad \text{and} \quad D_n = \frac{N}{V} \tag{2}$$

where N is the number of neurons per unit volume V. If we assume that each dendrite is conic and/or cylindrical in shape, then dendritic length is

---

[1]This position is contrary to the "concurrent development" hypothesis of Rakic, Bourgeois, Eckenhoff, Zecevic, and Goldman-Rakic (1986). However, Rakic et al. (1986) and subsequent studies by his group (Bourgeois, Goldman-Rakic & Rakic, 1994; Zecevic & Rakic, 1991) relied strongly on the assumptions of linear regression, which may have prevented observing oscillations in their own data. For example, significant nonlinear regression fits and strong Fourier components can be obtained by Fourier analysis and nonlinear regression of the published data in Rakic et al. (1986) and the other papers just cited (Thatcher, unpublished observations). An interesting aspect of the "concurrent" hypothesis is that it is all-or-none, that is, either cerebral development involves a single event or it involves multiple events, and therefore significant nonlinearities do not support a concurrent hypothesis.

directly related to dendritic surface area S (e.g., the equation for surface area of the sides of a cylinder and a conic is $S = 2\pi rL$). Thus, there is a direct relationship between the surface area of dendritic arborization in squared microns and neuronal packing density in the number of neurons per cubic millimeter or $S = 1/D_n$, as per Equations 1 and 2. We can extend these relations and define synaptic packing density in which the density D_s of synapses per unit somato-dendritic surface area is:

$$D_s = \frac{N}{S} \tag{3}$$

where N is the number of synapses and S is somato-dendritic surface area in square millimeters.

Postnatal Development of Pyramidal Cell Dendrites

Many factors can influence cell packing density. Three of the most important measures are (a) cranial volume (determined by skull expansion), (b) neural cell body size (or volume), and, if we assume that the development of the vasculature and glia are to support the development and function of neurons, then (c) dendritic length and dendritic ramification. In order to specifically measure the contribution made by dendrites, Schade and Groeningen (1961) studied the growth and arborization of the dendrites of the human frontal cortex by measuring the number of dendrites leaving the cell body, the number of points of ramification of the dendrites, and the number of dendrite endings within zones of concentric circles separated by 25 μm. They found that the total number of dendrites increased from birth until about 2 years and then remained unchanged. However, the number of points of ramification within the zones as well as dendritic length increased after birth and throughout the early childhood and adolescent periods up to adulthood. For example, the degree of ramification of pyramidal cell dendrites increased by a factor of 13.6 times from birth to adulthood, whereas the total length of the pyramidal cell dendrites increased by a factor of 33 times (Schade & Groeningen, 1961). This represents a very considerable increase in the total dendritic surface area and, thus, an increase in the area available for synapse formation from birth to adulthood. Because dendritic surface area and/or arborization is inversely related to neuronal packing density (Equation 3), these data support the assumption that the amount of dendritic arborization and synaptic packing density is not a constant and fixed postnatal value, but dendritic surface area changes in a nonlinear manner in both the temporal and spatial domains as a function of postnatal age.

POSTNATAL OSCILLATIONS IN HUMAN EEG DEVELOPMENT

Cortico-Cortical Connections and EEG Coherence

Coherence is mathematically analogous to a cross-correlation in the frequency domain. It is a measure of the degree of "phase synchrony" or "shared activity" between spatially separated generators (Bendat & Peirsol, 1980; Glaser & Ruchkin, 1976; Otnes & Enochson, 1972). The application of coherence measures to the human scalp EEG have shown that EEG coherence reflects the coupling between neocortical neurons (Lopez da Silva, Pijn, & Boeijinga, 1989; Nunez, 1981; Thatcher, McAlaster, Lester, Horst, & Cantor, 1983; Tucker, Roth, & Blair, 1986). Recently, a "two-compartmental" model of EEG coherence was developed by Thatcher et al. (1986) and later replicated and extended by Pascual-Marqui, Valdes-Sosa, and Alvarez-Amador (1986). This equation was based on Braitenberg's (1978) two-compartment analysis of cortical axonal fiber systems in which compartment A is composed of the basal dendrites that receive input primarily from the axon collaterals from neighboring or "short-distance" pyramidal cells and compartment B is composed of the apical dendrites of cortical pyramidal cells that receive input primarily from "long-distance" intracortical connections. The short-distance A system primarily involves local interactions on the order of millimeters to a few centimeters, whereas the long-distance B system involves long-range interactions on the order of several centimeters, which represent the majority of white matter fibers. These two systems exhibit two different network properties. System A, due to the variable depths of the basal dendrites, is not involved in reciprocal loop processes but rather in a diffusion type of transmission process. In contrast, system B, due to reciprocal connections and invariant apical dendrite terminations, is involved in long-distance feedback or loop systems (Braitenburg, 1978; Pascual-Marqui et al., 1988; Thatcher et al., 1986).

The following mathematical equation was developed to describe the magnitude and slope of decline of human EEG coherence with interelectrode distance (Thatcher et al., 1986):

$$\text{Coherence} = A_i e^{-kd} + B_i e^{kd} \sin kd \qquad (4)$$

where A_i and B_i are amplitude parameters and k and d are parameters of frequency (Hz) and scalp interelectrode distance in centimeters, respectively. The first term on the right-hand side of Equation 4 corresponds to the operation of the short-distance A system, and the second term corresponds to the operation of the long-distance B system.

Although the magnitude of EEG coherence with interelectrode distance can be understood by the Thatcher et al. (1986) equation, changes in the development of coherence over long spans of time (i.e., months and years) require additional consideration. The developmental changes in EEG coherence in a large group of subjects reflects changes in the mean coupling between connected neuronal networks. For example, if we assume that volume conduction has been controlled, then we can postulate a relationship between EEG coherence and two primary factors: (a) the number of cortico-cortical connections between neural assembles, and (b) the synaptic strength of connections between neural assembles (the terms *cortico-cortical connections* and *intracortical connections* are considered synonymous). This relationship is described as:

$$\text{Coherence} = C_{ij} \times S_{ij} \qquad (5)$$

where C_{ij} is a connection matrix of the number or density of connections between neural systems i and j, and S_{ij} is the synaptic strength of those connections. The latter equation provides a logical means by which developmental changes in EEG coherence can be interpreted in terms of changes in the number and strength of connections between assemblies of neurons (Pascual-Marqui et al., 1988; Thatcher et al., 1986, 1987). For example, according to Equation 5, increased coherence is due to either an increase in the number and/or strength of connections and, conversely, decreased coherence is due to a decreased number and/or reduced strength of connections. Among the neurophysiological mechanisms that could be responsible for the changes in the numbers or strengths of connections are axonal sprouting, synaptogenesis, mylenation, expansion of existing synaptic terminals, pruning of synaptic connections, presynaptic changes in the amount of neurotransmitter, and changes in the postsynaptic response to a given neurotransmitter (see discussions by Purves, 1988, and Huttenlocher, 1984).

Growth Spurts and Oscillations in EEG Coherence Development

Thatcher (1992a, 1993) defined growth spurts in EEG coherence as age-specific peaks of velocity or those postnatal ages where there was a maximum increase in mean coherence as measured by the first derivative of the developmental time series. The point of maximum increase in EEG coherence (i.e., peak velocity) was considered to reflect an increase in the number and/or strength of connections between two or more intracortical systems as per Equation 5. The criteria for defining a peak in velocity as a growth spurt were that (a) only EEG coherence trajectories that loaded >.80 on a factor were evaluated and (b) the first derivative must exhibit a positive peak. The criterion of "in-phase" developmental trajectories was generally satisfied by a significant loading on a given factor (Thatcher, 1991). That is, each factor represents the commonality between developmental trajectories of EEG coherence and therefore, by definition, a factor reflects "in-phase" activity by a positive loading and antiphase by a negative loading. High loading trajectories were consider important because they reflect shared activity between specific intracortical connection systems and not localized or spurious changes. The velocity was selected rather than the second derivative (acceleration) or peaks in mean coherence itself because velocity reflects the point in time when growth or change in coherence is at a maximum. The second derivative reflects the time of onset of a growth spurt as well as points of inflection. However, the second derivative is more susceptible to noise and may or may not eventually lead to a positive first-derivative peak or to a significant increase in mean coherence. Mean coherence values represent the target or endpoint of the growth spurt as measured by the first derivative. However, the endpoint is when growth or change is at zero, and therefore maximum mean coherence values were not used to define a growth spurt.

A four-point least-squares procedure was used to compute the first derivative (i.e., velocity) or instantaneous rate of change in EEG coherence means from the 436 children in each developmental time series (Savitzky & Golay, 1964). The first four points (mean ages of 0.513–1.292 years) were used to estimate the derivatives, and these points were set to zero. Therefore, no estimates of growth spurts prior to 1.495 years of age were made. Figure 5.2 shows the velocity curves from the subgroupings of electrode pairs that had the highest loadings (e.g., >.80) on the first five factors in the theta frequency band. These factors accounted for a total of 65.7% of the variance. Factor 1 accounted for 22.3% of the variance, factor 2 accounted for 12.9% of the variance, factor 3 accounted for 10.4% of the variance, factor 4 accounted for 10.8% of the variance, and factor 5 accounted for 9.3% of the variance (Thatcher, 1991). Left temporal-frontal and left parietal-frontal developmental trajectories loaded on factor 1, right temporal-frontal developmental trajectories loaded on factor 2, bilateral local frontal trajectories loaded on factor 3, left occipital frontal trajectories loaded on factor 4, and bilateral posterior cortical trajectories loaded on factor 5. Periodic "in-phase" activity was present at different ages for each of the five factors. The fact that multiple electrode combinations were often involved indicated that the "growth spurts" or "in-phase" activity reflected the involvement of relatively large numbers of neuronal systems over relatively short periods of time (e.g., 6 months to 1 year).

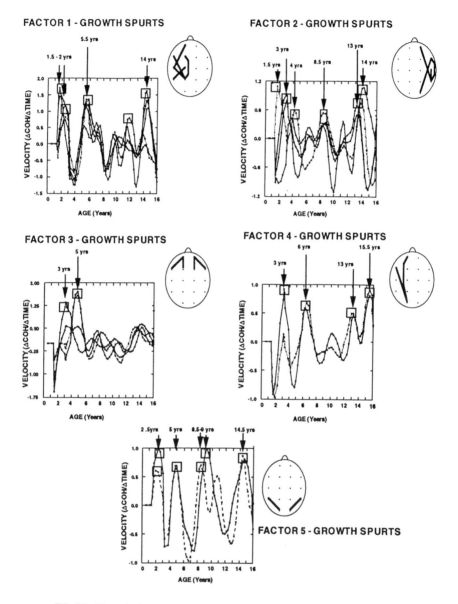

FIG. 5.2. The velocity curves or the first derivatives (mean coherence/time) of the developmental trajectories of mean EEG coherence from the sub-groupings of electrode pairs that had the highest factor loadings (e.g., >.80) (Thatcher, 1991). Growth spurts were defined by a positive peak in the first derivative (i.e., a postnatal time of maximum growth) in multiple interelec-trode combinations. Since each of the trajectories loaded heavily on a factor (i.e., >.80) this was considered sufficient evidence that a trajectory represented "in-phase" or anatomical synchrony of growth. From Thatcher (1994a). Adapted by permission.

Phase Transitions About Ages 6 and 10 Years Postnatal

As seen in Fig. 5.3, between the age of 5 and 7 years and 9 and 11 years a sudden change in the mean trajectory occurred. This sudden changes in the developmental trajectories, referred to as phase transitions or bifurcations, involved the sequence from in-phase to out-of-phase oscillations in the left hemisphere at age 6–7 and from out-of-phase to in-phase oscillations at age 9–11 in the right hemisphere (see arrows). The phase transitions were widespread and were observed in numerous pairs of interelectrode combi-

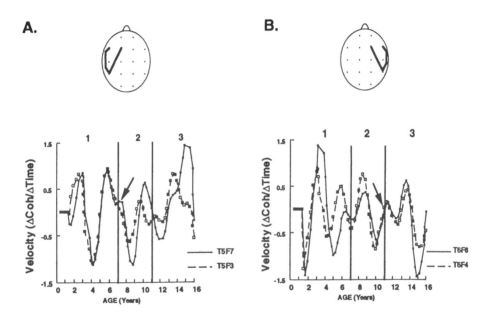

FIG. 5.3. (A) Velocity curves (mean coherence/time) from left-hemisphere dorsal medial-frontal to lateral-temporal (F3-T5) and from lateral-frontal to lateral-temporal (F7-T5). The developmental trajectories were "in phase" from 1.5 years to approximately 5 years (cycle 1). At approximately 7 years (see arrow) the trajectories began to exhibit "out of phase" relations. The x axis is age in Julian years (see Thatcher et al., 1987, for method of computing Julian years). (B) Velocity curves (mean coherence/time) from right-hemisphere dorsal medial-frontal to lateral-temporal (F4-T6) and from lateral-frontal to lateral-temporal (F8-T4). The developmental trajectories were "out of phase" from 1.5 years to approximately 9 years (cycle 3). At approximately 9–11 years (see arrow) the trajectories began to exhibit "in-phase" relations. The x axis is age in Julian years (see Thatcher et al., 1987, for method of computing Julian years).

nations. However, they were most pronounced and consistent from lateral and medial frontal cortical regions. A spatial gradient in the velocity of EEG coherence was evident for phase transitions in the lateral to medial plane. In the left hemisphere, for example, the age 7 phase transition was marked by two poles of apparently competing intracortical systems; the first pole was lateral-frontal to lateral-temporal (F7-T5) and the second pole was medial frontal to lateral-temporal (F3-T5). Prior to age 5, both intracortical poles were in-phase; however, around age 6–7 the medial and lateral fronto-temporal systems phase shifted and formed two separate subsystems (see Fig. 5.4A).

A phase transition with a spatial gradient was also present in the right lateral and right medial fronto to lateral temporal regions during the age 9–11 years period (see Fig. 5.4B). This right-hemisphere phase transition, however, was different than the earlier left-hemisphere phase transition because it was marked by an apparent integration or phase synchrony of previously differentiated or asynchronous right lateral-temporal trajectories. Another example of the phase transition at age 5–7 is seen in Fig. 5.4 from the left fronto-parietal electrodes (i.e., F7-P3). Mean percent coherence (i.e., coherence × 100) versus age is shown in Fig. 5.4A, in which there are oscillations around a homeorhetic line (dashed line) and a slow decline in coherence from 1.5 to approximately 5 years. At approximately 6 years there is a large jump in mean percent coherence with a new set of damped oscillations and a second homeorhetic line from age 7 to 16. Figure 5.4B shows this phase transition in phase space where the first derivative (y axis) is plotted against mean percent coherence (x axis) and the age axis (z axis) is extended. The phase transition is seen as a "cusp" between the ages of 5 and 7 years (Gilmore, 1981; Thom, 1975).

Cyclic Microcycles of Development

Figure 5.5 is a summary of the ages and durations of "in-phase" activity for the five factor groupings shown in Figure 1.[2] An iterative and sequential anatomical pattern of growth spurts was evident. For example, at age 1.5 years growth spurts were relatively localized (e.g., 6 cm interelectrode distances) and confined to the left parietal and left central to left lateral-temporal regions. At age 2.5 years there was a lengthening along the anterior-posterior dimension (e.g., 12 cm interelectrode distances) with a lateral-to-medial rotation of parietal-frontal relations to include left parietal to left dorsal

---

[2]Although most of the first-derivative peaks were single points, several peaks were broad involving more than one point. Therefore, for clarity only approximate ages of first derivative peaks are represented in the text and figures. Because Julian ages were used (Thatcher et al., 1987), the designation of the age of a first-derivative peak was the 6-month period it was nearest to.

LEFT FRONTAL-PARIETAL DEVELOPMENT (F7-P3)

A.

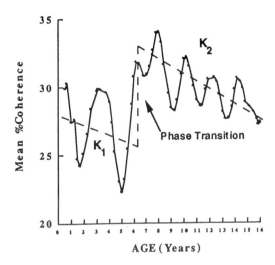

B.

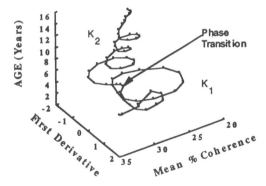

FIG. 5.4. (A) Mean percent EEG coherence (i.e., coherence × 100) in the theta frequency band from left lateral frontal-parietal regions (i.e., F7-P3) from 6 months to age 16. Two modes of oscillation, mode one from birth to approximately age 5 and mode two from approximately age 7 to age 16, are fitted by regression lines K_1 and K_2. The phase transition between the two developmental states of equilibria is represented by the line connecting K_1 to K_2. (B) Two-dimensional phase portrait represented in three dimensions by extending the phase space over age. This figure demonstrates that there are two-limit cycles or phase states of EEG coherence oscillation in the left fronto-parietal (i.e., P3-F7), which are spirals with different radii and frequencies over the life-span. From Thatcher (1991). Adapted by permission.

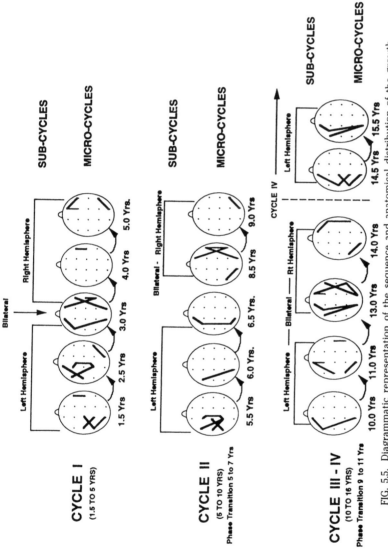

FIG. 5.5. Diagrammatic representation of the sequence and anatomical distribution of the growth spurts shown in Fig. 5.1. Lines connecting two electrode locations correspond to the electrode locations in Fig. 5.1 for the various developmental trajectories that loaded (>.80) on the first five factors (Thatcher, 1991). Microcycles were defined by a developmental sequence involving an anterior-posterior lengthening of interelectrode distances and a lateral-medial rotation that cycles from the left hemisphere to bilateral to right hemisphere in approximately 4-year periods. The microcycles were grouped into subcycles and the subcycles were grouped into cycles as defined by the age 5–7 and age 9–11 bifurcations.

medial-frontal regions (i.e., P3-F3 and T3-F1). At age 3 years there was a further lengthening of intracortical relations along the anterior-posterior dimension (e.g., 18 to 24 cm interelectrode distances) with continued involvement of dorsal medial-frontal to posterior cortex. This sequence of lengthening along the anterior-posterior dimension and rotation along the lateral-to-medial dimension between 1.5 and 3 years was repeated again between ages 5.5 and 6.5 years and finally again between 14.5 and 15.5 years and is referred to as *microcycles* of cortical development. The label of a pattern as a microcycle or a subcycle is used to emphasize the presence of a cyclical pattern. The important point, whether a sequence is labeled as a microcycle or a subcycle, or as a stage or substage, is that sequential developmental processes were nested within cyclic anatomical patterns.

Each EEG coherence growth spurt was marked by a different set of differentiated and integrated intracortical subsystems that represented an iterative sequence of cortical reorganizations. That is, there was a sequential reordering of different subgroupings of cortical connection systems at specific postnatal ages. For example (see Fig. 5.6), the left parietal-temporal pattern (i.e., P3-T3) at 1.5 years was repeated at 5.5 years and again at 14.5 years; the left frontal pole-occipital pattern (i.e., O1-F1) at 6.5 years was

MODEL CORTICO-CORTICAL CONNECTION SYSTEM

FIG. 5.6. A model of cortico-cortical connection development. (A) Diagram of left frontal pole regions (i.e., Fp1), which is competing with left occipital (i.e., O1) for synaptic influence on the parietal cortex. That is, connections from Fp1 and O1 converge onto P3, where they compete for the available synaptic binding sites on the dentrites and/or cell body of parietal neurons. (B) An expansion of the synaptic environment for the competing connection systems shown in (A). The carrying capacity for synaptic influence is a function of the amount of parietal dendritic-somatic area on which synapses can form and the amount of trophic growth factor. Synapses originating from the frontal and occipital regions converge onto the parietal dendro-somatic surface, where they compete for contact and influence of the parietal neurons. From Thatcher (1994b). Adapted by permission.

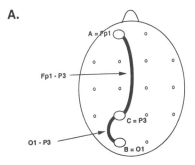

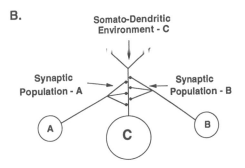

repeated at 13 and 15.5 years; the bilateral occipital-posterior temporal pattern (i.e., O1/2-T5/6) at 2.5 years was repeated at 5 and 14.5 years; the right frontal-posterior cortical pattern (F2-T6 and F8-O2) at 3 years was repeated at 8.5 years and 13 years; and so on.

A NONLINEAR SYNAPTOGENIC MODEL
OF CEREBRAL DEVELOPMENT

The results of the developmental EEG studies (Epstein, 1980; Hudspeth & Pribram, 1990, 1991; Matousek & Petersen, 1973; Thatcher, 1989, 1991, 1992a, 1993; Thatcher et al., 1987) raise a number of critical questions. Among these questions are:

1. What are the physiological bases for the oscillations in human EEG over the developmental lifespan?
2. What are the mechanisms by which growth spurts in EEG occur?
3. What is the nature of the phase transitions that occur between brain regions that exhibit different oscillations?
4. If life-span oscillations reflect important physiological processes, then do different modes and locations of oscillation contribute to the development of different aspects of human cognition?

To begin the search for the answers it is reasonable to begin with fundamental biological and ecological models that are capable of explaining the presence of oscillations in populations of neurons. Among the most adaptable ecological models are where two populations are competing for a common food supply (Gause, 1934; Gause & Witt, 1935; Volterra, 1926) and/or population models involving prey–predator relationships (Holling, 1959, 1966; Lotka, 1925; Nicholson & Bailey, 1935; Soloman, 1949; Volterra, 1926). These two models are mathematically related, primarily by the strength of the competitive coupling (Berryman, 1981; Getz, 1984; Real, 1977). In order to adapt these models to cortical development we must assume:

1. A common niche for synapses is the somato-dendritic surface area expressed in squared micrometers (see Equations 1–3).
2. Cortico-cortical connection systems can compete and/or cooperate for the available somato-dendritic surface area upon which synaptic connections are formed.
3. Competing and/or cooperating cortico-cortical connection systems from different brain regions can coexist within a given cortical region,

such that displacement of connections from region 1 by connections from region 2 can occur.

In order to specify the dynamics of synaptic population interaction, three levels of analysis are considered: (a) the synaptic level, (b) the axonal-dendritic level, and (c) the synaptic population level.

The Synaptic Level

It is generally agreed that the mature synapse represents the endpoint of a continuous and dynamic process of growth and degeneration in which both postsynaptic and presynaptic mechanisms operate in the embryogenesis, maintenance, and regression of synapses (Purves, 1988). On the one hand, mature neuronal networks are believed to be genetically specified in which the environment merely triggers preestablished programs and sequentially stabilizes specific synaptic connections (Weisel, 1982). On the other hand, a growing number of scientists believe that genetic programs only grossly specify synaptic configuration, with the activity of the nervous system largely specifying the fine details of connectivity (Brown, Holland, & Hopkins, 1981; Purves & Lichtman, 1985; Zucker, 1982). Among the strongest proponents of the latter view are Changeux and Danchin (1976), who postulated that genetic mechanisms specify main categories or sets of connections by producing a surplus or redundant number of synapses and that activity-dependent factors select which of this redundant set will become stable and survive. According to this model, the genetic program allows for an initial overproduction of synapses but during maturation a significant fraction regress. They argue that when synaptic contacts first form, they exist under three states: labile (L), stable (S), and regressed (D). The labile state may become either stabilized (L → S) or irreversibly regressed (L → D) with regrowth represented by (not → L). A critical feature of Changeux and Danchin's (1976) model is that the transitions of synapses from labile to stable or labile to regressed are regulated in an "epigenetic" manner by both presynaptic and postsynaptic activities. Although the molecular mechanisms are not precisely known, it is widely believed that environmentally driven neurotransmitters are involved in the anterograde or presynaptic side (Lo & Poo, 1991; Purves, 1988) and genetically driven nerve growth factors are involved in the retrograde or postsynaptic side (Changeux & Danchin, 1976; Montague, Gally, & Edelman, 1991; Vogel & Davies, 1991). Of course other factors emitted by nerve terminals must also be considered, such as ATP and some enzymes or polypeptide hormones (Becker, 1991; Raffioni, Bradshaw, & Buxser, 1993) that provide "energy" for development. For the development of complex patterns of synapses on somas and dendrites, internal "coupling factors" are postulated as a way to explain the regular spacing of synapses (Stent,

1973). Thus, for simplification one can postulate that although environment and genetics interact on both the pre- and postsynaptic sides, the presynaptic side is more strongly influenced by environmental factors and the postsynaptic side is more strongly influenced by genetic factors. We can represent the relation between synapses and the supply of energy necessary to sustain their existence, such as trophic nerve growth factor NGF or ATP, as:

$$D_e = \frac{N}{E} \qquad (6)$$

where N is the number of synapses, E is the concentration of subsistence and maintenance substance such as NGF, and D_e is the density of subsistence and maintenance substance per unit synapse (see Equations 24 and 25 for more detailed definitions).

The Axonal-Dendritic Level

Figure 5.6 (top) is a representation of two synaptic populations A and B converging on a common somato-dentritic area C. The projections A and B represent multiple axons with multiple branches containing multiple synaptic connections. There are shared spatial locations on the dendrites of C in which the synaptic species from population A cooperates and/or competes for occupancy with the synaptic species from population B. The bottom illustration is an example of cortico-cortical connection systems representing A, B, and C; for example, lateral frontal to parietal cortico-cortical connections (F7-P3) are A, occipital to parietal cortico-cortical connections (O1-P3) are B, and C is the somato-dendritic domain of the left parietal region (P3) where the cortico-cortical connections A and B converge. It is at this location of convergence that competition for available dendritic space and limited energy resources emerges (see Equations 24 and 25).

Neural Population Level

Given the factors and arrangements at the synaptic and axonal-dendritic levels described earlier, a mathematical model of the ontogenesis of synaptogenesis was developed. This model is based on modifications of the Lotka-Volterra equations as described by Milsum (1968), Gilpin and Ayala (1973), and Berryman (1981). The following sections represent an adaptation of Berryman's (1981, 1990) population dynamics model as applied to cortico-cortical synaptic systems. Figure 5.7 is a representation of the dynamical interactions within and between cortico-cortical synaptic systems as depicted in Fig. 5.6. There are four major kinds of relations and interactions between synaptic connection systems: (a) independent, (b) competition, (c) cooperation, and (d) predator/prey. These categories of interaction can be

DYNAMIC CORTICAL SYNAPTIC CONNECTION MODEL

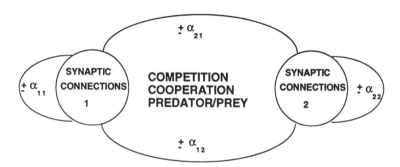

FIG. 5.7. Ecological model in which synapses arising from two different cortical regions interact for influence on a third cortical region. The interaction can be of four types: independent, cooperative, competitive, and predator–prey, depending upon the sign and magnitude of the interaction coefficients a_{ii}, which are divided into intrasynaptic interaction coefficients, such as a_{11} and a_{22}, and intersynaptic interaction coefficients, such as a_{12} and a_{21}. From Thatcher (1994b). Adapted by permission.

depicted by the sign and magnitude of the interaction coefficients a_{ii}, which are divided into intrasynaptic interaction coefficients, such as a_{11} and a_{22}, or intersynaptic interaction coefficients, such as a_{12} and a_{21}. Independence is when a_{12} and a_{21} are zero, competition is when a_{12} and a_{21} are both negative, cooperation is when a_{12} and a_{21} are both positive, and predator/prey is when a_{12} is negative and a_{21} is positive (see Equations 27–30).

In the sections to follow, the details of how these population interactions are modeled for cortical synaptic connections are established by an examination of the mathematical structure of neural population dynamics.

Nonlinear Dynamics of Intrasynaptic Interactions

We define a *population* of synapses as a group or set of synapses with a common origin and a common somato-dendritic termination point. In other words, axonal terminations that arise from neural cell bodies in location A and terminate on location C represent a population of synapses (see Fig. 5.6). Let the number of synaptic connections in a population at time t be represented by $N(t)$ and those present one time period previously by $N(t - 1)$. Further, let the number of synaptic connections grow or increase at an average rate of b over the time interval $t - 1$ to t. It follows that the number of synaptic connections present in the population at time t must be

$$N_t = N_{(t-1)} \times b \tag{7}$$

If we start at time zero with a population of $N(0)$ synaptic connections, and assuming that the rate of growth does not change, then we can calculate the growth of synaptic connections over several time increments by the equation

$$N_t = N_{(t-1)} \times b^{\Delta t} \tag{8}$$

where Δt is the number of time increments. We can write Equation 8 in its more familiar exponential form by taking natural logarithms, setting $B = \log_e(b)$, and taking antilogs to arrive at

$$N_t = N_{(t-\Delta t)} \times \exp(B \times \Delta t) \tag{9}$$

Equation 9 is a solution of the well-known differential equation of exponential growth or the "Malthusian law" as described in

$$\frac{dN}{dt} = N \times B \tag{10}$$

In addition to growth of synaptic connections we must assume that connections die or are displaced. To incorporate this feature into the model a growth parameter r is defined as

$$r = b - d \tag{11}$$

where r is the rate of change in synaptic connections, b is the birth or creation of synaptic connections, and d is the death or displacement of synaptic connections. We can substitute $R = \log_e(r)$ for B in Equation 9 when $\Delta t = 1$ to yield

$$N_t = N_{(t-1)} \times \exp(R) \tag{12}$$

Using Equation 12 we can calculate population growth as a stepwise, or recursive, process and estimate the rate of change by

$$R = \log_e[N_t] - \log_e[N_{(t-1)}] \tag{13}$$

where R is the rate of growth and N_t and $N_{(t-1)}$ are the estimated densities of synaptic connections at two sequential points in time.

Limits to Growth

It is obvious that populations of synapses cannot grow indefinitely and must eventually be limited by shortages of trophic nerve growth factor (NGF), space, or other essential resources. This idea can be formalized by considering a population of N synaptic contacts in which each individual synapse requires W units of a critical resource, say, a trophic nerve growth factor, to keep it alive and to be replaced when it dies. If the total nerve growth factor available per unit time is F, there will be surplus trophic growth factor for synaptic growth when F is larger than the subsistence demand of the population $W \times N$. In other words, the population will grow (i.e., $R > 0$) when the demand/supply ratio is less than unity, that is, $(W \times N)/F < 1$. In contrast, the population will decline (i.e., $R < 0$) when $(W \times N)/F > 1$, and the population will remain constant at steady state equilibrium (i.e., $R = 0$) when the demand/supply ratio is unity, that is, $(W \times N)/F = 1$. We can see from Equation 12 that the population will also be in equilibrium when $R = 0$, because $\exp(0) = 1$ and, therefore, $N_t = N_{(t-1)}$. A simple expression for the relationship between rate of growth R and the demand/supply ratio $(W \times N)/F$ is

$$R = A - C \times \left(\frac{W \times N}{F} \right) \tag{14}$$

where A is the intercept of the line with the R axis at $N = 0$ and C is the slope of the line. Because $R = 0$ when $(W \times N)/F = 1$, then $A = C$ when $R = 0$ (i.e., $0 = A - C$ or $A = C$). Because $A = C$ when $R = 0$, Equation 8 can be written

$$R = A - \left(\frac{A \times W \times N}{F} \right) \quad \text{or} \quad R = A \times \left(1 - \frac{W \times N}{F} \right) \tag{15}$$

We can further reduce the number of parameters in this equation by letting the equilibrium value of $N = K$, which occurs when $R = 0$, so that

$$0 = A \times \left(1 - \frac{W \times K}{F} \right) \quad \text{or} \quad K = F/W \tag{16}$$

In other words, the equilibrium density, K, is equal to the supply of essential resources F divided by the subsistence demand W. This parameter reflects the density of synapses that can be sustained indefinitely by a constant supply of nerve growth factor and available somato-dendritic space and is referred to as the *carrying capacity of the synaptic environment* (K). Substituting K for F/W in Equation 15 yields

$$R = A \times \left(1 - \frac{N}{K} \right) \tag{17}$$

This equation expresses R, the rate of change in the number of synapses, as a function of the synaptic density, N, and the carrying capacity of the synaptic environment, K.

Genetics as "Experience-Independent" and Environment as "Experience-Dependent" Development

The synaptic carrying capacity can be modeled to contain dynamical properties itself. This is important in order to account for both genetical and environmental aspects of development as they may operate at subcellular or DNA levels as well as at extracellular levels. The approach we choose to model the dynamics of genetics and environment is based on Greenough and colleagues' "experience-dependent and -independent" models of cortical development (Black & Greenough, 1986; Greenough, Black, & Wallace, 1987) in which the carrying capacity could be modified depending on the supply and demand of nerve growth factor (NGF) and somato-dendritic surface area. Let us assume that the carrying capacity of the synaptic environment K is a function of both the concentration of nerve growth factor and the available somato-dendritic space on which synapses can be formed, or $K =$ NGF + SPACE. Let us further assume that the ratio between the supply and demand of these components is controlled by both experience-dependent and experience-independent influences at all levels of development and that environment and genetics are always interrelated and additive. We can model such a relationship by representing experience-independent and experience-dependent influences on different axes of a complex variable Z, where $Z = x + iy$ with experience-independent influences represented by the x or real variable and the experience-dependent influences represented by the imaginary variable iy.

However, for the sake of simplicity, in the following sections the complex representation of experience-dependent and experience-independent influences is not formally modeled or simulated. Although this is necessary given the limits of space, it should be noted that interesting and complicated dynamics evolve from these equations when the complex variable is used. For the moment, let us substitute the functional relationship (Equation 17) for R in Equation 12, in which we get a discrete-time analog of the well-known Verhulst (1938) logistic equation,

$$N_i = N_{(t-1)} \times \exp\left[A \times \left(1 - \frac{N_{(t-1)}}{K}\right)\right] \tag{18}$$

more commonly seen as the differential equation

$$\frac{dN}{dt} = R \times N \times \left(1 - \frac{N}{K}\right) \quad \text{where } R = A \tag{19}$$

The logistic is a fundamental equation of linear population dynamics, containing the basic elements of positive feedback population growth and negative feedback constraints on growth. It assumes that R is linearly related to population density, that negative feedback occurs without a time delay, and that the system is characterized by a single equilibrium point. These assumptions are overly restrictive and do not allow for the richness of behavior observed in the development of cerebral cytoarchitecture and the developmental EEG literature. In order to adapt Equations 18 and 19 we need to account for synaptic growth in a variable environment that involves delayed nonlinear negative feedback. We also need to account for "stages" or "discontinuities" in development as represented by two or more equilibria or domains of attraction.

Based on Gilpin and Ayala (1973) and Berryman's (1990) formulation, we can adapt Equation 18 to describe synaptic growth far from equilibrium in a variable or stochastic environment as

$$R = A \times \left[1 - \left(\frac{N(t-1)}{K} \right)^Q \right] + V[0,S] \tag{20}$$

where V is a standard deviate of a normally distributed variable with mean 0 and standard deviation S. Increasing the value of S will increase the amount of random "noise" in the environment. We can also adapt Equation 18 so that the slope of the feedback function is not constant and, in fact, is proportionally stronger at either high or low densities (i.e., is nonlinear). For example, when competition is strong near to the carrying capacity then the R function will get steeper as it approaches the carrying capacity; that is, it will be convex. When negative feedback is more intense at low synaptic densities then the R function will have a concave form. We can represent nonlinear feedback by adding an exponent Q to the demand/supply ratio, where Q is referred to as the coefficient of curvature of the logistic equation. When $Q > 1$ the R function will become convex and when $Q < 1$ it will become concave (Berryman, 1990).

Equation 20 is self-regulatory if it is assumed that there is no delay or only a negligible delay between the time that the population N reaches its limit K and the time for the establishment of the appropriately corrected value of the synaptic productive rate. However, as pointed out by Hutchinson (1948), if there is a time lag T so that the rate dN/dt at time T is determined by the delay $N_{(t-T)}$, then oscillations will be present in the equation. We can incorporate time lags into the logistic equation by letting R be a function of $N_{(t-T)}$, where T is the delay in the negative feedback response; that is

$$R = A \times \left(1 - \frac{N_{(t-T)}}{K} \right) + V[0,S] \tag{21}$$

Finally, we can use Tong's (1978) and Berryman's (1990) formulations to adapt Equation 20 to contain two equilibria or basins of attraction that are separated by an unstable equilibrium point, sometimes referred to as an escape threshold or separatrix. To accomplish this we generalized the logistic R function as

$$R = A_i \times \left(1 - \frac{N_{(t-1)}}{L_i}\right) \times \left[1 - \left(\frac{N_{(t-1)}}{K_i}\right)^{Q_i}\right] + V[0,S] \qquad (22)$$

$$i = 1 \text{ when } N_{(t-1)} > E$$
$$i = 2 \text{ when } N_{(t-1)} < E$$

where L and K are the carrying capacities of the lower and upper equilibrium states respectively, E is the escape threshold or separatrix, and the subscript i indexes the parameters of the upper ($i = 1$) and lower ($i = 2$) equilibria. Thus, when synaptic density is above the escape threshold, E, trajectories are drawn toward the upper equilibrium, and when density is below the threshold, trajectories are attracted to the lower equilibrium. In nonlinear dynamics the separatrix E forms the unstable point of a saddle to which trajectories move toward limit sets or basins.

Nonlinear Dynamics of Intra- and Intersynaptic Interactions

A crucial aspect of this model concerns the availability and demand for resources, which are defined by the number of synapses and the availability of dendritic space on which synapses are formed and the availability of trophic growth factors. It is the interrelations between demand for and availability of these resource that determine the nature of the nonlinear dynamics of the model.

To explore this aspect of the model let us first write Equation 17 as

$$R = A - \beta N_{(t-1)} \qquad (23)$$

where $\beta = A/K$ is the negative effect of a set of cortico-cortical synaptic connections on its own rate of increased connectivity. We can call this an intrasynaptic effect because it represents the effects of intraspecific competition between members of the same cortico-cortical connection system. However, because there is a finite amount of resources from which synapses can be formed, it is necessary to modify Equation 23 to take into account both dendritic space and the amount of trophic nerve growth factor. Therefore, let us extend Equation 23 so that

$$R_i = A_i - G_i \frac{N_i}{S_i} - H_i \frac{N_i}{E_i} \qquad (24)$$

where N_i is the density of the ith set of cortico-cortical connections, G_i is a measure of the demand for somato-dendritic space for that set of connections, H_i is a measure of the demand for food or trophic growth factor for that set of connections, S_i is a measure of the available somato-dendritic space for that set of connections, and E_i is the amount of trophic growth factor available for that set of synaptic connections i. In this variation of the logistic model, the carrying capacity can be determined by both available somato-dendritic surface area (S_i) expressed in square millimeters and/or the concentration of trophic nerve growth factor (E_i) expressed in micromoles, whereas the parameters G_i and H_i specify the demands of the average synapse for these resources, respectively.

As described in more detail in the next section, the concepts of competition, cooperation, and predator/prey interactions between two populations emerge by expanding Equation 24 to two interrelated equations and varying the ratios of the various elements of Equation 24. For example, we can write Equation 24 for two populations as Equations 25a and 25b:

$$R_1 = A_1 - G_1 \frac{N_1}{S_1} - H_1 \frac{N_1}{N_0} \tag{25a}$$

$$R_2 = A_2 - G_2 \frac{N_2}{S_2} - H_2 \frac{N_2}{N_1} \tag{25b}$$

These equations state that the rates of growth of the two populations R_1 and R_2 vary as a function of their respective intercepts A_1 and A_2 minus the respective demands for space G_1 and G_2 and the ratio of the density of synapses $(N_1$ and $N_2)$ to the available dendritic space $(S_1$ and $S_2)$. Most importantly, R_1 and R_2 are also related to the respective demand for food (and/or trophic factor) H_1 and H_2 and the ratio of the density of synapses (N_1, N_2, N_0) to the available food as supplied by population N_2 to N_1 in Equation 25b and between population N_1 and a basic trophic level N_0 in Equation 25a. In other words, the rate of growth of population 2 is dependent upon the density of synapses of population 1, because population 1 serves as a source of food for population 2.

Competition, Cooperation, and Predator–Prey Interactions Between Cortico-Cortical Synaptic Connections

A simplification of the model shown in Equations 24 and 25 can yield a product model of competition, cooperation, and predator/prey. For example, let us consider that somato-dendritic space and nerve growth factor for the intraspecific interactions of a given population of cortico-cortical connections are constant and set β in Equation 23 to α_{ii} where:

$$\alpha_{ii} = \frac{G_i}{S_i} + \frac{H_i}{E_i} \qquad (26)$$

which allows us to reduce Equation 24 to Equation 23.

With this simplification it is possible to introduce the effect of another or different set of cortico-cortical synaptic connections. We use the notation of the interaction coefficients α_{ii} to be consistent with Fig. 5.7:

$$R_1 = A_1 - \alpha_{11}N_{1,(t-1)} \pm \alpha_{12}N_{2,(t-1)} \qquad (27)$$

where α_{11} is the coefficient or weighting for the intraspecific effect of N_1 on itself and α_{12} is the coefficient or weighting for the effect of the second set of synaptic connections, N_2, on the rate of increase of N_1, or the interspecific effect. The sign of the coefficient α_{12} determines whether the interaction between sets of synaptic connections is competitive, cooperative, or exploitive.

Equation 27 is a variation of the Lotka–Volterra equation, in which predator/prey interactions are dependent on the product of predator to prey. However, as pointed out by Berryman (1990), there are problems with the simplified product model of Equation 27. For example, according to Equation 27 the rate of increase in synaptic connections is dependent only on the density of the other set of synaptic connections and does not take into consideration the possibility that growth of a given synaptic connection system may depend on its own density and not just the density of another synaptic system. In other words, the rate of change in synaptic connections can also be expressed as a ratio of predators to prey or N_2/N_1 as in Equations 25a and 25b. We call this the *ratio-dependent variation of the model* and the formulation in Equation 27 is the *product-dependent variation of the model*. In subsequent analyses of the model both the product-dependent and the ratio-dependent forms of the model are evaluated and compared to determine which is the best fit and possibly to infer which dynamic is most prevalent in the development of cortico-cortical connection systems. In the equations to follow, however, only the ratio-dependent variation is presented. In order to derive the product-dependent variation one simply changes the ratio (e.g., N_2/N_1) to a single species as in Equation 27. By setting both dendritic space and the nerve growth trophic levels constant, the equations can be simplified to the ratio of the two synaptic connection systems where one is either cooperating or competing with the other. For this purpose, let us set the exploited population as N_1 and the exploiting population as N_2. In this manner competition, cooperation, and predator/prey interactions can be described by three similar equations that differ only in the ratio that determines the interspecific interaction. For example, beneficial effects are signified by the ratio of a population of synaptic connections to a population of benefactor connections, N_2/N_1, and harmful effects are represented by the ratio of the exploiting synaptic population (i.e., N_2) to the synaptic population that is displaced or exploited (e.g., the prey), N_2/N_1. The following three equations described these interrelated conditions.

Competition Between Cortico-Cortical Synaptic Systems

Competition can be represented as follows:

$$R_1 = A_1 - \alpha_{11}N_1 - \alpha_{12}\frac{N_2}{N_1} \tag{28a}$$

$$R_2 = A_2 - \alpha_{22}N_2 - \alpha_{21}\frac{N_1}{N_2} \tag{28b}$$

Equations 28a and 28b are symmetrical in that each set of synaptic connections has a negative effect on the other so that the two equations are structurally balanced. Zero growth isocline analyses in which $R = 0$ for each synaptic connection group show the conditions of stability and instability in Equations 28a and 28b (Berryman, 1990). For example, competitive coexistence is possible only when $\alpha_{11}\alpha_{22} > \alpha_{12}\alpha_{21}$; for all other conditions competitive annihilation or exclusion will occur in which one synaptic species or group of synaptic connections is succeeded by more successful competitors.

Cooperation Between Cortico-Cortical Synaptic Systems

Cooperation between two sets of cortico-cortical synaptic connections is described with the following two equations:

$$R_1 = A_1 - \alpha_{11}N_1 - \alpha_{12}\frac{N_1}{N_2} \tag{29a}$$

$$R_2 = A_2 - \alpha_{22}N_2 - \alpha_{21}\frac{N_2}{N_1} \tag{29b}$$

The only difference between the equations for competition and the equations for cooperation is the ratio of synaptic densities that determines the interspecific interaction (Berryman, 1990). As in the case of competition, the feedback structure of cooperation is symmetrical but involves positive rather than negative interactions between the two sets of synaptic connections. However, this has no effect on the overall feedback structure of the system because the product of the two positive interactions also produces a positive feedback loop.

Predator/Prey Relations Between Cortico-Cortical Synaptic Systems

The equations for exploitation or predator–prey interactions are represented by the following two equations

$$R_1 = A_1 - \alpha_{11}N_1 - \alpha_{12}\frac{N_2}{N_1} \text{ (Prey population)} \qquad (30a)$$

$$R_2 = A_2 - \alpha_{22}N_2 + \alpha_{21}\frac{N_2}{N_1} \text{ (Predatory population)} \qquad (30b)$$

Notice that the interspecific effect on the exploited population is determined by the same predatory/prey ratio. These two ratio-dependent equations represent, more generally, sets of synaptic connections that are harmed by the interaction (i.e., competing with or being exploited by). In the predator/prey relationship the feedback structure is asymmetrical because one set of synaptic connections benefits whereas the other suffers from the association. This produces an overall negative feedback loop that has a stabilizing effect on the two synaptic connections' interaction. However, an intrinsic time lag in the feedback loop can give rise to cyclical oscillations characteristic of many predator–prey interactions.

We can expand Equations 28, 29, and 30 to explicitly include supply and demand for dendritic space as well as the supply and demand for trophic nerve growth factor as per Equations 24 and 25. We can also write a general model (Berryman, 1990) for the ratio-dependent equations in terms of their carrying capacities and the nonlinear coefficients of curvature, Q, such as

$$R_i = A_i \left[1 - \left(\frac{N_i}{K_i}\right)^{Q_i} \right] - \frac{\alpha_{ij}N_j}{N_i + F} \qquad (31)$$

where N_j and N_i represent the exploiting and exploited populations, respectively. The three types of interactions expressed by this general equation are represented in Fig. 5.7.

FIT OF MODEL TO EEG COHERENCE TRAJECTORIES

A stepwise procedure was used to evaluate individual and combinations of EEG coherence developmental trajectories and to determine the best fit of the data to both the product-dependent and the ratio-dependent variations of the model. The first step was to evaluate the dynamics, stability, and sensitivity of the population model for single cortico-cortical connection systems. In these analyses intrahemispheric EEG coherence trajectories in the theta frequency band (right hemisphere = 28, left hemisphere = 28) were evaluated for the presence of two or more equlibria (i.e., the presence of a separatrix and basins of attraction, see Equation 22), the magnitude of time delays, and the magnitude and direction of nonlinearity as measured by the coefficient of curvature. The second step was to evaluate the two population dynamics of EEG coherence developmental trajectories in short-/short-distance electrode pairings (e.g., F1-F7 vs. F1-F3; $N = 14$) and short-/long-distance electrode pairings (e.g., F1-F3 vs. F1-O1; $N = 30$) in both the left and right hemisphere. The goal was to evaluate the goodness of fit to the EEG coherence trajectories using the model of two populations as independent, competing, cooperating, and/or in a predator–prey mode of interaction (see Fig. 5.7). This involved a least-squares regression analysis to fit the R function, using both the product-dependent variation and the ratio-dependent variation, followed by simulation of the best fitting model using deterministic and stochastic simulations. The mode of interaction as competitive, cooperative, predator–prey, or independent (i.e., no significant interaction) was determined based on Equation 31. The type of two-population interaction each pair of EEG coherence trajectories fell into was determined by the sign of the coefficients, the R^2, and the probability values (i.e., $p < .05$). Once the category of interaction was determined (excluding the independent interactions), the dynamics of the model were further evaluated by isocline analyses in which the structure of the isoclines, the phase-space trajectories, and the time series plots were compared.

Global Characteristics: Limit Cycles and Bifurcations

The phase-space trajectories were characterized by (a) sigmoid-type logistic growth or (b) limit-cycle behavior or (c) spiral trajectories that tended to converge toward a limit cycle. Many of the trajectories could be characterized as two or more equilibria separated by an escape threshold or separatrix. From 1.5 to 5 years of age the separatrix occurred primarily in right frontal and right fronto-temporal regions around the ages of 3–4 years. Between the ages of 5 and 7 years the separatrix occurred primarily in the left fronto-temporal and left fronto-parietal regions, and a third group of separatrix bifurcations was seen in the right fronto-temporal regions around the ages of 9–11 years. Because of the complexity of the analyses, especially when two or more separatrixes were involved, the following presentation concerns only the range from 1.5 to 5 years of age. This age range only contained, at most, one separatrix, and it provides for a detailed and simplified analysis.

The fits of all of the EEG developmental trajectories were statistically significant ($p < .05$) using the single-population equations. In 100% of the cases time delays at T_3 and/or T_2 yielded higher R^2 values than at a time delay of T_1. The highest R^2 values at T_3 or T_2 ranged from 41.78% in F3-C3 to 99.9% in F1-F3.

Frontal Cortical Regions as Predators and Posterior Cortical Regions as Prey

The mode of interaction between EEG cortico-cortical developmental systems could be explained most frequently and with the highest amount of variance accounted for in the predator–prey mode (e.g., 37/44 = 86.05% in the left hemisphere and 21/44 = 48.5% in the right hemisphere). The next most prevalent mode of interaction was of the competitive type, although competitive interactions occurred exclusively in the right hemisphere (12/44 = 27.2% of right-hemisphere pairings and 0% of left-hemisphere pairings). The least frequent modes of interaction were the independent (5/44 = 11.63% of left hemisphere and 6/44 = 13.63% of right hemisphere) and cooperative modes (2/44 = 4.65% of left-hemisphere pairings and 4/44 = 9.09% of right-hemisphere pairings), respectively. Clear differences in the anatomical distribution of the various modes were present. In general, the predator–prey modes occurred in the anterior-to-posterior plane, with frontal regions only being the predators and only the posterior cortical regions the prey. The independent and cooperative modes tended to occur in the medio-lateral plane and the competitive modes occurred, primarily, in right local frontal and right fronto-temporal regions.

Figure 5.8 shows an example of actual mean EEG coherence data (A) and simulated data (B) for Fp1-P3 and O1-P3 competitive dynamics (see Fig. 5.6). In this case the least-squares regression fit of the model to the actual mean EEG coherence data had an R for P3-O1 = 97.41% and for Fp1-P3 = 94.97%. According to the model there is a continuous cycling of synaptic abundance followed by synaptic pruning in both frontal and posterior cortical regions. However, it is believed that the mechanisms of pruning are somewhat different because the frontal regions are directly responsible for the synaptic organization and reorganization in posterior cortical regions (Thatcher, 1994b). The synaptic sequence, as diagrammed in Fig. 5.8B, is: *Stage one*, at approximately 1.5 years, is when long-distance frontal-posterior synaptic influences are at a low and at the same time short-distance posterior cortical synaptic influences are at a high or surplus. At this age there is minimal frontal cortical reorganization of posterior regions with previously formed frontal connections being influential. *Stage two*, at approximately 2.5 years, is when short-distance posterior cortical synaptic influences are on the decline and long-distance frontal-posterior synaptic influences are increasing and becoming significantly more influential on posterior cortical neural networks. *Stage three*, at age approximately 3.8 years, appears when long-distance frontal synaptic influence and reorganization are at a maximum; however, there is a diminishing supply of "virgin" local posterior cortical synapses, and thus frontal influence begins to decline. *Stage four*, at approximately 5.5 years, is when long-distance frontal-posterior cortical synaptic

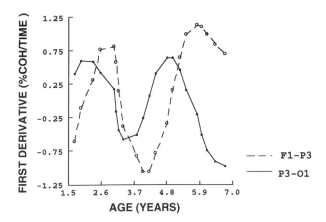

A.

EXPERIMENTAL DATA

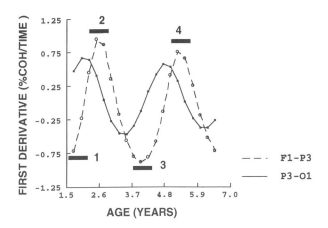

B.

SIMULATED DATA

FIG. 5.8. Comparison of (A) actual first derivatives of mean EEG coherence from the frontal-parietal (F1P3) and parietal-occipital (P3O1) regions to (B) simulated first derivative values based upon the predator/prey model described by Equation 31. The least-squares regression fit of the model (Equation 25) to the actual mean EEG coherence data had for P3-O1 $R^2 =$ 97.41% and for Fp1-P3 $R^2 =$ 94.97%. From Thatcher (1994b). Adapted by permission.

influences are on the decline, and short-distance posterior cortical influences are on the rise—that is, restocking the supply of posterior cortical synapses that the frontal lobes can later "replace" or "reorganize."

DISCUSSION

The results of the model simulations and regression fits to the trajectories of EEG coherence development demonstrate the feasibility of applying an ecological model of predator–prey interaction to explain the dynamics of human cerebral development. For example, in the single population analyses statistically significant regression fits ranged from 33% to 99% of the variance. The adequacy of the two-population model was also established by the accuracy of the simulations and the consistency of the signs of the coefficients in which 86.36% of the total number of regression fits were statistically significant ($p < .05$), whereas 86.05% and 47.7% of the left- and right-hemisphere models, respectively, were of a predator–prey type with frontal regions always being the predator and posterior cortical regions always being the prey. Attempts were made to reverse the signs of the coefficients and to force the posterior cortical regions to be the predator; however, the fit process always failed to converge.

Cytological Analogs of Synaptic Predation

The three primary forms of ecological interactions are cooperation, competition, and predator–prey. Of these the predator–prey interactions are the most pervasive and stable, being present in a very wide range of biological situations and levels of interaction. The pervasiveness and stability of predator–prey interactions stem from the maintenance of a dynamic equilibrium through the mutual dependence of both cooperation and competition of the two interacting species. There are four types of ecological predation, each of which is equivalent when expressed in their simplest mathematical forms. *Herbivores* are animals that prey on plants or their fruits or seeds, and although the plants eaten are often not killed they may nevertheless be damaged. *Carnivores* prey on herbivores or other carnivores. *Parasitism* is a variant on predation, and involves the parasite laying eggs on or near the host, which results in reduced fertility, fecundity, and growth rates of the host. Finally, *cannibalism* is a form of predation involving just one species, with predator and prey often being the adults and young, respectively. It is important to note that prey death is not always necessary for predator reproduction, especially in the case of parasites and herbivores.

The adaptation of an ecological predator–prey model to cortical synaptogenesis does not require the exact specification of the predator–prey type because identical mathematical forms pertain to each of the four different categories of interaction. However, given the long cycle times of cerebral dynamics (e.g., months and years), a somewhat gentle form of predation, similar to a herbivore or parasite, would represent a more appropriate ecological model. According to this model, synaptic reorganization would involve a displacement and/or absorption of existing synapses by successfully competing synapses.

Cycles of Development: The Issue of Discontinuous Development

According to the model the frequency of oscillation in EEG coherence developmental trajectories is a function of the time delay t, the rate of growth r, the carrying capacity K, and the stochastic noise or variability ($V[0]$) (see Equation 22). The parametric evaluation of the model showed 91.3% of the time delays were three steps, 8.7% were two steps, and 0% were only a time delay of 1 step. Three-step time delays are characteristic of predator–prey interactions where there are intervening biological variables governing the predator–prey interaction. One- and two-step time delays are more characteristic of competitive and cooperative dynamics. An important feature of the frequency of oscillations in EEG coherence was their relative invariance within a phase period, for example, from birth to age 7 or age 7 to 16, with sudden shifts in frequency usually occurring when there were sudden changes in the homeorhetic mean value of oscillation such as in Fig. 5.4. Such coordinated changes in frequency and the homeorhetic mean can occur very simply by changing the carrying capacity. As specified earlier, carrying capacity would be most strongly influenced by changes in skull growth and/or cell packing density. It is significant that dendritic surface area is inversely related to neuronal packing density (Bok, 1959; Jerison, 1973; Wright, 1934; see Equations 1, 2, and 3). By the age of 6 years there is measurable cortical neuronal cell death (Cowan et al., 1984; O'Leary, 1987), whereas skull volume has increased from approximately 30% at birth to approximately 90% of adult value by age 6 (Blinkov & Glezer, 1968). The postnatal loss of neurons and simultaneous increase in skull volume result in a large decrease in neuronal packing density (Blinkov & Glezer, 1968; Rabinowicz, 1979). However, neuronal packing density, and thus the cortical dendritic surface areas available for synaptogenesis, reaches an asymptote near the age of 6 years. The transition from rapid growth to asymptotic stability, in which limits in synaptogenesis are at a new high, may contribute to a shift in the global equilibria of the EEG trajectories observed around the age of 5–7 years. A decrease in cortical packing density due to skull growth near the time of puberty may contribute to the second transition or bifurcation observed around the age of 10–11 years.

In general, the dynamics of intracortical development modeled in this study support modern neo-Piagetian models of cognitive development (Case, 1985, 1987; Fischer, 1980; Fischer & Farrar, 1987; Fischer & Pipp, 1984; Pascual-Leone, 1976; Van Geert, 1991). Specifically, children's thought processes proceed through time-bound cycles between birth and 16 years of age with each cycle divided into a number of subcycles, and the structure of one cycle or subcycle hierarchically emerges from those of the previous cycle or subcycle (Case, 1985, 1987). Although Fischer and Case differ in the exact timing of cycles and in their emphasis on the relative importance and meaning of different cycles, these two workers have done a commendable job of formulating cyclical theories of behavioral development. The data from the present study strongly support Fischer's and Cases' theories by pointing out some of the physiological processes that may underlie the emergence of "stages" of child development. One of the most important contributions by the neo-Piagetians, especially Fischer and Case, is their perception of cycles as opposed to simply stages of child behavioral development. A *cycle* is defined by events that repeat themselves in the same order and over approximately the same interval of time. In contrast, a *stage* is a discrete process or step. There are many examples in biology whereby cycles of growth give rise to an outward manifestation of stages. For example, organisms that construct nests or hives on a seasonal basis often produce step-like structures. It is argued in this chapter that the presence of stages in cognitive development is merely the outward manifestation of underlying cycles of brain growth and that the underlying neurophysiological gradients and cycles are the engines that drive cognitive development. Thus, human cognitive development contains both continuous and discontinuous processes. One possible source of the stages in cognitive development is the fact that different regions of the brain develop at different ages. Although a cyclic process drives differential anatomical development, the outward manifestation of qualitatively different behaviors is due, in part, to the growth of different neural structures at different ages.

Bifurcations, Phase Transitions, and Punctuated Equilibria

The dynamics of the bifurcations or phase transitions are similar to those observed in competitive nonlinear oscillator systems in which opposing forces imperceptibly build up until a sudden differentiation or bifurcation occurs (Thom, 1975). The sudden changes in mean EEG coherence observed at 3–4 years (see Thatcher, 1992b), 5–7 years, and 9–11 years satisfy many of Gilmore's catastrophe flags (Gilmore, 1981) and exhibit characteristics of a "fold" or "cusp" catastrophe (Thom, 1975; Van der Maas & Molenaar, 1992). A clear example of a cusp catastrophe is seen in Fig. 5.4, in which the P3-F7

EEG coherence trajectory exhibits a fold and sudden jump between 5 and 7 years. The Gilmore (1981) catastrophe flags of "modality," "sudden jump," "hysteresis," and "frequency shifts" were present in many of the EEG coherence developmental trajectories. The presence of a bifurcation or catastrophe suggests that the underlying dynamics can be modeled by gradient systems and vector fields of the form $\mathbf{x} = -U(x)$ for $\mathbf{x}$ in $\mathbf{R}^k$ in which competition and cooperation between forces are responsible for the dynamics and the stable equilibria (Gilmore, 1981; Thompson & Stewart, 1986). The presence of formal catastrophe dynamics is also important for modeling "schemata" development using the ideas and notation of Rumelhart and colleagues (Rumelhart, Smolensky, McClelland, & Hinton, 1986).

Functional Interpretation of Frontal Lobe Synaptic Competition and Predation

What is the functional significance of the frontal regions being exclusively the predators and fierce competitors in the dynamic cycle of synaptic surplus followed by synaptic pruning? One interpretation is that the frontal regions control or significantly influence the pruning phase of the synaptic development of posterior cortical regions. That is, frontal synaptic influence significantly determines which synapses will survive and which will be lost during the developmental sculpting process. A hierarchical integration of cortical resources periodically occurs, forming a frontal lobe mediated spiral of ever-cascading competencies. This process is nonlinear in both space and time and is manifested behaviorally by relatively sudden changes in cognitive competence. The appearance of discontinuous development is often characterized as "sensitive periods" or "growth spurts" (Cicchetti, 1990, 1993; Fischer, 1983). According to the present model, sensitive periods reflect the nonlinear manifestation of a underlying and continuous growth process (Thatcher, 1992a, 1992b, 1994a).

Genetic Versus Environmental Influences

As noted earlier, the positive first derivatives of mean EEG coherence change were defined as reflecting the synaptic surplus phase whereas the negative first derivative was defined as reflecting the synaptic pruning phase (Thatcher, 1992a, 1993, 1994a). One would expect that genetic factors would have a strong influence on the synaptic surplus phase and that environmental factors would have a strong influence on the synaptic pruning phase. That is, genetics has the less variable task of turning genes on and off, whereas the environment and the demands placed on the individual are highly variable and complex. It follows that because the individuals in these studies live in diverse environments one would expect greater variance in the first derivative of EEG coherence during the pruning phase than during the surplus phase. Figure 5.9 shows two examples of the relationship between the variance of the first derivative of mean EEG coherence versus the actual first derivatives of mean EEG coherence. A 180° phase reversal is strongly present in which variance is greatest during the negative first derivatives or the synaptic pruning phases, and it is small during the positive first derivatives or the synaptic surplus phases. High EEG coherence variance of the negative first derivative is precisely what is expected if environmental factors dominate the pruning phase and genetic factors dominate the surplus phase.

Figure 5.9B illustrates the proposed cycle of synaptic surplus followed by synaptic pruning in which the pruning phase is strongly influenced by the frontal lobes according to the model in Fig. 5.6 (i.e., the F1-P3 and O1-P3 model). Both frontal and posterior cortical regions exhibit cycles of synaptic surplus followed by synaptic pruning; however, the frontal regions directly displace or remove posterior cortical synapses, whereas the posterior cortical regions do not displace the frontal synapses. Instead, the growth of frontal synapses is dependent on the presence of posterior cortical synapses. Thus, when there is a reduced supply of posterior cortical synapses, frontal synaptic influences decline, and vice versa. The posterior cortical synaptic surplus phase is a type of "restocking" of the supply of posterior cortical synapses that the frontal lobes can subsequently "replace" or "reorganize" based on environmental exigencies.

Neural Plasticity, Sensitive Periods, and Psychopathology

The cyclic reorganization model of human brain development explicitly integrates neural plasticity with sensitive periods. That is, each cycle of synaptic surplus followed by pruning represents a sensitive period in anatomically localized and interconnected brain regions. Thus, sensitive periods are continually occurring because they are driven by a diffusion wave of anatomically circulating nerve growth factor. A staging or discontinuous aspect of this process arises because of inherent nonlinearities in both space and time. Spatially the nonlinearities arise because of the segregation of differentiated function in distributed ensembles of neurons. The functionally differentiated anatomy of the brain guarantees spatial nonlinearities as the wave of growth hormone sweeps across domains of cells. Thus, stages or sensitive periods are present because functionally differentiated regions of the brain develop at different ages. A stage-plateau sequence in cognitive development is an outward manifestation of both the continuous and discontinuous aspects of the process. Each stage or period represents rapid synaptic growth within functionally differentiated neural systems and, as a

MEAN & VARIANCE OF EEG COHERENCE DEVELOPMENT ARE INVERSELY RELATED

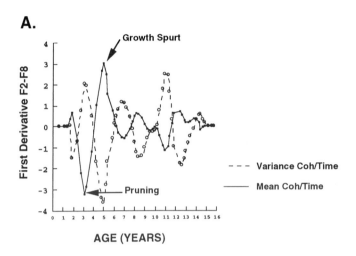

A.

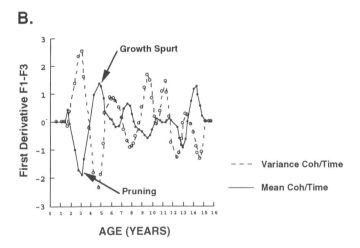

B.

FIG. 5.9. The first derivatives of the mean and variance of EEG coherence from male children for two different cortical regions (A, F2-F8; B, F1-F3). A 180° phase reversal is strongly present in which variance is greatest during the negative first derivatives or the synaptic pruning phases and small during the positive first derivatives or the synaptic surplus phases. From Thatcher (1994b). Adapted by permission.

consequence, neural plasticity involves the genetically driven overproduction of synapses and the environmentally driven maintenance and pruning of synaptic connections. As emphasized in previous sections, it is predicted that the subcortical synaptic drives on the frontal lobe as well as cortico-cortical connections with the frontal lobes along plays a crucial role in development, especially in the process of synaptic pruning and synaptic selection.

ACKNOWLEDGMENTS

I am indebted to Rebecca A. Walker for her assistance in the typing and construction of the paper. This article was supported by a grant from the Henry M. Jackson Foundation (No. JFC36285006, R. W. Thatcher, Principal Investigator).

REFERENCES

Becker, L. E. (1991). Synaptic dysgenesis. *Canadian Journal of Neurological Science, 18*, 170–180.

Bendat, J. S., & Piersol, A. G. (1980). *Engineering applications of correlation and spectral analysis.* New York: John Wiley & Sons.

Berryman, A. A. (1981). *Population systems: A general introduction.* New York: Plenum Press.

Berryman, A. A. (1990). *Population dynamics: A workbook for POPSYS software.* Pullman, WA: Ecological Systems Analysis.

Black, J. E., & Greenough, W. T. (1986). Induction of pattern in neural structure by experience, Implications for cognitive development. In M. E. Lamb, A. L. Brown, & B. Rogoff (Eds.), *Advances in developmental psychology* (Vol. 4, pp. 1–50). Hillsdale, NJ: Lawrence Erlbaum Associates.

Blinkov, S. M., & Glezer, I. I. (1968). *The human brain in figures and tables.* New York: Plenum Press.

Bok, S. T. (1959). *Histonomy of the cerebral cortex.* Amsterdam: Elsevier.

Bourgeois, J., Goldman-Rakic, P. S., & Rakic, P. (1994). Synaptogenesis in the prefrontal cortex of rhesus monkeys. *Cerebral Cortex, 4*, 78–96.

Braitenberg, V. (1978). Cortical architectonics: general and areal. In M. A. B. Brazier & H. Petsche (Eds.), *Architectectonics of the cerebral cortex* (pp. 16–32). New York: Academic Press.

Brown, M. C., Holland, R. L., & Hopkins, W. G. (1981). Excess neuronal inputs during development. In D. R. Garrod & J. D. Feldman (Eds.), *Development in the nervous system* (pp. 112–130). Cambridge: Cambridge University Press.

Case, R. (1985). *Intellectual development: Birth to adulthood.* New York: Academic Press.

Case, R. (1987). The structure and process of intellectual development. *International Journal of Psychology, 22*, 571–607.

Changeux, J.-P., & Danchin, A. (1976). Selective stabilisation of developing synapses as a mechanism for specification of neuronal networks. *Nature, 264*, 705–712.

Cicchetti, D. (1990). The organization and coherences of socioemotional, cognitive, and representational development: Illustrations through a developmental psychopathology perspective on down syndrome and child maltreatment. In R. Thompson (Ed.), *Nebraska symposium on motivation: Socioemotional development* (pp. 259–366). Lincoln: University of Nebraska Press.

Cicchetti, D. (1993). Developmental psychopathology: Reactions, reflections, projections. *Developmental Review, 13*, 471–502.

Conel, J. L. (1955). *The postnatal development of the human cerebral cortex: Vol. V. The cortex of the fifteen-month infant.* Cambridge, MA: Harvard University Press.

Conel, J. L. (1959). *The postnatal development of the human cerebral cortex: Vol. VI. The cortex of the twenty-four-month infant.* Cambridge, MA: Harvard University Press.

Conel, J. L. (1963). *The postnatal development of the human cerebral cortex: Vol. VII. The cortex of the four-year child.* Cambridge, MA: Harvard University Press.

Conel, J. L. (1967). *The postnatal development of the human cerebral cortex: Vol. VIII. The cortex of the six-year child.* Cambridge, MA: Harvard University Press.

Cowan, W. M. (1979). The developing brain. In *The brain.* San Francisco: Freeman.

Cowan, W. M., Fawcett, J. W., O'Leary, D. D., & Stanfield, B. B. (1984). Regressive events in neurogenesis. *Science, 21*, 1258–1265.

Edelman, G. M. (1987). *Neural Darwinism: The theory of neuronal group selection.* New York: Basic.

Epstein, H. T. (1980). EEG developmental stages. *Developmental Psychobiology, 13*, 629–631.

Finkel, L. H., & Edelman, G. M. (1989). The integration of distributed cortical systems by reentry: A computersimulation of interactive functionally segregated visual areas. *Journal of Neuroscience, 9*, 3188–3208.

Fischer, K. W. (1980). A theory of cognitive development: The control and construction of hierarchies of skills. *Psychological Review, 87*, 477–531.

Fischer, K. W. (1983). Developmental levels as periods of discontinuity. In K. W. Fischer (Ed.), *Levels and transitions in children's development* (pp. 76–96). San Francisco: Jossey-Bass.

Fischer, K. W. (1987). Relations between brain and cognitive development. *Child Development, 57*, 623–632.

Fischer, K. W., & Farrar, M. J. (1987). Generalizations about generalization: How a theory of skill development explains both generality and specificity. *International Journal of Psychology, 22*, 643–677.

Fischer, K. W., & Pipp, S. L. (1984). Processes of cognitive development: Optimal level and skill acquisition. In R. J. Sternberg (Ed.), *Mechanisms of cognitive development* (pp. 45–80). New York: Freeman.

Fox, N. A., & Bell, M. A. (1990). Electrophysiological indices of frontal lobe development. In A. Diamond (Ed.), *The development and neural bases of higher cognitive functions* (pp. 677–698). New York: New York Academy of Sciences.

Gasser, T., Jennen-Steinmetz, C., Sroka, L., Verleger, R., & Mocks, J. (1988). Development of the EEG of school age children and adolescents. *Electroencephalography and Clinical Neurophysiology, 69*, 100–109.

Gause, G. F. (1934). *The struggle for existence.* Baltimore: Williams & Wilkins.

Gause, G. F., & Witt, A. A. (1935). Behavior of mixed populations and the problem of natural selection. *American Naturalist, 3*, 596–609.

Getz, W. M. (1984). Population dynamics: A per-capita resource approach. *Journal of Theoretical Biology, 108*, 623–643.

Gilmann, R. (1981). *Catastrophe theory for scientists and engineers.* New York: John Wiley & Sons.

Gilpin, M. E., & Ayala, F. J. (1973). Global models of growth and competition. *Proceedings of the National Academy of Science (USA), 70*, 3590–3593.

Glaser, E. M., & Ruchkin, D. S. (1976). *Principles of neurobiological signal analyses.* New York: Academic Press.

Greenough, W., Black, J., & Wallace, C. (1987). Experience and brain development. *Child Development, 58*, 539–559.

Henrikson, C. K., & Vaughn, J. E. (1974). Fine structural relationships between neurites and radial glial processes in developing mouse spinal cord. *Journal of Neurocytology, 3*, 659–675.

Holling, C. S. (1959). The components of predation as revealed by a study of small mammal predation of the European pine sawfly. *Canadian Entomologist, 91*, 293–320.

Holling, C. S. (1966). The functional response of invertebrate predators to prey density. *Memoirs of the Entomological Society of Canada, 48*, 1–86.

Hudspeth, W. J., & Pribram, K. H. (1990). Stages of brain and cognitive maturation. *Journal of Educational Psychology, 82*, 881–884.

Hudspeth, W. J., & Pribram, K. H. (1991). Physiological indices of cerebral maturation. *International Journal of Psychophysiology, 2*, 19–29.

Hutchinson, G. E. (1948). Circular causal systems in ecology. *Annals of the New York Academy of Sciences, 50*, 221–246.

Huttenlocher, P. R. (1979). Synaptic density in human frontal cortex: Developmental changes and effects of aging. *Brain Research, 163*, 195–205.

Huttenlocher, P. R. (1984). Synapse elimination and plasticity in developing human cerebral cortex. *American Journal of Mental Deficiences, 88*, 488–496.

Huttenlocher, P. R. (1990). Morphometric study of human cerebral cortex development. *Neuropsychologia, 28*, 517–527.

Huttenlocher, P. R., & de Courten, C. (1987). The development of synapses in striate cortex of man. *Human Neurobiology, 6*, 1–9.

Jerison, H. J. (1973). *Evolution of the brain and intelligence*. New York: Academic Press.

Levay, S., Stryker, M. P., & Shatz, C. J. (1978). Ocular dominance columns and their development in layer IV of the cat's visual cortex. A quantitative study. *Journal of Comparative Neurology, 191*, 1–51.

Lo, Y.-J., & Poo, M.-M. (1991). Activity-dependent synaptic competition in vitro: Heterosynaptic suppression of developing synapses. *Science, 254*, 1019–1022.

Lopez da Silva, F., Pijn, J. P., & Boeijinga, P. (1989). Interdependence of EEG signals: Linear vs. nonlinear associations and the significance of time delays and phase shifts. *Brain Topography, 2*, 9–18.

Lotka, A. J. (1925). *The elements of physical biology*. Baltimore: Williams & Wilkins

Matousek, M., & Petersen, I. (1973). Frequency analysis of the EEG background activity by means of age dependent EEG quotients. In P. Kellaway & I. Petersen (Eds.), *Automation of clinical electroencephalography*. New York: Raven Press.

McAlaster, R. (1992). Postnatal cerebral maturation in Down's syndrome children: A developmental EEG coherence study. *International Journal of Neuroscience, 65*, 221–237.

Milsum, J. H. (1968). *Positive feedback*. New York: Pergamon Press.

Montague, P., Gally, J. A., & Edelman, G. M. (1991). Spatial signaling in the development and function of neural connections. *Cerebral Cortex, 1*, 199–220.

Nicholson, A. J., & Bailey, V. A. (1935). The balance of animal populations. *Proceedings of the Zoological Society of London, 3*, 551–598.

Nunez, P. (1981). *Electric fields of the brain: The neurophysics of EEG*. New York: Oxford University Press.

O'Leary, D. D. M. (1987). Remodelling of early axonal projections through the selective elimination of neurons and long axon collaterals. In G. Bock & M. O'Connor (Eds.), *Selective neuronal death* (pp. 113–142). New York: John Wiley & Sons.

Otnes, R. K., & Enochson, L. (1972). *Digital time series analysis*. New York: John Wiley & Sons.

Pascual-Marqui, R. D., Valdes-Sosa, P. A., & Alvarez-Amador, A. (1988). A parametric model for multichannel EEG spectra. *International Journal of Neuroscience, 40*, 89–99.

Pascual-Leone, J. (1976). A view of cognition from a formalist's perspective. In K. F. Riegel & J. Meacham (Eds.), *The developing individual in a changing world*. The Hague: Mouton.

Piaget, J. (1952). *The origins of intelligence*. New York: International University Press.

Piaget, J. (1971). *Psychology of intelligence*. New Jersey: Littlefield, Adams.

Piaget, J. (1975). *Biology and knowledge* (2nd ed.). Chicago: University of Chicago Press.

Purves, D. (1988). *Body and brain: A trophic theory of neural connections*. Boston: Harvard University Press.

Purves, D., & Lichtman, J. W. (1985). *Principles of neural development*. Sunderland, MA: A. Sinauer Associates.

Rabinowicz, T. (1979). The differentiate maturation of the human cerebral cortex. In F. Falkner & J. Tanner (Eds.), *Human growth: Neurobiology and nutrition* (pp. 97–123). New York: Plenum Press.

Raffioni, S., Bradshaw, R. A., & Buxser, S. E. (1993). The receptors for nerve growth factor and other neurotrophins. *Annual Review of Biochemistry, 62*, 823–850.

Rakic, P. (1985). Limits of neurogenesis in primates. *Science, 227*, 1054–1056.

Rakic, P., Bourgeois, J., Eckenhoff, M. F., Zecevic, N., & Goldman-Rakic, P. S. (1986). Concurrent overproduction of synapses in diverse regions of the primate cerebral cortex. *Science, 232*, 232–235.

Real, L. (1977). The kinetics of functional response. *American Naturalist. 111*, 289–300.

Rumelhart, D. E., Smolensky, P., McClelland, J. L., & Hinton, G. E. (1986). Schemata and sequential thought processes in PDP models. In J. L. McClelland & D. E. Rumelhart, *Parallel distributed processing* (Vol. 2). Cambridge, MA: MIT Press.

Savitzky, A., & Golay, M. J. E. (1964). Smoothing and differentiation of data by simplified least squares procedures. *Analytical Chemistry, 36*, 1627–1639.

Schade, J. P., & Groeningen, V. V. (1961). Structural development of the human cerebral cortex. *Acta Anatomica, 47*, 79–111.

Soloman, M. E. (1949). The natural control of animal population. *Journal of Animal Ecology, 18*, 1–35.

Sporns, O., Tononi, G., & Edelman, G. M. (1991). Modeling perceptual grouping and figure-ground segregation by means of active reentrant connections. *Proceedings of the National Academy of Sciences (USA), 88*, 129–133.

Sporns, O., Tononi, G., & Edelman, G. M. (1994). Neural models of cortical integration. In R. Thatcher, M. Hallett, T. Zeffiro, E. John, & M. Huerta (Eds.), *Functional neuroimaging: Technical foundations*. New York: Academic Press.

Stent, G. (1973). Internal coupling determines the spacing of dendrites. *Proceedings of the National Academy of Sciences (USA), 70*, 997–1012.

Thatcher, R. W. (1989, March). *Nonlinear dynamics of human cerebral development*. Paper presented at First International Conference on Mechanisms of Mind (E. R. John, Organizer), Havana, Cuba.

Thatcher, R. W. (1991). Maturation of the human frontal lobes: Physiological evidence for staging. *Developmental Neuropsychology, 7*(3), 397–419.

Thatcher, R. W. (1992a). Cyclic cortical reorganization during early childhood development. *Brain and Cognition, 20*, 24–50.

Thatcher, R. W. (1992b). Are rhythms of human cerebral development "traveling waves"? *Behavior and Brain Sciences, 14*(4), 575.

Thatcher, R. W. (1993, April). *Cyclic cortical morphogenesis: A nonlinear synaptic population model*. (Abstr.) Biennial Meeting of the Society for Research in Child Development, New Orleans, LA.

Thatcher, R. W. (1994a). Cyclic cortical reorganization: Origins of cognition. In G. Dawson & K. Fischer (Eds.), *Human behavior and the developing brain* (pp. 232–268). New York: Guilford Press.

Thatcher, R. W. (1994b). Psychopathology of early frontal lobe damage: Dependence on cycles of postnatal development. *Developmental Pathology, 6*, 565–596.

Thatcher, R. W., Krause, P., & Hrybyk, M. (1986). Corticocortical association fibers and EEG coherence: A two compartmental model. *Electroencephalography and Clinical Neurophysiology, 64*, 123–143.

Thatcher, R. W., McAlaster, R., Lester, M. L., Horst, R. L., & Cantor, D. S. (1983). Hemispheric EEG asymmetries related to cognitive functioning in children. In A. Perecuman (Ed.), *Cognitive processing in the right hemisphere* (pp. 125–145). New York: Academic Press.

Thatcher, R., Toro, C., Pflieger, M. E., & Hallett, M. (1994). Human neural network dynamics using multimodal registration of EEG, PET and MRI. In R. Thatcher, M. Hallett, T. Zeffiro, E. John, & M. Huerta (Eds.), *Functional neuroimaging: Technical foundations*. New York: Academic Press.

Thatcher, R. W., Walker, R. A., & Giudice, S. (1987). Human cerebral hemispheres develop at different rates and ages. *Science, 236*, 1110–1113.

Thom, R. (1975). *Structural stability and morphogenesis*. Reading, MA: W. A. Benjamin.

Thompson, J., & Stewart, H. (1986). *Nonlinear dynamics and chaos*. New York: John Wiley & Sons.

Tong, H. (1978). On a threshold model. In C. H. Chen (Ed.), *Pattern recognition and signal processing*. Amsterdam: Sijthoff and Noordhof.

Tucker, D. M., Roth, D. L., & Blair, T. B. (1986). Functional connections among cortical regions: Topography of EEG coherence. *Electroencephalography and Clinical Neurophysiology, 63*, 242–250.

Van der Maas, H. L. I., & Molenaar, P. C. M. (1992). A catastrophy theoretical approach to stagewise cognitive development. *Psychological Review, 99*, 395–417.

Van Geert, P. (1991). A dynamic systems model of cognitive and language growth. *Psychology Review, 98*, 3–53.

Vaughn, J. E. (1989). Fine structure of synaptogenesis in the vertebrate central nervous system. *Synapse, 3*, 255–285.

Verhulst, P. F. (1938). Notice sur la loi que la population suite dans son accroissement. *Correspondence Mathematique et Physique, 10*, 113–121.

Vogel, K. S., & Davies, A. M. (1991). The duration of neurotrophic factor independence in early sensory neurons is matched to the time course of target field innervation. *Neuron, 7*, 819–850.

Volterra, V. (1926). Variazioni e fluttuaioni del numero d'individui in specie animali conviventi. *Memorial R. Academic Lincei Series, 6*(2), 26–43.

Weisel, T. N. (1982). Postnatal development of the visual cortex and the influence of environment. *Nature, 299*, 583–591.

Wright, R. D. (1934). Some mechanisms in the evolution of the central nervous system. *Journal of Anatomy, 69*, 86–88.

Zecevic, N., & Rakic, P. (1991). Synaptogenesis in monkey somatosensory cortex. *Cerebral Cortex, 1*, 510–523.

Zucker, R. S. (1982). Processes underlying one form of synaptic plasticity: Facilitation. In C. D. Woody (Ed.), *Conditioning*. New York: Plenum Press.

6

DYNAMIC MODELING OF COGNITIVE AND LANGUAGE DEVELOPMENT: FROM GROWTH PROCESSES TO SUDDEN JUMPS AND MULTIMODALITY

Paul van Geert
University of Groningen, The Netherlands

IN SEARCH OF A DEDUCTIVE PROCEDURE

Developmental models should allow their users to predict the course and form of developmental change, provided the relevant parameters and conditions are known. It is almost trivial that, if all relevant conditions for a particular prediction are alike, the resulting predictions should be similar. It should not be the case, for instance, that a prediction depends on who exactly is making that prediction, or on which moment it is made. To put it differently, a model should entail a deductive procedure that takes a certain number of conditions (parameters, values, etc.) as its input, and produces a specific prediction as its output. The problem with most of our developmental models, however, is that they hardly ever contain such a deductive procedure. The relationship between a model and its predictions is often loose and only intuitively established. Given the same sets of nontrivial conditions, different users will come up with different predictions. Often it is unclear what the relevant inputs to the procedure should be, which steps should be taken to arrive at a prediction, or how precise those predictions should be.

The deductive procedure, if any such exists, amounts to the formal specification of the relevant concepts and relationships in what is otherwise stated as a verbal description and conceptualization of development. It allows its user not only to make predictions given a certain set of empirical conditions, but also to explore the inherent possibilities of the model. That is, one can experiment with possible combinations of empirical conditions and investigate what the model would predict if such conditions were empirically fulfilled. Before going a little deeper into the issue of whether and why such theoretical experiments are useful, I present a short and necessarily incomplete overview of how predictions are carried out in most of the existing developmental models.

Prediction in Developmental Models

The simplest form of prediction is to foretell the occurrence of a specific developmental event at a certain time. For instance, attachment theorists predict the emergence of attachment and its characteristic behavioral patterns around the age of 8 months. This prediction is based on an empirical generalization of observations of attachment development in representative samples of children. There exists, as far as I can see, no core procedure in attachment theory that allows one to deductively infer that attachment must necessarily emerge at a specific moment in time, given a particular starting point and developmental conditions.

A second form of prediction is found with stage theories. Piaget's theory of the four major cognitive stages, for instance, describes a process of equilibration, which takes place in the form of irreversible jumps from one qualitative stage level to another. Theoretically, the prediction could be that a child's cognitive level changes literally overnight, as if it were a case of insect metamorphosis (Klausmeier, 1976). Piaget himself, however, introduced the concept of *décalage* to refer to the fact that such a literal sudden change was not to be expected (Piaget, 1955). The moment at which a particular cognitive content is assimilated with a newly discovered level varies widely over content domains. Yet Piaget emphasized the importance of the "structure of the whole," thus leaving the empirical investigator with considerable uncertainty as to what should be predicted from the theory, except for predictions based on generalizations of Piaget's empirical findings. Maybe the only, but nevertheless very important, thing that deductively follows from Piaget's theory is the fact that if developmental changes occur they should take the form of discontinuities (Van der Maas & Molenaar, 1992).

Approaches such as information-processing theory or the parameter-setting theory of language acquisition conceptualize development in terms of emerging rules that eventually coalesce into procedures. From a rule approach one would expect predictions in the form of all-or-none occurrence of activities governed by the rule at issue. For instance, a child uses the rule that a sentence *subject* is followed by a *verb* and not by an *object* (that is, the child has discovered that the mother tongue is a so-called S-V-O language). If a rule is a rule it either applies to its class or not. Thus, as soon as a rule has been discovered, or a parameter has been set, it must directly affect all contexts in which it is applicable. It is not unlikely, however, that the new rule is applied to new cases only and that the child continues to use the old form for already established sentence formats. The latter eventually fade away only gradually. Thus, a rule or parameter-setting model is compatible both with a prediction of sudden and of gradual change, or eventually with a combination of both (Ruhland, Wijnen, & Van Geert, 1995).

In standard developmental psychology, formal, deductive prediction is generally confined to those areas where the assumptions of differential psychology are valid. The regression model is a case in point. If the distribution of the values of two variables in a population is described by a regression line with an x coefficient m and a constant y intercept b, any dependent y value (e.g., school results) can be predicted for any independent x value (e.g., a test score) by simply applying the equation $mx + b = y$. The standard error term can be used to predict the distribution of values around the calculated y value. The regression model (which I merely use as an example) is in itself not a developmental model, because it does not directly address change. Only if the independent value is sufficiently closely related to a function that unfolds in time can the regression model be employed to model and therefore predict development. For instance, if the independent variable is the amount of experience a child has with some kind of problem, and the amount of experience is a constant function of time, the regression model can be turned into a developmental model, predicting a dependent variable (such as the child's score on a particular problem-solving test) as a function of time. It goes without saying that the regression model amounts to an extremely simple model of development. Yet it is about the only formal, deductive model we have that applies to a sufficiently large number of cases and contexts (I leave aside exponential models or exponential growth models, which obey approximately the same logic; see Hoeksma, van den Boom, Koomen, & Koops, 1997; Willett, 1994).

The regression model, if applied to time-dependent variables, is the simplest possible conceptualization of development: Developmental properties increase across time. It is an example of a deductive model: It consists of a formal procedure (a simple mathematical equation) and it has a generative character (it can take any numerical value as its input and compute the result for those particular values). It is a dynamic model if one of the inputs (the x value) is a function of time.

In the next section I discuss a few general properties of developmental models and argue that they are similar to those of dynamic models in general. These properties may lead toward a richer and more valid dynamic formalization than the simple regression model (which is not to say that the regression model should be abandoned; in many cases it may still provide us with the best and most parsimonious explanation of the data).

Developmental and Dynamic Models

Properties of Developmental Models. First and foremost, a developmental model describes and explains change. A model that described only a series of successive properties of behavior, across the life span, for instance, is not developmental. Whatever properties it wishes to distinguish, the model should be capable of explaining why and how some later property comes about as a consequence of an earlier one.

Second, developmental models select a particular time scale and level of aggregation onto which they anchor both the empirical phenomena of interest and the explanatory concepts and mechanisms. This selection often amounts to a particular combination between interacting time scales, or interacting levels of aggregation. For instance, a model such as Piaget's relates events at the time scale of intentional activity to events at the level of stage and life-span developmental changes (Van Geert, 1990). Another example is biopsychological models, which combine events at the level of child–environment interaction with phenomena occurring at the neuronal substrate.

Third, developmental phenomena are explained on the basis of a few canonical mechanisms, such as Piaget's equilibration or cognitive conflict concepts (Van Geert, 1988).

The fourth, and very important, property is that of iteratively applied mechanisms or explanatory principles. Development proceeds by a process that takes the result of a previous developmental event as its input, and produces a new developmental property, or state, as its output. For instance, solving a problem will eventually change the child's problem-solving rules. The next problem the child is confronted with will be solved on the basis of this altered rule set. Although this property seems a little trivial at first, it will turn out to be of utmost importance. In fact, it is the iterative character of the processes that shows the clearest distinction with mere time based models, such as the regression model. It is not time that is the major variable. It is the recursive activity of developmental mechanisms that accounts for the dynamics.

Next, developmental theories often invoke nonlinear principles. For instance, if the result of some experience depends crucially on the moment and context in which it occurs, it is no longer possible to predict its effect on the basis of a simple linear model like the regression model. It is true that particular forms of nonlinearity, especially those that invoke context dependency, can often be treated as if they boil down to error or coincidental variance, superposed on a basically linear model. But many of the more interesting phenomena, such as the sudden jumps toward a new level of processing that Piaget described, cannot be set aside as coincidental variation. They are truly nonlinear phenomena, and require proper explanatory concepts that reckon with this particular property.

Finally, developmental change is often viewed as a succession of actual change and relative stability. In dynamic terms, developmental processes are described as evolutions away from and toward attractor states or local equilibria.

From a Developmental to a Dynamic Model. Whenever a model has the properties mentioned and its concepts are not too vaguely described, it can be transformed into a deductively applicable, formal dynamic model. Before explaining how such transformation can be carried out, let me first discuss what I see as a common misunderstanding.

It is often implicitly assumed that a dynamic model explaining developmental processes must, by necessity, be a model of the brain or of some functionally similar associative learning network. Although there is a lot of extremely interesting work done with connectionist nets, for instance, they are not in themselves the ultimate and only dynamic models (see, e.g., Plunkett & Sinha, 1992, for a discussion of developmental theory and connectionist network building). In principle, a connectionist net is a generalized associative learning model. To illustrate the difference with a dynamic developmental model in general, I refer to a recent attempt at dynamically modeling Vygotsky's concept of the zone of proximal development (ZPD) (Van Geert, 1994b). The Vygotsky model describes the dynamic interaction between a learner and a tutor. The learner receives help and support from a tutor, whereas the tutor adapts the help to the learner's increasing (or eventually decreasing) level of skill. The dynamic model is not concerned with how exactly the learner comes to understand and incorporate the help and information given by the tutor. Neither does it concern itself with the question of how the tutor learns to understand the pupil's behavior as an expression of a particular developmental level. This is far from saying that the latter problems are trivial or uninteresting. The point is that it is possible to build interesting and revealing dynamic models at a level that takes the underlying processes of learning and the still deeper levels of neural processing for granted.

The transformation of an existing developmental model into a deductively applicable dynamic model takes place along the following lines.

The first step is to rewrite the essential concepts and conceptual relationships in the form of a flow chart. The flow-chart representation is quite common in developmental model building, but that is the point where the formalization usually stops.

The second step is to specify the components of the flow chart. The blocks normally correspond with variables, which are either overt or covert. The overt variables can be specified in the form of empirical observables, such as test scores or estimations of "true scores" or "true levels." The covert variables, which usually amount to theoretical variables, can be quantified in the form of an estimated level (e.g., a level that accounts for the probability that a child will encounter a cognitive conflict, for instance, if one were to model Piaget's theory of cognitive development). The formalization of the relationships between the variables is a more difficult task, however. In general, relationships in a flow chart specify either conditions or contributions. For instance, nonverbal understanding of objects and object categories are a necessary prerequisite, that is, a condition, for the learning of words (Gopnik & Meltzoff, 1987, 1992). What I mean by *contribution* is that one variable makes either a positive or a negative contribution to the occurrence or presence of another. For instance, the lexicon makes a contribution to the development of multiword sentences in that the more words the child knows, the more words the child will syntactically combine into sentences (note that, like all my examples, this is just an example of a theoretical statement, not of a theoretical or empirical fact about development).

In order to formalize and specify both the conditions and the contributions, one needs a general theory of how psychological variables come about and change. The simplest general theory is one that assumes plain linear increase. Thus, if a variable A positively contributes to a variable B, then the more there is of A, the more there will be of B. The most complex general theory is, probably, one that builds a complete neuronal, sensorimotor, and social interactional model of the postulated psychological processes. Assuming that the simplest model is just too simple, and the complex one is too complex, we may ask ourselves at which level of abstraction an efficient model should be conceptualized. In practice, one can choose a model that stays as close as possible to the simple side of the problem. That is, one tries to design a model that describes developmental processes in terms of increases or decreases in the chosen variables. This is the approach I have followed thus far and that I have used to model theories as well as empirical processes (see Van Geert, 1994a, for an overview). In the next section I give a short overview of it. The second possible choice is to stay a little closer to the underlying neuronal processes. This is the approach of connectionist modeling. Connectionist models are, of course, not literal models of the brain. They capture an essential aspect of the brain, however—namely, the principles of networking and parallel processing.

DYNAMIC GROWTH MODELS

General Principles of Dynamic Growth Models

Growth is a widespread property of living matter. It applies to biological phenomena such as body or population size, but also to organizational phenomena, such as economic growth. In various papers I have argued that developmental changes in a great many developmental variables can be conceived of as a form of growth. Growth is an autocatalytic process, in that it regulates its own progress. Growth occurs only if sufficient resources are available. In the case of psychological variables, such as a knowledge or skill level, those resources are of different kinds. Examples of resources are the available information, but also social support during a learning process and internal resources such as speed and quality of information processing and the size of working memory. Resources may vary considerably, but they are always limited. The resource limitation sets an upper level to a potential growth process and explains why growth in some variable or other leads to an attractor state.

Growth is an iterative process: The next level of a variable depends on some preceding level and on a certain amount of invested resources. Thus, the cause of a succeeding growth level is a preceding growth level and the effect that level has on the currently available resources. I also assume that in most processes of psychological growth, such as the growth of a child's lexicon or the growth of abstract understanding, there is a certain delay between causes and effects. Finally, because the growth of most psychological variables depends on their interaction with the environment, I assume that growth processes can best be conceptualized as discrete processes. Each discrete step in the growth process amounts to an actual confrontation between the level that is already achieved and a particular problem or application of the variable whose growth it determines. Examples of such "confrontations" are problem-solving situations, communicative interactions, and so forth.

The growth of a specific variable is either supported or hampered by the growth of other ones. For instance, nonverbal gesturing in infants may compete with the infants' verbal communication, especially if the nonverbal gesturing is reinforced by the environment. In fact, one can argue that a psychological system in an environment, for instance, the cognitive and behavioral system of an infant living in a particular culture and social environment, behaves very much like an *ecological system*. An ecological system is nothing but a network of interacting units, which are in mutual support or competition with each other.

The basic equation used for simulating growth processes is the following:

$$L_{t+n} = L_t + L_t{}^p r(1 - L_t/K) + L_t{}^p(\textstyle\sum u_i J_t) \tag{1}$$

where L_{t+n} and L_t are the levels of a particular variable at time t and $t + n$, respectively (n is the length of the delay). The exponent p specifies to what extent the growth rate is affected by the already attained level L. If $p = 0$, growth is determined only by the unutilized resources, that is, by the distance between the actual level and the equilibrium level. If $p = 0$, the growth process behaves like the classical learning curves. If $p = 1$, growth is determined both by the unutilized resources and by the level already achieved. The canonical growth form in this case is S-shaped. If $p > 1$, for instance, if $p = 2$, growth depends on the unutilized resources, on the level attained, and on an additional linear function of the attained growth level, for instance, an increased speed of processing the information needed.

The K variable is the so-called carrying capacity level. It determines the equilibrium that the growth level will eventually attain. The value of K depends on the sum of all resources invested in a growth process, with the exception of resources covered by the support function $\Sigma\, dS_i$.

The function $\Sigma\, dS_i$ is the sum of all additional supportive and competitive influences on L. In most of the growth networks I worked on so far, I made a distinction between support or competition that depends linearly on the level of some supporting or competing variable, and support or competition that depends on the amount of resources consumed or produced by the growth or decay of a related variable. For instance, we shall see that the growth of multiword sentences is supported by the number of words the child already knows, that is, by the size of the child's lexicon. However, time and effort spent on learning new words, that is, on increasing the lexicon, may eventually come at the cost of time and effort the child could have spent in learning new rules for sentence formation (later we shall see that the relationship may also be supportive instead of competitive). If both r and p are zero, the model degenerates to a simple linear influences model: The growth of L is reduced to whatever it receives from supporting variables (or loses from competing ones).

What does this general growth model add to a flow-chart conceptualization? Assume I have an extremely simple developmental model, consisting of a variable A and a variable B and that contains only one relationship, namely, a positive effect of B on A. When I apply the growth model to this simple flow chart, I implicitly add the following assumptions. The first is that the change in A (and eventually B) amounts to an iterative process. I justify this added assumption by referring to the fact that most, if not all, developmental models postulate mechanisms that are in their very essence iterative. The second added assumption is that I supplement the arrow representing a support from B to A by a reflexive arrow on A. This follows from my assumption that developmental change is a growth process: I assume that A will change even if the support from B is lacking. If I have reasons to believe that B is growing itself, I must also add a reflexive arrow to B, accounting for the growth of B. If the growth of B depends largely on the same kind of resources that A feeds on, I must complement the hypothesized supportive relationship by a (transient) competitive one. The latter specifies to what extent the actual growth of A is either hampered or favored by the eventual growth in B.

In the following section I illustrate this account of development with an example from language acquisition.

A Model of Language Growth

Structure of the Model.   Language acquisition is an ideal field for longitudinal or, more precisely, time-series research. Linguistic data are easy to obtain. Because most children are enthusiastic speakers, it suffices to hang a microphone in a room and to tape their spontaneous utterances. The observation of the behavior is almost completely unobtrusive, and frequent observation has no distorting effect on the developmental process. Moreover, linguistics has an extremely well-developed system for describing and categorizing language, in terms of words, word classes, and syntactic phenomena. Thus there is hardly a problem of interobserver reliability (unless one monitors a very young child whose utterances pose phonological difficulties). Finally, language data are also extremely rich, ranging from phonological to lexical, semantic, and syntactic aspects.

The Groningen Primary Language Project has collected corpora from eight children, ranging from approximately 16 to 32 months of age. The corpora are based on observation sessions every 2 weeks of 1 hr carried out in the child's home. Transcription of the data was done on the basis of the Childes convention, which guarantees transparant data exchange with other studies, for instance, from different languages. The aim of the project I report on was to see whether a model of connected growers could account for the observed curves in the field of syntactic and morphosyntactic development (Ruhland & Van Geert, 1995; Ruhland et al., 1995).

Structuralist theories of language acquisition, such as Chomsky's theory of parameter setting (Chomsky, 1980, 1981), are interested in qualitative precedence relations among certain structural phenomena. For instance, if a child uses structure x, then the child should also use structure y and y must precede x. There are no predictions as to which quantitative pattern is expected here. The first major account of quantitative patterns in language acquisition was made by Roger Brown in the early 1970s (Brown, 1973). Since then, theoretical accounts of those quantitative patterns have been limited to dynamic growth theory (Van Geert, 1991, 1993) and connectionist modeling (Ellman, 1993; Plunkett, Sinha, Moller, & Strandsby, 1992; Rumelhart & McClelland, 1993).

The project I describe here focuses on important markers of syntactic structure in sentences, namely, function words and the occurrence of finite verbs. Examples of function words are pronouns (*you*, *me*), determiners (*the*, *a*), and prepositions (*up*, *on*). Function words form a so-called closed class. That is, there is a fixed number of them, and no new ones are created (which differs from open-class words like nouns—the word *megabyte*, for instance, is a recently created noun). Function words have important syntactic functions, somewhat similar to the functions of finite verbs. Their use is strongly rule governed. We may expect that because they are so closely related to deep linguistic rules, their emergence in language takes the form of a sudden jump instead of a gradual and slow increase.

Our data supported the claim that in about half of the subjects, function words in particular emerged suddenly and in combination with one another (i.e., pronouns came at about the same time as determiners, for instance). We found that the so-called cubic version of the logistic growth function (with $p = 2$) produced a very good fit of the data in several children (Ruhland & Van Geert, 1995). The next thing we wanted to know was whether the growth of function words was systematically related with other aspects of language. Because function words and finite verbs have a somewhat similar function in the structuring of the sentence (they provide a structure of slots in which to put noun phrases) we expected that the growth of function words would be related. Because verbs occur earlier in acquisition than function words, we postulated that a certain level of productive use of finite verbs should be a precondition to the emergence of function words. We also expected that the level of finite verb usage would be a supportive factor in the growth of function word production.

Function words and finite verbs are highly specific linguistic phenomena that require a considerable amount of linguistic differentiation in terms of syntactic categories and rules. We also wanted to know whether these refined categories were related to such overall characteristics of early language as the size of the child's lexicon and the mean length of the child's utterances. It has been widely found that children do not start to form multiword utterances (beginning with two-word sentences) before they have built up a minimal lexicon (of at least 50 words on average). Because there is no logical reason for this fact (a child could start to form two-word sentences as soon as the child knows two words; the only thing the child has to do is omit the pause between two successively uttered words), we postulated that a certain size of the lexicon is a conditional prerequisite to the growth of multiword sentences. Moreover, it can be argued that the level of lexical knowledge is a supportive factor in the production of multiword sentences. Finally, because multiword sentences rely heavily on resources such as limited working memory, we assumed that the growth in sentence length would stand in a mutually supportive relationship to the syntactic elements that are used to structure those sentences. Examples of such elements are finite verbs and function words. Thus we postulated a set of symmetrical support relationships between the level of multiword sentences, and the productive use of finite verbs and function words, respectively. Figures 6.1, 6.2, and 6.3 show the conditional prerequisite and support relationships between our four "growers," namely, the lexicon,

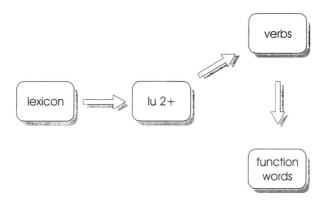

FIG. 6.1. Conditional precursor relations among four linguistic variables.

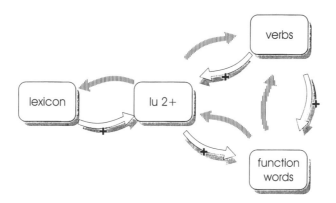

FIG. 6.2. Model of level support relations; only the white arrows made a significant contribution to the model.

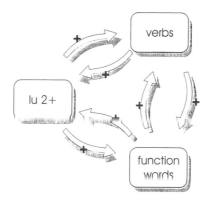

FIG. 6.3. Model of growth support relations.

multiword sentences, finite verbs, and function words. As far as the multiword sentences are concerned, we soon found out that the mean length of utterance (MLU), which is the classical indicator of multiword sentence use, had little explanatory value in our model. That is, in the corpora that we inspected, MLU increased basically linearly, often with salient, random-like variation. It then turned out that an alternative measure, the percentage of sentences with two or more words (LU2+), was a much more sensitive variable. That is, its occurrence is more directly related to structural variables such as finite verbs and function word use.

Empirical Data and Growth Model. In order to run a simulation of the data shown in Fig. 6.4, which were taken from observations of a single child, Peter, we started with four difference equations (see Cats & Ruhland, in press, for details). Three (LU2+, FinVerb, and FuncWord) were based on the general growth equation (Equation 1). The fourth (Lexicon) was a simple growth equation lacking the support term. The reason for omitting the support term was that we postulated that none of the three additional variables had a significant effect on the growth of the lexicon, or, more precisely, that the contribution of each of those was not significantly bigger than that of any other contribution term, such as parental help, effort, attention, memory load, and so forth. In that case the support term is entirely covered by a single carrying capacity parameter K (see Van Geert, 1991, 1994a, for more details).

In order to specify the support term in each of the three additional variables, one has to fill out a matrix specifying how each variable affects any other one. For instance, in the matrix there is a cell [LU2+; FinVerb] specifying how the level of utterances with two or more words affects the level of finite verb use. It is possible to confine oneself to the matrix relating the growth levels. This is sufficient if the simulation problem basically amounts to explaining how the equilibrium level of one variable depends on the (equilibrium) level of another (it is easy to prove that the support term determines the equilibrium level).

Earlier I explained that it is not only the level of one variable that eventually affects the growth of another, but also the growth in the first may influence the growth in the other. More precisely, the actual growth process consumes limited resources such as time, effort, and attention, eventually at the cost of other growth processes. This particular form of competition will have a significant effect only if the resource consumption is really massive. Such massive consumption, for instance of time, sometimes occurs in language development. For instance, right after the discovery of some particular rule or phrase structure principle, some children tend to repeat those new structures endlessly for some time. At that moment there is

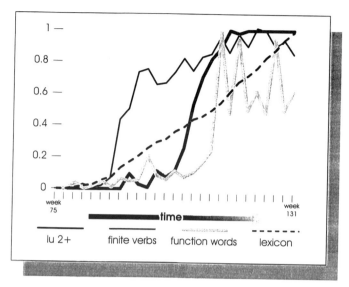

FIG. 6.4. Data from Peter: percentage of sentences with two or more words, number of finite verbs and function words, cumulative lexicon; all variables are scaled to maximum = 1.

hardly any time left for other structures, or almost no attention is invested in other structures that are on the verge of discovery. However, the opposite condition is equally probable. Imagine one variable that directly depends on the other, which is probably the case with function words (or finite verbs, for that matter) and the occurrence of sentences longer than two words. A function word or finite verb tends to create an empty slot (or empty slots) in a sentence, where nouns or noun phrases could fit in. For instance, when the child wants juice, the child may say *juice*, but if he uses the verb *give-me* (I assume it's just a single verb for the child) the child will probably have to add *juice* and thus create a two-word sentence in order to become understandable. Thus it is possible that all resources (attention, time, effort, help, etc.) invested in one linguistic aspect, such as finite verbs, will also be to the benefit of another variable (such as LU2+).

The simplest way to start a growth simulation is to see whether a model can be built that predicts the next observation from the preceding one. Because the data are based on every 2 weeks observation sessions, the model should try to predict all observed levels based on the observed levels from two weeks earlier. This means, implicitly, that the assumption is made that language growth in this area has a feedback delay of 2 weeks (or, to put it differently, that it takes about 2 weeks before the effects of learning processes become observable). This particular assumption is based on no

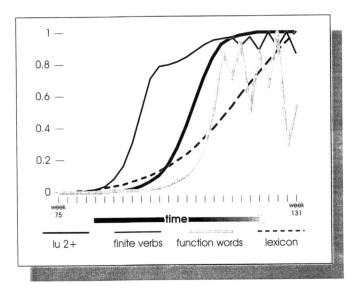

FIG. 6.5. Dynamic growth modeling of LU2+ sentences, finite verbs, function words, and lexicon.

evidence at all; it is just a convenient simplification (although in earlier models I found that the 2-week delay provides good fits with the data; see Van Geert, 1991).

It turned out that this initial approximation produced remarkably good fits of the empirical data (see Fig. 6.5). In order to arrive at the present parameter values, we first tried various combinations, and then zoomed in on combinations of values that seemed promising. Finally, the parameters producing the best fits were found by looking for minima in a matrix of sums of squared differences between observed and modeled data. More recently, we started to use software packages designed for fitting complex nonlinear models (e.g., *Magestic*). These estimation programs look for the set of parameter values that produce the least amount of deviation from the empirical data.

The fact that the modeled curves are very similar to the empirical data does not necessarily mean that the present growth model is psychologically valid. It could of course just be an accidental hit. I should add, however, that the probability that it is a purely accidental success is very small, given the degrees of freedom with 4 times 27 data points. Thus, for whatever the model is worth, we may conclude that it supports the hypothesis that the four linguistic variables at issue are obeying the principle of growth and that their growth patterns are mutually connected (although, in a purely Popperian fashion, it does not refute the hypothesis that there exist other models and conceptualizations that might produce an even better fit).

Problems With the Growth Model

I have already noted that the model, in spite of its attractive properties, is only a first and rough approximation. In this section I discuss several problems; the first concerns the model's resolution properties, and the second the model's stability in the face of random variation. The next three problems all deal with what I would like to call the *locality* of the model: the fact that it is valid only for a limited time span, the limited number of relationships it focuses on, and finally, the fact that it is limited to a single subject.

The Resolution Problem. In essence, a growth model refers to a continuous process (Banks, 1994). In some (probably rare) cases it will be discrete, for instance, in the case of insect population growth, if the parent population dies and leaves eggs that will hatch the next season (May, 1976). I have argued that language or cognitive growth can be conceived of as semidiscrete processes, if growth depends on "learning events." By learning events I understand those activities in which a skill is acted out and altered as a consequence of its effect. Thus, each time a child uses or notices a particular linguistic form, that form either gets further consolidated or loses some of its strength (which is the case with transient linguistic forms, such as the two-word-sentence strategy). It is clear that these discrete language events are far more frequent than the two-weekly observations on which the modeling has been based. A fully elaborate growth model should therefore operate at the time level of linguistic events, which eventually amounts to simulations of a couple of thousand steps, instead of the present 27. The assumed delay in the learning effect would then have to be accounted for in terms of actual time delays.

It is quite implausible, however, that a delay of, for instance, 2 weeks is indeed a discrete time delay. It is highly unlikely that the effect of a learning event that occurred 2 weeks ago suddenly and completely pops up today. It is much more likely that the delay is a matter of spreading out the delay over a longer time stretch. For instance, the weight of each past learning event could be specified by a normal distribution, with its maximum value at around 2 weeks before the actual growth level. A completely randomized, delayed grower has a cyclical attractor that covers an entire phase space range surrounded by a maximal cycle. If one plots every nth point (for n the time delay) in the simulated time series, the result is quite similar to a chaotic oscillation in a discrete logistic model, such as the one used in our first model simulation.

At present, I have no definite answer to the question as to what the resolution of model simulations should be. However, if a first approximation based on the interobservation time produces a good fit, one should not stick to that resolution level. One should also test models with similar time delays and an increasing number of simulation steps, ideally up to the point where the number of steps is about equal to the steps one assumes also occur in reality.

The Stability Problem.   The model specified in Equation 1 describes the general principle of growth. It is a deterministic model. In reality, it is highly unlikely that growth occurs under deterministic conditions. Unless the parameters depend on a very high number of contributing factors (thus averaging out the fluctuations in each of them), they will tend to vary according to influences that are captured neither by the model nor by empirical observation. Those influences then behave like random terms, affecting the value of all the levels and parameters involved in the model. We have seen that the model simulation produced a very nice fit of the empirical data. It did so under purely deterministic conditions. In order to test the robustness of this (nevertheless preliminary) model we should randomize all the terms involved and investigate the amount of deviation from our original results. If the variation is within reasonable limits the model is acceptable. If the variation overlaps considerably with what other, very different, models would have produced, the model should be rejected.

In order to test the stability of the model, all parameters were multiplied by a random term with the following form

$$(1 + (\text{rand} - \text{rand}) \cdot d) \qquad (2)$$

which can be viewed as a rough approximation of a normally distributed set of random numbers with average of zero, standard deviation d times 0.4, a minimum of $1 - d$ and a maximum of $1 + d$. The function *rand* is a random number between 0 and 1, picked from an even distribution; the d parameter specifies to what extent the random numbers affect the parameter to which the randomization operator applies.

With a d parameter of 0.1–0.2 the original model seems to behave rather well, in that it stays closely to the qualitative pattern of change found in the empirical data. However, this observation is completely intuitive and no statistical tests have been run so far. There is one exception, however, which is related to the graph of the function words. In order to obtain the strong oscillation, a high growth rate has been chosen, the effect of which is quite unstable. In some cases, oscillations occur that are about as big as the maximal growth range (which is between 0 and 1 in this model). Such an extreme oscillation is quite improbable, although one should realize that the empirical oscillations are nevertheless quite substantial (up to about 0.6 of the growth range).

The Problem of the Model's Temporal (or Diachronical) Range. It is not difficult to realize that the present model claims no validity beyond the rather limited stretch of time covered by the empirical observations. The functional significance of a variable such as "number of sentences equal to or longer than two words" is limited to the early stage of syntactic development. It loses its meaning as a predictor of language growth as soon as other and more complex syntactic constructions emerge. A question arises as to the temporal range of such models: How far do they extend beyond the empirical observations? Are they valid within the period covered by our observations? It is not improbable, for instance, that the LU2+ variable is already losing much of its significance by the end of our observation series.

In order to explain the eventual growth and decay of relationship parameters we would have needed a considerably more complicated model. The complicated model must explain why, for instance, the LU2+ parameter loses its effect, and which new variables take over. The problem is, however, that if all the parameters needed to make the growth model run are growers themselves, an exponential explosion of the number of parameters occurs, which makes such complex models hardly if at all manageable (in a completely specified growth model with N variables, the number of parameters needed is N^2; in practice this number is greatly reduced because many of these parameters are about zero and need not be considered).

Given this problem, it is conceivable that growth models are low-level specifications of higher level models of self-organizational growth. Farmer (1990) made a distinction between transition dynamics, parameter dynamics, and graph dynamics. Transition dynamics concern the actual low-level changes described in the growth model of linguistic variables, for instance. The parameter dynamics explain changes in the nature and magnitude of the parameters involved. They address questions such as: Why does the effect of LU2+ on function words first increase and then decrease to virtually zero? The graph dynamics explain the emergence of new linguistic variables, which also require new parameter and transition dynamics. So far, most if not all of the modeling work, growth as well as connectionist modeling, has been focusing on the transition dynamics.

The Problem of the Model's Synchronical Range. In the preceding section we discussed the time extension of the model; how far the model should extend its claims across the temporal dimension. In models with fast parameter dynamics, the answer is probably "maybe not more than just a few weeks." This section deals with how many variables should be connected in the network. In the present model I related four variables. The selection among a great many potential variables was based on linguistic grounds. For instance, we hypothesized that function words and finite verbs must affect each other's growth, because they both fulfill comparable syntactic structuring functions in sentences. In addition to linguistic (or psychological) theory, the criterion of parsimony should play a significant role here. In principle, linguistic theory relates every aspect of language to every other one, although it can also be used to rank the relationships in terms of importance or strength. The question then becomes: What is the smallest possible number of linguistically strong relationships that still produces a good fit with the empirical data?

The problem with this question is, however, that there is no standard trade-off between an increasing number of dynamic variables (and associated parameters) and the resulting curve fits. In polynomial curve fitting, for instance, we know that the curve fit increases with increasing numbers of parameters. This fact allows us to define algorithms that compensate for number of parameters used (e.g., Akaike's Information criterion). In a dynamic model, however, the dynamic parameters obtain values that depend on the set of mutual dynamic interactions. It often occurs that the introduction of an additional dynamic parameter significantly reduces the fit of a model. In summary, it is the model builder's decision as to whether or not a certain increase in model fit warrants the introduction of yet another dynamic variable (always provided that it is at least supported by a valid theory, e.g., a linguistic theory of language acquisition).

The Problem of Variability Among Individual Subjects. The model presented so far has been based on the data obtained from a single child. Although individual variation is a central feature of dynamic growth models, that variation should neither extend beyond the limits of the model itself, nor should it involve parameter values with signs opposite to the theoretically supported ones. For instance, if there exist linguistic justifications for the fact that function words and finite verbs maintain a positive relationship, one should not allow individual variation that assumes a negative relationship among the two (unless there are other and stronger theoretical arguments to support that).

Let me first present the data obtained with a second child in the same age range (see Fig. 6.6). The patterns for lexical growth and function words are highly similar. In the second child (Josse), however, growth of finite verbs and LU2+ sentences started significantly earlier than in the child (Peter) on whose data the original model has been based. Simply substituting the observed initial state values in the original model produces a reasonable fit for the new data, in that most of the overall properties are maintained (a linear increase for the lexicon, a jump followed by an oscillatory pattern with the function words, oscillatory change in both LU2+ and finite verbs). What is lacking, however, is the characteristic increase pattern in LU2+, and particularly in the finite verbs. The latter show a considerable oscillation in the first half of the growth curve, followed by a stable second

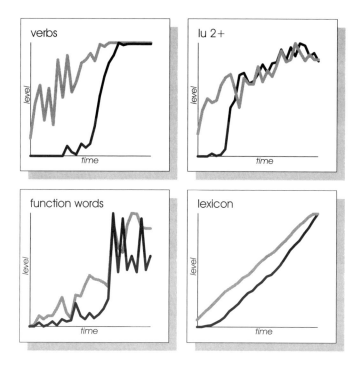

FIG. 6.6. Comparison between data from Peter (black) and Josse (grey).

half. In the first data set, finite verbs showed a quiet, S-shaped increase toward a stable end state (i.e., end state within the confinements of the present data series).

Let me try to speculate a bit further about the potential causes of the oscillatory pattern in the second child. It seems that in the second child, Josse, finite verbs grow precociously. By *precocious* I mean growth in the absence of sufficient resources. It seems that in the early stage of finite verb growth in Josse's data, a structural component supporting the grammatically correct use of finite verbs is still lacking or, more probably, still underdeveloped. For instance, let me assume that the proficient use of finite verbs, and of any other syntactic category, for that matter, depends on the child's ability to use all syntactic categories correctly (that is, with correct position and **inflection**) Let me call this variable Cat (correct category use) and assume that Cat supports VFin (finite verbs). It follows that the equilibrium level for VFin is specified by the equation

$$\mathrm{Eq}[\mathrm{VFin}_{t+1}] = K_{\mathrm{VFin}}(r_{\mathrm{VFin}} + d \cdot \mathrm{Cat}_t)/r_{\mathrm{VFin}} \tag{3}$$

where K_{VFin} is the carrying capacity of VFin in the absence of Cat, r_{VFin} is the growth rate of Vfin, d is a support parameter, and Cat_t the level of the variable

Cat at time t (see Van Geert, 1991, 1994a, for further explanation on this equation). From Equation 3 it follows that the equilibrium level of VFin will increase as long as the growth of Cat continues. If the growth rate of VFin is very high (e.g., because there is strong support from some other variable), VFin will start to oscillate around its increasing equilibrium point. A comparable process could eventually explain the pattern of increase and decrease in the first half of Josse's data set.

It is easy to see that it is not only the first half of the growth pattern of VFin that differs among the data sets, but also those of LU2+ and function words. However, we don't need to invoke additional growth variables to explain the latter differences. In the original model, function words, LU2+, and finite verbs were related in the form of a mutual support network. It follows then that if one variable, which in this case is the finite verb level, shows precocious growth, the related variables function words and LU2+ must profit from that. This explains why the first half of the growth levels of both function words and LU2+ is higher in Josse than they are in Peter.

Figure 6.7 shows the result of a simulation based on an altered version of our original growth model. The alteration consists of a carrying capacity function for the finite verbs, which is still increasing during the first half of the time series, after which it reaches a stable level. Although the modeled series resembles the observed series quite well, there are a number of points one should keep in mind. In the first place, the simulations are based on a randomized model—that is, the parameter and initial state values vary randomly, with a maximum variation of 20% of the fixed parameter value (the fixed parameter value is the value defined in the parameter list). A considerable number of the simulations produce oscillations that are either much bigger or much smaller than the empirically observed ones. However, if the real process has a random character similar to the randomization in the model, the latter will produce a fit *function* (instead of, e.g., a single fit in the form of a sum of least squares). The fit function is probably something like a normal distribution of sums of least squares, which in the case of an ideal fit should be high and narrow. Second, the simulation is based on the rough approximation introduced in the beginning, namely, a model in which the observation interval corresponds with an iterative step. I have already explained that a more realistic model should capture the iterative steps as they occur in reality, namely, steps based on the actual use of the linguistic variables in question. Finally, the observed values of finite verb use reach a stable maximum in the second half of the observed period, whereas the simulated curve continues to oscillate around its (local) maximum.

The Problem of Curve Fitting. The theoretical curves presented in this chapter and several other papers (Van Geert, 1991, 1995) have been based on an intuitive fitting procedure. A first estimation of the parameters is

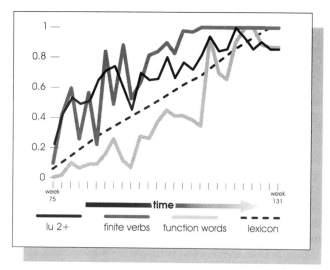

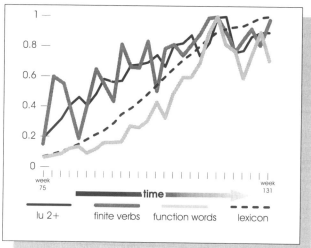

FIG. 6.7. Comparison between data (top) from Josse and modeled series (bottom).

based on applying a simple logistic growth equation with $p = 1$, $d = 0$, and $K = 1$ to each of the empirical growth curves. It is trivial that if E_t and E_{t+1} are two successive data points of, for instance, the function words graph represented on a scale ranging from 0 to 1, the growth rate $r_{t/t+1}$ of Equation 1 is

$$(E_{t+1} - E_t)/[E_t(1 - E_t)] = r_{t/t+1} \qquad (3)$$

If we have a model in which the parameter d governs the effect of supportive and competitive growers, the following equation holds:

$$r_{t/t+1} = r + d_a A_t + d_b B_t + \cdots \tag{4}$$

For A_t and B_t the empirical data points at time t for variables A and B, respectively. The parameters r, d_a, d_b, and so on can then be estimated by comparing successive values of $r_{t/t+1}$, reckoning with the values of A, B, and so forth. The best fits can be obtained by defining matrices of least-squares values corresponding with combinations of parameter values. This is a laborious procedure that eventually leads to local optima, that is, to combinations of parameter values that provides the best fit. It is likely, however, that these connected growth models have several such local optima—that is, that there is more than one solution to the problem of which parameters produce the best fit with the data. The eventual existence of more than one optimal solution is consistent with the ecological nature of the developmental interactions assumed in the growth model.

More formal solutions to the problem of fitting group data to growth models have been discussed by Willett (1994) and Eckstein and Shemesh (1992). Cooney and Constas (1993) focused on the question of whether fluctuations in the data from learning experiments and data from individual language corpora converged on some sort of attractor. They found that data on lexical growth exhibit a fractal property that may be described by a simple dynamic model such as the logistic growth model. Recently, considerable progress was made by Molenaar and Raymakers (chapter 12, this volume) with a filtering technique that estimates parameter values of growth models. The technique is applicable to time-series data with a relatively small number of data points, which is characteristic of most of the repeated observations designs from studies on early language development.

A MODEL OF DISCONTINUOUS STAGES

Sudden Jumps and Multistability

Evidence for Developmental Discontinuity. By their very nature, growth models are continuous. That is, for any two points on a growth curve, there exists a point in between that specifies the level at the intermediate time point. The delay effects that I expect to occur with psychological growth are due to the fact that such growth may depend on discrete learning events and to the fact that the effect of such events requires a certain amount of time to become consolidated. Van der Maas and Molenaar (1992) and Hopkins and Van der Maas (in press) argued that there exists a significant number of developmental phenomena for which the continuity assumption does not hold. They contended that development occurs in the form of discrete changes, which can be described, formalized, and empirically tested with the aid of catastrophe theory. For a few children from our longitudinal research project, there is evidence that the growth of function words takes the form of a so-called cusp catastrophe (Ruhland & Van Geert, 1995). With function words, we found evidence for the catastrophe flag "sudden jump," but only weak or inconclusive evidence for additional flags such as bimodality or anomalous variance. The cusp catastrophe amounts to a sudden jump toward a new equilibrium. This means that at a certain point in time the function words variable has two potential equilibria, an old one, which is probably close to zero, and a new one, which is close to the adult use of function words. At a certain moment, the use of function words increases rapidly and then levels off at its new attractor. It is important to note that although the surface form of this process of increase is very similar to a logistic growth process (e.g., especially if $p = 2$), it is essentially different. In a logistic growth process, there is only one equilibrium level (the carrying capacity level K). In a cusp catastrophe model, however, there are two, and although the move toward the new equilibrium level may resemble the move toward the K level in a growth process, the essential difference between the two lies in the presence of two stable modes (two equilibria) in the cusp catastrophe. If function words, or finite verbs, for that matter, are indeed governed by bi- or multimodality, as is the claim in catastrophe theoretic dynamics (Hopkins & Van der Maas, in press; Van der Maas, 1993; Van der Maas & Molenaar, 1992) a growth model is at best an approximation of a surface property of the process. Is it possible for a growth model to capture the eventual bi- or multimodal aspect of developmental change?

Push-Me-Pull-You Models. A push-me-pull-you model is based on the assumption that in most developmental and learning models the attractor state is actively manipulated and adapted to the current growth level of a grower. Vygotsky's model of the zone of proximal development (ZPD), for instance, is based on the idea that children learn to do new things because they did those same things before with the help of a more competent person. This person must have adapted the level of help and support to the (developing) ability or skill level of the child. As a result of this help, the child's level increases. In order to remain functional, the help and support level must increase proportionally, until finally some upper limit is reached.

The basic idea behind a push-me-pull-you model is that the carrying capacity of the grower stays within a certain, "attractive" distance from the grower's level. The carrying capacity increases in response to the increase in the growth level. With this basic principle, it is possible to define dynamic models of Vygotsky's zone of proximal development (Van Geert, 1994b), but also of phenomena such as the emergence of attachment (Van Geert, 1997b). These models have an interesting property that is lacking in the classic growth model, namely, bimodality. They contain control parameters that govern the rate of adaptation of either the grower or the carrying capacity in response to changes in either the "puller" (the carrying capacity) or the "pusher" (the growth level). It remains to be investigated, however, whether this bimodal state is an instantiation of a cusp catastrophe or not.

Distributed-Weight Models. In all the previously discussed models, ranging from the classical logistic to the push-me-pull-you models, the grower (e.g., the level of function word use) has only one value at a particular moment in time. That value may oscillate chaotically, remain stable, or turn around in a cycle, but at any point in time there is one and only one value. The model I present in the next section is based on a principle of distributed knowledge and can have several potential levels at a time.

A Model of Discontinuous, Stagewise Growth

The Representation of Skill or Knowledge. The model makes a distinction between the internal knowledge or skill representation and the actual expression of the knowledge, in the form of a problem-solving activity, for instance. The internal representation consists of a list of random numbers, each of which represents a particular problem-solving skill or knowledge item. The numbers basically function as addresses, referring to certain cognitive representations, mechanisms, or conditions.

Let me first explain how a random number can be thought to represent a skill or knowledge, both in a symbolic representational system and in a connectionist, subsymbolic network. In a symbolic conceptualization, skills or knowledge may be represented in the form of a finite set of symbolic markers. Because it is a physical symbol system, all we require the markers to do is distinguish one representation from another (Fodor, 1980; Newell, 1980). Thus we can represent any skill or knowledge item as a binary string. Each slot in the string represents a particular feature. If the number in that particular slot is 1, the feature is present, and absent if the value is 0. It is also possible to assume that the features are developmentally or conditionally ordered. This means that slots at the left can obtain a value 1 only if slots at the right have (or once had) a value 1 (see Van Geert, 1992). In summary, a random decimal number can be mapped (eventually after truncation) onto a binary number. That binary number stands in a one-to-one relationship with a symbolic binary feature representation of a particular skill or knowledge item. A much simpler solution to the problem of how a number may represent a (cognitive) content is to reduce the distinction between all possible contents to a distinction in terms of developmental complexity. Differences in developmental complexity are based on a great number of developmentally significant variables or dimensions that constitute an abstract multidimensional space. In this space, any cognitive content (or any other developmentally relevant content for that matter) can be represented by its distance from the imaginary origin of this abstract space. The distance is, of course, a one-dimensional property (more details can be found in Van Geert, 1997a). In this way, a single number on the distance dimension specifies the set of all contents that share this particular developmental distance specification, that is, all contents with the same developmental level.

A similar reasoning holds for a subsymbolic representation, for instance, a connectionist network. In such a network, a skill or knowledge item is represented by a particular activation pattern. A binary coding can be used to specify which nodes in the network are active and which are not. It suffices again that each slot in the binary number refers to a particular node (e.g. the first slot is the node with the number 1, the second slot to the left is node 2, and so forth). The difference between any two decimal numbers corresponds with a particular difference between activation nets. That difference is of course greater if the difference between the numbers is greater.

Internal Representation and External Action. If a number n represents a particular representation of a skill or knowledge item, it can also be used to represent a problem that can be solved by invoking that skill or knowledge item. Thus, in order to see whether a knowledge system can solve a certain problem, we present that problem in the form of a number. The probability that the system solves the problem can be set to a function of the distance between the problem number and the closest number available in the internal representation. The simulation of a problem-solving activity thus amounts to a process of finding the best resembling number in a list of stored numbers (the internal representations), and then running a simple randomized decision procedure. Trivial as this process undoubtedly is, it suffices for us to simulate a basic aspect of development, namely, learning through experience.

In summary, the model contains an array of numbers that represent knowledge, for instance, the knowledge of a particular 4-year-old child. The model makes no assumptions whatsoever as to the exact nature of this knowledge: It suffices that levels of knowledge can be distinguished from one another and ordered along a developmental scale. The system's internal array contains a list of knowledge items (the numbers), beginning with the earliest ones (comparable with Piaget's basic reflexive action patterns present at birth) and ending with the most recently acquired form of knowledge. In order to represent the developmental level of the system, that is, in order to specify which kind or level of problems the system will be able to solve, the knowledge-representing numbers are coupled with a weight factor. The weight factor corresponds with the probability that a certain level or type of skill or knowledge will be actualized.

A Conceptualization of "Developmental Level." There are two ways in which the system's current developmental level can be defined. The first refers to the highest level of understanding the system is capable of. This corresponds with the highest value in the system's array of knowledge-specifying numbers. Thus one way for development to proceed is by extending this array with higher and higher levels of knowledge or understanding. The second criterion refers to the weight factors associated with each of the knowledge representations. We know that subjects seldom function at their maximal competence level; in fact, it usually requires a lot of experimental effort to put a subject in a condition such that he or she can do so. Thus there exists a level of "habitual" action, that is, a level that corresponds with what a particular subject does under "normal" circumstances. This level is specified by the weight factors, because they correspond with the probability that a subject will perform the associated action (more precisely, an action at a specific level of development). If we plot the weight factors along the ordered set of knowledge-representing numbers, the child's developmental level is specified by the peak in the weight figures. There is no essential objection against a series of weights with more than one peak. For instance, if the weight plot shows two peaks that are approximately equal in height, we know that the system is at present in a bistable state, with each of the peaks corresponding with a potential developmental state or level.

Development can now be quantified (i.e., within the confinements of the present model) in the form of the movement of the weights peak over the ordered series of problem or skill representations. For instance, if the peak moves slowly in the beginning, then faster in the middle, and slowly again at the end, we have a form of development that closely resembles the S-shaped increase of logistic growth. If the peak literally jumps from one place to the other, skipping the intermediate peak levels, we have a model of a sudden jump. If two (or more) peaks are present at the same time, the system is characterized by a bi- or multimodal state. In summary, the present conceptualization of growth and development allows for continuous as well as discontinuous growth patterns (a detailed explanation of the model is given in Van Geert, 1997a).

A Conceptualization of Developmental Progress. Assume that our system is presented with a particular problem, in the form of a number N_P (I call this the problem number or P-number). How will the system find out which skill or knowledge item it has to retrieve in order to solve that problem? That is, which number N_R (which I call the representation number or

R-number) will it have to retrieve, such that the comparison between N_P and N_R leads to the output "Problem Solved!"? Recall that the probability that the problem N_P is solved is a random function of the difference between N_R and N_P.

In the present model, the retrieval of the "solution," that is, of a particular type of action, is as simple as can be. The system just retrieves the type of problem-solving behavior or knowledge it is good at. Thus, if its developmental level is L (whatever that may mean), it produces a problem solution of type L. This is basically what people always do (and cannot refrain from doing): If confronted with a problem they produce a solution of a kind they can manage, one they are familiar with.

Technically, the retrieval process runs as follows. Each time the system is asked for a particular activity, it multiplies each of the weights in the knowledge array with a particular random number. It then decides which multiplication gives the highest result, and then selects the associated knowledge number for output.

The basic idea behind the present model is that *development is a combination of a conservative and a progressive tendency.* It is conservative in the sense that it tries to keep what it already has. It is progressive in the sense that it tries to adapt to environmental requirements, that is, to the nature of the problems with which it is presented. This combination of progressive and conservative tendencies is characteristic of most, if not all, developmental theories. In Piaget's model, for instance, we see it instantiated in the contrast between assimilation (conservative) and accommodation (progressive) or the tendency toward equilibrium (conservative) followed by disequilibrium (progressive).

The conservative aspect is modeled as follows. Whatever R-number is retrieved is also rewarded, simply because it has proven to be the "strongest" one. Its reward is an increase in its weight factor, in accordance with a preestablished increase function. The reward is randomized, in order to account for the fact that actions can have various levels of success, ranging from no success at all (in which case the reward is zero) to complete success (in which case the reward is maximal). The increase in the weight factor is specified in the form of the logistic growth equation we encountered earlier. It shows that models of growth and models of discontinuous change can be combined in a natural way.

The progressive aspect is modeled in a different way. It is assumed that the environment poses problems and challenges of all kinds, that is, with problems that require all possible levels of development and understanding. If the problem (or, in general, the experience provided by the system's environment) is within a certain optimal distance from what the system is currently capable of understanding (the highest current level of knowledge represented in the system), the system is allowed to extend its knowledge array with a representation of that new, "accessible" problem or experience. In addition, the weight factor associated with that level is also increased.

The following example illustrates both the conservative and the progressive principle. For instance, imagine the family dog who tries to steal a cookie a child is holding in his hand. The child may say something like "cookie dog." In terms of the model, his two-word-sentence action is rewarded or reinforced, because of the conservative principle. That is to say, whatever mechanism is responsible for the production of two-word utterances is further consolidated or strengthened. The child's parent, however, expands this two-word sentence by saying "Is that naughty dog trying to steal your cookie?" Although it is quite unlikely that the child is capable of understanding this sentence in its full syntactic complexity, the child will nevertheless pick up some of the syntactic structure, for instance, the nested syntactic structure {dog [steal <(your) (cookie)>] }, which is a Subject–Verb–Object structure that lies well beyond the simple two word sentences the child is actually producing. If this is the first time the child actually explicitly notices an S-V-O structure, he will add that structure to his array of "understandable" syntactic structures. This, however, does not necessarily imply that the child will also *use* this structure in speech. It may still take quite some time before he will do so.

An important property of the model is that the rewards are distributed. Thus the retrieved R-number (with the maximal output number) is rewarded and so are its neighbors. The smaller the difference with the retrieved R-number, the higher the probability that this neighbor will be rewarded. The distributed reward function can be made such that the reward either is spread across a considerable range or is confined to neighbors that have only a minute difference with the winner.

We have seen, however, that rewards are given not only to the retrieved number, but also to the R-number that is closest to the given problem, that is, the P-number. The neighbors of that R-number also profit from the reward, and the extent to which they are rewarded depends on their distance to the best fitting R-number.

Basic Simulation Results. The most interesting simulation results occur when the conservative and progressive parameters are balanced. If we plot the system's output, which has the form of numbers referring to specific levels, the developmental process shows a few dramatic discontinuities. That is, the system remains in a dynamic equilibrium for some time, corresponding with a relatively narrow band within which the outputs vary. It then suddenly jumps toward a much higher level, without any intermediate levels occurring (see Fig. 6.8). The jump often takes the form of a transient oscillation between the old and the new level, after which the system again settles into a narrow band of variation, that is, a new stage. It is easy to

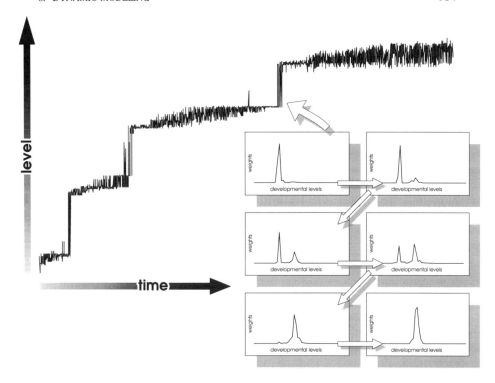

FIG. 6.8. Model of stagewise increase; jumps take the form of discontinuous, bimodal changes.

show that the jump is a real discontinuity by plotting the progressive changes in the array of weights associated with the knowledge numbers. Figure 6.8 shows the change in weights occurring in the vicinity of a jump. We see that before the jump the weights are concentrated in a single spike, which remains constant for as long as the system maintains its present stage. The spike then rather abruptly recesses. Meanwhile, a new spike starts to grow at a marked distance from the first one. When both spikes are at about the same height, the system is in a bimodal response state, corresponding with the oscillation between the old and new activity levels. Then the new spike takes over, and the old one disappears completely.

The stages themselves have a number of interesting properties. First, their number characteristically varies between three and six, which corresponds with the number of stages distinguished in various classical stage theories. Second, the intervals between successive jumps tend to increase in a logarithmic way, which is very similar to the increase in stage length that Piaget and the neo-Piagetians have described. Third, the stages themselves often contain a few substages, that is, strictly separated bands within the overall band of stage-specific variation. The existence of substages is reminiscent of a fractal pattern of change, that is, a pattern that is scale-invariant. If the frequency of the discontinuities is plotted against their magnitude, the resulting graph follows a power distribution, which is an indication of the fractal nature of the pattern.

Finally, the transitions have a number of properties that are highly similar to the catastrophe indicators that Van der Maas and Molenaar (1992) described. We have already seen that the model shows sudden jumps and the associated bimodal distributions. The latter occur in the form of real bimodal behavior in the vicinity of the transition. Because the moment of occurrence of a jump is a random event that lies within certain limits of variation, the variance occurring in a group of simulated curves typically increases dramatically around the discontinuities, also because individual curves display genuine bimodal behavior. Around the jump, the system also shows the property of critical slowing down: The weights, which represent the strengths of the associated types of action, are dramatically decreased in the neighborhood of the discontinuity. If the model is changed such that it can accommodate the principle of a control variable governing the inputs, it shows hysteresis in that the point at which jumps occur depends on the direction in which the control variable has been made to vary. Finally, the model parameters can be altered in such a way that they account for conditions and contexts of development that differ from the "Piagetian" case that I have described so far. For instance, it is possible to introduce the effect of an educational environment that tries to adapt its teaching and guidance to the child's developmental needs. Different parameter sets produce qualitatively different patterns of change that correspond with various patterns found in empirical research (see Van Geert, 1997a, for a full description of parameter sets and simulation results).

SUMMARY

In this chapter I have argued that empirical growth phenomena such as the growth of linguistic variables in spontaneous speech recordings of children can be modeled with the aid of a connected growers network. The network is in fact a small ecological system, where increase or decrease is understood on the basis of mutual support or competition among the linguistic variables involved.

Although the simulated curves came quite close to the empirically observed ones, the model still suffers from a lot of problems. One problem lies in what I called the *resolution* of the model: How dense should the steps be distributed over the growth simulation in order to arrive at a valid representation of the empirical growth process? A second problem concerns the stability of the solution in the face of random variation of parameters and conditions. Other problems concern the diachronical and synchronical limitations of the model. How far does it extend in developmental time? Are all four variables involved really needed, or should more variables be taken into account. Finally, is the model based on the observations made with a single child applicable to other children?

A disadvantage of growth models is that they cannot explain sudden equilibrium jumps and bi- and multimodality, phenomena that are likely to be characteristic features of development in general. I have presented two kinds of models that could eventually overcome (part of) this problem. The first was a so-called push-me-pull-you model, which differentiated a growth variable into a growing attractor and a growing variable. Attractor and variable are mutually dependent: Both grow as a consequence of the growth in the other. The second kind of model, which I discussed in more detail, consisted of a distributed growth model, which made a distinction between an internal representation state and the resulting external behaviors. This model shows interesting properties, such as discontinuous jumps and the stagewise character of developmental change. The discontinuities have a fractal character. Moreover, the model naturally displays a great number of the qualitative indicators characteristic of a cusp catastrophe.

REFERENCES

Banks, R. B. (1994). *Growth and diffusion phenomena*. Berlin: Springer.

Brown, R. (1973). *A first language: The early stages*. London: Allen & Unwin.

Cats, M., & Ruhland, R. (in press). Simulatie van vroege Taalontwikkeling [Simulation of early language development]. *Tijdschrijft voor Informatica en modelbouw*.

Chomsky, N. (1980). *Rules and representations*. Oxford: Blackwell.

Chomsky, N. (1981). *Lectures on government and binding*. Dordrecht: Foris.

Cooney, J. B., & Constas, M. A. (1993). On determining the dimension of discontinuities in human learning and development. In M. L. Howe & R. Pasnak (Eds.), *Emerging themes in cognitive development: Vol. 1. Foundations* (pp. 154–191). New York: Springer.

Eckstein, S., & Shemesh, M. (1992). Mathematical models of cognitive development. *British Journal of Psychology, 45*, 1–18.

Ellman, J. L. (1993). Learning and development in neural networks: The importance of starting small. *Cognition, 48*, 71–99.

Farmer, J. D. (1990). A rosetta stone for connectionism. *Physica D, 42*, 153–187.

Fodor, J. (1980). Fixation of belief and concept acquisition. In M. Piattelli-Palmarini (Ed.), *Language and learning: The debate between Jean Piaget and Noam Chomsky* (pp. 142–161). Cambridge, MA: Harvard University Press.

Gopnik, A., & Meltzoff, A. (1987). The development of categorization in the second year and its relation to other cognitive and linguistic developments. *Child Development, 58*, 1523–1531.

Gopnik, A., & Meltzoff, A. (1992). Categorization and naming: Basic level-sorting in eighteen-month-olds and its relation to language. *Child Development, 63*, 1091–1103.

Hoeksma, J. B., van den Boom, D. C., Koomen, H. M. Y., & Koops, W. (1997). Modeling the sensitivity-attachment hypothesis. In W. Koops, J. B. Hoeksma, & D. C. van den Boom (Eds.), *Development of interaction and attachment: Traditional and non-traditional approaches* (pp. 157–168). Amsterdam: North Holland.

Hopkins, B., & Van der Maas, H. (in press). Catastrophe theory and developmental transitions. *British Journal of Developmental Psychology*.

Klausmeier, H. J. (1976). Conceptual development during the school years. In J. T. Levin & V. L. Allen (Eds.), *Cognitive learning in children: Theories and strategies* (pp. 5–29). New York: Academic Press.

May, R. M. (1976). Simple mathematical models with very complicated dynamics. *Nature, 261,* 459–467.

Newell, A. (1980). Physical symbol systems. *Cognitive Science, 4,* 135–183.

Piaget, J. (1955). Les stades du développement intellectuel de l'enfant et de l'adolescent [The stages of intellectual development in the child and the adolescent]. In P. Osterrieth, J. Piaget, R. De Saussure, J. M. Tanner, H. Wallon, R. Zazzo, B. Inhelder, & A. Rey (Eds.), *Le problème des stades en psychologie de l'enfant: Symposium de l'Association de Langue Française* (pp. 33–42). Paris: Presses Universitaires de France.

Plunkett, K., & Sinha, C. (1992). Connectionism and developmental theory. *British Journal of Developmental Psychology, 10,* 209–254.

Plunkett, K., Sinha, C., Moller, M. F., & Strandsby, O. (1992). Symbol grounding or the emergence of symbols? Vocabulary growth in children and a connectionist net. *Connection Science, 4,* 293–312.

Ruhland, R., & Van Geert, P. (1995). Jumping into syntax: Evidence from closed class words. *British Journal of Developmental Psychology.*

Ruhland, R., Wijnen, F., & Van Geert, P. (1995). An exploration into the application of dynamic systems modeling to language acquisition. In F. Wijnen & M. Verrips (Eds.), *Amsterdam series in child language development, 4,* 107–134.

Rumelhart, D., & McClelland, J. (1993). On learning the past tense of English verbs. In P. Bloom (Ed.), *Language acquisition: Core readings* (pp. 423–471). Cambridge, MA: MIT Press.

Van der Maas, H. (1993). *Catastrophe analysis of stage-wise cognitive development: Model, method and applications.* Doctoral dissertation, University of Amsterdam.

Van der Maas, H., & Molenaar, P. (1992). A catastrophe-theoretical approach to cognitive development. *Psychological Review, 99,* 395–417.

Van Geert, P. (1988). The concept of transition in developmental models. In W. Baker, L. P. Mos, H. V. van Rappard, & H. J. Stam (Eds.), *Recent trends in theoretical psychology* (pp. 225–236). New York: Springer.

Van Geert, P. (1990). Theoretical problems in developmental psychology. In P. Van Geert & L. Mos (Eds.), *Annals of theoretical psychology: Developmental psychology* (pp. 1–54). New York: Plenum.

Van Geert, P. (1991). A dynamic systems model of cognitive and language growth. *Psychological Review, 98,* 3–53.

Van Geert, P. (1992). [Towards a calculus for developmental theories.] Unpublished.

Van Geert, P. (1993). A dynamic systems model of cognitive growth: competition and support under limited resource conditions. In L. B. Smith & E. Thelen (Eds.), *A dynamic systems approach to development: Applications* (pp. 265–331). Cambridge, MA: MIT Press.

Van Geert, P. (1994a). *Dynamic systems of development: Change between complexity and chaos.* New York: Prentice Hall/Harvester Wheatsheaf.

Van Geert, P. (1994b). Vygotskyan dynamics of development. *Human Development, 37,* 1–20.

Van Geert, P. (1995). Growth dynamics in development. In R. F. Port & T. Van Gelder (Eds.), *Mind as motion: Explorations in the dynamics of cognition* (pp. 331–337). Cambridge, MA: Bradford Books/MIT Press.

Van Geert, P. (1997a). A dynamic systems model of basic developmental mechanisms: Piaget, Vygotsky and beyond. *Psychological Review* (submitted).

Van Geert, P. (1997b). The development of attachment and attachment-related competences: A dynamic model. In W. Koops, J. B. Hoeksma, & D. Van den Boom (Eds.), *Development of interaction and attachment: Traditional and non-traditional approaches* (pp. 233–258). Amsterdam: North Holland.

Willet, J. (1994). *Growth models in development.* Paper presented at the Conference of the Jean Piaget Society, Chicago.

7

THE DYNAMICAL AND STATISTICAL PROPERTIES OF COGNITIVE STRATEGIES: RELATIONS BETWEEN STRATEGIES, ATTRACTORS, AND LATENT CLASSES

Han L. J. van der Maas
University of Amsterdam

Cognitive developmental psychology is faced with new developments in the mathematical theory of nonlinear dynamic systems and in psychometrics. The incorporation of these developments in current theorizing in cognitive developmental psychology is a complex matter, but one whose importance has been emphasized repeatedly (Butterworth, 1993; Molenaar, 1986; Rindskopf, 1987). The new mathematical understanding of nonlinear dynamic systems and the application of resulting ideas and techniques in an amazing number of disciplines might be called a revolution in study of change (Gleick, 1987). New fundamental relationships have emerged between chaos and unpredictability, nonlinearity and self-organization, strange attractors and fractals, disequilibrium and sudden qualitative changes, and between limit cycles and oscillatory behavior.

A key concept in nonlinear dynamic systems theory is the concept of attractor, stable state, mode, or equilibrium (viewed here as synonyms). Given constant values of a set of independent variables, dependent or behavioral variables seek stable states. Such stable states or attractors can change suddenly in a number of well-defined ways when independent variables change continuously.

It has been noted that the nonlinear terminology can be too easily applied to many common phenomena. Yet, in the study of motor development, for instance, it has been shown that the interpretation of states or coordinated movements in terms of attractors goes beyond its apparent metaphorical character. By using perturbations the stability of attractors can be tested and systematic manipulations of independent variables lead, as predicted, to sudden jumps between attractors (for a standard example, see Kelso, 1984). In the case of cognitive development the interpretation of modes or attractors is less straightforward. Because identification of attractors in terms of (measurable) cognitive states is only the start of applying nonlinear dynamic system theory, agreement on this point is a prerequisite for any interpretation.

The new development in psychometrics concerns modern test theory as opposed to classical test theory. In fact, this development is not that new, and this is equally true for nonlinear dynamics. However, the transfer of a new technique to particular domains of inquiry can be a slow process. In the 30 years of Rasch modeling it is the case that successful applications in cognitive developmental psychology are still rare. The Rasch model is the most famous example of modern test theory and is a special case of an item response model that in turn is a special case of a latent structure model (Clogg, 1988, 1994; Hagenaars, 1990). The new concept is the latent variable, as an alternative for the sum score, which has very attractive characteristics like, for instance, specific objectivity (Rasch, 1980; see also Mellenbergh, 1994).

Models for all kinds of special cases have been developed concerning different measurement levels of observed variables, kind and number of latent variables, and type of experimental hypothesis. The unification of these models has been very successful for models of continuous observed and latent variables in the form of the LISREL model (Jöreskog & Sörbom, 1988). For dichotomous observed variables and continuous latent variables, item response theory forms a general approach (Hambleton & Swaminathan, 1985; Mellenbergh, 1994). If both observed and latent variables are categorical, then latent class analysis is appropriate (McCutcheon, 1987).

In contrast to other latent structure models, latent class analysis concerns latent categorical classes, groups, or types. This means that for a test consisting of dichotomous (or polytomous) items we can choose to construct a continuum (or factor or one-dimensional latent trait), or to construct a typology. We elaborate the advantages of the latter option for the statistical test of both the concepts of strategy and attractor. First, we consider the relation between the strategy concept in cognitive developmental psychology and the concept of attractor in nonlinear dynamic system theory on a conceptual level.

COGNITIVE DEVELOPMENTAL PSYCHOLOGY
AND NONLINEAR DYNAMIC SYSTEM THEORY

An interesting aspect is that the concepts of nonlinear dynamic system theory are to a certain degree well known in cognitive developmental psychology. The dominant theoretical position in the history of cognitive developmental psychology is the Piagetian. In this theory equilibration has an important place. The Piagetian theory is remarkably consistent with nonlinear dynamic system theory with regard to dynamics. Many authors have recognized this and have directly related Piagetian concepts with concepts of the various traditions in nonlinear dynamic system theory, for instance, chaos theory (Van Geert, 1991), catastrophe theory (Preece, 1980; Saari, 1977; Van der Maas & Molenaar, 1992), synergetics (Thelen, Kelso, & Fogel, 1987), nonequilibration thermodynamics (Garcia, 1992), and dynamic system theory (Keating, 1990; Lewis, 1994).

Piaget saw equilibration as a process leading from states of equilibrium to other qualitatively different states, and passing through multiple "nonbalances" and reequilibrations. Because these new equilibria are generally better, he wrote of self-organization (Piaget, 1978, pp. 3–4). This statement is in full agreement with modern mathematical views on the progressive change of complex systems. The same close similarity can be seen between Waddington's epigenetic landscapes and, for instance, the potential functions of catastrophe theory (Saunders & Kubal, 1989).

So, on a theoretical level the application of nonlinear dynamic system theory to cognitive developmental psychology seems very straightforward. Unfortunately, there are a number of complications. First, the history of cognitive developmental psychology has seen many serious attacks on, or, at least, attempts to revise, the Piagetian theory. Second, the Piagetian theory concerns more than just the concept of equilibration. It is unclear for which parts of this theory nonlinear dynamic system theory is relevant. The implications of this relationship are yet not fully understood. Third, and perhaps most importantly, it is still unclear how the idea of self-organization should be tested empirically.

Most alternative developmental theories reject the idea of equilibration, or at least do not incorporate it. Hence, an empirical test that demonstrates its presence would have implications for cognitive developmental psychology. However, the application of nonlinear dynamic system theory to the Piagetian equilibration theory on a very abstract level, although of interest, does not lead to empirical tests. Brainerd's (1978) historical complaint about the lack of discriminatory empirical predictions is not immediately resolved.

The abstractness of most concepts, the generality of certain claims, and the vagueness of theoretical predictions are all factors that hamper empirical testing. However, this is generally not true for domain-specific Piagetian models (and for many proposed elaborations of the Piagetian theory) that concern the acquisition of single cognitive competencies. The rather general competencies, subsystems, structures, and so on are then taken as much more specific concepts like operations, rules, strategies, and so on. On this level the same laws of equilibration operate. If we take, for instance, conservation acquisition, the Piagetians usually distinguish between four progressive, more or less stable states, each characterized by a specific cognitive operation or strategy (Piaget, 1978). There are many (more or less) valid ways to assess strategies. Hence, we suggest making the link between cognitive developmental psychology and nonlinear dynamic system theory on this level by the claim that strategies are, when viewed from a dynamical point of view, modes or attractors of complex nonlinear systems (see, e.g., Amit, 1989).

If we do not take the Piagetian theory as a starting point, this proposal is still relevant. Almost all alternative models of conservation acquisition apply the concept of strategy in some form or other. It is not practical in the present context to give an overview of the application of the strategy concept in social science.[1] For the present purposes, it is not necessary to be very precise as the idea of strategies as attractors in nonlinear dynamic system theory is very general. It is general in the sense that it does not pertain to a certain process model, cognitive theory, or a subset of cognitive behavior. Strategies, rules, operations, and others can therefore explicitly be taken as synonyms.

What are the implications of viewing strategies as attractors? It implies that a strategy is a stable improbable organization of unknown underlying capacities, processes, or neural structures. It concerns a certain locally stable configuration of an unknown number of unknown possibilities (the unknown state space) recognizable by the behavior of certain order or state variables. Strategies refer to coherent cognitive behavior on an emergent level. In nonlinear dynamic system theory, it is not necessary to identify all unknown lower order subsystems, or to choose a certain architecture or cognitive process model. Behavior is studied on the emergent level (Kelso, Ding, & Schöner, 1993).

It implies also that this unlikely organization of the cognitive system of many degrees of freedom has certain equilibrium characteristics. A strategy has a stability that can be studied by perturbations. A strategy can be brought so far out of equilibrium that it falls apart or transforms into an another strategy in a discontinuous manner. In general, strategy behavior may encompass all phenomena studied in nonlinear dynamic system theory

---

[1]Amirkhiabani and Hendry (1994) reviewed the strategy concept in cognitive psychology. In contrast to its numerous applications there are only a few attempts to give a general definition (Turtune, 1987). According to Klauer (1988), a strategy is a plan of a sequence of actions to attain a prespecified goal. According to Bruner, Goodnow, and Austin (1956), a strategy refers to a pattern of decisions in the acquisition, retention, and utilization of information that serves to meet certain objectives. According to Turtune (1987), researchers in fields such as language development and production systems (artificial intelligence, AI) agree that (a) cognitive strategies are learned, (b) they involve manipulating and coordinating organized mental systems and mechanisms, (c) they are flexible, and (d) they may be conscious or voluntary (see also Siegler & Jenkins, 1989). Concerning assessment of strategies, Brainerd (1973), Ericsson and Simon (1980), and for a different view Smith (1992) are relevant references. See also the last section of this chapter.

(Van Geert, 1991). There are also consequences for the interpretation of reaction times, another source of behavioral data. A possible interpretation implies that we take reaction time as equilibration time (local or global relaxation time, see Kelso et al., 1993). Simply stated, when a subject is faced with a task, a strategy emerges and is executed at the moment it has reached a specific degree of stability.

The stability of strategies by perturbations was studied by Piaget by means of, for instance, countersuggestion. In fact, Piaget provided explicit descriptions of the stability of strategies in these terms. In present cognitive developmental psychology this idea has almost disappeared. We do not generally view training manipulations, feedback, generalization tasks, and such as perturbations. Yet, if a child gets confused by $6 + 5$ whereas the child can solve $4 + 5$ by counting fingers, a description in terms of instability may be very useful.

The absence of this general perspective on cognitive development is due, in part, to the rejection of the discontinuity hypothesis. Discontinuity is seen as one of the most problematic aspects of the Piagetian theory (Flavell, Miller, & Miller, 1993). However, this rejection should be reconsidered in the light of the recent popularity of the discontinuity concept (or phase transition) in physics, chemistry, biology, and embryology. We must realize that discontinuities do not pertain solely to general stages. They can also occur within domain-specific development where they might be detected more easily.

This recognition of attractor states in applications of nonlinear dynamic system theory does not follow a scientific procedure but can be checked afterward. This problem is known as "finding the bad state variables (in catastrophe theory) or order variables (in synergetics)." Checking afterward is important and feasible. If, for instance, we propose that sleeping stages are attractors, then a number of characteristic behaviors, like sudden jumps and hysteresis, should occur. The same is true of strategies. However, we do not elaborate here on the evidence for these characteristics in cognitive developmental psychology (see Van der Maas & Molenaar, 1992). We limit the discussion to the possibilities of collecting evidence that meets the requirements of modern psychometrics.

Following two independent lines of reasoning we show that latent class analysis can be used to test the hypothesis of a cognitive attractor. One line of reasoning concerns nonlinear dynamic system theory, and the other concerns cognitive developmental psychology.

ATTRACTORS AND PSYCHOMETRICS

The statistical application of nonlinear dynamic system theory to cognitive developmental psychology, and generally in social science, meets with various difficulties. First, mathematical equations of the system under study are not usually available. Second, given that we have identified the relevant variables, we cannot usually measure them on a ratio or interval scale. Third, if we can measure them we often cannot do so with a sufficiently high sample rate and for a sufficiently lengthy period.

For instance, to obtain reliable estimates of the dimension of deterministic chaos requires highly reliable dense and long time series, such as are usually only obtained with physiological or physical variables (Robertson, Cohen, & Mayer-Kress, 1993; Mayer-Kress et al., 1988). This limitation applies to a lesser extent to bifurcation theory, in which prototypical changes in attractor states are studied. In social science bifurcation theory is known as catastrophe theory. This theory is based on a classification of structurally stable bifurcations that depend on the number of dependent and independent variables (for references to introductory literature and for an example of an application to cognitive development see Van der Maas & Molenaar, 1992).

It is useful to relate catastrophe models to regression models. In univariate linear regression the value of the dependent variable, determined by the value of an independent variable, varies between certain statistical boundaries. It is thought that there is an optimal value, approximated by the regression line, but that all kinds of unsystematic factors perturb this optimal state. This optimal state can be seen as a quadratic minimum, reflected in the expectation of normally distributed error. The regression line shows the continuous change of a single quadratic minimum along the values of the independent variable. Nonlinear regression models do not differ in essence in this respect, because here too a single quadratic minimum changes in a continuous—for instance, logistic—way.

In catastrophe theory the same type of optimality is studied. Systems locally seek the state that minimizes some function of energy, cost, dissonance, and so on. However, the continuous changes of independent variables now involve sudden jumps to other existing quadratic minima, splittings of quadratic minima in two or more stable and unstable states, or even oscillatory behavior. A discontinuity in catastrophe models occurs by the disappearance of one quadratic minimum and the emergence of a distinct new, stable state under continuous variation of independent variables.

The cusp model in catastrophe theory concerns the behavior of a quartic function (instead of a quadratic function in regression analysis) controlled by two independent variables. The model is formulated as an apparently simple mathematical equation ($Y^3 - XY - Z = 0$, where Y is the dependent and X and Z are the independent variables). It is even possible to translate this equation to an equivalent stochastic probability distribution and apply maximum likelihood estimation to fit data of measured independent and dependent continuous variables (Cobb & Zacks, 1985). However, attempts to fit data meet with some difficult problems concerning scaling (Hartelman, Van der Maas, & Molenaar, 1995).

To explain this difficulty the comparison with regression analysis is again useful. The cusp model is like the most basic linear regression model without any parameters (both intercept and slope equal zero; see Morse Lemma in Poston & Stewart, 1978). The in principle (or better, qualitative) relation between the variables is all that is stated, without even referring to the sign (positive or negative) of this relation. Linear and nonlinear scalings of variables result in various types of regression models. Each can be tested. For the selection of the best regression model, however, theory is needed. That is, if we apply regression analysis, we have a prespecified hypothesis of the type of scaling (logarithmic, quadratic, linear, number of variables, interaction effects, etc.). The same is true for the cusp. The cusp equation only specifies the principal relation between two independent and one dependent variable. Hence, we cannot expect that in case of catastrophe models a computer program can test all types of nonlinear scalings hierarchically. The same type of prespecified hypothesis is needed to statistically fit the cusp model to the data.

To simplify this discussion we now focus on the behavioral variable only. An important prediction of catastrophe models is multimodality, in it simplest form bimodality. In terms of statistical distributions this means that there should be two or more peaks in the frequency distribution of scores on the dependent variable. At first sight the application of mixture distribution techniques (Everitt & Hand, 1981) seems best because these techniques possess straightforward statistics and allow for hierarchical testing of the number of peaks. However, two problems occur. First, these are parametric techniques,[2] and hence we must choose beforehand which type of distribution applies to each peak of the mixture. Second, mixture distribution techniques can test for the presence of a mixture of two (e.g., normal) distributions in which the variance strongly differs, whereas the means are equal. The resulting mixture has only one peak and is not bimodal. The first problem is relevant for stochastic catastrophe analysis in general. The cusp model does not predict the shape of the distribution of each of the peaks beyond the fact that they exist. Nonparametric techniques might prove useful, because then prior knowledge concerning the distributions is not required.

Bimodality is a well known criterion in cognitive developmental psychology, and reported for a large number of cognitive developmental tasks. The test score on these generally Piagetian tasks is the sum score of a number of incorrectly or correctly solved items, such as categorical data. In some rare cases we have scores on an interval or ratio scale for each item, for instance, when children have to give a quantitative prediction (Thomas,

---

[2]This is not necessarily true. There are mixture models for categorical data too. As Everitt and Dunn (1988) discussed, it is possible to formulate the latent class model in terms of a finite mixture density. In this chapter we assume that mixture techniques concern mixtures of normal and binomial distributions.

1989). In this case, the mixture techniques can be used. The sum scores of typical tests in cognitive developmental psychology are, however, in the best case, ordinal. Here the latent structure models are useful.

The indirect procedure is to construct a latent trait, estimate person and item parameters, and test whether item parameters are uniformly distributed and person parameters bimodally. With the present techniques this can be done in a single procedure (Mislevy & Bock, 1986; Mislevy & Wilson, 1995). The justification of this method is that the person parameters are characterized by a scale level that is higher than the sum scores. That means the distances between scale points are no longer arbitrary.

The direct procedure is more simple. We can fit latent class models to the categorical item responses and search for modes in the multinomial distribution directly. Each latent class forms a mode in this distribution. By equality restrictions we can force the latent class model to have a one-dimensional latent trait as in the indirect procedure (ordered classes, see Clogg, 1988), but this is not necessary.

The direct procedure is of great importance. Latent class analysis (LCA) provides very effective statistical tools to test for multimodality that require quite unproblematic assumptions. As a data analytic technique, LCA can be compared to cluster analysis in that both search for underlying groups or types. But LCA has significant advantages. These include maximum likelihood estimation, well-behaved statistics, and an enormous model flexibility. Hagenaars (1990) argued that LCA can be seen as a modified LISREL approach for categorical data. McCutcheon (1987) concluded: "LCA provides a powerful and flexible method for analyzing the causal structure of relations among qualitative measures without requiring assumptions about the normality of variables distributions" (p. 80). Hence we can test for multimodality and many other things even if our measurements are not on interval or ratio scales. Of great importance are also the development of latent class models for time series (for an overview, see Langeheine, 1994).

To demonstrate the advantage of this procedure we consider the classical example of multistable perception. In the perception of certain figures (like the Necker cube) two distinct attractors exist (in case of the Necker cube: hollow and solid). Several catastrophe models have been proposed for this phenomenon, all predicting hysteresis if certain stimulus characteristics are systematically increased and decreased in strength. This means that the switches between hollow and solid should take place for different values of the so-called bias, depending on the direction of change in this control parameter. For instance, seven items are constructed with increasing levels of bias and administered to two groups of subjects. One group is tested with items with increasing bias and the other with decreasing bias. They should switch between attractors for different levels of bias, such as on different items.

In measuring the behavioral variable we encounter an important problem: The perception of the stimulus is binary. The problem is that a continuous measure of the dependent variable seems necessary to overcome the criticism of explicit a priori discontinuous behavior (Zahler & Sussmann, 1977), and to allow for the application of Cobb's technique for fitting data to the catastrophe model. For these reasons some researchers ask subjects to judge stimuli on a continuous scale, for instance from −10 to 10 (Stewart & Peregoy, 1983), which seems to be a highly artificial procedure. However, the criticism of explicit a priori discontinuous behavior can be rejected for binary data too because of hysteresis, and by LCA we can fit hysteresis models to binary data. We will not go into the discussion of Sussmann and Zahler's criticism. It suffices to say that discontinuities are indeed a direct consequence of dichotomous measurement whereas hysteresis is not. The alternative Sussman and Zahler model (Sussmann & Zahler, 1978) of discontinuous change does not predict hysteresis.

In a Necker cube experiment by Ta'eed, Ta'eed, and Wright (1988), half of the subjects answer items in one sequence (left-to-right group) whereas the other half answer them in the opposite sequence (right-to-left group). A latent class model, based on Proctor's model (see McCutcheon, 1987), is specified in Table 7.1.

The parameters a and b are the conditional probabilities of answering hollow before and after the switch. That is, a should be large and b should be small. Other constraints are possible, for instance, $a = 1 - b$ or b(class 1) = c and b(class 2) = d. The choice of constraints takes place as in other scale models in LCA (see Clogg, 1988). A manifest direction variable is included and fixed at 1 and 0 in computation. This means that subjects of the left-to-right group can only switch on the right side of the sequence of items, that is, on item 5, 6, or 7. Subjects of the right-to-left group can only switch on items 1, 2, 3, and 4. The alternative model does not have these restrictions. The more restrictive model is nested under the alternative

TABLE 7.1
A Simple Latent Class Model for Hysteresis

	LP	i1	i2	i3	i4	i5	i6	i7	Direction
Class 1	p1	a	a	a	a	a	a	a	1 (i1 to i7)
Class 2	p2	a	a	a	a	a	a	b	1 (i1 to i7)
Class 3	p3	a	a	a	a	a	b	b	1 (i1 to i7)
Class 4	p4	a	a	a	a	b	b	b	1 (i1 to i7)
Class 5	p5	a	a	a	b	b	b	b	0 (i7 to i1)
Class 6	p6	a	a	b	b	b	b	b	0 (i7 to i1)
Class 7	p7	a	b	b	b	b	b	b	0 (i7 to i1)
Class 8	p8	b	b	b	b	b	b	b	0 (i7 to i1)

Note. i1 to i7 are items within increasing bias; a, b are conditional probabilities. Direction is used as a grouping parameter with fixed conditional probabilities. LP are latent class proportions, $\Sigma p = 1$. Expected values of estimates are $a \approx 1$, $b \approx 0$. In the alternative model the grouping parameter is not fixed.

model so that the restriction of hysteresis can be tested statistically (using a likelihood ratio test).

Analyses of simulated data show that this procedure works quite well. Data were simulated according to a stochastic differential equation based on the cusp model of catastrophe theory (Cobb & Zacks, 1985).

STRATEGIES AND PSYCHOMETRICS

There exists a long and complex discussion in cognitive developmental psychology and psychometrics concerning the testability of cognitive strategies. The measurement of proportional reasoning is a good example of this discussion. A famous task to assess proportional reasoning is the balance scale (Siegler, 1981).

In this task children are shown a balance scale with discrete weights at pins at different distances from the center. They have to judge whether the scale is well balanced or that one of the sides will go down. The torque, that is, the difference in product of weights and distances, is the correct cue. Researchers seem to agree that the assumption of strategies is necessary, although they disagree importantly in how to unveil these strategies.

Piaget required verbal justifications to determine which strategy is used by a given child. However, this so-called clinical approach has been heavily attacked and at present nonverbal methods are preferred (Brainerd, 1973; Miller, 1976). Siegler's (1981) rule assessment methodology is a good example of a nonverbal approach. Siegler proposed the use of six item types that differentiate among four rules that are quite similar to the Piagetian substages. The idea is that systematic errors on these item types (each four items) reflect the strategy used (see also Tatsuoka, 1983).

Siegler used a rather informal way to score response patterns. Criteria like 20 out of 24 according to one of the four rules are arbitrary from a psychometric point of view. However, a suitable choice of a statistical model for this type of rule assessment was not obvious. Factor-analytic and latent-trait models both assume continuous latent dimensions. Although both can handle dichotomous data, they assume that subjects can be ordered on one or more latent continua. The strategy concept seems to conflict with this basic assumption.

Two examples illustrate the problems of applying latent trait theory to balance scale data. Wilson (1989) applied an extension of the Rasch model to detect transitions in the development of balance scale reasoning. Wilson's model concerns the ordering and discrimination of substages in discontinuous development by group membership parameters. This method only worked for the rule I to rule II transition, although statistical results were not presented. Moreover, young subjects were excluded and even one item type was left out because this item type, conflict weight, was easier to solve using rule I than using rule III, which violates the assumption of unidimensionality. Some technical problems can be solved by reformulating the model as a linear latent-trait model (LLTM, Fischer, 1992). Recently, Mislevy and Wilson (1995) proposed an improved Saltus model based on marginal maximum likelihood estimation.

The second example concerns a more indirect method to apply the LLTM (Fischer, 1973). Van Maanen, Been, and Sijtsma (1989) discussed reasons why Spada's (1976) application of the LLTM did not fit balance scale data. The item parameter is a weighted sum of the cognitive processes involved in each item type. The authors note two strong requirements for the LLTM. First, there should be an underlying continuous latent trait as in the Rasch model. Second, all subjects should use the same strategy. Van Maanen et al. see the latter requirement of an universal cognitive process as a major problem. The first and second requirement are closely related. Their solution is to discriminate strategy groups first, by means of cluster analysis, and then apply the LLTM to each cluster separately. Although the cluster solution seems readily interpretable in terms of Siegler's rules, the LLTMs still do not fit. In their discussion of the paper they make a very interesting remark: "In this research the standard deviation of the raw scores in the four strategy homogeneous groups is relatively small in every case" (p. 284). This is problematic because all subjects are then scaled within a rather small interval. The reason they give seems valid: "A strategy homogeneous group consists of subjects which generate in principle the same answer pattern" (p. 284).

This is where the first requirement of Rasch-like models is violated. In case of multiple strategies there is no one-dimensional continuous latent trait. The authors conclude that "after all one can argue that an analysis of the data with a latent class model should be preferred" (p. 284).

This is exactly the point we are trying to make. Cognitive strategies should be detected by nonverbal methods in which response patterns to multiple tasks or items are collected. The analysis of these response patterns should take place by models of typologies, clusters, and, in view of their advantages, by latent class models. Technically, some special latent trait models can be quite similar to latent class models. In the last years several mixed models have been proposed (Rost, 1990; Mislevy & Verhelst, 1990; Mislevy & Wilson, 1995) in which both the concepts of class and trait are applied. Although much progress can be expected in this field, the general statement that strategies should be modeled by latent classes seems valid. From the point of view of interpretation the relation between strategies and latent classes is very direct.

In the literature some nice examples of the application of latent class analysis to rule and strategy detection on other cognitive tasks can be found in Bergan, Towstopiat, Cancelli, and Karp (1982), Dayton and Macready (1983), Macready and Dayton (1994), and Rindskopf (1987). A simple model for balance scale data is shown in Table 7.2.

TABLE 7.2
A Simple Latent Class Model for Balance Scale Data

Rule	LP	Item Types					
		CB	CD	CW	D	W	B
I	p1	b	b	a	b	a	a
II	p2	b	b	a	a	a	a
III	p3	c	c	c	a	a	a
IV	p4	a	a	a	a	a	a

Note. I to IV are rules defined by Siegler. Item types are a conflict balance item (CB), a conflict distance item (CD), a conflict weight item (CW), a distance item (D), a weight item (W), and a balance item (B); $p1$ to $p4$ are the proportions of the mutually exclusive latent classes associated with rules; a to c are conditional probabilities specifying the probability of a correct response for each class for each item; and $p1$ to $p4 \in [0,1]$, $\Sigma p = 1$, $a, b, c \in [0,1]$. Expected values of estimates: $a \approx 1$, $b \approx 0$, and $c \approx \frac{1}{3}$.

There are three reasons why this model is too simple. First, although it is in exact agreement with Siegler's (1981) model, it does not fit empirical data. The equalities are too restrictive, rule III should be replaced by more advanced guessing strategies, and other rules, like the famous addition rule, exist (Jansen & Van der Maas, in press). Second, each of the item types consists of four or five items, implying cross-tables of millions of cells. Analyses of more than six to eight items are not practical with present techniques. A solution might be to arrange the balance scale test in five parts, where each part consists of one item of each type. We can fit latent class models to each part, and even fit latent Markov models (Langeheine, 1994) to test for learning effects within one test session. Third, these analyses require lots of data (hundreds of subjects). Such datasets are rare. This is more a practical problem (for all latent structure models).

Jansen and Van der Maas (in press) applied latent class analysis to the data set of Van Maanen et al. (1989). They fitted models to sets of items of all item types as well as to sets of items of a single item type. In Table 7.3 the parameter estimates of a model of four classes for five conflict balance

TABLE 7.3
Latent Class Model of Responses to the Conflict-Balance Items

Class	Latent	CB1	CB2	CB3	CB4	CB5
1	.36	.00	.00	.00	.00	.00
2	.26	.28	.28	.28	.28	.28
3	.25	.88	.88	.88	.88	.88
4	.13	.31	.31	.82	.82	.31

Note. $N = 472$. CB1, 2, 3, 4, 5 are conflict-balance items 1, 2, 3, 4, and 5. From Jansen and Van der Maas (in press). Reprinted by permission.

items are shown. This model has χ^2 of 30.9 with 24 degrees of freedom and is the best fitting model according to the AIC and BIC indexes. Class 1, 2, and 3 can be identified as rule I, III, and IV, whereas class 4 fits the addition rule (because only the third and the fourth item can be correctly solved by addition).

CONCLUSION

In cognitive developmental psychology the strategy concept is generally accepted and applied as a domain-specific unit of analysis (Siegler & Jenkins, 1989). It can be found in many research areas, tests, theories, and models, making up a large but fragmented body of knowledge on cognitive strategies. Debates focus on different aspects of the strategy concept. These concern their symbolic or nonsymbolic nature, their development, their place in cognitive architectures and process models, and their empirical detection.

The proposed link between the strategy and the attractor concept is well connected with current cognitive and psychometric research. Some see nonlinear dynamic system theory as incompatible with current research traditions, and argue for an entirely new approach. In our proposal, there is in fact a high degree of compatibility. We see nonlinear dynamic system theory as an additional theoretical framework, concerning the change of strategies or strategy development.

In this respect, we have an old research tradition in which reequilibration, self-organization, and perturbation of cognitive operators play a central role. One could say that there is nothing new. With regard to the intentions this is true, but instead of Piaget's informal equilibration theory we can now apply the formal mathematical notions of nonlinear dynamic system theory, and instead of arbitrary scoring procedures for rules we now have formal statistical tests.

We have shown that besides the conceptual link between strategies and attractors, a link to the concept of latent classes can be made. We presented two arguments that LCA is the most direct psychometric model for both strategy and attractor detection, respecting the categorical level of most of cognitive developmental psychology data. Viewing attractors, strategies, and latent classes as equivalent gives us a practical connection between cognitive developmental psychology, nonlinear dynamic system theory, and psychometrics.

ACKNOWLEDGMENT

The research of Dr. H. L. J. van der Maas has been made possible by a fellowship of the Royal Netherlands Academy of Arts and Sciences.

REFERENCES

Amirkhiabani, G., & Hendry, G. D. (1994). Cognitive strategies. *Perceptual and Motor Skills, 78,* 491–500.

Amit, D. J. (1989). *Modelling brain function: The world of attractor neural networks.* Cambridge, England: Cambridge University Press.

Bergan, J. R., Towstopiat, O., Cancelli, A. A., & Karp, C. (1982). Replacement and component rules in hierarchically ordered mathematics rule learning tasks. *Journal of Educational Psychology, 74,* 39–50.

Brainerd, C. J. (1973). Judgements and explanations as criteria for the presence of cognitive structures. *Psychological Bulletin, 79,* 172–179.

Brainerd, C. J. (1978). The stage question in cognitive-developmental theory. *Behavioral and Brain Sciences, 2,* 173–213.

Bruner, J. S., Goodnow, J. J., & Austin, G. A. (1956). *A study of thinking.* New York: Wiley.

Butterworth, G. (1993). Dynamic approaches to infant perception and action: Old and new theories about the origin of knowledge. In L. B. Smith & E. Thelen (Eds.), *A dynamic systems approach to development* (pp. 171–187). Cambridge, MA: MIT Press.

Clogg, C. C. (1988). Latent class models for measuring. In R. Langeheine & J. Rost (Eds.), *Latent trait and latent class analysis* (pp. 173–205). New York: Plenum Press.

Clogg, C. C. (1994). Latent class models. In G. Arminger, C. C. Clogg, & M. E. Sobel (Eds.), *Handbook of statistical modeling in the behavioral and social sciences* (pp. 311–360). New York: Plenum Press.

Cobb, L., & Zacks, S. (1985). Applications of catastrophe theory for statistical modelling in the biosciences. *Journal of the American Statistical Association, 80,* 793–802.

Dayton, C. M., & Macready, G. B. (1983). Latent structure analysis of repeated classifications with dichotomuous data. *British Journal of Mathematical and Statistical Psychology, 36,* 189–121.

Ericsson, K. A., & Simon, H. H. (1980). Verbal reports as data. *Psychological Review, 87,* 215–251.

Everitt, B. S., & Dunn, G. (1988). Log-linear modelling, Latent class analysis, or correspondence analysis. In R. Langeheine & J. Rost (Eds.), *Latent trait and latent class analysis* (pp. 109–127). New York: Plenum Press.

Everitt, B. S., & Hand, D. J. (1981). *Finite mixture distributions.* London: Chapman and Hall.

Fischer, G. H. (1973). The linear logistic test model as an instrument in education research. *Acta Psychologica, 37,* 359–374.

Fischer, G. H. (1992). The "Saltus" model revisited. *Methodika, 6,* 87–98.

Flavell, J. H., Miller, P. H., & Miller, S. (1993). *Cognitive development.* Englewood Cliffs, NJ: Prentice Hall.

Garcia, R. (1992). The structure of knowledge and the knowledge of structure. In H. Beilin & P. Pufall (Eds.), *Piaget's theory: Prospects and possibilities* (pp. 21–37). Hillsdale, NJ: Lawrence Erlbaum Associates.

Gleick, J. (1987). *Chaos: Making a new science.* New York: Penguin Books.

Hagenaars, J. A. (1990). *Categorical longitudinal data.* Newbury Park, CA: Sage.

Hambleton, R. K., & Swaminathan, H. (1985). *Item response theory: Principles and applications.* Boston: Kluwer-Nijhoff.

Hartelman, P., Van der Maas, H. L. J., & Molenaar, P. C. M. (1995). *Stochastic catastrophe theory.* Manuscript submitted for publication.

Jansen, B. R. J., & Van der Maas, H. L. J. (in press). A statistical test of the rule assessment methodology by latent class analysis. *Developmental Review.*

Jöreskog, K. G., & Sörbom, D. (1988). *LISREL VII: A guide to the program and applications.* Chicago: SPSS, Inc.

Keating, D. P. (1990). Developmental processes in the socialization of cognitive structures. *Entwicklung und Lernen: Beiträge zum symposium anläßlich des 60. Geburtstages von Wolfgang Edelstein*. Berlin: MaxPlanck Institut für Bildungsforschung.

Kelso, J. A. (1984). Phase transitions and critical behavior in human bimanual coordination. *American Journal of Physiology: Regulatory, Integrative and Comparative Physiology, 15*, 1000–1004.

Kelso, J. A. S., Ding, M., & Schöner, G. (1993). Dynamic pattern formation: A primer. In L. B. Smith & E. Thelen (Eds.), *A dynamic systems approach to development* (pp. 13–50). Cambridge, MA: MIT Press.

Klauer, K. J. (1988). Teaching for learning-to learn: A critical appraisal with some proposals. *Instructional Science, 17*, 351–367.

Langeheine, R. (1994). Latent variables Markov models. In A. von Eye & C. C. Clogg (Eds.), *Latent variables analysis: Applications for developmental research* (pp. 373–398). Thousand Oaks, CA: Sage.

Lewis, M. D. (1994). Reconciling stage and specificity in neo-Piagetian theory: Self-organizing conceptual structures. *Human Development, 37*, 143–169.

Mayer-Kress, G., Yates, F. E., Benton, L., Keidel, M., Tirsch, W., Pöppl, S. J., & Geist, K. (1988). Dimensional analysis of nonlinear oscillations in brain, heart, and muscle. *Mathematical Biosciences, 90*, 155–182.

Macready, G. B., & Dayton, C. M. (1994). Latent class models for longitudinal assessment of trait acquisition. In A. von Eye & C. C. Clogg (Eds.), *Latent variables analysis: Applications for developmental research* (pp. 245–273). Thousand Oaks, CA: Sage.

McCutcheon, A. L. (1987). *Latent class analysis*. Sage University Paper Series on Quantitative Applications in the Social Sciences, Series No. 07-064. Beverly Hills, CA: Sage.

Mellenbergh, G. J. (1994). Generalized linear response theory. *Psychological Bulletin, 115*, 300–307.

Miller, S. A. (1976). Nonverbal assessment of Piagetian concepts. *Psychological Bulletin, 83*, 405–430.

Mislevy, R. J., & Bock, R. D. (1986). *PC-BILOG: Item analysis and test scoring with binary logistic models*. Mooresville, IN: Scientific Software, Inc.

Mislevy, R. J., & Verhelst, N. (1990). Modeling item responses when different subjects employ different solution strategies. *Psychometrika, 55*, 195–215.

Mislevy, R. J., & Wilson, M. (1995). Marginal maximum likelihood estimation for a psychometric model of discontinuous development. *Psychometrika, 61*, 41–72.

Molenaar, P. C. M. (1986). On the impossibility of acquiring more powerful structures: A neglected alternative. *Human Development, 29*, 245–251.

Piaget, J. (1978). *The development of thought: Equilibration of cognitive structures*. Oxford: Blackwell.

Poston, T., & Stewart, I. (1978). *Catastrophe theory and its applications*. London: Pitman.

Preece, P. F. W. (1980). A geometrical model of Piagetian conservation. *Psychological Reports, 46*, 143–148.

Rasch, G. (1980). *Probabilistic models for some intelligence and attainments tests*. Chicago: University of Chicago Press.

Rindskopf, D. (1987). Using latent class analysis to test developmental models. *Developmental Review, 7*, 66–85.

Robertson, S. S., Cohen, A. H., & Mayer-Kress, G. (1993). Behavioral chaos: Beyond the metaphor. In L. B. Smith & E. Thelen (Eds.), *A dynamic systems approach to development* (pp. 119–150). Cambridge, MA: MIT Press.

Rost, J. (1990). Rasch models in latent classes: an integration of two approaches to item analysis. *Applied Psychological Measurement, 14*, 271–282.

Saari, D. G. (1977). A qualitative model for the dynamics of cognitive processes. *Journal of Mathematical Psychology, 15*, 145–168.

Saunders, P. T., & Kubal, C. (1989). Bifurcations and the epigenetic landscape. In B. Goodwin & P. Saunders (Eds.), *Theoretical biology: Epigenetic and evolutionary order drom complex systems* (pp. 16–30). Edinburgh: Edinburgh University Press.

Siegler, R. S. (1981). Developmental sequences within and between concepts. *Monographs of the Society for Research in Child Development, 46*(2), 84.

Siegler, R. S., & Jenkins, E. (1989). *How children discover new strategies.* Hillsdale, NJ: Lawrence Erlbaum Associates.

Smith, L. (1992). Judgements and justifications: Criteria for the attribution of children's knowledge in Piagetian research. *British Journal of Developmental Psychology, 10*, 1–23.

Spada, H. (1976). *Modelle des Denkens und Lernens.* Bern: Huber.

Stewart, I. N., & Peregoy, P. L. (1983). Catastrophe theory modeling in psychology. *Psychological Bulletin, 94*, 336–362.

Sussmann, H. J., & Zahler, R. S. (1978). A critique of applied catastrophe theory in the behavioral sciences. *Behavioral Science, 23*, 383–389.

Ta'eed, L. K., Ta'eed, O., & Wright, J. E. (1988). Determinants involved in the perception of the Necker cube: An application of catastrophe theory. *Behavioral Science, 33*, 97–115.

Tatsuoka, K. K. (1983). Rule space: an approach for dealing with misconceptions based on item response theory. *Journal of Educational Measurement, 20*(4), 345–354.

Thelen, E., Kelso, J. A. S., & Fogel, A. (1987). Self-organizing systems and infant motor development. *Developmental Review, 7*, 39–65.

Thomas, H. (1989). A binomial mixture model for classification performance: A commentary on Waxman, Chambers, Yntema, and Gelman (1989). *Journal of Experimental Child Psychology, 48*, 423–430.

Turtune, J. E. (1987). Social influences on cognitive strategies and cognitive development: The role of communication and instruction. *Intelligence, 11*, 77–89.

Van der Maas, H. L. J., & Molenaar, P. C. M. (1992). Stagewise cognitive development: An application of catastrophe theory. *Psychological Review, 99*, 395–417.

Van Geert, P. (1991). A dynamic systems model of cognitive and language growth. *Psychological Review, 98*, 3–53.

Van Maanen, L., Been, P. H., & Sijtsma, K. (1989). The linear logistic test model and heterogenity of cognitive strategies. In E. E. Roskam (Ed.), *Mathematical psychology in progress* (pp. 267–288). Berlin: Springer-Verlag.

Wilson, M. (1989). Saltus: A psychometric model of discontinuity in cognitive development. *Psychological Bulletin, 105*, 276–289.

Zahler, R. S., & Sussmann, H. J. (1977). Claims and accomplishments of applied catastrophe theory. *Nature, 269*, 759–763.

III

DEVELOPMENT OF COMMUNICATION

8

Nonlinear Dynamics of Brain Regions and the Design of Neuronal Growth-Cycle-Based Cognitive Tasks

Pieter H. Been

University of Groningen

Cognitive development depends on the maturation of intracortical connections and the differentiation of cortical subsystems (Thatcher, 1994). As far as cognitive development has been considered in this dependency, (neo)Piagetian theories have been predominant. The established relationship between Piagetian stages and cortical development is based on the observation that there are cycles in both developmental processes that can be loosely tied together (Hudspeth & Pribram, 1990; Thatcher, 1994). Neural network models of cognitive processes (Grossberg, 1982, 1988) open the way to relate cortical and cognitive development in a more rigorous fashion because in such models cortical developmental parameters such as synaptic density can be incorporated at an aggregated level (Cowan & Ermentrout, 1978). The inherent cognitive complexity of Piagetian tasks seems to make the establishment of a rigorous connection between cognitive and cortical development prohibitive. By complexity is meant that numerous cognitive subprocesses are involved. The first implication of this observation is that modeling at the neural network level is not within our scope for the time being. The second is that the many cognitive subprocesses involved are related to different cortical subsystems, with each subsystem characterized by different cortical maturation cycles. In such a case demonstration of clear-cut relationships becomes difficult.

To simplify matters one could proceed in a bottom-up fashion, as exemplified here. The strategy is to select a brain region that fulfills two prerequisites: It shows a clear-cut maturation cycle, and it performs a cognitive process that can be modeled at the neural network level. As we shall see, the parieto-occipital region of the brain that allows selective spatial attention in visual information processing is a good candidate for this approach. In working our way up from the neuronal level to behavior we need a nonlinear dynamic model, because most processes in the brain are inherently nonlinear (Grossberg, 1982). First, the nonlinear dynamic properties of the model, such as hysteresis, are studied during real-time processing at a microscopic time scale during different input conditions. The different input conditions mimic different cognitive tasks. The output of the model is related to real-time cognitive behavior in the form of evoked potentials, reaction times (RTs), and errors. This opens the way to put the model to empirical tests, as has been partially done. Second, the incorporation of developmental cortical parameters—as well as of disturbed cognitive development suspect of underlying physiological deficiencies in the brain(congenital dyslexia)—is used for predictions of cognitive development at the macroscopic time scale.

The approach adopted here is somewhat different from that adopted in other studies of nonlinear dynamic phenomena in development (Thatcher, 1994; Van der Maas & Molenaar, 1992). Instead of looking for nonlinear phenomena in observations, observations are predicted from nonlinear models proceeding from an *"Ansatz."*

THE PARIETO-OCCIPITAL
AND TEMPORAL REGION

Maturation

One of the most clearly shaped cortical maturation cycles shows up in the electroencephalographic (EEG) frequency spectrum in the parieto occipital region of the brain, as computed by Hudspeth and Pribram (1990) on the data of a cross-age sample from Matouček and Petersén (1973). Hudspeth and Pribram used the sum of the squared vector lengths of the amplitudes in a number of EEG frequency bands.

Figure 8.1 shows the amplitude of the frequency band (normalized for the amplitudes in the other frequency bands) and its first derivate ("velocity") recomputed from the same data. The growth spurts in the maturation cycle, as exhibited most clearly by the velocity, correspond nearly exactly with growth spurts in EEG coherence in the nearby parieto-temporal region (Thatcher, 1994, p. 237, Fig. 8.1), which may be considered a sign of increment of intracortical synaptic relays. The same observation applies to the amplitude of the EEG frequency spectrum in the α band (Been, 1994). Because learning is reflected in an increase in the volume of synaptic knobs or the number of synaptic relays (Cotman & Lynch, 1990) the relationship

Relative amplitude EEG in the alpha band

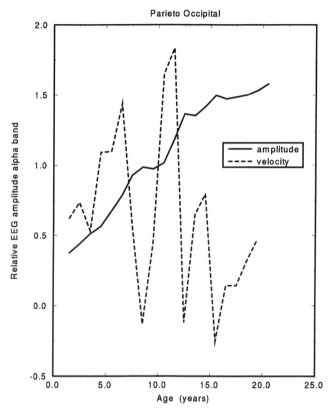

FIG. 8.1. Development of amplitude of EEG and its first derivative (velocity) in the α band.

with development, be it maturational or induced by the environment, is established by these measurements.

Function

The occipital, posterior parietal, and temporal areas of the brain are involved in visual information processing. The areas are connected by the two main pathways of the visual system: the magno- and parvocellular pathway. Starting at the level of the retinal ganglia, both pathways project via the LGN to the occipital cortex (Livingstone & Hubel, 1988). From the occipital area the parvo pathway projects to the temporal area and the magno pathway to the parietal occipital area (Mishkin, Ungerleider, & Macko, 1983). Although both pathways probably interact, a number of distinct functions can be assigned to them. The parvo pathway provides, for instance, for color vision and pattern recognition, is sensitive to high spatial frequencies in patterns, and has a high threshold for contrast. Some functions assigned to the magno pathway are movement perception, sensitivity to low spatial frequencies, high contrast sensitivity, and storage of the spatial location of visual patterns (Livingstone & Hubel, 1988). As far as contrast sensitivity is involved, an important observation from the dynamical point of view is that the magno system saturates at low contrast levels whereas the parvo system does not saturate for contrast levels. Saturation means leveling off of response: The system works in a nonlinear fashion. The parvo system, showing no signs of saturation, may be considered to work linearly (Livingstone & Hubel, 1988; Previc, 1990).

Because of the pattern recognition function of the parvo pathway and the spatial location function of the magno pathway, Mishkin et al. (1988) distinguished the two pathways as the "what" and "where" systems respectively. The global architecture of both systems is sketched in Fig. 8.2.

Mishkin et al. assumed that only feedforward pathways are involved. Because it is well known that intracortical processes feed back from late to early processes (Zeki, 1993; Zeki & Shipp, 1988), feedback pathways between the areas have been added. Such an arrangement also explains the oscillatory nature of intracortical processes (Thatcher, 1994), as we see later.

We now have a global sketch of the architecture of the where and what system and some indications of their (non)linear properties. Both systems interact to provide a mechanism for early processes in selective visual spatial attention as studied in psychological experimental research.

Disturbances

At least some reading-disabled children show disturbances in the functioning of the magno system. The afterimage of presented stimuli persists longer in the reading disabled, which could be a symptom of a decreased inhibition of the parvo system by the magno system (Lovegrove, Heddle, & Slaghuis, 1980; Slaghuis & Lovegrove, 1986, 1987). In addition, reading-disabled children are less sensitive to contrast, especially at lower spatial frequencies (Lovegrove et al., 1982; Martin & Lovegrove, 1984). The magno path is very sensitive to contrast and more sensitive to low spatial frequencies than the parvo path, and this is also a sign of disturbed functioning of the magno pathway of reading-disabled children. Furthermore, dyslexic children are less able in the detection of visual flicker stimuli presented at high flicker rates (Brannan & Williams, 1988). Normally the magno system has high temporal resolution, so again this is a sign of impoverished magno processing in dyslexics. According to Winters, Patterson, and Shontz (1989), 75% of dyslexics suffer from disturbances in the magno system.

Autopsies of congenital dyslexics show cytoarchitectural distortions in the cortex (Galaburda, 1983; Kemper, 1984), which may be caused by excessive testosterone production during fetal life (Geschwind, 1983). If brain

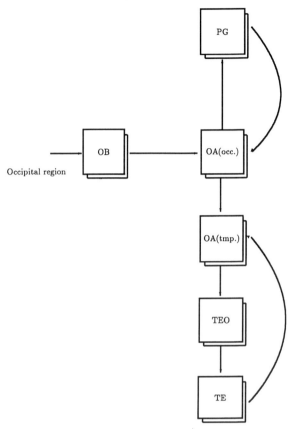

FIG. 8.2. Global architecture of the where and what system. Abbrevations according to Mishkin et al. (1983). TE(O): temporal cortex, OC: occipital cortex, PG: parietal cortex. Correspondence of OC and intermediate areas OA, OB, and TEO with nomenclature of the visual system in parentheses (Zeki, 1993): OA (V3, V4, V5), OB (V2), and OC (V1). OA(occ.): OA occipital. OA(tmp.): OA temporal.

structures relayed by the magno path suffer from cytoarchitectural distortions, such as a lowered density of neurons, this places an upper bound on the possible number of synaptic relays. This hypothesis, reflecting a congenital disturbance of neural development in dyslexics, is adopted here.

SELECTIVE ATTENTION IN VISUAL INFORMATION PROCESSING

Attention in the visual system is a well-studied subject both from the psychological and the physiological point of view (Kosslyn & Anderson, 1992; Van der Heijden, 1992). At least two mechanisms play a role in selective attention in the visual system, although there are probably more (Alport, 1989). Processes that arrange for global attention are left out of consideration.

First, selective attention in the visual system depends on the required (motor) response. An explanation is that higher order (late) processes feed back to lower order (early) processes (Mesulam, 1981; Van der Heijden, 1992).

Second—and this is the process we are interested in—selective attention plays a role during early information processing in the visual system and is probably dependent on sensory representations in the posterior parietal cortex (Mesulam, 1981). The phenomenon of selective attention shows up in cue stimulus paradigms. Cues given at the same location as the subsequent stimulus, with an interval between, say, 100 and 400 msec, speed up recognition times of stimuli. A typical result is that longer intervals go with shorter recognition times and that the effect levels off at longer cue stimulus intervals (Eriksen & Murphy, 1987; Remington & Pierce, 1984).

If early selective attention in visual information processing is dependent on sensory representations in the parietal lobe, then the where system is involved.

Now, the challenge is to specify a dynamic model, incorporating the architecture and physiological properties of the where and what system, that can explain the leveling off facilitation of cues in stimulus recognition experiments. When in addition new phenomena can be predicted and demonstrated, this will corroborate the model.

DYNAMIC MODEL

Architecture

In Fig. 8.3 an approximated architecture of the where and what system is represented as a graph of dynamic model of a neuronal net. The relay to area TEO in the inferior temporal cortex in Fig. 8.3 is left out for reasons of parsimony. In this context it is supposed that the what loop in the dynamic model provides for pattern recognition and that the where loop of the model is sensitive to the spatial location of patterns. The variables in the boxes represent (evoked) potentials, which are related to RTs and errors at the behavioral level (John, 1977; Ritter, Simson, Vaughan, & Friedman, 1979).

The upper box is the where system; the lower box is the what system. The straight lines represent excitatory feedforward connections. The curved lines are inhibitory feedback loops. The where box contains two loops that are interconnected by an inhibitory pathway. This pathway arranges for lateral inhibition, because it is well known that the visual system shows

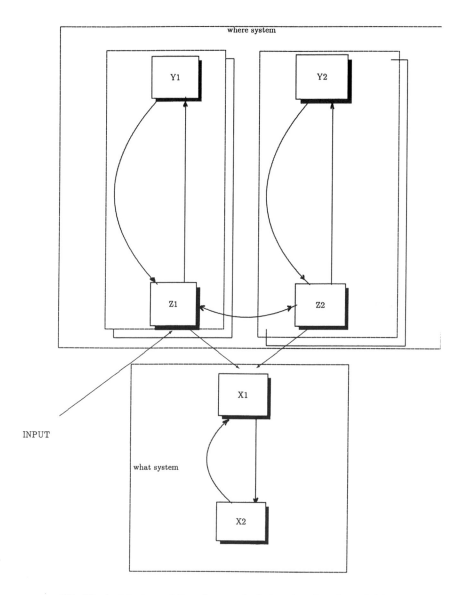

FIG. 8.3. Architecture of the where and what system transformed into a dynamic model. Correspondence with the cortical areas in Fig. 8.2: Input received from OB; z_i: OA occipital; y_i: PG; x_1: OA temporal; x_2: TE.

on-center, off-surround mechanisms (Grossberg, 1982). The two loops of the
where system correspond with different spatial locations in the visual field.
Input at location z_1 activates the where loop z_1-y_1, which inhibits the z_2-y_2
loop. The evoked potential in z_1 is determined by the input, and the activity
of both where loops. This activity is transferred to the what loop by means
of x_1; the evoked potential in the what loop may be in- or decreased, causing
enhanced or deprived pattern recognition. Increment occurs when stimuli
are presented with short intervals at the same location. When subsequent
stimuli are presented at different locations a decrement in the what loop
caused by lateral inhibition may occur. In this way the where system makes
some parts of the visual field more sensitive and other parts less sensitive
for the detection of subsequent patterns. Selective attention to specific
locations in the visual field is the result.

Because of the inhibitory feedback the loops in the minor boxes in the
where system—and the loop in the what system—are oscillators. The frequency of these oscillations depends on the strength of the pathways and
is called the *eigen frequency*. The concept of eigen frequency is important
in this context and recurs often.

The oscillators in the where system may be considered nonlinear, mim-
icking the saturation effects in the magno system. The what system is a
linear oscillator. The couplings are linear coefficients, because the what
system behaves linearly from the dynamic point of view.

Differential Equations

Starting from the neuronal level, Cowan and Ermentrout (1978, Equation
2.50) derived equations that describe the global behavior of neuronal nets
containing excitatory and inhibitory neurons:

$$\dot{x} = -x + 2\varepsilon_{11}\phi(x) - 2\varepsilon_{12}\phi(y) + I_1 \tag{1}$$

$$\dot{y} = -y + 2\varepsilon_{21}\phi(x) - 2\varepsilon_{22}\phi(y) + I_2 \tag{2}$$

The x and y represent the voltages in the excitatory and inhibitory net,
respectively. Decay is incorporated in the model by the $-x$ and $-y$ terms.
The dimensionless parameters ε_{ij} determine the amount of inhibition (ε_{12},
ε_{22}) or excitation (ε_{21}, ε_{11}). The I_i represents an externally applied input. A
sigmoid (S-shaped) function

$$\phi(z) = \frac{q_0}{r+1}\{1 + \exp[-v(z-\theta)]\}^{-1} - p \tag{3}$$

arranges for the spreading of the voltage z with parameters q_0, which is
mean charge per impulse delivered by a neuron; r, the mean refractory

period of neurons in milliseconds; v, a constant fixing the mean sensitivity of neurons; θ, the mean threshold voltage of the neurons; and p, a constant to fix the rest potential.

The dimensionless parameters ε_{ij} are composites of the following parameters

$$\varepsilon_{ij} = b\rho\tau v q_0 \sigma / (r+1)C \tag{4}$$

attached to the physical units, where b is the mean number of synaptic connections from all neurons in the net to any given neuron; ρ is the packing density of neurons in the net; τ the product of estimated membrane resistance (R) of neurons times the estimated membrane capacitance (C) of neurons; v the constant fixing the estimated sensitivity of neurons to input; q_0 the mean charge of the neurons delivered per impulse; σ the boundary of the distance within which synaptic connections are supposed to occur; and r the estimated refractory period of neurons.

It is obvious that the mean number of synaptic connections (b) and the packing density of neurons (ρ) are parameters of interest in this context, because they are related to learning.

The equations can be used as general building blocks for the composition of models tailored to the execution of specific cognitive processes. Using the equations of Cowan and Ermentrout as building blocks the dynamics of the model architecture in Fig. 8.3 is described by the following six first-order differential equations.

$$\dot{x}_1 = z_1 + z_2 - ax_2 \tag{5}$$

$$\dot{x}_2 = -bx_1 \tag{6}$$

$$\dot{y}_1 = 2\varepsilon_1 \phi(z_1) \tag{7}$$

$$\dot{y}_2 = 2\varepsilon_1 \phi(z_2) \tag{8}$$

$$\dot{z}_1 = -\delta z_1 - 2\varepsilon_2 \phi(y_1) - 2\varepsilon_3 \phi(z_2) + I \tag{9}$$

$$\dot{z}_2 = -\delta z_2 - 2\varepsilon_2 \phi(y_2) - 2\varepsilon_3 \phi(z_1) \tag{10}$$

The first two equations (5 and 6) describe the workings of the what system; these equations are linear. The voltage levels x_1 and x_2 are multiplied by the coefficients a and b. Equations 7 and 9 describe the first loop of the where system, and equations 8 and 10 the second loop. The loops mutually inhibit by the parameter ε_3. The couplings in the where system are nonlinear by the choice of the S-shaped ϕ function. The δ parameter arranges for damping in the system.

Learning, development, and deficiencies can be incorporated in the dynamic model by a suitable choice of the ε_i parameters, which reflects the number of synaptic relays.

The symbol I represents the input into the system. The choice of a function for I depends on the cognitive process that is modeled. Possible choices for I are a single or double pulse of the form $t \exp(-t)$ (Rall, 1967) or a periodic pulse in the form of a cosine wave, $F \cos(\omega t)$, with F representing input force, ω angular input frequency, and t time. These choices of I are model equivalents of the following cognitive tasks.

A single pulse applied to the model is equivalent to single-pattern processing, such as a word or letter. A cue stimulus paradigm (before the stimulus is presented a location cue is provided) can be modeled by a double pulse. A periodic pulse with fixed or slightly varying frequencies (cosine wave) is an idealization of the process of reading. After each succeeding saccade a group of letters is processed. Also, an oddball paradigm can be modeled by a periodic pulse. In an oddball task a target should be detected among a train of stimuli. Finally, random input with widely varying frequencies is considered as the resting state of the visual system (eyes closed).

Simulations, Predictions, and Empirical Evidence

Single Pulse. When a single pulse is applied to the model, z_1 of the magno loop shows a damped oscillation, which reflects the eigen frequency. More synaptic relays (e.g., $\varepsilon_i = 8$) go with a higher eigen frequency and amplitude of the oscillations compared to a lesser synaptic density (e.g., $\varepsilon_i = 4$) (Been, 1994). The effect is transferred to the parvo loop by the $z_1 - x_1$ pathway. Thus the model predicts higher amplitudes in evoked potentials, which are positively correlated with RTs (Ritter et al., 1979) and with the probability of correct response (John, 1977) as a result of development and learning. Because the single pulse condition in the model is equivalent to single pattern recognition at the psychological level, development and learning should show up in higher amplitudes of evoked potentials, faster RTs, and diminished error rates. The hypothesis that the reading problems of dyslexics in a substantial number of cases may be caused by developmental disturbances in the magno pathway predicts diminished evoked potentials during pattern recognition, longer RTs, and increased error rates for this group compared to normal reading subjects. This is indeed observed (Ciesielski, 1989; Legein & Bouma, 1981).

Double Pulse. Figure 8.4 shows the behavior of the model at z_1 after applying a double pulse with the interval between two pulses varied. This input condition is comparable with a cue stimulus paradigm with variable intervals between cue and stimulus.

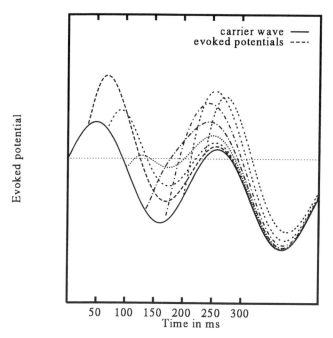

FIG. 8.4. Cue as carrier wave for the subsequent stimulus in a cue stimulus
paradigm with variable intervals.

The oscillation induced by the first pulse (cue) acts as a carrier wave for
the second pulse (stimulus). Thus, with variable cue stimulus intervals a
sinusoidal relationship between cue stimulus intervals and evoked potential
is predicted. The prediction holds for stimuli presented at the location of
the cue. When the subsequent stimulus is presented off the location of the
cue a phase shift in the carrier wave is predicted due to lateral inhibition.
Thus, a phase shift is predicted when the cue effect is compared for stimuli
on cue location and stimuli off cue location. We have demonstrated these
predicted relationships in reaction time experiments and evoked potential
studies with cue stimulus intervals varied between 40 and 200 msec with
steps of 14 msec (Kubat, 1997). Thus the exponential relationship between
cue-stimulus interval and RTs reported in earlier experimental studies (Eriksen & Murphy, 1987; Remington & Pierce, 1984) may be considered an
approximation of the more detailed picture predicted by the dynamic model.

Because the oscillation frequency of the carrier wave induced by the
magno system determines the sinusoidal relationship between cue stimulus
intervals and the evoked potentials and RTs, the eigen frequency of the
where system can be derived from this relationship by simply counting the
number of oscillations in a fixed interval. A typical result is an eigen frequency of about 8 Hz for adults without reading problems.

Periodic Pulse With Random Frequency: Power Spectra. From the assumption that random input from cortical areas outside the visual system represents the resting state of the visual system (eyes closed), the model predicts that the amplitude of the spontaneous EEG is at a maximum in the neighborhood of the eigen frequency of the system. This prediction is derived from the resonance property of oscillators: The amplitude of the output of an oscillating system reaches its maximum when the input frequency is near the eigen frequency (Halliday & Resnick, 1966). Because the eigen frequency of the model is determined by the number of synaptic relays, the maximum amplitude of the model output shifts to higher frequencies as a result of learning and development. This is illustrated by Fig. 8.5, which shows the power spectra computed on the model output for high and low synaptic density conditions. The power peak shifts to higher frequencies

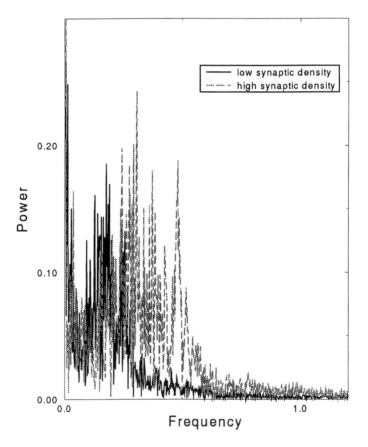

FIG. 8.5. Power spectra derived from model output show a shift of the power peak to higher frequencies when the number of synaptic relays in the model is increased.

when the synaptic model density is increased. In this way the model can explain the shifting of the maximum amplitude of the EEG in the parieto, occipital, and temporal region in Fig. 8.1 to higher frequency bands as age increases.

Periodic Pulse With Fixed or Slightly Varied Frequency: Attractors. A phase portrait of one loop in the where system can be obtained by plotting the evoked potential in the two populations of neurons z_i and y_i as time evolves. When a periodic pulse is delivered to the model below the eigen frequency a phase portrait with one attractor results. This is a sign of regular behavior: The input pulse is converted to an ouput pulse with the same characteristics. When the frequency of the imput pulse is in the neighborhood of the eigen frequency, irregular behavior of the magno loop can be seen. Figure 8.6 shows the phase portrait and output of the magno loop in this condition. Sometimes the signal sustains: A location cue is intruded in the ongoing recognition process. Sometimes the signal collapses: A location cue is missed. Such irregular behavior shows up in a phase portrait with two attractors. When the system remains in the lower attractor the systems collapses; in the upper attractor the system sustains. This behavior at a fixed input frequency is preserved when the input frequency is slightly varied in a random fashion.

The behavior of the nonlinear magno loop is passed to the linear parvo loop. Sometimes the system collapses (a feature is missed) and sometimes it sustains (a feature is intruded). Such omissions and intrusions are typical for the reading process of dyslexics (Critchley, 1964). The hypothesis of a reduced synaptic density in dyslexics offers the explanation that during reading the input frequency is in the neighborhood of their eigen frequency. The eigen frequency of dyslexics can be estimated at 3 Hz, which is equivalent to the typical speed of reading: After fixation times between 200 and 500 msec a saccadic jump of the eye brings the next text fragment on the fovea (Been, 1994).

Periodic Pulse With Systematically Varied Frequency: Hysteresis. A derived proof for irregular (nonlinear) dynamics—which is open to statistical test—can be obtained by the phenomenon of hysteresis, called jump resonance by electrical engineers (Shinners, 1979).

As we have seen, irregular dynamics shows up when a periodic input is applied with a frequency in the neigborhood of the eigen frequency of the system. Jump resonance in a dynamic system can be induced by applying a periodic input with increasing or decreasing frequencies in the neighborhood of the eigen frequency. At decreasing or increasing frequencies of the input signal the amplitude (and phase) of the output signal will change with a sudden jump. The point of change is different for the decreasing and increasing frequency condition. Hysteresis is shown in the phase portrait

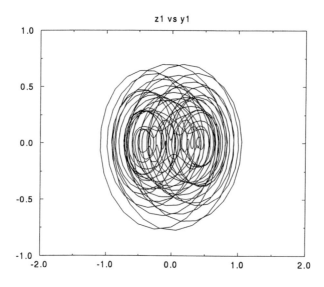

z1 vs y1

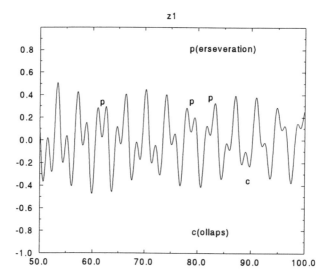

z1

FIG. 8.6. Behavior of z_1 of the magno loop with periodic forcing in the neighborhood of the eigen frequency. Phase portrait (above) and output signal (below). The phase portrait shows two attractors. When the system stays in the left attractor the output signal collapses. Staying in the right attractor means that the output signal sustains. Because the output signal is passed to the parvo loop omissions (because of collapse) and perseverations (sustaining signal) in pattern recognition occur. Parameter values: $a = b = 5$, $\varepsilon_1 = \varepsilon_2 = 17$, $\varepsilon_3 = .1$, $\delta = .03$, $F = 1.5$, $\omega = 1.5$, $v = .8$, $\theta = 0$, $p = .5$.

of the variables z_1 and y_1 in Fig. 8.7, obtained by applying a varying periodic pulse to the model. The sudden changes in amplitude are clearly visible. At increasing input frequency the amplitude rises with a sudden jump in the right part of the phase portrait. In the decreasing frequency condition the sudden rise of amplitude is in the left part of the phase portrait. Furthermore, in the range between both sudden jumps the amplitude in the decreasing frequency condition exceeds the amplitude of the increasing frequency condition.

The change of amplitude is a stable characteristic of the phase portrait. Thus, we can predict that the average amplitude of the evoked potential (and thus reaction times and error rates) will be different in the increasing and decreasing frequency condition. The upper part of Fig. 8.8 of averaged amplitudes obtained in the hysteresis condition demonstrates this. A bifurcation in amplitudes can be seen. The critical presentation frequency at which the bifurcation occurs is in the neighborhood of the eigen frequency of the neuronal net (Hale, 1969; Zeeman, 1977).

This prediction can be tested statistically on the output of human cognitive systems that process stimuli presented with increasing (decreasing) frequency in the neighborhood of the eigen frequency, by means of analysis of variance or regression techniques. A significant interaction between presentation frequency per se and the increment or decrement of the presentation frequency should be observed.

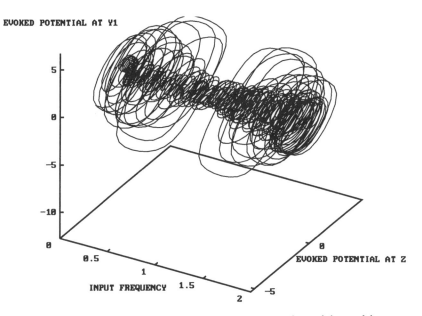

FIG. 8.7. Phase portrait of jump resonance in the magno loop of the model. Input frequency is increased from left to right and decreased from right to left.

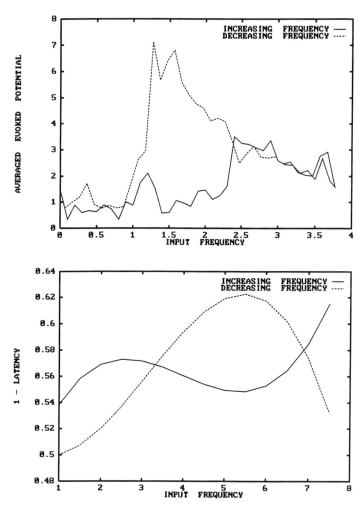

FIG. 8.8. Bifurcations. The upper part of the figure shows the averaged amplitude of model output in the de- and increasing frequency condition. Decreasing frequencies result in higher amplitudes in the hysteresis range. Model predictions are corroborated by the bifurcation in RTs obtained from a same location oddball task performed by a dyslexic reader in the lower part of the figure.

Apart from the desirable property that a formal test of a proposed dynamic model is made possible, the jump resonance phenomenon offers another advantage: There is no need for continuous sampling of the output signal. The phenomenon predicts the most probable (average) amplitude of the evoked potential of the cognitive system, given an increasing or decreasing presentation frequency. Obviously, averaged amplitudes of evoked potentials and related measures as reaction times can be obtained by stratified sampling, with the strata being defined by the presentation frequency per se and the increment or decrement of the presentation frequency. This opens the way for testing the phenomenon in reaction time tasks because the amplitude of the evoked potential is reflected in reaction times and error rates.

It is expected that the eigen frequency of a neuronal net is reflected in the dominant frequency of the EEG in rest. In the parieto-occipital regions this frequency is estimated to be about 8 Hz in normal adult readers and in at least some dyslexics about 3 Hz. Therefore, to induce jump resonance in feature detection in dyslexic readers the presentation frequency of stimuli should be varied in the 3 Hz neighborhood, and for normal adult readers in the 8 Hz neighborhood. These presentation rates are too fast to require a reaction to every stimulus presented. This problem can be circumvented by the use of an oddball paradigm: A stimulus train containing some targets is presented; the requirement is to react to targets only. When the stimulus train is divided into blocks containing one target with a fixed presentation rate and the presentation rate is varied between blocks, stratified sampling of reaction times and errors is possible.

To test whether the bifurcation induced by jump resonance shows up in reaction time tasks, the following variations of an oddball task are appropriate.

In the first variation a train of stimuli, containing a target, is presented with increasing or decreasing frequencies on the same location. Frequencies are varied between 1 and 12 Hz. In this case the where and what systems receive input with the same frequency. Thus, if jump resonance shows up this can be due to both the where and the what systems, although we expect that jump resonance occurs first in the where system (it is a property of nonlinear systems) and is passed to the linear what system. To disentangle the dynamics of the where and what systems an oddball variation can be designed that delivers different frequencies to the what and where systems. Stimuli are presented at a random location in a 3×3 matrix. Thus, the input frequency to the what system remains the same, whereas the input frequency to the where system is reduced to 1/9 (considerably below the eigen frequency). When jump resonance shows up in the same location variety and vanishes in the random location variety, the phenomenon may be ascribed to the where system.

The prediction of bifurcation has been tested by looking for a significant interaction between the increasing or decreasing condition and the input frequency by means analysis of variance. Dependent variables are reaction times and errors (Been, 1994).

In about 60% of dyslexic readers we have found a significant interaction and bifurcations between 2 and 4 Hz. The lower part of Fig. 8.8 shows an example. With 90% of normal adult readers we obtained significant interactions and bifurcations in the 7–10 Hz range. These observations apply to the same-location oddball paradigm.

In the random-position oddball paradigm all interactions are not significant. Jump resonance may be attributed to the where system, as expected.

DISCUSSION

The preceding paragraphs have demonstrated the feasibility of designing cognitive tasks executed by specific cortical regions by means of dynamic models of neuronal networks. Using the (non)linear properties of the model dynamics involved, the central concept of eigen frequency allows for differential predictions concerning the execution of these tasks in relation to learning and development. As far as the parieto, occipital, and temporal regions of the cortex are involved, the growth spurts in the maturation cycles of these cortical areas are indicators of an increasing eigen frequency, due to an increase in the number of intracortical synaptic relays.

As we have seen, there is a relationship between eigen frequency and

1. Amplitude of the spontaneous EEG in the α band
2. The oscillation frequency of the relationship between cue stimulus interval and behavioral measures in a cue stimulus paradigm
3. The fixed or slightly varied input frequency during periodic pattern recognition and the occurrence of two attractors in the EEG
4. The systematically varied input frequency during pattern recognition and the input frequency at which a bifurcation shows up in behavioral measures due to the phenomenon of hysteresis

Relationship 1 is an established fact, and relationship 3 is probably difficult to establish because of the low signal–noise ratio in the raw EEG. However, relationships 2 and 4 can be easily related to development in transversal and longitudinal studies, relating cortical growth spurts to differences in cognitive behavior. As far as disturbed cognitive development in reading is involved this already has been partially done. Neuronal growth-cycle-based cognitive tasks may in this way offer a new supply to establish relationships between cortical growth cycles and cognitive tasks in addition to (neo)Piagetian tasks.

REFERENCES

Alport, A. (1989). Visual attention. In M. I. Posner (Ed.), *Foundations of cognitive science* (pp. 631–682). Cambridge, MA: MIT Press.

Been, P. H. (1994). Dyslexia and irregular dynamics of the visual system. In K. P. van den Bos, L. S. Siegel, D. J. Bakker, & D. J. Share (Eds.), *Current directions in dyslexia research* (pp. 93–116). Lisse: Swets and Zeitlinger.

Brannan, J., & Williams, M. (1988). Developmental versus sensory deficit effects on perceptual processing in the reading disabled. *Perception and Psychophysics, 44,* 437–444.

Ciesielski, K. T. (1989). Event-related potentials in children with specific visual cognitive disability. *Neuropsychologia, 27*(3), 303–313.

Cotman, C. W., & Lynch, G. S. (1990). The neurobiology of learning and memory. In P. D. Eimas & A. M. Galaburda (Eds.), *Neurobiology of cognition*. Cambridge, MA: MIT Press.

Cowan, J. D., & Ermentrout, G. B. (1978). Some aspects of the "eigenbehavior" of neural nets. In S. A. Levin (Ed.), *Studies in mathematical biology. Part I: Cellular behavior and the development of pattern* (pp. 67–116). Washington, DC: Mathematical Association of America.

Critchley, M. (1964). *Developmental dyslexia*. London: William Heineman.

Eriksen, C. W., & Murphy, T. D. (1987). Movement of attentional focus across the visual field: A critical look at the evidence. *Perception and Psychophysics, 42*(3), 299–305.

Galaburda, A. (1983). Developmental dyslexia: Current anatomical research. *Annals of Dyslexia, 33*, 41–53.

Geschwind, N. (1983). Biological associations of left-handedness. *Annals of Dyslexia, 33*, 29–39.

Grossberg, S. (1982). *Studies of mind and brain*. Dordrecht: D. Reidel.

Grossberg, S. (Ed.). (1988). *Neural networks and natural intelligence*. Cambridge, MA: MIT Press.

Hale, J. K. (1969). *Ordinary differential equations*. New York: John Wiley & Sons.

Halliday, D., & Resnick, R. (1966). *Physics*. New York: John Wiley & Sons.

Hudspeth, W. J., & Pribram, K. H. (1990). Stages of brain and cognitive maturation. *Journal of Educational Psychology, 82*(4), 881–884.

John, E. R. (1977). *Neurometrics: Clinical applications of quantitative electrophysiology*. Hillsdale, NJ: Lawrence Erlbaum Associates.

Kemper, T. L. (1984). Asymmetrical lesions in dyslexia. In N. Geschwind & A. M. Galaburda (Eds.), *Cerebral dominance. The biological foundations* (pp. 75–89). Cambridge, MA: Harvard University Press.

Kosslyn, S. M., & Anderson, R. A. (Eds.). (1992). *Frontiers in cognitive neuroscience*. Cambridge, MA: MIT Press.

Kubat, K. (1997). *Evoked potentials and dynamics of the visual system* (working title). Doctoral dissertation, University of Groningen.

Legein, C. P., & Bouma, H. (1981). Visual recognition experiments in dyslexia. In G. T. Pavlidis & T. R. Miles (Eds.), *Dyslexia research and its applications to education* (pp. 165–175). Chichester: John Wiley and Sons.

Livingstone, M., & Hubel, D. (1988). Segregation of form, color, movement, and depth: Anatomy, physiology, and perception. *Science, 240*, 740–749.

Lovegrove, W. J., Heddle, M., & Slaghuis, W. L. (1980). Reading disability: Spatial frequency deficits in visual information store. *Neuropsychologia, 18*, 111–115.

Lovegrove, W., Martin, R., Bowling, A., Blackwood, M., Badcock, D., & Paxton, S. (1982). Contrast sensitivity functions and specicfic reading disability. *Neuropsychologia, 20*, 309–315.

Martin, R., & Lovegrove, W. (1984). The effects of field size and luminance on contrast sensitivity differences between specifically reading disabled and normal children. *Neuropsychologia, 22*, 73–77.

Matouček, M., & Petersén, I. (1973). Frequency analysis of the EEG in normal children and adolescents. In P. Kellaway & I. Petersén (Eds.), *Automation of clinical electroencephalography* (pp. 75–102). New York: Raven Press.

Mesulam, M. M. (1981). A cortical network for directed attention and unilateral neglect. *Annals of Neurology, 10*, 309–325.

Mishkin, M., Ungerleider, L. G., & Macko, K. A. (1983). Object vision and spatial vision: Two cortical pathways. *Trends in Neurosciences, 6*, 414–417.

Previc, F. H. (1990). Functional specialization in the lower and upper visual fields in humans: Its ecological origins and neurophysiological implications. *Behavioral and Brain Sciences, 13*, 519–575.

Rall, W. (1967). Distinguishing theoretical synaptic potentials computed for different soma-dendritic distributions of synaptic inputs. *Journal of Neurophysiology, 30*, 1138–1168.

Remington, R., & Pierce, L. (1984). Moving attention: Evidence for time-invariant shifts of visual selective attention. *Perception and Psychophysics, 42*(3), 393–399.

Ritter, W., Simson, R., Vaughan, H. G., & Friedman, F. (1979). A brain event related to the making of a sensory discrimination. *Science, 203*, 1358–1361.

Shinners, S. M. (1979). *Modern control system theory and application*. Reading, MA: Addison-Wesley.

Slaghuis, W., & Lovegrove, W. (1986). The critical duration in spatial-frequency-dependent visible persistence and specific reading disability. *Bulletin of the Psychonomic Society, 24*, 416–418.

Slaghuis, W., & Lovegrove, W. (1987). The effect of field size and luminance on spatial-frequency-dependent visible persistence and specific reading disability. *Bulletin of the Psychonomic Society, 25*, 38–40.

Thatcher, R. W. (1994). Cyclic cortical reorganization. Origins of human cognitive development. In G. Dawson & K. W. Fischer (Eds.), *Human behavior and the developing brain* (pp. 232–266). New York: Guilford.

Van der Heijden, A. H. C. (1992). *Selective attention in vision*. London: Routledge.

Van der Maas, H., & Molenaar, P. C. M. (1992). Stagewise cognitive development: An application of catastrophe theory. *Psychological Review, 99*(3), 395–417.

Winters, R. L., Patterson, R., & Shontz, W. (1989). Visual persistence and adult dyslexia. *Journal of Learning Disabilities, 22*, 641–645.

Zeeman, E. C. (1977). Duffing's equation in brain modelling. In E. C. Zeeman (Ed.), *Catastrophe theory* (pp. 293–301). Reading, MA: Addison-Wesley.

Zeki, S. (1993). *A vision of the brain*. Oxford: Blackwell.

Zeki, S., & Shipp, S. (1988). The functional logic of cortical connections. *Nature, 355*, 311–317.

9

DYNAMICAL SYSTEMS AND THE STRUCTURE OF BEHAVIOR

Darren Newtson
University of Virginia

Everyday action consists of a succession of dynamical systems at the point of intersection between the person and the environment. This fact has profound implications for its analysis in psychological terms. At least one way to get "beyond the metaphor" of dynamical systems theory is to take it literally as a theory of behavior. As a theory, it then does precisely what good theory is supposed to do: It identifies variables and new phenomena that one had, under the assumption of other viewpoints, simply overlooked. Occasionally, it elevates a phenomenon thought trivial from another theoretical viewpoint to a more centrally important place. Occasionally, it frames a theoretical or empirical issue thought important from other theoretical viewpoints as in fact a triviality.

The great strength of the dynamical systems viewpoint, of course, is its emphasis on patterning in time. The approach is especially adept at identifying hidden patterns in apparently random series of measurements. Other effects of thinking in terms of the theory are more subtle, but no less important. Dynamical analyses, for instance, require dynamical variables, and dynamical variables are variables that are always present, even if zero. Thus one is led to think of phenomena in terms of variables with a range of values, as opposed to, say, category memberships. One must also consider the behavior of the system as a whole, with all of its variables, if one is to visualize or plot its phase space. Because dynamical systems may be multistable, one need not postulate an outside variable whenever the behavior of the system one is considering changes its behavior; one recognizes the possibility, at least, that some structures and some changes in structure may be emergent system properties. Complex behavior might reflect the interaction of many variables, but might also result from the interaction of just a few variables in chaos.

It has been estimated that every human speaker says, around once each day, a sentence that has never been uttered before. A similar claim might be made for the sequencing of action in individual behavior. Role theory, for example, failed because the inherent flexibility and creativity of everyday behavior eluded succinct description (cf. Sarbin & Allen, 1968). A great appeal of dynamical systems theory for many psychologists is that nonlinear models allow for deterministic systems to produce just such creative patterning in their behavior. Such creativity may be produced by systems in chaos, in which the system visits sequences of states in a fixed phase space in an order that is sensitively dependent on—we could say adapted to—the local conditions of the system. Thus nonlinear systems provide an exciting alternative way of thinking about the emergence of such phenomena that goes beyond existing approaches.

The goal of dynamical approaches is typically to understand a complex set of phenomena as due to an underlying order in its phase space, knowable by its underlying dimensionality and its shape. Such understanding is usually expressible most precisely as a mathematical equation, or model, and the analysis of alternative forms of such models is another important contribution of the theory. Such analyses can often show one the potential range of phenomena a model can address, and can identify the crucial assumptions within it.

In what follows then, I should like to review a large body of findings on the problems of everyday action perception, organization, and coordination in view of the implications of dynamical systems theory. Some of these findings preceded the theory, and could only be made sense of after its formulation. Others were directly suggested or implied by the theory itself, taken as a model of ongoing behavior.

Gallistel (1980) was one of the first to revive the problem of the units of action, citing the early formulations of behavior units such as coupled oscillators in the work of von Holst, Weiss, and Donald Wilson. These investigators showed that dynamical systems occur in the behavior of quite primitive organisms, and do not depend on sophisticated central control systems for their emergence. Kelso and his colleagues (Kelso & Clark, 1982; Salzman & Kelso, 1987; Schöner & Kelso, 1988), Thelen and her colleagues (Fogel & Thelen, 1987; Thelen & Fogel, 1989), Michael Turvey (1977, 1990), and the psychologist Robert Shaw (Shaw & Bransford, 1977) all argued that dynamical systems exist in everyday human behavior. These analyses have in common the view that ordinary actions result from the cycling of what have been termed *coordinative structures*—organized, constrained systems of limb and muscle groups—in selective interaction with properties of the environment to produce stable, recognizable actions.

If action consists of the cycling of systems produced by coordinative structures, then three kinds of action sequences may immediately be postulated:

1. The repetitive cycling of a constant system, as in walking
2. Repetitive cycling of a system with a constant variable set, but with parameter modifications, as in handwriting
3. Successions of different systems, with intermittent shifts as the content of each action changes

IMPLICATION I: INTERMITTENCE OF REORGANIZATION

The first important implication of adopting the dynamical system as the unit of analysis is that ongoing behavior should contain intermittent points of reorganization that define the boundaries between actions. If one asks competent perceivers of behavior to partition a behavior sequence into its component actions, as I have (Newtson, 1973, 1976; Newtson, Engquist, & Bois, 1976, 1977), one finds consistent agreement across subjects in the temporal location of action unit boundaries. The detection of such boundaries is somewhat variable over subjects, but, in most instances, not a lot of precision is required for veridical perception. If we are watching someone playing catch, we see the person alternate between coordinative structures required for throwing and for catching; in order to follow the event, we do not need to detect the shifts very precisely unless, of course, we are one of the participants. The nature of each coordinative structure is visible for most of the duration of its cycle, although it seems easiest for subjects to identify it at its initiation.

Such points of reorganization have been termed *breakpoints*. Intervening intervals between breakpoints are termed *nonbreakpoints*. Our studies have shown that slides of breakpoints are better recognized after viewing an event than are slides of nonbreakpoints. This is true for adults, as well as for children down to 5 years of age (Newtson & Engquist, 1976; Newtson, Gowan, & Patterson, 1980). Breakpoint slides provide a striking, comic-strip-like summary of the action sequence, although children are unable to use this property effectively until around age 7 (Engquist, 1982). In addition, adult perceivers are much more able to detect the deletion of film frames at breakpoints in ongoing films than they are able to detect frame deletions at nonbreakpoints (Newtson & Engquist, 1976).

One basic issue for the perception of action concerns the perception of intent. Heider (1958), in his classic formulation of the problem, argued that intent was given directly by perceptual information. He gave the example of a "mass–spring" system, in which a mass, suspended from a spring, would return to its position due to the persistent pattern of forces in the system. Perception of similar patterning, argued Heider, could account for the direct perception of convergence on a goal characteristic of intentional behavior. In contemporary terms, we could now say that Heider postulated that some actions would have a perceptible attractor in their phase space, and that the attractor defined the intention of the action. Heider stressed that the perceptual field itself was extended in time, and did not consist of a static pattern. Consistent with Heider's observations, perceivers can make causal attributions for actions simultaneously with the discrimination of the actions, and the causal discriminations are just as reliable as the discriminated action-unit boundaries (Newtson et al., 1976).

Further investigations emphasized that the process of action discrimination relies very little, if at all, on cognitive processes (Newtson, 1980; Lassiter, 1988). Perceivers can readily discriminate and interpret breakpoint information under a variety of cognitive loads, although such manipulations can reduce memory for the events. These data were most puzzling from a cognitive point of view, which assumed that action perception proceeds from the categorization of lower level movement patterns. Breakpoints do not, after all, provide a ready guide to the encoding of behavior into action categories.

Instead, the data point to a higher level, abstract kind of perceptual information, which exists in events at the action-by-action, event-by-event level. Not coincidentally, it is this property of behavior that makes film editing possible. One can readily delete sequence contents at nonbreakpoints without disrupting event comprehension. This explains how an editor can produce a simple continuity of events from a shot sequence in which large discontinuities of movement occur between each shot. The dictum in film editing is, "When in doubt, cut on the action." In our terms this means that shots may always be linked by cutting from one breakpoint to the next.

IMPLICATION 2: BEHAVIOR SHOULD DISPLAY A SPIKE-LIKE STRUCTURE OVER TIME

A second implication for the structure of behavior follows from the notion of coordinative structures. If different actions require different coordinative structures, then the intermittent reorganizations at action unit boundaries should be detectable by measures of bodily position change. If, as seems likely, changes between different coordinative structures require greater reorganization than changes that occur during the cycling of the structure, then action unit boundaries should correspond to intermittent bursts, or spikes of change in time.

To evaluate the relation between the surface structure of the behavior stream and perceived action units, I used a movement notation originally developed as a productive dance notation (Eshkol, 1973). It was adapted to animal behavior by Golani (1976, 1992), and is called the Eshkol–Wachmann movement notation. This system represents the body as a stick figure, and records the angle of each limb or body segment relative to its pivot joint in two planes. One may make these static position descriptions at some constant time interval (we use ½ or 1 sec), and then compare successive codings to generate profiles of change in time (Newtson et al., 1976). The simplest procedure, we have found, is to simply trace a stick figure from a video monitor onto a transparency, and then to compare transparencies from successive coded intervals, making a 0–1 judgment as to whether each of 15 limb or body segments has changed in joint angle (Newtson, Hairfield, Bloomingdale, & Cutino, 1987). Two additional features, weight distribution and orientation to the camera, are also recorded. The result is a vector of 17 zeros and ones that can be used to plot the pattern of change in bodily organization over time. Coding reliabilities in the range of .90 and up are readily achievable with a few minutes' practice. If the coding seems crude, keep in mind that (a) it can discriminate 2^{17} different positions, and (b) the behavior stream has fractal dimensions, and the appropriate level of temporal resolution is dependent on that property (cf. Newtson, 1994).

Factor analyses of such codings readily detect the occurrence of coordinative structures in everyday behavior (Newtson et al., 1977, 1987). The grouping of body parts into structures that change together is one readily detectable structural property of the behavior stream. No general "human movement pattern," however, can be shown to exist. Instead, various parts are organized for the purpose of various tasks, and different sequence contents readily produce different factor structures.

If one simply sums the changes in coding features to produce an overall index of position change, one can readily confirm the correspondence between bodily reorganizations and perceived action-unit boundaries. Figure 9.1 shows the average values obtained for seven sequences of a variety of action contents (e.g., setting a table, shelving books, answering and talking on a phone, clearing a table, making stick figures, taking a test, constructing a toy tower). The figure thus shows the "average" profile of an action in the behavior stream, analogous to a graph of an "average" word in sound. Although such an "average action" may be no more meaningful than an "average word," it does provide a check, at least, to uninformed assertions about the structure of action in ongoing behavior—a topic about which psychologists and philosophers have asserted much, assumed much, and that has in fact been investigated very little. The general shape of a perceived action unit is as depicted in Fig. 9.1. This general shape was found in initial studies by Newtson et al. (1976), and replicated over entirely different sequences by Newtson et al. (1987).

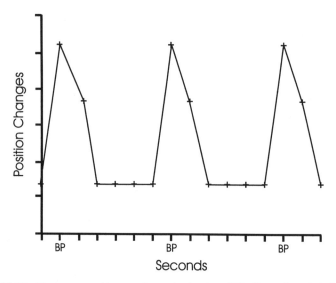

FIG. 9.1. The structure of "average" perceived actions (BP indicates boundaries).

Figure 9.2 shows the second-by-second profile of a single sequence, in which a person pinned letters and numbers on a bulletin board. The regular, rhythmic characteristic of the latter sequence is not accidental, as Engquist, in her doctoral dissertation, made the sequence with a regular pattern, using trained dancers and a metronome, in order to match it precisely to a second sequence with a different content (Engquist, 1982). Inspection of the individual records of our other sequences, however, showed persistent apparent periodicity as well.

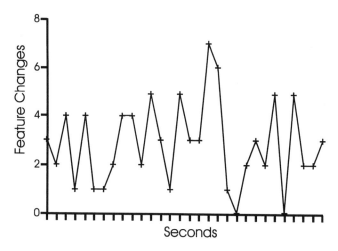

FIG. 9.2. The structure of a simple behavior sequence.

One criticism of this work that came up repeatedly was that these analyses invariably employed repetitive action. After some time trying—and failing—to come up with nonrepetitive action sequences, I got it. If actions consist of the cycling of coordinative structures—of dynamical systems—repetition is a fundamental property of ongoing behavior. Consider the amount of cycling required, for example, to enact the "McDonald's script." It is immediately apparent that close coding of almost any normal behavior sequence will turn up repetitive structures.

Accordingly, we conducted spectral analyses of all of the sequences that we had analyzed (Newtson et al., 1987). In every instance that we have analyzed so far, spectral analysis has confirmed that position change in ordinary action is significantly periodic. In other words, the behavior stream contains a wave of reorganization as one of its structural properties.

When we analyzed these records, moreover, we expected that breakpoint frequency would be about the same as position change frequency. To our surprise, breakpoint frequency was always about twice as fast as position change frequency. Waves are marvelously organized structures. Among their intriguing properties is the fact that they only contain two independent amplitudes per cycle, and it is this property—termed the wave sampling theorem—that allows digital recording systems to precisely specify sound on the basis of intermittent samples. When we applied the mathematical function—termed the translation function—to the amplitudes obtained at breakpoint intervals, we found that we could do a pretty good job of recreating the observed sequence from this information alone.

As a control, we attempted reconstruction from nonbreakpoints and found that it could not be done. Coherence analysis showed that in every one of the sequences analyzed the breakpoint sequence was highly (and significantly) coherent with the coded sequence, even though less than 8% of the intervals were used.

If there is an independent level of structure in action that is perceived directly, then it would seem to consist of specifications of the wave characteristics of the other's behavior. This would suggest, in turn, that the wave characteristics of the other should figure in some way in the regulation of social interaction. It also raises the clear possibility that processes of social "cognition," whereby the categorical status of individual actions is identified (cf. Vallacher & Wegner, 1985), are a subsequent and often optional and unnecessary step in the regulation of social behavior.

IMPLICATION 3: THERE ARE WAVES OF INFORMATION IN BEHAVIOR

The physicist Robert Shaw (1981) demonstrated that the phase space of a system provides a measure of its information content. Changes in the phase space of a system constitute flows of information into or out of a system. If breakpoints are points of change in the phase space of dynamical action systems, then they are points of information flow. The waves that we have observed, then, are not merely waves of position change, but waves of information.

The idea is simply that a system with a fixed or constant phase space has a constant information value: The nominal uncertainty of any observed state is the log of $1/n$, where n is the number of distinguishable states of the system. If n remains constant, the information value of observations of its states remains the same over repeated observations. If there are internal constraints in the system, of course, some information flows may occur as the probability of different internal states fluctuates, but in general we might expect such flows to be small in comparison to those that result when the state space itself is altered. A completely repetitive action sequence in which all states are equiprobable would have zero change in its information value over time, and hence zero information flow. Wholly repetitive behavior, then, does not display an information wave; flow in time is zero.

Changes in a parameter of one of the variables in a system would either expand or shrink the state space. This is the kind of information flow induced in what have been termed "quasi-repetitive" action sequences. Hollerbach (1981) provided an analysis of handwriting that shows how the skill begins with a simple oscillator to produce a script "e," which then undergoes a series of parameter modifications (e.g., to produce a script "l") that allow the entire set of letters to be produced.

Complex action sequences consisting of a succession of different action systems would, as a result of the successive modifications of phase spaces, show large flows of information at breakpoints. Flows could be in the direction of increased or decreased information value. Shaw (1981) demonstrated, moreover, that chaotic sequences show simultaneous inflow and outflow of information. The spikes that occur in position change, then, are not simply spikes of movement, but are spikes of information flow. Hence the waves that we have identified are waves of information, visible to observers but not dependent on observation for their existence. As Salzman and Kelso (1987) noted, the organization of action is contained in its "surface structure."

Our analyses of ongoing behavior show that ordinary "complex" action sequences display constant parameters of amplitude, frequency, and phase relations over different action contents (Newtson et al., 1987). Frequency of the behavior wave is clearly a matter of the pace of the action. The amplitude of an information wave is a little less intuitive. Think of a vibrating object; it has a mean position, just like any variable mean. It also has an amplitude of variation in position, or of vibration. This is precisely the notion that the standard deviation is derived from, and is the measure of variance in behavior. Amplitude in the behavior wave, then, refers to its variance; in one study, for example, we used the number of different coding categories in each 5-sec interval as a measure of this property (Newtson, 1993). Antisocial adolescents, often thought to be "hyperactive," were in fact found to act at the same frequency as normals, but to display greater amplitude, or variance, in their behavior. This property could account for impressions of hyperactivity in these children precisely because the increased novelty of their behavior would cause it to attract observers' attention.

An important implication for the understanding of interpersonal behavior results from these considerations. The mere presence of another person, when that person is acting, contributes a pulsating information source to the perceptual field of the other. Environmental variables, while rich in information, are not typically dynamic except in relation to the actor's own behavior. The behavior of others, in consequence, is highly salient. "Behavior," as Heider (1958) observed, "engulfs the field."

IMPLICATION 4: ACTION INDUCES INFORMATION FLOW FOR THE ACTOR

The analysis of the optical flow induced by the behavior of the perceiver and its important role in specifying the environment was, of course, the basis of J. J. Gibson's fundamentally important contribution to our understanding of perception (Gibson, 1966, 1979). Yet, as Cutting (1986) pointed out, information theory has been of little use to Gibsonian theory. At least one part of the difficulty of applying information theory to perception has been the formulation of information analyses in terms particularly appropriate to cognitive theory. Thus the information value of an observation is given as a function of the set size from which it came, postulating a categorical framework constructed by the perceiver (Garner, 1962, 1974). Information theory was developed to analyze communication systems, and its concepts, such as Shannon and Weaver's formula for average information transmission, readily lend themselves to communication contexts. The kinds of information flows psychological information theorists have been concerned with are those due to differences in state probabilities within fixed state spaces (cf. Attneave, 1959; Garner, 1962).

Shaw's (1981) use of information concepts in the context of dynamical systems is profoundly different. Shaw treated information as an objective property of the environment. He noted, "Information, like energy, is a profound primitive concept, and as such cannot be defined as a combination of elemental constituents. It can, however, be defined operationally and given a measure" (p. 83). In other words, information is an objective property of the environment and, Shaw pointed out, the phase space is a measure of the objective information content of a system. The fact that one needs to specify some set size to operationalize its measurement does not make it a subjective property, constructed by the perceiver, any more than the need to adopt a frame of reference for the measurement of velocity converts that property to a psychological one. If one measures the position of a pendulum, the information value of the observation depends on the precision of one's measurement, because that determines the number of states that one can discriminate in its phase space. Similarly, the information value of a sensory dimension in a perceptual array depends on the perceptual threshold of the perceiver for differences on that dimension. The presence in any array of a minimum of two discriminable values on that dimension defines the existence of information on it.

The application of information theory to the analysis of the perceptual layout that would be appropriate for a Gibsonian analysis would be in terms of the nominal uncertainty of the array. Suppose that, at any given time, the array consists of a set of what we might term *indicators*—any sensory dimension on which at least two values can be discriminated, such as an edge. We could think of the nominal uncertainty of the array as simply a log function of the number of such indicators. The actual uncertainty of an array without structure would be equal to this value. As Gibson pointed out, the indicators in an array are highly structured; in an unambiguous layout, the quantity of information in the array is much less than the nominal uncertainty, as a result of environmental structure. Indeed, in a completely specified array, actual uncertainty may be zero. Such an array would be perfectly predictable. If the observer moves, some of the specifications change, but just as in Shaw's (1981) constant-size phase spaces, the total information value of the field does not change. For example, if the observer takes a step, some specifications are lost, some new ones are gained, but the location of the observer in the room is still one of a constant-size set of such possible locations. The specifications of the layout of the room will change, but there will be invariant relations among them that preserve knowledge of the relative positions of the walls, floor, and so forth. Such transformations are, in Shaw's (1981) terms, informationally static.

If an action creates some uncertainty, or ambiguity in the array, another action may eliminate it. This is the Gibsonian alternative to constructive perception. Gibsonians typically analyze arrays that are informationally static, and in which actual uncertainty is zero. Even a dynamic array, it should be noted, contains zero information flow if the phase space of movement remains constant.

If there are information waves in behavior, however, arrays with persons also include information sources that are not static, but display stably varying flows of information. The perceptual field, in other words, contains not only invariants with zero information flow, but variables with positive but stable fluctuations in information value.

If we think of the set of specifications in the perceptual field at any one time as a population, then each action is like a generation in that population. Some specifications are lost, some are gained, and some survive. Models of population dynamics, such as the logistic equation, may be used as direct models of the dynamics of information flow in the perceptual-action system. The rate of information flow in the perceptual field would be equivalent to the replacement rate in a population, defined as births minus deaths. The nominal uncertainty of the environment would equal the carrying capacity of the environment. Given the discrete nature of information, and the inter- mittence of reorganization in behavior, the logistic difference equation may be the most suitable model for such an analysis.

If one takes the growth of the population of specifications as being density dependent, as seems likely, then the simple difference equations such as those given by May (1981) for single populations would be appropriate for the analysis of perceptual information flow for a solitary actor. That equa- tion is as follows:

$$x_{t+1} = rx_t(1 - x_t) \tag{1}$$

where $x = N/K$, N being the population and K being the carrying capacity of the environment; r is the replacement rate in the population, births minus deaths.

The behavior of this equation is well known. It is multistable, going from steady states at low flow values through a sequence of periodic regimes, and then arriving at chaotic patterning. Because information flow would be a log function of the number of variables in the array, one can simply insert those values into the formula as the value of r, the replacement rate. It is quite possible, therefore, that the waves that we have observed in behavior would disappear at high and low flow rates. One is reminded of Miller's famous number for the things that can be kept in mind, 7 plus or minus 2 (Miller, 1956); it may be entirely coincidental, but flow rates for more than 8 variables produce waves, with chaotic states emerging at around 12 vari- ables in the field (i.e., using the log to the base two of these numbers as r).

The old dictum that the function of the perceptual system is to render the environment predictable is in need of qualification. An active system cannot expect to reduce uncertainty to zero in a dynamic world; the function of the perceptual-action system, properly considered, must be to maintain stability of information flow, not to eliminate it.

In any event, these considerations point to the possibility that the infor- mation waves that exist in behavior need not depend on some information- processing, wave-generating mechanism. Instead, they may readily emerge from the dynamic interaction of the person with the environment, and from the interaction of the person with other persons.

IMPLICATION 5: WAVES COUPLE, OR INTERACT

If two persons are in each other's presence, and are performing normal actions, one might expect to observe mutual influence. Each person experiences a pulsing information state due to that person's own action, and a pulsing information source in the behavior of the other. At minimum, one would expect mechanical sorts of interactions to occur between the two actors. In fact, the effects of *compresence*, as it has been termed, are well documented (Zajonc, 1965). When two persons perform simple tasks in each other's presence, an increase in performance occurs, so-called *social facilitation*. When tasks are complex, task performance is reduced, producing *social interference*. Although various cognitive explanations have been put forward for these effects—and no doubt cognitive consequences ensue—one might also expect that persons performing simple tasks would tend to entrain each other, excluding idiosyncratic behaviors. Such entrainment has, in fact, been observed under conditions of social facilitation (Kelley & Thibaut, 1968). Performers of complex tasks, which are more difficult to entrain, could be expected to suffer destructive interference due to the presence of the other, resulting in decreased task performance.

The simplest way to observe the interfering effects of behavior waves is to imitate someone. Such imitation is an annoyance, of course, precisely because it interferes with the ongoing behavior of the other person.

A more interesting approach to coaction situations, however, is in terms of the logistic model just discussed. If persons do experience information waves in behavior consistently with the model, then extensions of the model to relations between multiple populations can be used to cast light on the consequences of mutual influence. The relation between the perceptual-action fields of two persons is like the mutualism relation between animal populations. Increased information flow in the behavior of one person is evident as an enrichment of the perceptual field of the other. The effect is that of the classic "flower–pollinator" relation between populations: the more flowers, the greater is the carrying capacity of the environment for bees, and vice versa.

One can readily model this situation, using the simple difference equations for mutualism between populations (cf. May, 1981). These explorations show that the most minimal influence between two such systems is sufficient to produce entrainment between the behavior waves of two systems. Difference equations for mutualism between two populations are given by May (1981), as follows:

$$N_{1(t+1)} = rN_{1t}\left\{1 - [N_{1t}/(K_1 + aN_{2t})]\right\} \tag{2}$$

$$N_{2(t+1)} = sN_{2t}\left\{1 - [N_{2t}/(K_2 + bN_{1t})]\right\} \tag{3}$$

where r and s are the growth parameters of the populations N_1 and N_2, respectively. The model requires that $ab < 1$. The a and b parameters specify the degree to which growth in one population directly enhances the carrying capacity of the environment of the other. With as little mutual effect as 0.0001 for the mutualism coefficients a and b, clear-cut attractors exist at in-phase and antiphase relations for the two systems (Newtson, 1993).

Such a finding is, for a social psychologist, a most exciting one. The two most basic forms of human coaction—in-phase coordination and turn-taking alternation—can be accounted for as an emergent property of the interaction of information flows. Conversation, for example, can be conceived not merely as a sequence of speaking turns, where two speakers alternate according to switching signals, but as a dynamic process whose structure is an emergent property of the behavior of the two persons.

Newtson (1993) found that as mutualism between two persons increases, a series of increasingly elaborate, strange attractors emerges in the behavior of the two systems. This series was dubbed a *courtship series* because it plausibly displayed changes in a relationship pattern that could accompany increasing intimacy between two persons.

Population dynamics may thus provide a fruitful source of models for the study of interpersonal relationships in general. Dominance relations, for example, may be modeled by setting the levels of mutual gain in the preceding system at highly unequal values. Under these conditions, the model produces highly constrained, predictable behavior from the low-gaining mutualist, with flexible, chaotic patterning in the behavior of the high-gaining mutualist.

Models for competitive and exploitative relations are also readily available. Psychologists often fail to appreciate, for example, how unstable purely competitive relations really are; one system almost invariably drives the other to extinction. Purely competitive models seem unlikely to provide general models of interaction patterning. A more realistic model would incorporate at least some competition, or conflict, along with mutualism effects. In our simulations we have examined just such a mixed model of competition and mutualism, using the following equations:

$$N_{1(t+1)} = rN_{1t}\left\{1 - [(N_{1t} + c_{21}N_{2t})/(K_1 + aN_{2t})]\right\} \tag{4}$$

$$N_{2(t+1)} = sN_{2t}\left\{1 - [(N_{2t} + c_{12}N_{1t})/(K_2 + bN_{1t})]\right\} \tag{5}$$

where r and s are the growth parameters of the populations N_1 and N_2, as before, and a and b are mutualism coefficients, also as before. In addition, however, the effect of the competitor is, in effect, to make each population larger to the degree that the competitor consumes the same resources. The coefficients of competition, then, c_{12} and c_{21}, indicate the degree to which the competitor population overlaps in its consumption of environmental resources. As was the case with the mutualism coefficients, both must be less than one in this model.

We computed simulations of this model under varying sets of parameters in order to explore the properties of two systems coupled in this manner. In general, the sequence of attractors noted by Newtson (1993) for purely mutualist systems was replicated, with one important difference: If levels of competition were low, but not minuscule (e.g. around 0.10 to 0.20), the level of mutualism that the system would tolerate was much higher. That is, purely mutualist systems tolerate a maximum of 0.3 to 0.4 mutualism before mutual flows begin to interfere with each other and decline. One might interpret that as a "sharing limit" for the overlap of variables for the two systems, or as a kind of limit on the benefits of intimacy. With some conflict in the system, however, much higher levels of coupling—in the range of 0.7 and 0.8—can be tolerated without loss of flow. In other words, a little conflict is necessary if the relationship is to achieve high levels of intimacy. Figure 9.3 shows the attractor that emerges at mutualism levels of $a = b = 0.8$, $c_{21} = c_{12} = 0.16$ (at $r = s = 3.17$; $K_1 = K_2 = 75$, iterations 25–250 from 64 evenly distributed initial conditions).

Information flow for one system is on the x axis, and for the other is on the y axis. In-phase behavior would show a line with a positive slope; antiphase coupling would be shown by a negative slope. Lead-lag relations show up as a circle on these plots. The attractor in Fig. 9.3 shows the kind of elaborate and complex attractor that can emerge in these systems. The attractor shows a smaller loop embedded in a larger circle; the system may traverse this circle in either direction, indicating that lead-lag relations may vary readily. More complicated loops emerge at high levels of joint flow. This relationship would have two distinct regimes of interaction, one a

FIG. 9.3. Strange attractor for mixed mutualist/competitor system.

widely varying one and a second less variable regime. The system, compared to others, spends little time at mutual in-phase and antiphase behavior; one partner or the other is always in charge.

A second question concerned the nature of highly unequal relationships. Predator–prey models provide suggestive analogies to exploitative relationships, and produce regular cycles of booms and busts for the two parties. Given a mixed model of information flow in relationships, one wonders what one would have to do—what kind of transformation is necessary—to create that kind of pattern in one of these relationships. In fact, a regular cyclic pattern of boom and bust can be generated in these relationship systems. If one sets the mutualism parameters at extremely unequal values (e.g., 0.99 for a and 0.01 for b), and competition indices at unequal values as well (e.g., $c_{21} = 0.16$ and $c_{12} = 0.08$), one obtains the attractor in Fig. 9.4. Movement around the attractor is unidirectional, showing a phase lead for the dominant mutualist. This system shows a low-dominant partner who is in fact a more effective competitor than the high dominant partner. The inequality of competitive effectiveness seems to be critical for the emergence of the cyclic pattern; at equal values, the system spirals in to a point in its joint state space. Thus a normal relationship could, these equations imply, become an abusive one if mutualism becomes extremely unequal, but the low mutualist partner is a more adept competitor than the other. The image of a dull-witted husband dominating a more intelligent wife comes to mind, with abuse occurring when he detects that she has outwitted him.

These models are, of course, highly speculative and unrealistic. Nonetheless, they serve the purpose of demonstrating that it is possible that interaction and relationship structures may emerge from the dynamics of inter-

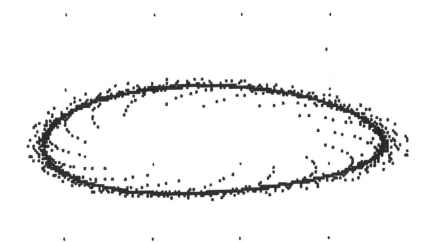

FIG. 9.4. Attractor for unequal mutualists and unequal competitors.

dependent information flows. Although many have speculated about "family systems" and "the dynamics of relationships" and "group dynamics" as powerful determinants of a great many phenomena, few can say what such things consist of, how they might be measured, and what variables might determine their behavior. The present approach shows, if nothing else, that these concepts allow one to define these questions in a straightforward manner. We have extended these equations to three-person systems and produced models of the dynamics that would occur in families with children as well.

Whether or not such patterning actually occurs in interaction is an empirical matter. A very large amount of data from dyadic interactions from a variety of instances would be required to confirm the presence of elaborately structured attractors. Empirical investigations of the coupling of behavior waves in a variety of interactions (Newtson et al., 1987) do show clear bands of significant frequencies in the behavior of interactants that are coherent with each other. "Conventional" measures of interaction structure, it should be noted, are limited almost entirely to speaking turns in conversation (e.g., Dabbs & Ruback, 1987), or to the frequency of occurrence of limited categories of nonverbal gestures. No general theories of behavior coordination besides the present one exist. Thus, when two women unloading boxes from a pickup truck were found to have a significant periodicity in their overall behavior waves at about 24.5 sec that was highly coherent and in phase, this confirmed the hypothesis of wave coupling, but did not speak to other research on face-to-face interaction (cf. Duncan & Fiske, 1977).

Although rhythm in action and synchrony in interaction are often assumed, they can be very difficult to demonstrate. One reason for optimism about the present approach is that it so readily identifies periodicity in behavior. Movement analyses, it should be noted, may not turn up periodicities as readily. If you expect that all of the current statements allow the word *movement* to be substituted for *action* or *position change*, you should be warned that you have misunderstood these analyses at a most fundamental level.

IMPLICATION 6: CONVERSATION IS REGULATED BY THE RELATIVE AMPLITUDE OF BEHAVIOR WAVES

Instead of viewing a conversation as a sequence of turn switches, then, according to some cognitive rule, we may see conversation as merely the coupling of two waves at antiphase. If wave amplitude is variance, the variance in the overall performance must increase during speech, and decrease during silences. Thus speaking could be part of the high-amplitude part of the wave, and listening must occur at the trough.

In order to detect such patterns, we recorded the amplitude of position change and the vocal intensity from 5 min of sample conversations between undergraduates. Position change was recorded with the Eshkol–Wachman procedure at ½-sec intervals. Vocal intensity was recorded by playing the sound track of the video recording into an oscilloscope, and scoring amplitude on an 8-point scale in each video frame. These values were then averaged over the ½-sec behavior coding interval to give a comparable vocal series of values. Position change and vocal intensity series were then analyzed both separately and as summed together for each person.

In one sequence analyzed, position change and vocal intensity within each person were positively related and significantly coherent. In general, the persons in this dyad were active, gesturing speakers and relatively quiet listeners. This is a common but not invariant pattern. Consistent with the findings of other investigators of conversation, however, the pattern of speaking turns did not reflect a simple alternation of equal speaking turn lengths (Jaffe & Feldstein, 1970). Overall spectral analyses of the behavior of each person showed broad bands of significant frequencies, but no simple organizing principle was apparent.

For a number of reasons, it seemed sensible to explore the relationship between information flows for each actor. Because flow is postulated to be a log function of the measured amplitudes, logs of the summed waves were taken. The ratio of flow between the two systems, then, would be given by the difference between these two values. The result for the first sequence analyzed is given in Fig. 9.5.

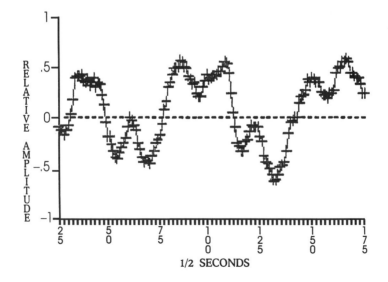

FIG. 9.5. The relative amplitude of behavior waves in a conversation.

As one can readily see, the conversational pattern was clearly reflected in the ratio of flow values. Speaking turns alternated according to a regular pattern, with an overlaid harmonic—we have termed it an "uhuh" harmonic, because of the interjections (verbal) and gestures (head nods) that typically occurred at these points. The sequence has a simple spectrum, with two significant values. One was at the frequency of total speaking turns (i.e., speaking turn for person 1 plus speaking turn for person 2) and the other was a harmonic of this frequency.

To those familiar with wave patterns, the pattern itself is readily recognizable. The pattern is that of the difference between two waves with a 3:1 frequency ratio. Closer inspection of the spectra of the individual vocal and gestural series clearly disclosed the basis of these patterns. The sequence consisted of a conversation between an urban female student and a rural male student. She seemed very calm, but spoke rapidly; he seemed fidgety and nervous, but spoke slowly. Her speech rate was three times his; his gesture rate was three times hers. Each apparently coupled their gesture rate to the speech rate of the other, and then let the difference in overall flow rate switch the interaction.

This hypothesis has been termed the *relative amplitude hypothesis of interaction organization*. It is that conversation is regulated by the relative amplitude, or magnitude, of information flow in the behavior waves of the participants, and that such regulation is an emergent rather than imposed pattern. Thus, for example, one can readily generate an "atlas" of speaking turn patterns that one would expect to observe between persons of varying speech rate ratios (see Newtson, 1994).

A number of phenomena become readily understandable from this perspective. It is well established that personal distance, eye contact, and interaction angle all play a role in interaction coordination. These variables are thought to serve somehow as nonverbal "communicators," but, paradoxically, they are substitutable for each other. From the present perspective, we can see that each of these factors serves an amplitude regulation function. One can increase one's amplitude relative to another by moving closer, talking more loudly, facing the person, and so on. By looking more or looking less, one can readily adjust the amplitude of the other in one's own field. Interaction angles can also be understood in terms of whether they facilitate or impede such amplitude adjustments.

Some other interaction phenomena become more understandable as well. One phenomenon often remarked on by coders of interaction is that of shadowing. Two persons in interaction will often mimic each other's posture; if one is tracking the difference between one's own wave and another's, it is probably simpler to perceive the difference if postures are symmetrical.

A second example is the occurrence of what we have come to term *bracing* postures. The easiest way to make relative flow simple to compute is to reduce one's own to zero; people do this by bracing themselves, as with the chin in one's hand. This has two effects: Besides simplifying comprehension for the observer, it increases the relative amplitude of the other's behavior, who is thus forced to simplify his or her behavior to maintain a constant pattern.

A third example is the occurrence of resonance phenomena. When two systems approach each other in frequency, the result is a tremendous boost in amplitude for both systems. The subjective feeling in conversation should be one of increased complexity, along with greater freedom of choice as a wider range of behavioral alternatives is made available. One should feel that one has many things to talk about. The result of a frequency mismatch, however, should be a feeling of constraint, of having little to talk about. This would provide a concrete basis for the claim that similarity facilitates interaction, insofar as similarity is similarity in frequency. Resonances also cause systems to selectively tune to each other. Whom one chooses to talk to in a group, for example, may depend on frequency matches.

A great many further implications for the organization of social interaction may be readily generated on this basis. This approach provides, for the first time, a model that can account for the patterning of ongoing interaction, including those conditions under which it will be predictable and those under which it will not be (i.e., under creative, chaotic regimes). It allows the classification not only of interactions, but also of types of relationships and models of relationship systems (cf. Newtson, 1993).

If we take dynamical systems theory as a theory of behavior, then it does precisely what we would hope a new theory would do. It orders old data, some of which was anomalous, it suggests new data, which let us frame new questions and test new hypotheses, and it provides superior alternative explanations for basic processes such as the organization of social interaction.

CONCLUSION

Despite the excitement generated by the development of dynamical systems theory, it has been difficult to generate research capitalizing on its promise. The situation is similar to that which occurred in the 1940s with the introduction of new ideas from cybernetics (Heims, 1994). From the first conferences on the new cybernetics in 1946 it was nearly 15 years to the systematic statements of cognitive psychology, such as that of Miller, Galanter, and Pribram (1960), and Neisser's widely read summary of initial programmatic research from that view did not appear until 1967, more than 20 years later (Neisser, 1967). Dating general awareness of dynamical systems theory as occurring in the mid 1980s, we should expect its assimilation into psychology shortly after the turn of the next century, with vigorous experimentation becoming the norm around 2005. This assumes, of course, that the rate of assimilation of new ideas will be the same; there are many reasons to be pessimistic.[1]

The problem then, as I think it is the problem now, was not just the difficulty of understanding the new ideas, but in assimilating them to psychological theory. As Heims (1994) pointed out, S-R psychology was skeptical of "teleological mechanisms" for two reasons. First, they seemed to put the cause of behavior in the present into the future, in the goal. The idea that information could exist inside the organism in the form of representations seemed highly artificial and abstract. Second, they produced circular causal patterns, as feedback mechanisms produced causal loops, which seemed at variance with the patterns of linear causation then thought to be characteristic of the physical sciences, and hence preferred. A more basic reason, however, was paradigmatic: The important phenomena of psychology in the 1950s were those of conditioning. Cognitive analyses were not persuasive because they did not produce more convincing analyses of conditioning.

Similarly, the important phenomena of the 1990s are those of information processing within the organism: encoding, representation, communication, and decision making. These are the important phenomena because the cognitive paradigm makes them so. What was important about cognitive theory was not that it led to new and better ways to conceptualize or analyze reinforcement schedules, but that it pointed to a new set of variables as basic to psychological phenomena. What is important about dynamical systems theory is not that it allows us new and better ways to apply cognitive theory, but that it takes us into new territory. It points to new variables and to new problems, and new ways of thinking about old phenomena.

The difficulty with dynamical systems theory right now is the same difficulty that cognitive theory faced in 1955. Give it 10 (or 20) years.

REFERENCES

Attneave, F. (1959). *Applications of information theory to psychology*. New York: Holt, Rinehart & Winston.

Cutting, J. E. (1986). *Perception with an eye for motion*. Cambridge, MA: MIT Press.

Dabbs, J., & Ruback, R. B. (1987). Dimensions of group process: Amount and structure of vocal interaction. In L. Berkowitz (Ed.), *Advances in experimental social psychology* (Vol. 20, pp. 2–37). New York: Academic Press.

Duncan, S., & Fiske, D. (1977). *Face-to-face interaction*. Hillsdale, NJ: Lawrence Erlbaum Associates.

Engquist, G. (1982). The development of behavior perception. In R. St. Clair & B. Hoffer (Eds.), *Developmental kinesics* (pp. 25–69). Baltimore: University Park Press.

---

[1]Dynamical systems theory tells us that the time it takes to make changes increases geometrically each time, so the paradigm change time may be 40 rather 20 years (cf. Kaufman, 1995).

Eshkol, L. (1973). *Moving, writing, reading*. Holon, Israel: Movement Notation Society.

Fogel, A., & Thelen, E. (1987). Development of early expressive and communicative action: Reinterpreting the evidence from a dynamic systems perspective. *Developmental Psychology, 23*, 747–761.

Gallistel, C. R. (1980). *The organization of action: A new synthesis*. Hillsdale, NJ: Lawrence Erlbaum Associates.

Garner, W. R. (1962). *Information and uncertainty as psychological concepts*. New York: John Wiley & Sons.

Garner, W. R. (1974). *The processing of information and structure*. New York: Halstead Press.

Gibson, J. J. (1966). *The senses considered as perceptual systems*. Boston: Houghton-Mifflin.

Gibson, J. J. (1979). *The ecological approach to visual perception*. Boston: Houghton-Mifflin.

Golani, I. (1976). Homeostatic motor processes in mammalian interactions: A choreography of display. In P. G. Bateson & P. H. Klopfer (Eds.), *Perspectives in ethology* (Vol. 2). New York: Plenum.

Golani, I. (1992). A mobility gradient in the organization of vertebrate movement: The perception of movement through symbolic language. *Behavioral and Brain Sciences, 15*, 249–308.

Heider, F. (1958). *The psychology of interpersonal relations*. New York: Wiley.

Heims, S. (1994). *The cybernetics group*. New York: Wiley.

Hollerbach, J. M. (1981). An oscillation theory of handwriting. *Biological Cybernetics, 39*, 139–156.

Jaffe, J., & Feldstein, S. (1970). *Rhythms of dialogue*. New York: Academic Press.

Kauffman, S. (1995). *At home in the universe: The search for the laws of self-organization and complexity*. New York: Oxford University Press.

Kelley, H. H., & Thibaut, J. W. (1968). Group problem solving. In G. Lindzey & E. Aronson (Eds.), *The handbook of social psychology* (Vol. 4, pp. 1–101). Reading, MA: Addison-Wesley.

Kelso, J. A. S., & Clark, J. (Eds.). (1982). *The development of movement control and coordination*. New York: Wiley.

Lassiter, G. D. (1988). Behavior perception, affect, and memory. *Social Cognition, 6*, 433–438.

May, R. M. (Ed.). (1981). *Theoretical ecology* (2nd ed.). Oxford: Blackwell.

Miller, G. A. (1956). The magical number seven, plus or minus two. *Psychological Review, 63*, 81–97.

Miller, G. A., Galanter, E., & Pribram, K. (1960). *Plans and the structure of behavior*. New York: Holt.

Neisser, U. (1967). *Cognitive psychology*. New York: Appleton-Century-Crofts.

Newtson, D. (1973). Attribution and the unit of perception of ongoing behavior. *Journal of Personality and Social Psychology, 28*, 28–38.

Newtson, D. (1976). Foundations of attribution: The perception of ongoing behavior. In J. Harvey, W. Ickes, & R. Kidd (Eds.), *New directions in attribution research*. Hillsdale, NJ: Lawrence Erlbaum Associates.

Newtson, D. (1980). An interactionist perspective on social knowing. *Personality and Social Psychology Bulletin, 6*, 520–531.

Newtson, D. (1990). Alternatives to representation or alternative representations: Comments on the ecological approach. *Contemporary Social Psychology, 14*, 163–174.

Newtson, D. (1993). The dynamics of action and interaction. In L. Smith & E. Thelen (Eds.), *Applications of dynamical systems theory to human development*. Cambridge, MA: MIT Press.

Newtson, D. (1994). The perception and coupling of behavior waves. In R. Vallacher & A. Nowack (Eds.), *Dynamical systems in social psychology*. San Diego, CA: Academic Press.

Newtson, D., & Engquist, G. (1976). The perceptual organization of ongoing behavior. *Journal of Experimental Social Psychology, 12*, 436–450.

Newtson, D., Engquist, G., & Bois, J. (1976). Reliability of a measure of behavior perception. *JSAS Catalogue of Selected Documents in Psychology* (MS # 1173).

Newtson, D., Engquist, G., & Bois, J. (1977). The objective basis of behavior units. *Journal of Personality and Social Psychology, 35*, 847–862.

Newtson, D., Gowan, D., & Patterson, C. (1980, September). *The development of action discrimination.* Paper presented at meeting of American Psychological Association, Montreal.

Newtson, D., Hairfield, J., Bloomingdale, J., & Cutino, S. (1987). The structure of action and interaction. *Social Cognition, 5,* 191–237.

Salzman, E., & Kelso, J. (1987). Skilled actions: A task dynamic approach. *Psychological Review, 94,* 84–106.

Sarbin, T., & Allen, V. (1968). Role theory. In G. Lindzey & E. Aronson (Eds.), *Handbook of social psychology* (Vol. 1, pp. 488–567). Reading, MA: Addison-Wesley.

Schöner, G., & Kelso, J. (1988). Dynamic pattern generation in behavioral and neural systems. *Science,* 25 March, 1513–1520.

Shaw, R. (1981). Strange attractors, chaotic behavior and information flow. *Z.Naturforsch., 36a,* 80–112.

Shaw, R., & Bransford, J. (1977). *Perceiving, acting, knowing.* Hillsdale, NJ: Lawrence Erlbaum Associates.

Thelen, E., & Fogel, A. (1989). Toward an action-based theory of infant development. In J. Lockman & N. Hazen (Eds.), *Action in social context* (pp. 221–248). New York: Plenum.

Turvey, M. T. (1977). Preliminaries to a theory of action with reference to vision. In R. Shaw & J. Bransford (Eds.), *Perceiving, acting, and knowing* (pp. 211–265). Hillsdale, NJ: Lawrence Erlbaum Associates.

Turvey, M. T. (1990). Coordination. *American Psychologist, 45,* 938–953.

Vallacher, R., & Wegner, D. (1985). *A theory of action identification.* Hillsdale, NJ: Lawrence Erlbaum Associates.

Zajonc, R. (1965). Social facilitation. *Science, 149,* 269–274.

10

MODELING INTERPERSONAL COORDINATION DYNAMICS: IMPLICATIONS FOR A DYNAMICAL THEORY OF DEVELOPING SYSTEMS

Richard C. Schmidt
College of the Holy Cross
University of Connecticut

Beth O'Brien
Tulane University

A significant aspect of development is that it occurs in a social context (Lockman & Hazen, 1989). The presence of other people and their role in the first years of our lives are so natural and omnipresent that it is easy to overlook the intricacy of the interpersonal coordination that must develop. The reason underlying this oversight is perhaps the unilateral nature of the coordination behavior in early care-provider/infant actions (i.e., care-provider implemented). However, as the infant develops a motor repertoire, the coordination goals necessarily become more mutual (as any parent can attest) and the intricacy of coordination involved becomes more obvious. The basis for the ensuing social coordination that develops is necessarily interpersonal motor coordination. The early dyadic activities of conversation and play are necessarily spatially and biomechanically constrained. For example, in order for child and adult to converse, or play pata-cake or peek-a-boo, there must be a coordination of the direction of gaze (Fogel, Nwokah, Hsu, Dedo, & Walker, 1993) if not limbs.

The goal of this chapter is to demonstrate how the development of interpersonal coordination might be modeled. In particular, it will examine whether the theory and method of the dynamical systems perspective used in the study of adult interpersonal motor coordination can be used to model the development of interpersonal coordination. One problem that needs to be overcome to successfully model any developing system is the degree of variability in the intrinsic functioning of such a system. That is, obviously, initial attempts at producing a movement pattern will be characterized by failures and half-successes. In principle, such variability could hamper attempts at providing an explicit formal model of a coordination behavior. A subsidiary goal of this chapter is to demonstrate that the dynamical systems perspective is sufficiently rich to model such systems in spite of the variability observed. In brief, the unstable behavior produced should have predictable characteristics if a dynamical control regime is underlying it. After an overview of dynamics and development, methods used for the dynamical study of interpersonal adult coordination are reviewed. How the problem of behavioral variability is overcome in this domain is edifying for dealing with developmental behavioral variability. The application of these methods to a developing interpersonal coordination is then proposed.

DYNAMICS AND DEVELOPMENT

Dynamical theory is used to model a physical system's properties of stability and change. It is a general theory that can be applied to physical systems whose behavior occurs at many space/time scales. Historically, it was developed to model the cosmological behavior of planets and galaxies (Ekeland, 1988), but more recently the understanding of the abstract, qualitative nature of dynamics has led researchers to apply these methods to complex systems at the chemical, biological, and social scales (Haken, 1977; Kugler & Turvey, 1987). The idea underlying these more recent applications is the fact that the complex systems are open systems—they are affected by flows of energy and information from their environment—and depending on their current relation to their surroundings they may take on different organizations. The goal is to mathematically model the organization of these systems (i.e., their stabilities) and their reordering under certain influences (i.e., their change). Importantly, dynamical theory provides a framework of methods that allow for the proposal of formal models that make predictions about the nature of physical systems' stabilities and change. Additionally, such formal models lead in a fairly straightforward manner to empirical tests of dynamical models.

Given dynamical theory's ability to model the reordering of physical systems, one can see why it has appealed to those investigating developing behavioral systems. Developing behavioral systems change in ontogenetic time. Described dynamically, one stable behavioral organization (e.g., walking in a toddler) "emerges" from another stable pattern (e.g., crawling in an infant). Understanding this process of behavioral change has a number of subsidiary questions. How can one understand what defines a behavioral stage? How can one understand the transition to a new one? What are the proximal causes for such a transition? Dynamical theory provides a general template for investigating emerging states in a physical system and, consequently, for understanding how these questions can be answered. Further, dynamical theory is general enough to model developmental change of systems that have different complexity or scale: The promise of dynamical theory is that single-organism behavioral development as well as interorganism behavioral development can be modeled using similar methods.

The foundational concept underlying the dynamical modeling of a complex open system is that of an *order parameter* (Haken, 1977). In brief, an order parameter is a measurable property that summarizes the quality of the organization of the system. It defines a metric whose values demarcate the qualitative states of system order. The measurement of the order parameter allows one to determine the mean state of the system and, by measuring the variability of the order parameter, the stability of that state. Of interest is how the mean and variance of the order parameter are influenced by external properties, namely, *control parameters*, that affect the state of the system. Perspicuous control parameters effect a weakening of a system's stable state, which often leads to the system's transition to a new stable state. The sudden quality of these transitions and their nonlinear rate of change has led them to be called phase transitions (Haken, Kelso, & Bunz, 1985) or catastrophes (Gilmore, 1981).

The now classic illustration of a dynamical model of a behavioral system is in found in interlimb coordination. Interlimb phasing has two natural modes. Limbs can be easily coordinated so that they are at the same place in the cycle at the same time—the in-phase mode or 0° relative phase—or so that they are in opposite places in the cycle at the same time—the antiphase mode or 180° relative phase. The two relative phase modes have been found to be differentially stable: The antiphase mode is less stable than the in-phase. The bimodality and differential stability of bimanual phasing have been observed in experiments where the 180° mode breaks down at higher frequencies of oscillation whereas the 0° mode does not (Kelso, 1984; Schmidt, Carello, & Turvey, 1990) and in experiments that measure the degree of steady-state fluctuation of the two modes (Schmidt, Shaw, & Turvey, 1993; Turvey, Rosenblum, Schmidt, & Kugler, 1986).

These properties have been explained as being a consequence of the dynamical nature of the control structure underlying bimanual coordination. The limb effector system acts identically to a regime of two coupled oscillators where the coupling strength between the oscillators decrease with increasing frequency. Haken et al. (1985; Schöner, Haken, & Kelso, 1986) employed a coupled oscillator regime with point attractors at relative phase angles of 0° and 180° to model the bimanual phasing properties. The dynamical description of relative phase angle (ϕ) between the two rhythmic units is defined by the differential equation:

$$\dot{\phi} = -\frac{dV(\phi)}{d\phi} + \sqrt{Q\varepsilon} \qquad (1)$$

where the rate of change of the relative phase angle ($\dot{\phi}$) is a function of the rate of change of the potential function,

$$V(\phi) = -a \, \cos(\phi) - b \, \cos(2\phi) \qquad (2)$$

and a stochastic noise term ε of magnitude Q. The minima of the potential function (where its rate of change is 0) indicate the stable relative phase patterns attainable by the coupled oscillatory regime. Figure 10.1 demonstrates that these stable points of the regime appear at the function minima of $\phi = 0°$ and $\phi = 180°$, and that the stable point at $\phi = 180°$ is less stable (i.e., more shallow) than that at $0°$. If one assumes that the ratio of the coupling strengths b/a decreases with increasing frequency, the steady state at $\phi = 180°$ (i.e., the local minimum of the equation at $180°$) disappears when b/a reaches a critical value of .25. The scaling of the control parameter leads to a weakening of the stable state at $\phi = 180°$. Hence, under the assumption that the coupling strength ratio decreases with increasing frequency, this

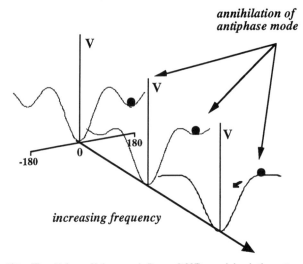

FIG. 10.1. The Haken, Kelso, and Bunz (1985) model of the attractors underlying bimanual, interlimb coordination. The potential function has attractor points (i.e., potential minima) at relative phase angles $0°$ and $\pm180°$ representing the in-phase and antiphase interlimb phase modes, respectively. Note how this model captures the differential stability of the coordination modes. First, the minima at $\pm180°$ are more shallow than those that at $0°$, denoting the lesser stability of the antiphase mode of interlimb phasing. Second, the minima at $\pm180°$ become more shallow, and finally disappear, with increasing frequency.

coupled oscillator dynamic predicts both the bimodality and differential stability observed in bimanual limb phasing.

The cause underlying the behavioral change in this interlimb phasing example is a combination of the weakening of the attractor at 180° (because of decreasing coupling strength) and the stochastic fluctuations (i.e., ε) that precipitate the new stable state. This is a general principle of dynamical control processes, namely, that variability is a natural part of systems that change behavioral mode and that fluctuations can lead to the exploration of new modes (Beek, 1989). The ramification of this point for modeling developing behavioral systems is obvious: Developing systems should be noisy because they are changing modes.

An example of the use of dynamical theory to understand the development of coordination is the ground-breaking research of Esther Thelen. In a series of studies (Thelen & Fisher, 1982; Thelen & Ulrich, 1991), Thelen and colleagues investigated infant leg movements that are the precursors to walking. She noted that interlimb leg movements performed on treadmills were coordinated early on, lost coordination for a time, and then regained it. She provided evidence that this emergence and loss of coordination can be explained as the behavior of a dynamical action system being scaled by changes in body weight—that is, body weight is functioning as a control parameter. In the early stage, the muscle tone of the infants' legs is great enough to rhythmically phase the limbs in a coordinated fashion. However, as the infant gains weight, the strength of the legs is no longer enough and coordinated interlimb phasing disappears. Finally, as the infant becomes more active and muscle tone improves, coordinated interlimb phasing reappears. In more recent work, Corbetta and Thelen (1994) studied the dynamical basis of changes from bimanual to unimanual reaching in first year of life. Their work demonstrates that the development of reaching involves the control of the activity of the contralateral arm: Initially the two arms are strongly coupled, and later they can be controlled independently. Thelen's research highlights that in order to understand the development of coordinated movement patterns, one must study more than the kinematics of limbs—namely, the dynamical "cooperative coupling of ensemble components" involved and how nonspecific properties can function as control parameters that change the modes of equilibrium of the cooperative coupling.

Although the past application of dynamical systems theory to developing systems has been quite promising, it has been metaphoric in nature, has lacked the formal modeling found in the adult interlimb phasing investigations, and consequently the interaction of prediction and experiment that a mathematical model can afford a research program. One reason that has prevented the use of formal models is that such models generally represent steady-state or stationary behavior, and developmental systems by their very nature produce behavior that is not steady and is nonstationary. So, for example, Equation 1 represents a dynamical system with steady-state behavior near 0° (in-phase) or 180° (antiphase) and temporary transitory behavior from the 180° steady state to 0° steady state. But in studying the leg kick precursors to walking in infants, one may see a somewhat arbitrary switching back and forth between these and other relative phase relations. And because this is naturalistic research with young infants, an experimenter cannot implement steady-state task constraints on the behavior, nor would the experimenter want to because that would obviate the naturalistic research questions (e.g., what are they doing at what developmental stage). Not only do the formal models as typically rendered not predict the nonstationary behavior of developing systems, typical methods of measurement are thwarted as well: Stationary statistical measures such as the mean and standard deviation are unenlightening summaries of the nonstationary patterns of behavior exhibited by developing systems or any system where the behavior is less stereotyped.

However, as we argue, nonstationarity of an order parameter alone does not require abandoning dynamical models. Indeed, dynamical models make predictions about what form the nonstationary behavior should take. To demonstrate this point and the methods of analysis of nonstationary relative coordination, we review research investigating adult between-person coordination.

THE DYNAMICS OF INTERPERSONAL INTERLIMB COORDINATION

Interpersonal interlimb coordination can be described on a continuum of task constraint. On the one hand, there are interpersonal coordinations such as in dance and in sports that are strongly task constrained in that the coordination is much practiced and has an explicit goal. Such coordination is intentional. On the other hand, there is interactional synchrony found in natural social interactions (e.g., conversations) that is only weakly constrained by the occurring task and is often unintentional. Research in social psychology (Newtson, Hairfield, Bloomingdale, & Cutino, 1987) suggests that there is a natural tendency for individuals to synchronize their movements without intending to, especially when the two individuals are either genetically or rapport bound (Bernieri, 1988; Bernieri, Reznick, & Rosenthal, 1988). This interlimb coordination occurs in conversation, between listener and lecturer, or in mother–child play. In interactional synchrony then, the coordination is implicit in another more explicit goal (e.g., sharing information in a conversation).

Although it has been proposed that interpersonal interlimb coordination across the task constraint continuum can be explained by dynamical processes of self-organization, past research has only explicitly tested this hypothesis in strongly constrained tasks in which intentional coordination is the goal. Such interlimb coordination is amenable to experimental investigation and formal dynamical modeling because the experimenter dictates the coordination pattern to be maintained. Hence, the order parameter that has been used to evaluate interlimb coordination, relative phase is, for the most part, stationary under typical parameterizations. To use von Holst's (1939/1973) terminology, the stationary relative phasing in such interlimb coordination represents *absolute coordination*. However, the problem of nonstationary coordination arises in trying to model the unintentional interlimb coordination between individuals in situations where the task constraint is weak. Through statistical (Condon, 1982) and perceptual measures (Bernieri et al., 1988), the analysis of such interactions reveals that individuals are entrained, albeit weakly. However, no one coordination pattern is apparent in these interactions, and hence the relative phasing is not centered around a constant value. Consequently, the variability of the coordination pattern is high and the mean states of this order parameter are not measures of equilibrium states. Indeed, the coordination system does not seem to be in a steady state at all. Therefore, as with developing systems, the standard methods of formal dynamical modeling are thwarted.

Kelso and colleagues (Kelso & Ding, 1994; Zanone & Kelso, 1990) pointed out that non-steady-state coordination behavior (what von Holst, 1939/1973, called *relative coordination*) can be produced by dynamical systems with weak attractor basins and intrinsic noise. Such dynamical systems demonstrate the property of *intermittency*: a constant change in state with an attraction to certain regions of their underlying phase space. Hence, it is possible that dynamical systems that demonstrate intermittency can in principle be used to model the noisy nonstationary behavior seen in weakly coupled systems such as naturally interacting dyads or developing interlimb control structures. In what follows, we review how intentional interpersonal coordination can be dynamically modeled using an intrapersonal coordination experimental paradigm and standard methods of dynamical modeling, and then demonstrate how the paradigm and dynamical model can be adapted to explore the nonstationary relative phasing of unintentional interpersonal coordination.

Intentional Interpersonal Coordination

The standard method that has been used to dynamically model interlimb coordination is to measure how coordinative mean states (e.g., of relative phase) and their variability change as external control parameters (e.g., frequency and inertial loadings of limbs) are manipulated. Interestingly, studies using this strategy for investigating intentional interpersonal coordination have demonstrated dynamical coordinative processes that are identical to those found in within-person coordination. Schmidt and Turvey (1994) used a rhythmic coordination paradigm previously used to investigate within-person coordination (see Kugler & Turvey, 1987) to evaluate intentional interpersonal interlimb coordination. In this methodology, two participants sitting side by side oscillated a weighted dowel (called a wrist-pendulum) in the sagittal plane using ulnar and radial flexion of their wrist (Fig. 10.2). What is manipulated is the differential inertial loading of the two wrist-pendulum systems. The two wrist-pendulum systems could be identical or different in their mass and length magnitudes. Such an inertial manipulation effectively scales the preferred frequency (eigenfrequency) of the oscillatory wrist movements (Kugler & Turvey, 1987; Turvey, Schmidt, Rosenblum, & Kugler, 1988), and the difference of the loadings between the two wrist-pendulum systems manipulates the difference between the preferred frequencies or the eigenfrequency difference of the pendulum pair. It is this property, the eigenfrequency difference, that has been used as an effective control parameter to manipulate order parameter (relative phase) dynamics.

Previous studies investigating the coordination of wrist-pendulums across the two wrists of a single person (see Schmidt & Turvey, 1995, for a review) investigated whether the steady-state (i.e., no frequency scaling) relative phasing of the wrist-pendulums would exhibit the predicted characteristics of a coupled oscillatory dynamical system such as that which had been used to model the breakdown of relative phasing (Haken, Kelso, & Bunz, 1985). That dynamical model predicts two properties if the eigenfrequency difference of the two oscillators is scaled. The first is fixed-point (attractor location) drift, which means that the mean relative phase exhibited by the oscillatory system moves away from the canonical values of 0° (for in-phase) and 180° (for antiphase coordination) in proportion to the eigenfrequency difference. Second, the model predicts that as the magnitude of the eigenfrequency difference increases, the stability of the system should decrease and fluctuation of the order parameter should increase. Both of these predicted dynamical characteristics have been affirmed in numerous intrapersonal

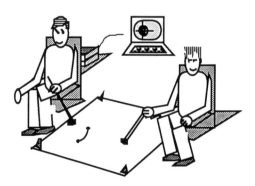

FIG. 10.2. The experimental arrangement used for studying interpersonal interlimb coordination.

wrist-pendulum paradigm studies (Schmidt & Turvey, 1995) supporting the hypothesis that control structures underlying the steady-state coordination of interlimb rhythmic movements within a person have a dynamical basis.

Schmidt and Turvey (1994) asked the related question of whether the dynamical principles involved in the intrapersonal coordination of rhythmic movements across the central nervous system (CNS) were sufficiently general to operate in the intentional visual coordination of movement between two people. In this study, three pairs of participants were told to visually coordinate the oscillations of their wrist-pendulums at a comfortable tempo in antiphase. Sixteen different wrist-pendulum pairs were used per participant pair. An exemplary relative phase time series (ϕ) from a typical trial is plotted in Fig. 10.3. Because the relative phase is centered around a mean value of about 180°, one can tell that a stable antiphase coordination was performed for the entire trial, yielding stationary relative phase time series. The coordination here is absolute coordination, and hence the mean state of the order parameter and its variability can reliably be used to determine whether the dynamical model predictions are affirmed. Summary graphs of these measures are depicted in Fig. 10.4. The left-hand graph demonstrates fixed-point drift, the drifting of the attractor location. As the eigenfrequency difference ($\Delta\omega$) of the pendulum pair is scaled away from 0, the mean relative phase of the system (ϕ) moves away from 180° such that the pendulum with the inherently faster eigenfrequency is leading in its cycle. The right-hand graph demonstrates the decreasing stability (increasing fluctuation) of the coupled oscillatory system as the eigenfrequency difference is scaled away from 0.

This study suggests that intentional interpersonal coordination can be understood in terms of the same dynamical processes of self-organization that underlie the coordination of limbs across the CNS: When two people intend to coordinate their rhythmic limb movements, the ensuing behavioral pattern is that of a dynamical coupled oscillatory system. It appears that

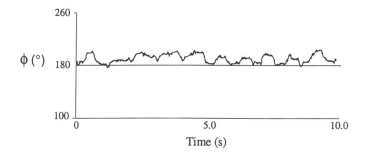

FIG. 10.3. A stationary interpersonal relative phase time series from an intentional coordination experiment (Schmidt & Turvey, 1994).

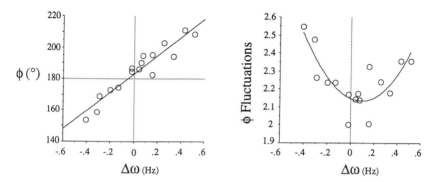

FIG. 10.4. Model predicted results from visual intentional interpersonal coordination experiment (Schmidt & Turvey, 1994): Fixed-point drift [left: $r^2(1,14) = .85$, $y = 0.17x + 0.05$, $p < .001$] and decreasing system stability [right: $r^2(1,14) = .47$, $y = 0.04x^2 + 0.04x + 2.3$, $p < .02$] as functions of the eigenfrequency difference ($\Delta\omega$) of two visually coupled wrist-pendulum systems (see text).

the participant pair has assembled a dyadic coupled oscillatory control structure to maintain their coordination.

Unintentional Interpersonal Coordination

The question remains, however, of whether natural interpersonal coordination where synchronous coordination is not an explicit goal has a dynamical basis. Although this suggestion has been made and metaphoric dynamical explanations have been given (e.g., Newtson et al., 1987), no formal dynamical modeling of interactional synchrony has been forthcoming. To be redundant, the problem with providing such a model is that, unlike intentional coordination where the experimenter dictates a particular coordination pattern to be maintained, the coordination pattern in unintentional coordination is not constant, and consequently, the order parameter used to evaluate interlimb coordination, relative phase, is nonstationary. This nonstationarity disallows the standard methods of dynamical modeling: the use of mean states and their fluctuations to determine attractor states and their strength (respectively). However, nonstationarity is expected of a dynamical system if its attractors are weak and the system contains a degree of inherent noise. What is needed are new methods of analysis to evaluate the nonstationary behavior to determine whether it indeed demonstrates intermittent attraction to weak equilibrium regions, that is, whether the coordination behavior demonstrates intermittency.

In particular, what needs to be investigated in unintentional interpersonal coordination is whether rhythmic movements are drawn to the relative phases of 0° and 180° that are indicative of the stable modes of the coupled oscillator dynamic underlying intentional interpersonal interlimb coordination. In order to investigate this, an experiment was performed that attempted to capture unintentional interactional synchrony in the laboratory though an adaptation of the wrist-pendulum paradigm previously described. Ten pairs of participants were recruited from undergraduate psychology classes to serve as subjects. The pairs sat facing the same direction and oscillated hand-held pendulums in the sagittal plane. The subject task was different for the two halves of a trial. During the first half of a trial, subject pairs were instructed to look straight ahead so that they could not see one another and to swing the pendulum at a comfortable rate that they could "perform all day." During the second half of a trial, subjects were told to look at the other subject's moving pendulum but maintain their preferred tempo from the first half of the trial. Each subject performed thirty 24-sec trials. The angular excursions of the two pendulums were collected and from these the time series of continuous relative phase was calculated (see Schmidt & Turvey, 1994, for calculation procedures). Of interest was whether on the second half of the trials (when visual information was available) the subjects would tend to entrain their movements unintentionally and whether this coordination is constrained by coupled oscillator dynamics that seem to guide intentional interpersonal coordination.

Inspection of the relative phase time series in Fig. 10.5 suggests no superficial difference between the first and second parts of the trial. If there is any entrainment in the second half of the trial, the coordination is not absolute but relative coordination. Compared to the Fig. 10.3, the relative phase measure is not centered around a constant value but is constantly changing through all possible states. It is, therefore, nonstationary. The mean and variance of relative phase would not in this case be revealing about the prospective underlying dynamical mechanisms. However, if there

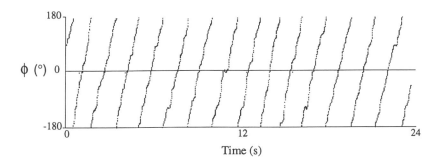

FIG. 10.5. A nonstationary interpersonal relative phase time series from an unintentional coordination experiment. In the first 12 sec of the trial, the participants were not visually coupled—they oscillated their pendulums not looking at each other. In the second 12 sec, the participants looked at the other person's pendulum but attempted to maintain their own preferred tempo.

is a weak dynamical coupling of the two movements yielding unintentional entrainment, one should be able to see evidence of intermittency. That is, if a coupled oscillator dynamic is constraining the behavior observed, then an attraction to the relative phases defined as fixed points for intentional interpersonal coordination (namely, 0° and/or 180°) should occur in the second half of the trial.

This intermittency of attraction can be evaluated in a number of ways. First, attraction to the fixed points in the second half of the trial should be indicated by a distribution of relative phase angles near the attractors at 0° and 180° that represents the dwell time in the attractor basin. Relatedly, because the rate of change of the relative phase ($\Delta\phi$) should slow down in the part of the trial that exhibits the intermittent attraction, $\Delta\phi$ should be less and should in particular decrease near the 0° and 180° fixed points in the second half of the trial.

To determine whether there was a greater concentration of ϕ near 0° and 180° in the second trial half, the ϕ time series (Fig. 10.5) were normalized into the 0–180° range. The number of relative phase values that fell within the nine 20° phase regions between 0° and 180° was calculated for each trial half. As anticipated, Fig. 10.6 (top) demonstrates that the distribution of relative phase is flat for the first trial half but has greater concentrations around 0° and 180° compared to the middle phase regions in the second trial half when visual information was available. Pairwise *t*-tests comparing the proportion of relative phases in each phase region reveal that the second trial half has significantly greater relative phases near 0° [0° to 20°: $t(299) = 6.25$, $p < .001$; 20° to 40°: $t(299) = 2.33$, $p < .05$] and significantly fewer in the phase regions between 0 and 180° [60° to 80°: $t(299) = 4.42$, $p < .001$; 80° to 100°: $t(299) = 5.00$, $p < .001$; 100° to 120°: $t(299) = 5.63$, $p < .001$; 120° to 140°: $t(299) = 3.01$, $p < .01$]. The concentration of the second trial half was not significantly greater or less near 180° [140° to 160°: $t(299) = 0.42$, $p > .05$; 160° to 180°: $t(299) = 0.03$, $p > .05$], however. These results suggest an attraction to the 0° region and a repulsion from relative phase angles between 0° and 180°. The lack of attraction from 180° can mean that either no attractor was present or that, if present, its attraction was too weak to be verified. In sum these findings can be interpreted as prima facie evidence for the existence in nonintentional interpersonal coordination of a coupled oscillator dynamic that produces fairly strong intermittent attraction to 0° and a weaker or nonexistent intermittent attraction to 180°.

Intermittent attraction can also be measured using a related index of attraction, $\Delta\phi$. If the two rhythmic movements periodically become entrained or phase locked, the rate of change of the relative phase ($\Delta\phi$) should decrease. In order to evaluate this possibility, the $\Delta\phi$ time series was calculated as $\phi_{n+1} - \phi_n$ (using the normalized ϕ time series). The results demonstrate that, indeed, the average $\Delta\phi$ was less for the second part of the trial

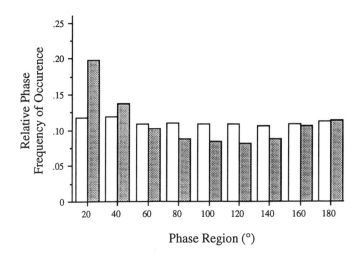

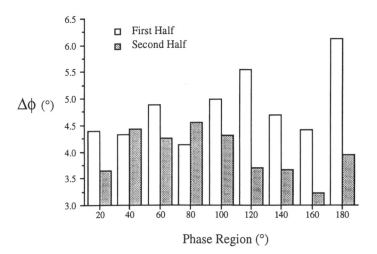

FIG. 10.6. Model-predicted intermittent attraction from an unintentional interpersonal coordination experiment. The rate of change of relative phase (Δφ) slows down near the 0° and 180° attractors of the Haken et al. (1985) model (bottom) only when visual information is available about the other's movement (second trial half). Relatedly, this intermittent attraction results in a greater frequency of occurrence of relative phase angles in these attractor regions (top).

than the first (3.97 vs. 4.83 °/sec), suggesting a slowing down of the relative phase change when visual information was available. To determine whether the decrease in relative phase was near the 0° and 180° attractor locations, the average $\Delta\phi$ was calculated as the relative phase passed through nine 20° relative phase regions between 0° and 180°. These mean rates of change across these regions for each trial half appear in Fig. 10.6 (bottom). The rates of change show no pattern across the relative phase regions for the first trial half. But for the second trial half, an inverted U-shape plot is revealed with minimum rates of change near 0° and 180°, which suggests that the system was being attracted to these regions. Pairwise t-tests comparing $\Delta\phi$ for each trial half revealed no significant differences ($p > .05$), however. The power of these tests may have been severely hampered by the variability associated with the $\Delta\phi$ time series.

The patterning of results portrayed in Fig. 10.6 suggests that an intermittent attraction can occur in unintentional interpersonal coordination at the attractor locations of a coupled oscillatory regime. It seems that "ghosts" of the attractor landscape used in intentional coordination behavior also constrain unintentional entrainment behavior and suggest that the mere presence of an information linkage without an explicit intention to coordinate is sufficient for the operation of these dynamical principles of self-organization. The methodological importance of these analyses is that in spite of the nonstationarity of the coordination order parameter, the dynamical basis of the variable behavior patterns can be resolved and predictions from a formal dynamical model can be made about the structure of the nonstationary behavior. The point is that one must move away from the standard measures of the coordination (order parameter) dynamics (i.e., means and variance) and look at the structure of the variance for signs of intermittent attraction. In brief, different methods are necessary for investigating coordination systems that by their very nature display variable behavior. Further, these methods can be applied to any system that has been proposed to have a dynamical basis, whether the system has variable behavior because it is complex (e.g., a social system) or has variable behavior because it is evolving (e.g., a developing system). In the next section, we distill from the preceding review of interpersonal coordination methodological steps necessary for studying the development of interpersonal coordination between a mother and infant.

DYNAMICAL MODELING OF DEVELOPING INTERPERSONAL COORDINATION

Recent work by Alan Fogel and colleagues (Fogel et al., 1993) investigated the role of posture and reaching in mother–infant interaction. It has been previously established that such interactions with very young infants (2–4 months) consist of predominantly mother–infant face-to-face gazing–*mutual gazing*. As the infant matures and becomes interested in inanimate environmental objects, facing away from the mother–*away gazing*–becomes an alternative behavioral mode.

Fogel et al. (1993) were interested in what sensorimotor factors precipitated the transition between these two developmental stages. One factor they found was the direction of the gaze of the infant. They found that mothers shifted the infant's position more when the infant was gazing away from them. Eventually as the infant matured, these mother-induced postural shifts were in the direction of the infant's gaze (i.e., away from the mother). Interestingly, the spatial relation of mother and infant in the face-to-face interaction is coconstructed–both mother and infant are involved in producing the final state. Another sensorimotor factor underlying the transition between these two developmental stages is the onset of reaching behavior. In some of the infants the match between gazing away and the mother's facing them away did not occur until after they began to reach. Hence, for these infants, their nonmother directedness was not substantially recognized in the dyadic system until the infant was able to have manual interactions with the surroundings.

Fogel et al. (1993) interpreted the development of this behavioral mode from the dynamical perspective. The coconstructive nature of the behavior–the fact that there is a mutual influence between the components of a system–is characteristic of a dynamical system. Fogel et al. (1993) suggested that "the dyadic match between infant gaze away and maternal holding of the infant facing away ... possibly (represents) a social attractor state ... (which) ... must await the ontogenetic emergence of at least two control parameters: (1) gazing away and (2) reaching" (p. 418). In this final section, we would like to suggest a modeling procedure based on the methods introduced to investigate adult unintentional interpersonal coordination that can be used to support the hypothesis that these mother–infant behavioral modes have a dynamical basis.

Qualitatively, the dynamical system that would produce these modes of interpersonal gaze is one that would have one attractor early (2–4 months) (representing the coordination pattern of mutual gaze) and two attractors later (representing the possible coordination patterns of mutual gaze and away gaze). The dynamical landscape of such a system can be represented by the potential functions in Fig. 10.7 (bottom). (Although the modeling here will be strictly qualitative, an explicit quantitative function representing these potential functions can also be provided.) Assuming that these attractors exist, what behavioral predictions can be made? What measurements can we make of the behavior to verify the existence of these interpersonal attractors?

The first step is to define an order parameter–a property that summarizes the quality of a coordinative state of interest. This step was tacit in

Angle of Relative Gaze

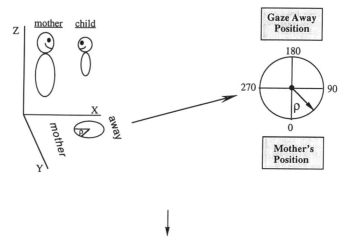

Dynamical Model

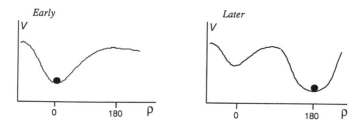

FIG. 10.7. The definition of the order parameter (top) proposed for investigating the coordination in mother–infant interaction and its development—the angle of relative gaze. The attractor landscapes (bottom) proposed to dynamically model the early (< 2 month) and later mother–infant relative gaze patterns (see text).

the unintentional interpersonal coordination research described earlier, because a perspicuous property, relative phase, that captures the interlimb coordinative states had already been defined. Because we are interested in the relationship of the gaze direction of the infant with respect to the postural position of the mother, the angle of *relative gaze* ρ as defined in Fig. 10.7 (top) is a good candidate. When ρ is near 0° it defines the mode of mutual gaze, whereas ρ near 180° defines the behavioral mode of away gaze.

Importantly, the angle of relative gaze must be able to be measured experimentally. Indeed, to evaluate its dynamical basis, one must be able to obtain a record of its change over time. Consequently, the time series of relative gaze must be acquired. It can be obtained by placing movement recording cameras (e.g., of a Peak Performance or Optotrak movement analysis system) on the ceiling to obtain the change in positions (i.e., the position time series) of the mother's head and the infant's head. Both front and back head positions would need to be acquired in order to determine the direction of gaze from the time series. The angle of relative gaze can be calculated from these head position time series. As for the experimental procedure, the natural 5-min interaction task used by Fogel et al. (i.e., have the mother sit in a chair for 5 min and play and talk to the baby as they would at home) would produce time series of sufficient length for a dynamical analysis.

Given the naturalistic task, one should expect the time series of relative gaze to be nonstationary. In terms of the dynamical landscape of Fig. 10.7 (bottom), the noise in the system (defined as forces coming from an external frame of reference) is so great that the system's state is pushed from the equilibrium positions at the bottom of the attractor wells. In spite of this nonstationarity of the order parameter, if interpersonal attractors for the behavioral modes of mutual gaze and away gaze exist, one should see intermittent attraction towards the values of $\rho = 0$ and $\rho = 180°$. Hence, after the order parameter has been defined and an experimental setup to measure it devised, one can use the methods described in the interpersonal coordination section to determine whether an intermittency of attraction occurs in the requisite portions of the dynamical landscape.

To do this one should first plot the distribution of the order parameter across the range of 0° to 180° to determine whether the states of the system are concentrated near the proposed attractor basins. If the interpersonal system indeed represents a social attractor state, then at early ages, one should see the relative gaze angle concentrated around $\rho = 0°$, and at later ages, one should see the relative gaze angle concentrated around $\rho = 0°$ and $\rho = 180°$ (Fig. 10.8). Second, the mean rate of change of the order parameter, $\Delta\rho$, should be calculated for different relative gaze regions (e.g., 20° intervals

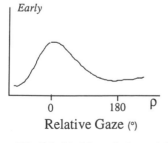
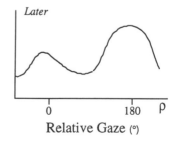

FIG. 10.8. Model predictions of the distribution of relative gaze angles for early (<2 month) and later mother–infant interaction if interpersonal attractors are underlying these coordination patterns.

between 0° and 180°). $\Delta\rho$ can be calculated as $\rho_{n+1} - \rho_n$. If the $\Delta\rho$ decreases near $\rho = 0°$ for younger ages and near $\rho = 0°$ and $\rho = 180°$ for older ages, then this is additional evidence of intermittent attraction—the gaze relation tends to slow down at these relative angles at these different ages. If ρ and $\Delta\rho$ are patterned in the predicted ways, then there is empirical support for interpersonal attractors underlying gaze direction in mother–infant interaction.

Having quantitatively captured the coordination dynamics has the added benefit that an index of the strength of the attractors can be calculated. The strength of the attractor is inversely related to the $\Delta\rho$ in the attractor region (i.e., the smaller the rate of change, the stronger the attractor). This measure would be useful in a number of ways because it quantifies the strength of a behavioral mode. First, this measure would provide a dynamical means of comparing the behavior of the different subjects and would provide a basis for grouping them into developmental stages. Second, this measure would provide a means of determining whether a given property is indeed functioning as a control parameter. Fogel et al. (1993) proposed that the infant abilities of gazing away and reaching operate as control parameters. One would expect to see a high correlation between the strength of a new behavioral mode and a quantitative index of a property (e.g., gazing away) whose change is underlying the emergence of the new behavioral regime.

CONCLUDING REMARKS

Developing systems are characterized by their change and the inherent variability of their behavioral patterns. Nonstationarity of the coordinative patterns are the rule rather than the exception. The dynamical system perspective offers a very rich set of concepts for modeling stability and change in physical systems. We have tried here to demonstrate, using our work on adult interpersonal coordination, that systems that exhibit very variable, nonstationary coordinative patterns can be dynamically modeled, as well as those that exhibit more stereotyped behavioral patterns. We have tried to demonstrate how the intermittent attraction found in weak dynamical systems can be a characteristic property of such nonstationary coordinative systems.

Using the Fogel et al. work on mother–infant interactions, we have proposed how this kind of dynamical system can be used in the study of inherently variable interpersonal developing systems. However, this method can also be used by developmental researchers to study the development of intrapersonal interlimb coordination (for an example of the development of clapping see Fitzpatrick, chapter 3, this volume). One theme of the method revealed here is an emphasis on modeling behavioral stabilities rather than behavioral transitions (Schmidt & Turvey, 1995). Although transitions between stages in development are important to understand, they are difficult to investigate given individual differences in development and the slow time scale of their evolution. The suggestion made here is to first verify the dynamical basis of stable (or not so stable) modes. As demonstrated earlier, this can be achieved by determining whether these modes exhibit the characteristic properties of attraction. Using the steady-state analysis of the behavioral modes as a basis, one can then turn to investigating the transition between two developmental states as dynamically based change.

ACKNOWLEDGMENTS

R. C. Schmidt was supported by Louisiana Board of Regents grant RD-A-23 during the preparation of this manuscript. My thanks to Paula Fitzpatrick who assisted with the research reported in this chapter.

REFERENCES

Beek, P. J. (1989). Timing and phase-locking in cascade juggling. *Ecological Psychology, 1*, 55–96.
Bernieri, F. J. (1988). Coordinated movement and rapport in teacher–student interactions. *Journal of Nonverbal Behavior, 12*, 120–138.
Bernieri, F. J., Reznick, J. S., & Rosenthal, R. (1988). Synchrony, pseudosynchrony, and dissynchrony: Measuring the entrainment process in mother–infant interactions. *Journal of Personality and Social Psychology, 54*, 243–253.
Condon, W. S. (1982). Cultural microrhythms. In M. Davis (Ed.), *Interaction rhythms: Periodicity in communicative behavior* (pp. 53–77). New York: Human Sciences Press.
Corbetta, D., & Thelen, E. (1994). Shifting patterns of interlimb coordination in infants' reaching. In S. Swinnen, H. Heuer, J. Massion, & P. Casaer (Eds.), *Interlimb coordination: Neural, dynamical and cognitive constraints* (pp. 413–438). San Diego: Academic Press.
Ekeland, I. (1988). *Mathematics and the unexpected.* Chicago: University of Chicago Press.
Fogel, A., Nwokah, E., Hsu, H., Dedo, J., & Walker, H. (1993). Posture and communication in mother–infant interaction. In G. J. P. Savelsbergh (Ed.), *The development of coordination in infancy* (pp. 395–422). Amsterdam: Elsevier.
Gilmore, R. (1981). *Catastrophe theory for scientists and engineers.* New York: Wiley.
Haken, H. (1977). *Synergetics: An introduction.* Heidelberg: Springer-Verlag.
Haken, H., Kelso, J. A. S., & Bunz, H. (1985). A theoretical model of phase transitions in human hand movements. *Biological Cybernetics, 51*, 347–356.
Kelso, J. A. S. (1984). Phase transitions and critical behavior in human bimanual coordination. *American Journal of Physiology: Regulatory, Integrative and Comparative, 246*, R1000–R1004.
Kelso, J. A. S., & Ding, M. (1994). Fluctuations, intermittency, and controllable chaos in biological coordination. In K. M. Newell & D. M. Corcos (Eds.), *Variability in motor control* (pp. 291–316). Champaign, IL: Human Kinetics.
Kugler, P. N., & Turvey, M. T. (1987). *Information, natural law and the self-assembly of rhythmic movement.* Hillsdale, NJ: Lawrence Erlbaum Associates.
Lockman, J. J., & Hazen, N. L. (1989). *Action in a social context.* New York: Plenum.

Newtson, D., Hairfield, J., Bloomingdale, J., & Cutino, S. (1987). The structure of action and interaction. *Social Cognition, 5*, 191–237.

Schmidt, R. C., Carello, C., & Turvey, M. T. (1990). Phase transitions and critical fluctuations in the visual coordination of rhythmic movements between people. *Journal of Experimental Psychology: Human Perception and Performance, 16*, 227–247.

Schmidt, R. C., Shaw, B. K., & Turvey, M. T. (1993). Coupling dynamics in interlimb coordination. *Journal of Experimental Psychology: Human Perception and Performance, 19*, 397–415.

Schmidt, R. C., & Turvey, M. T. (1994). Phase-entrainment dynamics of visually coupled rhythmic movements. *Biological Cybernetics, 70*, 369–376.

Schmidt, R. C., & Turvey, M. T. (1995). Models of interlimb coordination: Equilibria, local analyses, and spectral patterning. *Journal of Experimental Psychology: Human Perception and Performance, 21*, 432–443.

Schöner, G., Haken, H., & Kelso, J. A. S. (1986). A stochastic theory of phase transitions in human hand movement. *Biological Cybernetics, 53*, 247–257.

Thelen, E., & Fisher, D. M. (1982). Newborn stepping: An explanation for a "disappearing" reflex. *Developmental Psychology, 18*, 760–775.

Thelen, E., & Ulrich, B. D. (1991). Hidden skills: A dynamic systems analysis of treadmill stepping during the first year. *Monographs of the Society for Research in Child Development, 56*, v–104.

Turvey, M. T., Rosenblum, L. D., Schmidt, R. C., & Kugler, P. N. (1986). Fluctuations and phase symmetry in coordinated rhythmic movement. *Journal of Experimental Psychology: Human Perception and Performance, 12*, 564–583.

Turvey, M. T., Schmidt, R. C., Rosenblum, L. D., & Kugler, P. N. (1988). On the time allometry of coordinated rhythmic movements. *Journal of Theoretical Biology, 130*, 285–325.

von Holst, E. (1973). Relative coordination as a phenomenon and as a method of analysis of central nervous system function. In R. Martin (Ed. and Trans.), *The collected papers of Erich von Holst: Vol. 1, The behavioral physiology of animal and man* (pp. 33–135). Coral Gables, FL: University of Miami Press. (Original work published 1939)

Zanone, P. G., & Kelso, J. A. S. (1990). Relative timing from the perspective of dynamic pattern theory: Stability and instability. In J. Fagard & P. H. Wolff (Eds.), *The development of timing control and temporal organization in coordinated action* (pp. 62–92). Amsterdam: Elsevier.

METHODS IN DYNAMICAL SYSTEMS AND DEVELOPMENT

11

APPROXIMATE ENTROPY (ApEn) AS A REGULARITY MEASURE

Steven M. Pincus
Guilford, Connecticut

Time series are encountered frequently in diverse settings. One is often interested in time series for either of two important purposes: (a) to distinguish (discriminate) systems, based on statistical characteristics, or (b) to mathematically model systems. In both cases, effective statistics and models need to account for the sequential interrelationships among the data—study of autocorrelation and of power spectra is motivated by this recognition. In this chapter we focus on the first of these purposes, statistical discrimination, via a quantification of regularity of a time series. This approach also calibrates the extent of sequential interrelationships, from a relatively new perspective, based on quantifying a notion of orderliness (as opposed to "randomness") of the data.

Approximate entropy (ApEn) has been recently introduced as a quantification of regularity in time-series data, motivated by applications to relatively short, noisy data sets (Pincus, 1991). Mathematically, ApEn is part of a general development as the *rate of entropy* for an approximating Markov Chain to a process (Pincus, 1992). In applications to heart rate, findings have discrimated groups of subjects via ApEn, in instances where classical (mean, SD) statistics did not show clear group distinctions (Fleisher, Pincus, & Rosenbaum, 1993; Kaplan et al., 1991; Pincus, Cummins, & Haddad, 1993; Pincus, Gladstone, & Ehrenkrantz, 1991; Pincus & Viscarello, 1992; Ryan, Goldberger, Pincus, Mietus, & Lipsitz, 1994). In applications to endocrine hormone secretion data based on as few as $N = 72$ points, ApEn has provided vivid distinctions ($p < 10^{-8}$) between actively diseased subjects and normals, with nearly 100% specificity and sensitivity (Hartman et al., 1994; Siragy, Vieweg, Pincus, & Veldhuis, 1995; Veldhuis et al., 1995).

We next describe ApEn implementation and interpretation, indicating its utility to distinguish correlated stochastic processes, and composite deterministic/stochastic models. We discuss the key technical idea that motivates ApEn, that one need not fully reconstruct an attractor to discriminate in a statistically valid manner—marginal probability distributions often suffice for this purpose. We discuss why algorithms to compute, for example, correlation dimension and the Kolmogorov-Sinai (K-S) entropy often work well for true dynamical systems, yet sometimes operationally confound for general models. This contrast indicates the need for a thematically faithful modification of a parameter such as the K-S entropy for general applications so that visual intuition matches numerical results, for broad classes of stochastic processes as well as for dynamical systems. We provide a mechanistic hypothesis suggesting greater regularity in a wide range of evolving, complicated systems. Finally, we illustrate the statistical breadth of ApEn via several disparate time-series applications, both to actual "field" data (growth hormone within endocrinology, and Dow Jones stock index), and to theoretical models (coupled stochastic differential equations, and new rejection criteria for a variety of i.i.d. or "random" processes).

To illustrate the distinctions we are trying to quantify, contrast Fig. 11.1a versus 11.1b, Fig. 11.2a versus 11.2b, and Fig. 11.3, taken from the MIX(p) process discussed later, for which we see time series that apparently become increasingly irregular as we proceed from (a) to (d). Historical context frames this effort. Complexity statistics developed for application to chaotic systems and relatively limited in scope recently have been commonly applied to finite, noisy, and/or stochastically derived time series, frequently with confounding and nonreplicable results. This caveat is particularly germane to biologic signals, especially those taken in vivo, as such signals likely represent the output of a complicated network with both stochastic and deterministic components.

QUANTIFICATION OF REGULARITY

Definition of ApEn

Two input parameters, m and r, must be fixed to compute ApEn; m is the "length" of compared runs, and r is effectively a filter. Given N data points $\{u(i)\}$, form vector-sequences $x(1)$ through $x(N - m + 1)$, defined by $x(i) = [u(i), \ldots, u(i + m - 1)]$. These vectors represent m consecutive u values, commencing with the ith point. Define the distance $d[x(i),x(j)]$ between vectors $x(i)$ and $x(j)$ as the maximum difference in their respective scalar

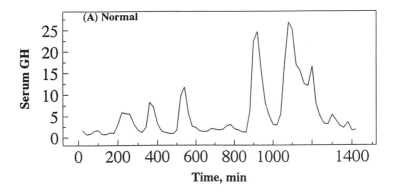

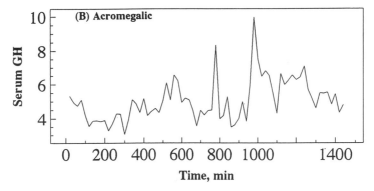

FIG. 11.1. Growth hormone (GH) serum concentrations, in milliunits/ml, measured at 5-min intervals for 24 hr ("fed" state): (a) Normal subject, mean concentration = 5.617, ApEn(2,0.20SD,288) = 0.341; (b) acromegalic subject, mean concentration = 4.981, ApEn(2,0.20SD,288) = 1.081.

components. Use the sequence $x(1)$, $x(2)$, ... $x(N - m + 1)$ to construct, for each $i \leq N - m + 1$, $C_i^m(r)$ = (number of $j \leq N - m + 1$ such that $d[x(i),x(j)] \leq r$) / $(N - m + 1)$. The $C_i^m(r)$ terms measure within a tolerance r the regularity, or frequency, of patterns similar to a given pattern of window length m. Define

$$\Phi^m(r) = (N - m + 1)^{-1} \sum_{i=1}^{N-m+1} \ln C_i^m(r)$$

where ln is the natural logarithm, and then define the *parameter*

$$\text{ApEn}(m,r) = \lim_{N \to \infty} [\Phi^m(r) - \Phi^{m+1}(r)]$$

Given N data points, we estimate this parameter by defining the *statistic* $\text{ApEn}(m,r,N) = \Phi^m(r) - \Phi^{m+1}(r)$. ApEn measures the likelihood that runs of

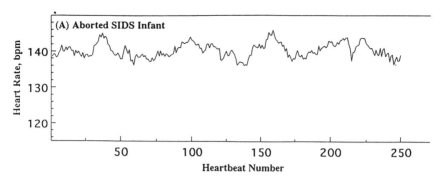

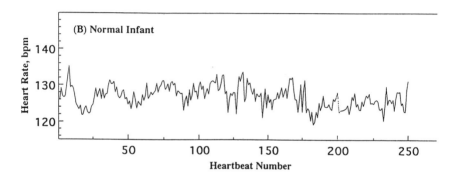

FIG. 11.2. Two infant quiet sleep heart rate tracings with similar variability and SD: (a) aborted SIDS infant, SD = 2.49 beats per minute (bpm), ApEn(2, 0.15SD,1000) = 0.826; (b) normal infant, SD = 2.61 bpm, ApEn(2,0.15SD,1000) = 1.463.

patterns that are close for m observations remain close on next incremental comparisons. Greater likelihood of remaining close, regularity, produces smaller ApEn values, and conversely. Upon unraveling definitions we deduce

$$-\text{ApEn} = \Phi^{m+1}(r) - \Phi^m(r)$$
$$= \text{average over } i \text{ of } \ln[\text{conditional probability}$$
$$\text{that } |u(j+m) - u(i+m)| \leq r$$
$$\text{given that } |u(j+k) - u(i+k)| \leq r \text{ for } k = 0, 1, \ldots, m-1] \qquad (1)$$

To develop a more intuitive, physiological understanding of this definition, a multistep description of the algorithm with figures is developed in Pincus and Goldberger (1994).

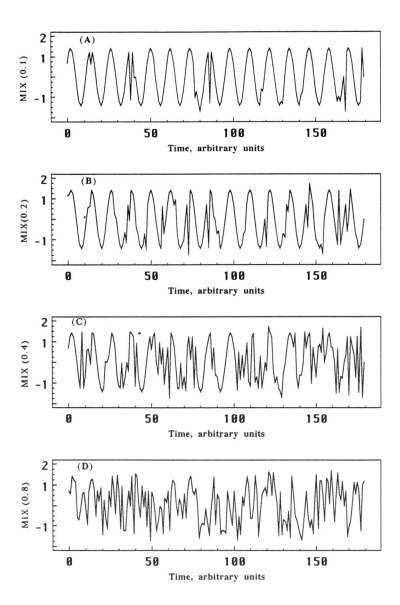

FIG. 11.3. MIX(p) model time-series output for four parameter values: (A) p
= 0.1; (B) p = 0.2; (C) p = 0.4; (D) p = 0.8. MIX(p) is a family of processes that
samples a sine wave for p = 0, samples independent, identically distributed
(i.i.d.) uniform random variables for p = 1, and intuitively becomes more
irregular as p increases. ApEn quantifies the increasing irregularity and
complexity with increasing p: for $m = 2$, $r = 0.18$, and $N = 1000$, ApEn(MIX(0.1))
= 0.436, ApEn(MIX(0.2)) = 0.782, ApEn(MIX(0.4)) = 1.455, and ApEn(MIX(0.8)) =
1.801. In contrast, the correlation dimension of MIX(p) was 0 for all $p < 1$, and
the K-S entropy of MIX(p) was ∞ for all $p > 0$. Thus even given no noise and
an infinite amount of data, these latter two measures do not discriminate the
MIX(p) family.

IMPLEMENTATION AND INTERPRETATION

The value of N, the number of input data points for ApEn computations, is typically between 75 and 5000. Based on calculations that included both theoretical analysis (Pincus, 1991; Pincus & Huang, 1992) and clinical applications (Fleisher et al., 1993; Hartman et al., 1994; Kaplan et al., 1991; Pincus et al., 1991, 1993; Pincus & Viscarello, 1992), we have concluded that for m = 1 and 2, values of r between 0.1 to 0.25 SD of the $u(i)$ data produce good statistical validity of ApEn(m,r,N). For such r values, we demonstrated the theoretical utility of ApEn($2,r,N$) to distinguish data on the basis of regularity for both deterministic and random processes, and the clinical utility in the aforementioned applications.

ApEn is typically calculated via a short computer code (see Appendix B in Pincus et al., 1991, for a FORTRAN listing). The form of ApEn provides for both de facto noise filtering, via choice of r (Pincus, 1991), and artifact insensitivity (Pincus et al., 1991), useful statistical properties for practical applications. On a Power Macintosh 6100 personal computer, given $N = 1000$ input points, the ApEn calculation consumes approximately 1 sec. This should be compared to computational run times for some of the "chaos" algorithms (e.g., Lyapunov spectrum), which often require hours on a supercomputer, even when correctly employed.

Importantly, despite algorithmic similarities, ApEn(m,r,N) is not intended as an approximate value of K-S entropy. It is imperative to consider ApEn(m,r,N) as a family of statistics; for a given application, system comparisons are intended with fixed m and r. For a given system, there usually is significant variation in ApEn(m,r,N) over the range of m and r (Pincus, 1991; Pincus & Huang, 1992).

A significant aspect of ApEn utility is that numerical calculation generally concurs with pictorial intuition, both for theoretical and clinically derived data. ApEn confirms differences that are visually "obviously distinct," as in the comparison of (a) versus (d) in Fig. 11.3, and provides information in subtler comparisons, distinguishing (c) from (d) in Fig. 11.3. Theoretical calculations for correlation dimension and K-S entropy (noted later) produce confounding results for the MIX(p) model of Fig. 11.3, and often for general stochastic and composite models. Clinically, illustrated in Fig. 11.3 for a fetal heart rate study (Pincus & Viscarello, 1992), abnormally low ApEn values not only indicate the visually apparent, regular heart rate tracing of an acidotic, distressed fetus measured 1 hr before delivery, but notably also the less visually apparent, modestly regular tracing measured early in labor. In an endocrine hormone secretion study (Hartman et al., 1994), ApEn discerned subjects in remission as intermediate between normal and actively diseased subjects ($p < .001$). Both these clinical results suggest the potential of a regularity statistic not only to confirm obvious findings, but to provide new diagnostic, possibly clinically predictive capability.

To enact direct comparisons of ApEn results, it is best to fix not only m and r, as indicated earlier, but also N (data length). The requirement to fix N is due to the statistical bias of ApEn (similar bias occurs for other complexity statistics); if one assumes a model form, corrections could typically be made to compare ApEn results for differing data lengths.

ApEn decrease frequently correlates with SD decrease. This is not a "problem," as statistics often correlate with one another, but there are times when we desire an index of regularity decorrelated from SD. We can realize such an index, by specifying r in ApEn(m,r,N) as a fixed percentage of the sample SD of the individual (not group, or fixed) subject data set, with possibly a different r for each subject (Pincus et al., 1993). We call this *normalized regularity*. Its utility was demonstrated, for example, in refining the differences between heart rate data from quiet and REM (rapid eye movement) infant sleep, two sleep states with markedly different overall variability (SD), by establishing that REM sleep has significantly greater normalized regularity (smaller normalized ApEn values) than quiet sleep has, which is juxtaposed with the more classical finding of much larger variability in REM sleep than in quiet sleep (Pincus et al., 1993). This thus enables us to determine if two processes are different both in variation (SD) and in normalized regularity. Choosing r in this manner allows sensible regularity comparisons of processes with substantially different SDs. In the aforementioned comparison, if REM sleep were a scale multiple of quiet sleep (the multiple given by the ratio of the respective overall variabilities), plus some translated mean heart rate, the normalized regularity ApEn values for REM and quiet sleep would be identical. Later, we employ normalized regularity to report highly significant scale-invariant distinctions between growth hormone secretory patterns of normal and acromegalic subjects, two groups with markedly different means and SDs.

The physiologic modeling of many complex systems is often very difficult; one would expect accurate models of such systems to be complicated composites, with both deterministic and stochastic components, and interconnecting network features. ApEn is a broadly applicable statistic in that it can distinguish many classes of systems, and can be meaningful applied to $N > 70$ data points. Via extensive Monte Carlo calculations we established that the standard deviation (SD) of ApEn(2,0.15 SD,1000) < 0.055 for a large class of candidate models (Pincus & Goldberger, 1994; Pincus & Huang, 1992; Pincus & Keefe, 1992). It is this small SD ("error bar") of ApEn that provides its utility to practical data analysis of moderate length time series.

RELATIVE CONSISTENCY—A VARIATIONAL PRINCIPLE

For many processes, ApEn(m,r,N) grows with decreasing r like $\log(2r)$, thus exhibiting infinite variation with r (Pincus & Huang, 1992). We typically observe that for a given time series, ApEn(2,0.1) is quite different from ApEn(4,0.01), so the question arises of which parameter choices (m and r) to use. The guidelines given earlier address this, but the most important requirement is consistency. For deterministic dynamical systems, we typically see that when K-S entropy(A) $\leq$ K-S entropy(B), then ApEn(m,r)(A) $\leq$ ApEn (m,r)(B), and conversely, for a wide range of m and r. Furthermore, for both theoretically described systems (Pincus, 1991; Pincus & Keefe, 1992) and those described by experimental data (Pincus et al., 1991, 1993), we have found that when ApEn(m_1,r_1)(A) $\leq$ ApEn(m_1,r_1)(B), then ApEn(m_2,r_2)(A) $\leq$ ApEn(m_2,r_2)(B), and conversely. This latter property also generally holds for parameterized systems of stochastic processes, in which K-S entropy is infinite. We call this ability of ApEn to preserve order a *relative property*. It is key to the general and clinical utility of ApEn.

From a theoretical perspective, the interplay between meshes [(m,r) pair specifications] need not be nice, in general, in ascertaining which of (two) processes is "more" random. In general, we might like to ask: Given no noise and an infinite amount of data, can we say that process A is more regular than process B? The *flip-flop pair* of processes implies that the answer to this question is "not necessarily": In general, comparison of relative process randomness at a prescribed level is best one can do (Pincus & Huang, 1992). Process A may appear more random than process B on many choices of partitions, but not necessarily on all partitions of suitably small diameter (r).

Fortunately, for many processes A and B, we can assert more than relative regularity, even though both A and B will typically have infinite K-S entropy. For such pairs of processes, denoted a *completely consistent pair*, whenever ApEn(m,r)(A) < ApEn(m,r)(B) for any specific choice of m and r, then it follows that ApEn(n,s)(A) < ApEn(n,s)(B) for all choices of n and s (Pincus & Huang, 1992). Visually, process B appears more random than A at any level of view. We indicate elsewhere a conjecture that should be straightforward to prove, providing a sufficient condition to insure that A and B are a completely consistent pair, and indicating the relationship to the autocorrelation function (Pincus & Goldberger, 1994).

RELATIONSHIP TO OTHER APPROACHES

The development of mathematics to quantify regularity has centered around various entropy measures. However, there are numerous entropy formulations, and many entropy definitions can be not related to one other (Pincus,

1991). K-S entropy, developed by Kolmogorov and expanded upon by Sinai, classifies deterministic dynamical systems by rates of information generation (Kolmogorov, 1958). It is this form of entropy that Grassberger and Procaccia (1983a), Eckmann and Ruelle (1985), and Takens (1983) estimated.

However, the K-S entropy was not developed for statistical applications, and has major debits in this regard. The original, primary motivation for this entropy was to determine when two Bernoulli shifts are isomorphic. Recall that the shift transformation σ is applied to infinite sequences in $\{(\ldots x_{-1},$ $x_0, x_1, \ldots)\}$, defined by $(\sigma x)_n = x_{n+1}$. For Bernoulli shifts, the x_i take values in an alphabet of finitely many symbols, each with positive weights, with the sum of all weights equal to 1. This shift formalizes the notion of bidirectionally infinite (independent) repetitive coin tossing with a finite state outcome. In proper context, the K-S entropy is applied by ergodic theorists to such well-defined theoretical transformations, for which no noise and an infinite amount of "data" are standard mathematical assumptions. Ornstein (1970) proved the important, deep result that two dynamical systems are isomorphic if and only if they have identical K-S entropy. Also, for dynamical systems, positive entropy implies chaos (Eckmann & Ruelle, 1985). But attempts to utilize K-S entropy for practical data analysis represent out-of-context application, which often generates serious difficulties, as it does here. K-S entropy is badly compromised by steady (even very), small amounts of nose, generally requires a vast amount of input data to achieve convergence (Ornstein & Weiss, 1990; Wolf, Swift, Swinney, & Vastano, 1985), and is usually infinite for stochastic processes. All these debits are key in the general setting, because time series arising from many complex networks likely are modeled by composite stochastic and deterministic systems.

ApEn was constructed along lines thematically similar to the K-S entropy, although with a different focus: to provide a widely applicable, statistically valid formula to distinguish data sets. The technical point motivating ApEn is that if joint probability measures for reconstructed dynamics describing each of two systems are different, then their marginal probability distributions on a fixed partition, given by conditional probabilities as in Equation 1, are likely different.

There exists a large literature on reconstructed dynamics for chaotic systems. Correlation dimension (Grassberger & Procaccia, 1983b), K-S entropy, and the Lyapunov spectrum have been much studied, as have techniques to utilize related algorithms in the presence of noise and limited data (Broomhead & King, 1986; Fraser & Swinney, 1986; Mayer-Kress et al., 1988). Even more recently, prediction techniques have been developed for chaotic systems (Casdagli, 1989; Farmer & Sidorowich, 1987; Sugihara & May, 1990). Most of these methods employ embedding dimensions larger than $m = 2$, as is typically employed with ApEn. Thus, in the purely deterministic dynamical system setting, they are more powerful than ApEn—in that they reconstruct the probability structure of the space with greater detail. However, in the general stochastic process setting, the statistical accuracy of the aforementioned parameters and methods appears to be poor, and the prediction techniques are not always defined.

Generally, changes in ApEn agree with changes in dimension and entropy algorithms for low-dimensional, deterministic systems. The essential points here, assuring broad utility, are that (a) ApEn can potentially distinguish a wide variety of systems: low-dimensional deterministic systems, periodic and multiply periodic systems, high-dimensional chaotic systems, stochastic and mixed (stochastic and deterministic) systems, and (b) ApEn is applicable to noisy, medium-sized data sets (Pincus, 1991; Pincus & Keefe, 1992). Thus ApEn can be applied to settings for which the K-S entropy and correlation dimension are either undefined or infinite, with good replicability properties as discussed later.

Relationship to Power Spectra and Phase Space Plots

Generally, smaller ApEn and greater regularity correspond in the spectral domain to more total power concentrated in a narrow frequency range, in contrast to greater irregularity, which typically produces broader banded spectra with more power spread over a greater frequency range. The two opposing extremes are (a) periodic and linear deterministic models, which produce very peaked, narrow-banded spectra, with low ApEn values, and (b) sequences of independent random variables, for which time series yield intuitively highly erratic behavior, and for which spectra are very broad-banded, with high ApEn values. Intermediate to these extremes are auto-correlated processes, which can exhibit complicated spectral behavior. These autocorrelated aperiodic processes can be either stochastic or deterministic chaotic. In some instances, evaluation of the spectral domain will be insightful, when pronounced differences occur in a particular frequency band. However, in many instances, differences at a prescribed frequency are less clear-cut (especially recalling that one typically is comparing spectral estimates, not the true spectra), yet the need for effective statistics to discriminate remains.

Also, greater regularity (lower ApEn) generally corresponds to greater ensemble correlation in phase space diagrams. Such diagrams typically display plots of some system variable $x(t)$ versus $x(t - T)$, for a fixed "time lag" T. These plots are quite voguish, in that they are often associated with claims that correlation, in conjunction with aperiodicity, implies chaos. A cautionary note is strongly indicated here. The labeling of bounded, aperiodic, yet correlated output as *deterministic* chaos has become a false cognate. This is incorrect; application of Theorem 6 of Pincus (1992) proves that any n-dimensional steady-state measure arising from a deterministic dynamical system model can be approximated to arbitrary accuracy by that from a stochastic Markov chain. This implies that any given phase space plot could have been generated by a (possibly correlated) stochastic model. The correlation seen in such diagrams is typically real, as is geometric change that reflects a shift in ensemble process autocorrelation in some comparisons. However, these observations are entirely distinct from any claims regarding underlying model form (chaos vs. stochastic process). Similarly, in power spectra, decreasing power with increasing frequency (often labeled $1/f$ decay) is also a property of process correlation, rather than underlying determinism or chaos (Pincus, 1994).

MIX(p): A FAMILY OF STOCHASTIC PROCESSES WITH INCREASING IRREGULARITY

We indicated earlier that statistics developed for truly chaotic settings are often inappropriate for general time-series application. Analysis of the MIX(p) processes (Pincus, 1991) vividly indicates some of the difficulties realized in applying such statistics out of context, and emphasizes the need to calibrate statistical analysis to intuitive sensibility. MIX is a family of stochastic processes that samples a sine wave for $p = 0$ and consists of independent, identically distributed (i.i.d.) samples selected uniformly ("completely randomly") from an interval for $p = 1$, intuitively becoming more random with increasing p. The four time series shown in Fig. 11.3 represent sample "realizations" of MIX(p) for the indicated values of p. Formally, to define MIX(p), first fix $0 \leq p \leq 1$. For all j, define

$$X_j = \sqrt{2} \, \sin(2\pi j/12) \tag{2}$$

$$Y_j = \text{i.i.d. uniform random variables on } [-\sqrt{3}, \sqrt{3}] \tag{3}$$

$$\begin{aligned} &Z_j = \text{i.i.d. random variables,} \\ &Z_j = 1 \text{ with probability } p, \\ &Z_j = 0 \text{ with probability } 1 - p \end{aligned} \tag{4}$$

Then define

$$\text{MIX}(p)_j = (1 - Z_j)X_j + Z_jY_j \tag{5}$$

The MIX(p) family is motivated by considering an autonomous unit that produces sinusoidal output, surrounded by a network of interacting processes that in ensemble produces output that resembles noise relative to the timing of the unit. The extent to which the surrounding world interacts with the unit could be controlled by a gateway between the two, with a larger gateway admitting greater apparent noise to compete with the base signal. Note that the MIX process has mean 0 and SD 1 for all p, so these moments do not discriminate members of MIX from one another. In conjunction with intuition, ApEn monotonically increases with increasing p, as indicated in the legend of Fig. 11.3.

In contrast, the correlation dimension of MIX(p) = 0 for $p < 1$, and the correlation dimension of MIX(1) = ∞ (Pincus, 1991). Also, the K-S entropy of MIX(p) = ∞ for $p > 0$, and = 0 for MIX(0). Thus both of these chaos statistics perform inadequately for this template process, even given an infinite amount of theoretical data: They do not distinguish members of MIX(p) from one another, and do not capture the evolving complexity change. We anticipate that many of the difficulties of the correlation dimension and the K-S entropy applied to MIX(p) are mirrored for other correlated stochastic processes. Stated differently, even if an infinite number of points were available, with no added "noise" atop MIX(p), we still could not use the correlation dimension or K-S entropy to distinguish members of this family. The difficulty here is that the parameters are identical, not that we have insufficient data or too much noise.

MARGINAL PROBABILITIES AND FULL RECONSTRUCTION

As noted earlier, full attractor (invariant measure) reconstruction is often unnecessary to distinguish processes. A primary data question is: Are data $\{X_i\}$ "atypical" (abnormal)? This is a discrimination question; the question of accurately modeling the process underlying $\{X_i\}$ is often much harder, but one that we may well be able to avoid. We think of marginal probabilities as partial process characterization, given by the small m and relatively coarse r in ApEn(m,r). The rationale is that we typically need orders of magnitude fewer points to accurately estimate these marginal probabilities than to accurately reconstruct the "attractor" measure defining the process. We now indicate what marginal probabilities are, and how they arise in time-series reconstruction.

A *joint probability measure* is a means of assigning probability to a region of space. Consider, for example, all points (x,y) such that $0 \le x,y \le 1$ (unit square). Define the joint measure for the density $f(x,y)$: the probability of (a subset of the square) $\mathbf{A} = \iint_{\mathbf{A}} f(x,y) \, dx \, dy$. Then define the *marginal density* of x, $f_X(x) = \int f(x,y) \, dy$ (analogously for y). It is essential to note that marginal probabilities of two processes may be equal while the joint probabilities are quite different. However, if two measures have distinctly different marginal probabilities, then that alone is sufficient to discriminate the measures.

Define the *conditional probability* of $X \in A$ given ($||$) $Y \in B$ as the joint probability that $X \in A$ and $Y \in B$ divided by the marginal probability that $Y \in B$; that is, $\int_B \int_A f(x,y) \, dx \, dy \, / \int_B f_Y(y) \, dy$. Marginal and conditional probability definitions extend to general numbers of variables. For application to time series, we study the joint distribution for n contiguous observations $\{X_m, \ldots, X_{m+n-1}\}$ as the n-variable measure. Complete steady-state description is given by expressions of the form of conditional probability ($u(j + m) \in A_m \, || \, u(j + 1) \in A_1, \ldots, u(j + m - 1) \in A_{m-1}$), for all integers m and sets A_i. The question of full reconstruction (embedding dimension n) is subsumed by a broader question, is a process nth order Markov? The general answer is, not necessarily; there may be no fixed n for which the process is characterized entirely by conditioning on n previous observations. However for fixed m, these marginal conditional probabilities contain a wealth of probabilistic detail about the underlying process, often allowing discrimination. Such probabilities form the building blocks of the K-S entropy, correlation dimension, and ApEn, by the probabilities

$$\{|u(j + m) - u(i + m)| \leq r \, || \, |u(j + k) - u(i + k)| \leq r$$
$$\text{for} \quad k = 0, 1, \ldots, m - 1\}. \tag{6}$$

In the K-S entropy, Lyapunov spectra, and correlation dimension, $m \to \infty$ (or to full embedding) and $r \to 0$, whereas ApEn stops short via small m and coarse r, sacrificing an attempt to reconstruct the full process dynamics. The trade-offs between the approaches to time-series reconstruction are statistical. Obviously bigger m and smaller r describe sharper parameter (probabilistic) detail. However, for each template vector $\{u(i), u(i + 1), \ldots, u(i + m)\}$, we estimate Equation 6 by A/B, where A is the number of j such that $|u(j + k) - u(i + k)| \leq r$ for $k = 0, 1, \ldots,$ and m, and B is the number of j such that $|u(j + k) - u(i + k)| \leq r$ for $k = 0, 1, \ldots,$ and $m - 1$. If either m is relatively large or r is too small, then both A and (importantly) B are small numbers; thus the estimate of Equation 6 by A/B is unreliable.

ApEn is related to a parameter in information theory, *conditional entropy* (Blahut, 1987). Assume a finite state space, where the entropy of a random variable X, $\text{Prob}(X = a_j) = p_j$, is $H(X) := -\Sigma p_j \log p_j$, and the entropy of a block of random variables $X_1, \ldots, X_n = H(X_1, \ldots, X_n) := -\Sigma\Sigma \cdots \Sigma p^n(a_{j1}, \ldots, a_{jn}) \log p^n(a_{j1}, \ldots, a_{jn})$. For two variables, the conditional entropy $H(Y||X) = H(X,Y) - H(X)$; this extends naturally to n variables. Closely mimicking the proof of Theorem 3 of Pincus (1991), the following theorem is immediate: For $r < \min_{j \neq k} |a_j - a_k|$, $\text{ApEn}(m,r) = H(X_{m+1} \, || \, X_1, \ldots, X_m)$; thus in this setting, ApEn is a conditional entropy. Observe that we do not assume that the process is mth order Markov, that is, that we fully describe the process; we aggregate the mth order marginal probabilities. The rate of entropy $= \lim_{n \to \infty} H(X_n || X_1, \ldots, X_{n-1})$ is the discrete state analogue of the K-S entropy.

However, we cannot go from discrete to continuous state naturally as a limit; most calculations give ∞. As for differential entropy, there is no fundamental physical interpretation of conditional entropy (and no invariance; Blahut, 1987, p. 243) in continuous state.

RECONSTRUCTED DYNAMICS—A COMPARISON OF TWO AUTOCORRELATED MAPS

Analysis of the MIX(p) processes indicates some of the theoretical difficulties realized in applying correlation dimension and K-S entropy statistics to general time-series (Pincus, 1991). Similar "confounding" results can be established for Gaussian processes, ARMA models, and more generally for weak-dependence processes, via proofs similar to that given by Pincus (1991).

Nonetheless, one might still consider applying an algorithm to compute, for example, the correlation dimension or K-S entropy, and should then query what the *operational* consequences are of application to a general correlated stochastic process. To understand the statistical limitations imposed by the choice of embedding dimension m and scaling parameter r, we can think of an (m,r) choice of input parameters as partitioning the state space into uniform width boxes of width r, from which we estimate mth order conditional probabilities. For state space such as $[-A/2, A/2]$, we would have $(A/r)^{m+1}$ conditional probabilities to estimate. Specifically, divide $[-A/2, A/2]$ into A/r cells; the ith cell $C(i)$ is the half-open interval $[x, x + r)$, where $x = -(A/2) + (i - 1)r$. Then define the conditional probability $p_{\text{ivect},j}$ for all length m vectors of integers ivect and integers j, ivect $= (i_1, i_2, \ldots, i_m)$, $1 \le i_k \le A/r$ for all k, $1 \le j \le A/r$, by $p_{\text{ivect},j} = \{$conditional probability that $u(k) \in C(j)$, given that $u(k - 1) \in C(i_1)$, $u(k - 2) \in C(i_2)$, $\ldots$, and $u(k - m) \in C(i_m)\}$. In the very general ergodic case, these conditional probabilities are given by limits of time averages.

For general stochastic processes, many of these conditional probabilities are nonzero, so we need to accommodate reasonable estimates of the $(A/r)^{m+1}$ conditional probabilities given N data points. If m is relatively large, or if r is too small, the number of probabilities to be estimated will be unwieldy, and statistical estimates will be poor for typical data set lengths.

In Pincus (1995) we operationally evaluate the issues in analyzing reconstructed dynamics for general stochastic processes, via a quantitative comparison of two processes, logis(3.6), the logistic map $f(x) = 3.6x(1 - x)$ and MIX(0.4), with embedding dimension $m = 2$ and a moderately coarse mesh width r that subdivides the state spaces into 20 equal-width cells. For logis(3.6), we observe an increasing and extreme sparseness of the set of (m + 1)-tuples for which the true conditional probabilities $p_{\text{ivect},j}$ are nonzero, as a function of m and r, which then affords large m and small r in conditional probability statistical estimation for these processes, even given relatively modest data lengths. This sparseness is representative of the strong dependence (Kolmogorov & Rozanov, 1960) seen in dynamical (often chaotic) systems, and it should not be surprising that algorithms that work well for such strong-dependence processes behave entirely differently for more commonly encountered weak-dependence processes. We conclude that for true dynamical systems, one can exploit the strong dependence by choosing large m, small r in algorithms, *en passant* estimating a fine-graded joint measure description. We also conclude that for the more general weak-dependence autocorrelated maps, the "diffuse" reconstructed dynamics manifest themselves by many poorly estimated conditional probabilities for $m \geq$ 3 and small r; further, many rare events produce added statistical bias. For these more general time-series models, it is imperative to be cautious, achieved by choosing small m (e.g., $m = 2$) and moderate width r, to insure replicability of a partial (dynamical) measure description.

A MECHANISTIC HYPOTHESIS FOR ALTERED REGULARITY

It seems important to determine a unifying theme suggesting greater signal regularity in a diverse range of complicated systems. We would hardly expect a single mathematical model, or even a single family of models, to govern a wide range of systems; furthermore, we would expect that in vivo, a physiologic signal would usually represent the output of a complex, multinodal network with both stochastic and deterministic components. Our mechanistic hypothesis is that in a variety of systems, greater regularity (lower ApEn) corresponds to greater component and subsystem autonomy and isolation. The idea is that in many contexts, "healthy" systems have good lines of communication, marked both by numbers of external influences that interact, and by the extent of this interaction. In such settings, disease and pathology would represent system decoupling and/or lessening external inputs, in effect isolating a central system component from its ambient universe. Crucial biologic messages in diseased states would either be slow to transmit and receive, or unable to arrive. From an output signal perspective, the base system would contribute a more dominant component of the observed time series.

This mechanistic hypothesis has been mathematically established via analysis of several very different, representational (stochastic and deterministic) mathematical model forms, conferring a robustness to model form of the hypothesis (Pincus, 1994; Pincus & Keefe, 1992). Restated contrapuntally, ApEn typically increases with greater system coupling and feedback, and

greater external influences, thus providing an explicit barometer of autonomy in many coupled, complicated systems.

Representative Model Confirming the Hypothesis

To give an explicit sense of how this hypothesis relates network and signal,
we discuss in part one of the models considered in Pincus (1994). This model
is an archetypal form of a multinodal, interconnected network, defined by
a coupled linear stochastic differential equation [linear ODE driven by random process input $\xi(t)$], from which one realizes bounded, autocorrelated,
yet aperiodic output. Stochastic differential equations are fundamental to a
variety of settings (Cox & Miller, 1965; Tuckwell, 1989). A typical assumption,
made later, is to let $\xi(t) = W'(\sigma^2)(t)$, white noise with parameter σ^2 (Brownian
motion). In particular, we want to study the effects on component output
of system coupling, and analyze the following reduced version of a two-node
network:

$$
\begin{aligned}
X''(t) + aX'(t) + bX(t) + KY(t) &= W'(\sigma^2)(t) \\
Y''(t) + aY'(t) + bY(t) + KX(t) &= W_1'(\sigma^2)(t)
\end{aligned}
\tag{7}
$$

Equation 7 is a coupled system of linear differential equations, with a and
b constants, and $W'(\sigma^2)(t)$ and $W_1'(\sigma^2)(t)$ white noise. We distinguish W and
W_1 simply to indicate that although they have the same distribution, they
are distinct processes. The term K indicates the extent of the coupling by
which X and Y are linked; when $K = 0$, the X and Y systems are free-running,
independent of one another. Increased coupling K imposes greater X contribution to the Y system, and conversely. Because we are interested in
studying component behavior, we analyze, for example, $X(t)$ solutions, viewing the system from the $X(t)$ perspective. We reduce Equation 7 to a single
differential equation by exploiting symmetry: For any a, b, K, and σ, the
(stationary) solutions $X(t)$ and $Y(t)$ must have identical distributions, assuming independence of W' and W_1'. It is relatively straightforward to then show
that the stationary X process must satisfy

$$
X''(t) + \alpha X'(t) + (\beta + K)X(t) = W'(\sigma^2)(t)
\tag{8}
$$

where α and β are functions of a and b alone (not of K).

Denoting $X''(t) + cX'(t) + dX(t) = W'(1)(t)$ by StoDE(c,d), the mechanistic
hypothesis will then be confirmed if we show that ApEn of StoDE($\alpha,\beta + K$)
increases with increasing K, for fixed a and b: Greater coupling will correspond to increased ApEn, and decoupling and greater component autonomy
will correspond to decreased ApEn. We illustrate this in Fig. 11.4 for $\alpha = 1$;
the procedure indicating how we numerically produced sample output time-

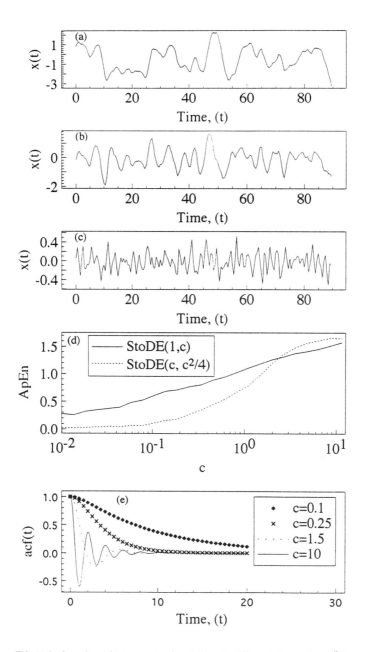

FIG. 11.4. Sample path time series for stochastic differential equation $X''(t) + aX'(t) + cX(t) = W'(1)(t)$, denoted StoDE($a$,$c$), with $a = 1$: (a) $c = 0.25$; (b) $c = 1.5$ (c) $c = 10$. (d) ApEn(2,0.2SD,1000) versus control parameters c in StoDE(1,c) and c in StoDE(c,$c^2/4$), the latter a linear-derivative term coupling analytically studied by Pincus (1994). (e) Autocorrelation functions acf(t) of stationary solution to StoDE(1,c) for values $c = 0.1$, $c = 0.25$, $c = 1.5$, and $c = 10$.

series solutions (realizations) for StoDE(c,d) is indicated in Pincus (1994). Time series of 1000 points for ApEn analysis were generated from realizations by sampling every 0.5 t-units.

Figure 11.4(a–c) displays sample StoDE($1,c$) realizations for three values of c, with greater apparent regularity corresponding to smaller values of c. This is quantified in Fig. 11.4(d), with ApEn monotonically increasing as c increases, confirming the general hypothesis. The assumption of $a = 1$ for studying StoDE(a,c) evolution is purely representational; similar monotonicity of ApEn with increasing c follows for other choices of $a > 0$.

We understand the monotonicity of ApEn in Fig. 11.4(d) by analyzing the autocorrelation functions acf(t) of solutions to Equation 8 analytically (Hoel, Port, & Stone, 1972; Pincus, 1994). Figure 11.4(e) shows the acf(t) for StoDE($1,c$) for the indicated values of c. The point is that for StoDE(a,c) with fixed $a > 0$, for any fixed, small value of t, acf(t) monotonically decreases for a large range of increasing c; there is smaller autocorrelation of StoDE(a,c) at any specified lag with increasing c. This observation is again consistent with the interpretation of ApEn as an ensemble parameter of autocorrelation.

APPLICABILITY TO ENDOCRINE HORMONE SECRETION DATA

In Pincus and Keefe (1992), the potential applicability of ApEn to endocrinology was examined, to discern abnormal pulsatility in hormone secretion time-series data. We next discuss results of ApEn analyses to a study of growth hormone (GH) secretion time-series data (Hartman et al., 1994).

Time series of serum GH in samples were obtained at 5-min intervals for 24 hr ($N = 288$ points) in three groups of subjects: (a) normal young adults ($N = 16$), both in fed and fasted (physiologically enhanced GH secretion) states; (b) acromegalics with active disease ($N = 19$); (c) acromegalics in biochemical remission ($N = 9$) following therapy (transsphenoidal surgery, radiation, bromocriptine). For each subject, we calculated normalized ApEn with both (a) $m = 1$, $r = .2$ SD and (b) $m = 2$, $r = .2$ SD (SD = individual subject time-series standard deviation). As indicated earlier, because normalized regularity is scale invariant, this allows sensible regularity comparisons, given the dissimilar mean and individual subject SD levels. We discuss the ApEn results with $m = 2$ here, displayed in Fig. 11.5; the $m = 1$ results are similar (Hartman et al., 1994).

Acromegalics with active disease had ApEn values (0.97 ± 0.18), which were significantly higher than normals in either the fed (0.33 ± 0.18, $p = .18 \times 10^{-12}$) or fasted state (0.48 ± 0.20, $p = .12 \times 10^{-7}$). All normal subjects, fed and fasted, had ApEn values <0.77; all but one acromegalic patient had ApEn values above 0.77. Thus ApEn separated acromegalic from normal GH secretion with both high sensitivity (95%) and high specificity (100%). Further-

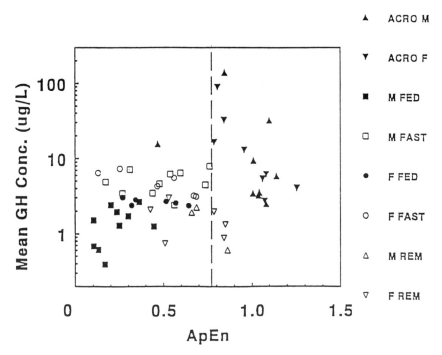

FIG. 11.5. Individual subject normalized ApEn (2,0.2SD) values versus mean
GH concentrations, logarithmic scale. Symbols are indicated on the right of the
figure; M and F are male, female; FED and FAST refer to controls, REM to
remissions, ACRO to active acromegalics. The broken line separates all but one
acromegalic with active disease from normal (both fed and fasted) subjects.

more, the one acromegalic patient with a lower ApEn value was somewhat
unusual in that he had McCune–Albright syndrome and was unable to un-
dergo transsphenoidal surgery due to severe sphenoid bone hyperostosis.
Acromegalic patients in biochemical remission had ApEn values (0.68 ± 0.16)
that were intermediate between those of acromegalics with active disease
and normal fed subjects ($p < .001$). Also, note that there is significant overlap
between (normal) fasted state and acromegalic growth hormone (GH) mean
level individual subject distributions, which reinforces the utility of analysis
beyond a "first-order" mean level in determining clinical state.

APPLICABILITY TO FINANCIAL TIME SERIES:
REJECTION OF i.i.d., LOGNORMAL RETURNS

Several economists have studied the application of "chaos" algorithms to
actual financial data, and have generally concluded that (a) there may be
some evidence of sequential correlation in the time series, but (b) these

algorithms have unsatisfactory statistical properties, and thus any quantitative conclusions must be lightly regarded. Ramsey and Yuan (1989) noted that actual error bars for these "statistics" are quite large, and that there is substantial bias in dimension algorithms with small (typically sized) data sets. Both Brock (1986) and Scheinkman and LeBaron (1989) applied these algorithms to distinguish random from deterministic systems. Brock concluded that evidence for chaos in post-war quarterly gross national product (GNP) data is weak. Scheinkman and LeBaron drew the cautious conclusion that stock return data are not compatible with a model where some of the variation comes from nonlinearities, as opposed to randomness. Hsieh (1991) concluded that although he provided strong evidence to reject the hypothesis of i.i.d. stock returns, the cause did not appear to be either regime changes or chaotic dynamics; rather, the cause appeared to be conditional heteroskedasticity.

We applied ApEn to stock market data to test the validity of the lognormal, independent increment assumption for returns, common to many models (e.g., Black & Scholes, 1973). We analyzed S&P 500 (SPX) index data from 22 distinct 1000-point periods during the years 1987–1988 (source: Tick Data, Inc., Lakewood, Colorado). The input time series $\{s_i\}$ were sequences of prices taken at 10-min intervals, obtained daily from the opening quotation at 9:30 a.m to the closing quotation at 4 p.m; thus we required 25-business-day contiguous blocks to comprise each 1000-point period. We were interested in incremental returns, and hence, to evaluate the null hypothesis, we applied ApEn to the time-series $\{u_i\}$ defined by $u_i = \log(s_{i+1}/s_i)$. During 1987–1988, the $\{u_i\}$ time series had a standard deviation of approximately 0.002; following the guidelines just given, we then calculated ApEn(2,0.0005,1000).

Before comparing theoretical calculations and empirical results, we recall the following. If the $\{u_i\}$ are an i.i.d. process of (normal) random variables, we can analytically compute the expected value of the parameter ApEn(m,r). This is given by Theorem 2, Equation 15, of Pincus (1991), which we now state.

Theorem: For an i.i.d. process with density function $f(x)$, with probability 1, for any m,

$$\text{ApEn}(m,r) = -\int f(y) \log \left(\int_{z=y-r}^{z=y+r} f(z)\, dz \right) dy \qquad (9)$$

Notice that Equation 9 is independent of m; this fact can be used to reject the i.i.d. hypothesis in settings with abundant data, as indicated later. For the lognormal return hypothesis under consideration, we calculate Equation 9 by setting $f(x) = N(\mu,\sigma)$, the normal density with specified mean and standard deviation. As a minor nuisance, the log term inside the integral prevents nice analytic calculations of Equation 9 in general, requiring straightforward numerical calculations instead.

However, to compare actual ApEn computations from data to theoretical calculations, it is crucial to remember that ApEn(m,r,N) provides a biased estimate of ApEn(m,r). Thus it is inappropriate to compare ApEn (2,0.0005,1000) values to ApEn(m,r) calculations from Equation 9. Instead, we performed Monte Carlo generation (50 replications per time period) of 1000 i.i.d. normally distributed values of specified mean and standard deviation to match those from each (of the 22) empirically derived $\{u_i\}$ time series, then computed ApEn(2,0.0005,1000) of this series. These ApEn values were compared to those from observed data. If the null hypothesis that SPX returns $\{u_i\}$ are independent normal random variables were valid, ApEn values from the Monte Carlo sequences should have nearly matched the ApEn values from the $\{u_i\}$ derived from the actual time series.

The average ApEn value calculated from data was 1.098, while the average ApEn value calculated from the theoretical Monte Carlo replications assuming the null hypothesis was 1.491. Furthermore, in all but one time period, the actual ApEn value was at least 0.3 less than that computed assuming the null hypothesis. For i.i.d. normal random variables with standard deviation given by that of $\{u_i\}$ as empirically determined, the standard deviation of ApEn(2,0.0005,1000) is between 0.02 and 0.05 (Monte Carlo simulations), consistent with error bars noted in an earlier section. Thus in 21 of the 22 time periods under study, the theoretical ApEn value given the null hypothesis is at least 6 ApEn standard deviations away from the calculated values from data, resulting in clear-cut rejection of this hypothesis. Also, it is notable that the one time period where theoretical and calculated ApEn values nearly agreed was 10/1/87 to 11/5/87, the period covering the stock market crash. Additionally, analogous calculations based on 5-min and 20-min returns produce very similar results, nearly 30% smaller computed ApEn values than those calculated from a lognormal i.i.d. assumption during all but the "crash" time period.

Although not directly studied, we further anticipate that ApEn could provide an economic indicator of change, independent of model considerations. Because ApEn is a marker of stability, change in its value could potentially forecast changing market conditions. Thus an investor might be advised to expect greater market instability, and might accordingly take a more cautious stance in financial decisions. As indicated earlier, the only time period of the 22 tested epochs for which empirical ApEn was as large as that for i.i.d. lognormal returns was the time interval around the 1987 stock market crash. It would be extremely interesting to see if empirical values of ApEn exhibited a distinct increase, on either long or short time intervals, immediately prior to this crash.

ApEn APPLICATION TO OTHER "RANDOM" MODELS

Two questions with extremely diverse potential applicability arise naturally from the approach just used to reject the i.i.d. lognormal hypothesis. These are:

1. Is a given time series governed by (a realization of) an i.i.d. model, with a distribution quite different from a Gaussian, and if so, can we give some characteristics of this distribution?
2. Is the i.i.d. assumption invalid altogether?

For a specific proposed distribution, we can mimic the preceding procedure, generate test sequences via Monte Carlo, and compare theoretical and empirical ApEn values: Either both sets of ApEn values are similar for a wide range of r, or the proposed model is invalid. Here we are interested in more general questions, and to draw meaningful conclusions, we assume for the remainder of this section that we have sufficient data to neglect the bias in ApEn, so that both $\text{ApEn}(1,r,N) \approx \text{ApEn}(1,r)$ and $\text{ApEn}(2,r,N) \approx \text{ApEn}(2,r)$ for a range of r values. For many familiar processes, $N \approx 5000$ appears to suffice for this purpose.

For the first question, we can generate a lower bound on $\text{ApEn}(2,r)$ for many different density functions $f(x)$, so that rejection of a proposed model follows from computed $\text{ApEn}(2,r,N)$ values significantly less than this lower bound. To produce such a lower bound, for a probability density function $f(y)$, and r, define

$$g(y) = -\log\left(\int_{z=y-r}^{z=y+r} f(z)\, dz\right) \qquad (10)$$

The integral inside the parentheses is the probability that the distribution is between $y - r$ and $y + r$; in particular, the value of the integral is between 0 and 1. Suppose, for all y, this integral is less than K. Then $g(y) > \log K$ for all y. So recalling Equation 9,

$$\text{ApEn}(m,r) = \int f(y)\left\{-\log\left(\int_{z=y-r}^{z=y+r} f(z)\, dz\right)\right\} dy \geq \int f(y) \log K\, dy = \log K \qquad (11)$$

To see this applied, consider normal density f, mean μ, and standard deviation σ. Let $r = 0.2\sigma$. Then $\int_{z=y-r}^{z=y+r} f(z)\, dz$ is maximized (bounded above as a function of y) when $y = \mu$; the integral has value $F(0.2) - F(-0.2)$, where F is the distribution function for the standard normal with 0 mean and unit variance. Then by Equation 11, $\text{ApEn}(m,r) \geq \log[F(0.2) - F(-0.2)] \approx 1.84$.

The choice of r approximately 0.2 standard deviations of the distribution is consistent with the guidelines given earlier; if we let $r = \sigma/3$, we bound ApEn(m,r) below by $\log[F(1/3) - F(-1/3)] \approx 1.35$.

This technique does not reject all i.i.d. distributions as candidate models, however, based on low ApEn values when r is chosen as a prescribed fraction of the standard deviation. Fat-tailed distributions can have very large standard deviations, so tying r to the standard deviation may bound $g(y)$ in Equation 10 only minimally away from 0. A representative example of such a fat-tailed distribution is given by the (truncated) probability density function $f(x) = K/(1 + |x|^3)$ for $|x| < e^{100,000}$, $f(x) = 0$ otherwise, where K is chosen to insure unit total mass (that the density integrates to 1). By symmetry, the mean of this distribution is 0, so the variance is $\int x^2 f(x)\, dx$, which approximately equals

$$2K \int_1^{e^{100,000}} (1/x)\, dx \tag{12}$$

which approximately equals $2K \log(e^{100,000}) \approx 200,000K$. From a straightforward estimate, $K > 0.1$, thus the standard deviation of this distribution is greater than 100. If we were to choose, for example, $r = 0.2 \times$ standard deviation, application of Equation 10 would give

$$g(0) < -\log\left(\int_{z=-20}^{z=20} f(z)\, dz \right) \tag{13}$$

Because $f(z)$ decreases like $1/|z|^3$, the inner integral is very nearly 1, so $g(0)$ is minimally larger than 0. The conclusion is thus: With high probability, relatively small empirical ApEn values cannot come from i.i.d. normal distributions, or other similar distributions, but may possibly represent fatter tailed i.i.d. random variables.

For the second question, ApEn provides a particularly elegant and efficient indicator of the validity of the i.i.d. assumption altogether. Assume that an underlying process is i.i.d. of unknown distribution. From Equation 9, ApEn(m,r) is independent of m for all r. Therefore for all r, ApEn$(1,r) = $ ApEn$(2,r)$. So compare ApEn$(1,r,N)$ and ApEn$(2,r,N)$ values, for r with minimal bias in the ApEn statistic; if these disagree by a nontrivial amount for some r, it is unlikely that the underlying process is i.i.d.

SUMMARY AND CONCLUSIONS

The principal focus of this chapter has been the description of a recently introduced regularity statistic, ApEn, that quantifies the continuum from perfectly orderly to completely random in time-series data. Several properties of ApEn facilitate its utility for biological time-series analysis:

1. ApEn is nearly unaffected by noise of magnitude below a de facto specified filter level.
2. ApEn is robust to outliers.
3. ApEn can be applied to time series of 100 or more points, with good confidence (established by standard deviation calculations).
4. ApEn is finite for stochastic, noisy deterministic, and composite (mixed) processes, these last of which are likely models for complicated biological systems.
5. Increasing ApEn corresponds to intuitively increasing process complexity in the settings of property 4.

This applicability to medium-sized data sets and general stochastic processes is in marked contrast to capabilities of "chaos" algorithms such as the correlation dimension, which are properly applied to low-dimensional iterated deterministic dynamical systems. The potential uses of ApEn to provide new insights in biological settings are thus myriad, from a complementary perspective to that given by classical statistical methods.

ApEn is typically calculated by a computer program, with a FORTRAN listing for a "basic" code referenced earlier. It is imperative to view ApEn as a family of statistics, each of which is a relative measure of process regularity. For proper implementation, the two input parameters m (window length) and r (tolerance width, de facto filter) must remain fixed in all calculations, as must N, the data length, to insure meaningful comparisons. Guidelines for m and r selection were indicated earlier. We have found normalized regularity to be especially useful, as in the growth hormone study discussed above; r is chosen as a fixed percentage (often 15% or 20%) of the subject's SD, rather than of a group SD. This version of ApEn has the property that it is decorrelated from process SD, in that it remains unchanged under uniform process magnification or reduction; thus we can entirely separate the questions of SD change and regularity change in data analysis.

ACKNOWLEDGMENT

I appreciate the SPX 500 data collection and empirical calculations performed by Roy DeMeo, as well as numerous discussions with him as to potential ApEn applicability to a variety of financial market time-series problems.

REFERENCES

Black, F., & Scholes, M. (1973). The pricing of options and corporate liabilities. *Journal of Political Economy, 8*, 637–653.
Blahut, R. E. (1987). *Principles and practice of information theory* (pp. 58–64). Reading, MA: Addison-Wesley.

Brock, W. A. (1986). Distinguishing random and deterministic systems: Abridged version. *Journal of Economic Theory, 40*, 168–195.

Broomhead, D. S., & King, G. P. (1986). Extracting qualitative dynamics from experimental data. *Physica D, 20*, 217–236.

Casdagli, M. (1989). Nonlinear prediction of chaotic time series. *Physica D, 35*, 335–356.

Cox, D. R., & Miller, H. D. (1965). *The theory of stochastic processes* (pp. 205–215). New York: John Wiley.

Eckmann, J. P., & Ruelle, D. (1985). Ergodic theory of chaos and strange attractors. *Reviews of Modern Physics, 57*, 617–656.

Farmer, J. D., & Sidorowich, J. J. (1987). Predicting chaotic time series. *Physical Review Letters, 59*, 845–884.

Fleisher, L. A., Pincus, S. M., & Rosenbaum, S. H. (1993). Approximate entropy of heart rate as a correlate of postoperative ventricular dysfunction. *Anesthesiology, 78*, 683–692.

Fraser, A. M., & Swinney, H. L. (1986). Independent coordinates for strange attractors from mutual information. *Physical Review A, 33*, 1134–1140.

Grassberger, P., & Procaccia, I. (1983a). Estimation of the Kolmogorov entropy from a chaotic signal. *Physical Review A, 28*, 2591–2593.

Grassberger, P., & Procaccia, I. (1983b). Measuring the strangeness of strange attractors. *Physica D, 9*, 189–208.

Hartman, M. L., Pincus, S. M., Johnson, M. L., Matthews, D. H., Faunt, L. M., Vance, M. L., Thorner, M. O., & Veldhuis, J. D. (1994). Enhanced basal and disorderly growth hormone (GH) secretion distinguish acromegalic from normal pulsatile GH release. *Journal of Clinical Investigation, 94*, 1277–1288.

Hoel, P. G., Port, S. C., & Stone, C. J. (1972). *Introduction to stochastic processes* (pp. 166–169). Boston: Houghton Mifflin.

Hsieh, D. A. (1991). Chaos and nonlinear dynamics: Application to financial markets. *Journal of Finance, 46*, 1839–1877.

Kaplan, D. T., Furman, M. I., Pincus, S. M., Ryan, S. M., Lipsitz, L. A., & Goldberger, A. L. (1991). Aging and the complexity of cardiovascular dynamics. *Biophysical Journal, 59*, 945–949.

Kolmogorov, A. N. (1958). A new metric invariant of transient dynamical systems and automorphisms in Lebesgue spaces. *Doklady Akademy Nauk. SSSR, 119*, 861–864.

Komogorov, A. N., & Rozanov, Y. A. (1960). On strong mixing conditions for stationary Guassian processes. *Theory of Probability and Applications, 5*, 204–208.

Mayer-Kress, G., Yates, F. E., Benton, L., Keidel, M., Tirsch, W., Poppl, S. J., & Geist, K. (1988). Dimensional analysis of nonlinear oscillations in brain, heart, and muscle. *Mathematical Biosciences, 90*, 155–182.

Ornstein, D. S. (1970). Bernoulli shifts with the same entropy are isomorphic. *Advances in Mathematics, 4*, 337–352.

Ornstein, D. S., & Weiss, B. (1990). How sampling reveals a process. *Annals of Probability, 18*, 905–930.

Pincus, S. M. (1991). Approximate entropy as a measure of system complexity. *Proceedings of the National Academy of Science USA, 88*, 2297–2301.

Pincus, S. M. (1992). Approximating Markov chains. *Proceedings of the National Academy of Science USA, 89*, 4432–4436.

Pincus, S. M. (1994). Greater signal regularity may indicate increased system isolation. *Mathematical Biosciences, 122*, 161–181.

Pincus, S. M. (1995). Approximate entropy (ApEn) as a complexity measure. *Chaos, 5*, 110–117.

Pincus, S. M., Cummins, T. R., & Haddad, G. G. (1993). Heart rate control in normal and aborted SIDS infants. *American Journal of Physiology, 264 (Regulatory & Integrative, 33)*, R638–R646.

Pincus, S. M., Gladstone, I. M., & Ehrenkranz, R. A. (1991). A regularity statistic for medical data analysis. *Journal of Clinical Monitoring, 7*, 335–345.

Pincus, S. M., & Goldberger, A. L. (1994). Physiological time-series analysis: What does regularity quantify? *American Journal of Physiology, 266 (Heart Circulatory Physiology, 35)*, H1643–H1656.

Pincus, S. M., & Huang, W. M. (1992). Approximate entropy: Statistical properties and applications. *Communications in Statistics- Theory and Methods, 21*, 3061–3077.

Pincus, S. M., & Keefe, D. L. (1992). Quantification of hormone pulsatility via an approximate entropy algorithm. *American Journal of Physiology, 262 (Endocrinology and Metabolism, 25)*, E741–E754.

Pincus, S. M., & Viscarello, R. R. (1992). Approximate entropy: A regularity measure for fetal heart rate analysis. *Obstetrics and Gynecology, 79*, 249–255.

Ramsey, J. B., & Yuan, H.-J. (1989). Bias and error bars in dimension calculations and their evaluation in some simple models. *Physics Letters A, 134*, 287–297.

Ryan, S. M., Goldberger, A. L., Pincus, S. M., Mietus, J., & Lipsitz, L. A. (1994). Gender- and age-related differences in heart rate dynamics: Are women more complex than men? *Journal of the American College of Cardiology, 24*, 1700–1707.

Scheinkman, J. A., & LeBaron, B. (1989). Nonlinear dynamics and stock returns. *Journal of Business, 62*, 311–337.

Siragy, H. M., Vieweg, W. V. R., Pincus, S. M., & Veldhuis, J. D. (1995). Increased disorderliness and amplified basal and pulsatile aldosterone secretion in patients with primary aldosteronism. *Journal of Clinical Endocrinology and Metabolism, 80*, 28–33.

Sugihara, G., & May, R. M. (1990). Nonlinear forecasting as a way of distinguishing chaos from measurement error in time series. *Nature, 344*, 734–741.

Takens, F. (1983). Invariants related to dimension and entropy. In *Atas do 13.Col. Brasiliero de Matematicas*, Rio de Janerio.

Tuckwell, H. C. (1989). *Stochastic processes in the neurosciences.* Philadelphia: SIAM.

Veldhuis, J. D., Liem, A. Y., South, S., Weltman, A., Weltman, J., Clemmons, D. A., Abbott, R., Mulligan, T., Johnson, M. L., Pincus, S., Straume, M., & Iranmanesh, A. (1995). Differential impact of age, sex-steroid hormones, and obesity on basal versus pulsatile growth hormone secretion in men as assessed in an ultrasensitive chemiluminescence assay. *Journal of Clinical Endocrinology and Metabolism, 80*, 3209–3222.

Wolf, A., Swift, J. B., Swinney, H. L., & Vastano, J. A. (1985). Determining Lyapunov exponents from a time-series. *Physica D, 16*, 285–317.

12

FITTING NONLINEAR DYNAMICAL MODELS DIRECTLY TO OBSERVED TIME SERIES

Peter C. M. Molenaar
University of Amsterdam
Pennsylvania State University

Maartje E. J. Raymakers
University of Amsterdam

Nonlinear dynamics is a capsule term referring to a variety of fields of research, including nonequilibrium thermodynamics (Nicolis & Prigogine, 1977), catastrophe theory (Thom, 1975), synergism (Haken, 1983), soliton theory (Toda, 1989), artificial neural network modeling (Grossberg, 1982), and chaos theory (e.g., Ott, 1993). These fields of research have provided us with profound new insights in the self-organizing capabilities and emergent pattern formation of temporal and spatiotemporal processes. Many concepts and techniques of nonlinear dynamics have found their way to the social sciences and have led to novel ways of conceptualizing the temporal organization of behavior. Among the many innovative applications of nonlinear dynamics in psychology we can discern a number of dedicated attempts to construct explicit causal models of time- or age-dependent processes. Examples are the predator–prey model of human cerebral development of Thatcher (chapter 5, this volume), the neural network model relating cortical and cognitive development proposed by Been (chapter 8, this volume), the catastrophe model of stagewise cognitive development of Van der Maas and Molenaar (1992; Van der Maas, chapter 7, this volume), the nonlinear growth models of Van Geert (1991; chapter 6, this volume), and the model of phase transitions in human hand movements of Haken, Kelso, and Bunz (1985). In each of these applications a nonlinear dynamical model has been specified that can explain the self-organizing tendencies of a particular psychological or developmental process. In this chapter the focus is on the way in which these models can be fitted to real data. More specifically, a flexible statistical technique is described with which the non-linear dynamical models concerned can be applied under a broad range of conditions.

Until now nonlinear dynamical modeling in psychology has proceeded in what might be called indirect ways. In contrast to the physical sciences there exists no established theoretical framework to guide the construction of psychological process models. Hence modeling has to proceed by the tentative postulation of a so-called *Ansatz*, a conjectured system of differential or difference equations that is expected to underly the temporal organization of an observed process. The validity of such an *Ansatz* then is investigated by means of computer simulation and/or mathematical analysis of the conjectured system, the results of which are to be compared with the observed characteristics of the real process under scrutiny. The next logical step would seem to be to fit a mathematical system model thus validated directly to observed process data, but to the best of our knowledge this has not yet been carried out.

Another indirect approach to accommodate uncertainty about the true underlying dynamical model of an observed process is to use more or less model-free techniques. Most applications of chaos theory in psychology have been dedicated to dimension estimation of so-called strange attractors that organize the steady-state behavior of nonlinear systems. This approach is especially popular in the analysis of brain function (cf. Basar, 1990). It is model-free in the sense that it does not require the specification of a mathematical model and only yields a limited characterization of the dynamical system underlying an observed process. In a similar vein, typical applications of catastrophe theory in psychology are model-free in that they do not require the specification of a mathematical model. Both dimension estimation and catastrophe theory owe their general range of application to deep mathematical theorems: Takens's embedding theorem (cf. Ott, 1993) and Thom's theorem (cf. Gilmore, 1981), respectively. Also, both approaches have given rise to fundamental issues regarding their applicability to noisy data (cf., respectively, Casdagli, Eubank, Farmer, & Gibson, 1992; Molenaar & Hartelman, 1996).

Within the confines of this chapter we neglect the many intriguing developments in the context of indirect and model-free aproaches, and instead restrict attention to the direct fit of parametric nonlinear dynamical models to noisy time series data. That is, we focus on parameter estimation in a given mathematical model of an observed process. Only in the final section do we touch on the important concomitant issues of model selection and model validation. Our basic tool is a recursive estimator for nonlinear dynamical models, a version of the so-called extended Kalman filter to be introduced in the next section. The presentation cannot be but schematic and tutorial, but is backed up with sufficient references to the rich literature on Kalman filtering. Moreover, on request the FORTRAN source code of our implementation of the extended Kalman filter can be obtained from the first author. In the remaining two sections we detail illustrative applications of the extended Kalman filter to parameter estimation in two nonlinear dynamical models: respectively, the model of phase transitions in human hand movement of Schöner, Haken, and Kelso (1986) and a simple version of Van Geert's (1991) nonlinear growth model.

RECURSIVE ESTIMATION IN (NON)LINEAR DYNAMICAL MODELS

The concept of recursive estimation is naturally linked up with the so-called state-space model. Hence we first introduce the linear state-space model and then define a recursive estimator for the state evolution in this model. The recursive estimator concerned is the famous Kalman filter, the workhorse of applied linear systems theory (e.g., Caines, 1988; Goodwin & Sin, 1984; Sage & Melsa, 1971). Next we consider the nonlinear state-space model and define an extended Kalman filter for recursive estimation of the state in this model. In closing this section we address some important characteristics of our implementation of the extended Kalman filter. This implementation is used in the applications to be described in the next two sections.

The Linear State-Space Model

Let $\mathbf{x}(t)$ denote a q-variate stochastic process called the state process, where t is understood to be integer-valued time: $t = 0, \pm1, \pm2, \ldots$ (henceforth vector- and matrix-valued variables are denoted by lower and upper case bold letters, respectively). Consider the following q-dimensional stochastic difference equation for $\mathbf{x}(t)$:

$$\mathbf{x}(t + 1) = \mathbf{A}_{t+1}\mathbf{x}(t) + \mathbf{w}(t + 1) \tag{1}$$

where $\mathbf{A}_t$ is a (q,q)-dimensional matrix with possibly time-varying elements and $\mathbf{w}(t)$ is a q-variate stochastic process called the innovations process. It is assumed that $\mathbf{w}(t)$ is a zero mean Gaussian process with covariance function:

$$E[\mathbf{w}(t),\mathbf{w}(t + u)'] = \delta(u)\mathbf{W} \qquad u = 0, \pm1, \ldots \tag{2}$$

where the prime denotes transposition and where $\delta(u) = 1$ if $u = 0$ and $\delta(u) = 0$ otherwise.

According to Equation 1 the state at time $t + 1$, $\mathbf{x}(t + 1)$, is a linear function of the state at the preceding time t, $\mathbf{A}_{t+1}\mathbf{x}(t)$, and of the innovations process. Such a model is referred to as a first-order autoregression in the time-series analysis literature (e.g., Hannan, 1970) and as a Markov model in the mathematical statistical literature on stochastic processes (e.g., Chung, 1982). The innovations process is taken to be a zero mean Gaussian process, which according to Equation 2 has zero serial correlations at lags u unequal to zero. Such a process is usually referred to as white noise. Together, Equations 1 and 2 descibe the evolution of the state in the linear state-space model. In general, however, the state $\mathbf{x}(t)$ will not be observed directly, but instead the observations $\mathbf{y}(t)$ consist of a linear combination of the q state dimensions corrupted by additive measurement noise $\mathbf{v}(t)$:

$$\mathbf{y}(t) = \mathbf{H}_t\mathbf{x}(t) + \mathbf{v}(t) \tag{3}$$

where $\mathbf{y}(t)$ is a manifest p-variate process and $\mathbf{H}_t$ is a (p,q)-dimensional matrix with possibly time-varying elements. It is assumed that $\mathbf{v}(t)$ is a p-variate zero mean Gaussian white noise process:

$$E[\mathbf{v}(t),\mathbf{v}(t + u)'] = \delta(u)\mathbf{V} \quad u = 0, \pm1, \ldots \tag{4}$$

Equations 1–4 constitute our definition of a linear state-space model. In closing this section, a few qualifications of this definition are given. First, both the innovations $\mathbf{w}(t)$ and the measurement errors $\mathbf{v}(t)$ have been required to be Gaussian white noise processes. This requirement is unnecessarily strict, however, and can be eased in various ways. For instance, it can be allowed that $\mathbf{w}(t)$ has nonzero serial correlations: $E[\mathbf{w}(t),\mathbf{w}(t+u)'] = \mathbf{W}(u)$, $u = 0, \pm1, \ldots$. Equivalently, the covariance function of $\mathbf{v}(t)$ can be allowed to be $\mathbf{V}(u)$, $u = 0, \pm1, \ldots$. For further details about the state-space model with serially correlated innovations and/or measurement errors, the reader is referred to Jazwinski (1970). In addition, it can be allowed that the covariance functions of $\mathbf{w}(t)$ and $\mathbf{v}(t)$ have time-varying elements, or, alternatively, that $\mathbf{w}(t)$ and/or $\mathbf{v}(t)$ are non-Gaussian processes (cf. Fahrmeir & Tutz, 1994). Second, according to Equation 1 the state evolution is a first-order autoregression; that is, the state at $t + 1$ only depends on the state at t. Yet $\mathbf{x}(t)$ is allowed to have the following form: $\mathbf{x}(t)' = [x(t), x(t - 1), \ldots, x(t - n)]$, implying that the state evolution actually depends on state values at n preceding time points. Hence by extending the dimension of the state, Equation 1 can accommodate autoregressions of arbitrary finite order. In fact, the option of extending the state dimension, in combination with judicious patterning of $\mathbf{A}_t$, ensures that Equation 1 can accommodate all possible linear process models. Third, and last, it is noted that in general the linear state-space model of a given process may not be unique. This is evident because the option to extend the dimension of the state at will yields a manifold of equivalent representations of the same given process. But even if it is insisted that the dimension of the state is minimal, there still may exist an infinity of equivalent instances of Equations 1–4 that are related to each other by a similarity transformation depending on an arbitrary nonsingular (q,q)-dimensional matrix. For further discussion of the lack of uniqueness of state-space models as well as procedures to determine the minimal dimension of the state, the reader is referred to Hannan and Deistler (1988).

The Kalman Filter

The state evolution constitutes, in psychometric jargon, a latent process. Hence for a given realization of the manifest process $y(t)$, $t = 1, 2, \ldots, T$, where we conveniently refer to such a finite realization as a *time series*, one has to estimate the latent time series $x(t)$, $t = 1, 2, \ldots, T$. As to this, several approaches can be followed, like the Bayesian, maximum likelihood, or least-squares approach. Quite distinct from this, however, an estimator obtained by each of these approaches can be implemented in a recursive or a nonrecursive way. For a nonrecursive implementation it is required that the complete manifest time series is available (referred to by Koopmans, 1974, as batch treatment of a historic time series). In contrast, in a recursive implementation the values of the manifest series are treated one after the other, in the order as they become available (usually referred to as online treatment of a time series in real time). Hence a recursive implementation of some estimator $\mathbf{F}$ of the latent state can be schematically represented as

$$\mathbf{x}(t+1\,|\,t+1) = \mathbf{F}_{t+1}[\mathbf{x}(t\,|\,t),\mathbf{y}(t+1),\mathbf{X}(t\,|\,t)] \qquad (5)$$

where $\mathbf{x}(t\,|\,t)$ denotes the estimate of $\mathbf{x}(t)$ given the information available at time t, and where $\mathbf{X}(t\,|\,t)$ is the covariance matrix of $\mathbf{x}(t\,|\,t)$. It is seen that the state estimate $\mathbf{x}(t+1\,|\,t+1)$ only depends on information available at the preceding time t, namely, $\mathbf{x}(t\,|\,t)$ and $\mathbf{X}(t\,|\,t)$, and the manifest process at time $t+1$. Hence the estimator (Equation 5) constitutes a first-order recursion and in that sense is compatible with the linear state-space model given by Equations 1–4.

The specific form of $\mathbf{F}_t[\cdot]$ depends on the estimation approach that is chosen. In his original work Kalman used an orthogonal projection approach (cf. Kalman, Falb, & Arbib, 1969), which in the present context corresponds to a least-squares approach (and also to a maximum likelihood approach, given the assumptions that the innovations $\mathbf{w}(t)$ in Equation 1 and measurement errors $\mathbf{v}(t)$ in Equation 3 are Gaussian processes). $\mathbf{F}_{t+1}[\cdot]$ then takes a particularly simple form involving the following set of matrix equations:

$$\mathbf{x}(t+1\,|\,t+1) = \mathbf{A}_{t+1}\mathbf{x}(t\,|\,t) + \mathbf{K}(t+1\,|\,t)[\mathbf{y}(t+1) - \mathbf{H}_{t+1}\mathbf{A}_{t+1}\mathbf{x}(t\,|\,t)]$$
$$\mathbf{K}(t+1\,|\,t) = \mathbf{X}(t+1\,|\,t)\mathbf{H}_{t+1}'[\mathbf{H}_{t+1}\mathbf{X}(t+1\,|\,t)\mathbf{H}_{t+1}' + \mathbf{V}]^{-1}$$
$$\mathbf{X}(t+1\,|\,t) = \mathbf{A}_{t+1}\mathbf{X}(t\,|\,t)\mathbf{A}_{t+1}' + \mathbf{W} \qquad\qquad (6)$$
$$\mathbf{X}(t+1\,|\,t+1) = [\mathbf{I} - \mathbf{K}(t+1\,|\,t)\mathbf{H}_{t+1}]\,\mathbf{X}(t+1\,|\,t)$$

The matrices $\mathbf{A}_t$, $\mathbf{H}_t$, $\mathbf{W}$, and $\mathbf{V}$ are taken from Equations 1–4. $\mathbf{K}(t+1\,|\,t)$ is a (q,p)-dimensional matrix called the gain, and $\mathbf{X}(t+1\,|\,t)$ is the (q,q)-dimensional covariance of $\mathbf{x}(t+1\,|\,t)$, that is, the estimate of the state at time $t+1$ given information available at time t. Together the matrix equations given by Equation 6 define the Kalman filter (KF) for given initial conditions $\mathbf{x}(0\,|\,0) = \mathbf{x}_0$ and $\mathbf{X}(0\,|\,0) = \mathbf{X}_0$.

To apply the KF, the following information has to be available a priori: $\mathbf{x}_0$, $\mathbf{X}_0$, $\mathbf{W}$, $\mathbf{V}$, and $\mathbf{A}_t$ and $\mathbf{H}_t$ for all time points t. It can be expected that in many applications some or even most of this information is lacking. As to this, it can be proved that, under rather general conditions, misspecifications of $\mathbf{x}_0$ and $\mathbf{X}_0$ only have limited and transient effects on the performance of the KF. The effects of misspecifications of the remaining a priori information can be quantified in so-called sensitivity analyses of the KF. The recursion equations used in such sensitivity analyses can be found in, for instance, Sage and Melsa (1971, section 8.4). Yet there are of course upper bounds to the degrees of misspecification that still will yield tolerable effects on the performance of the KF. In those cases where any a priori information about parameters in $\mathbf{W}$, $\mathbf{V}$, $\mathbf{A}_t$, and/or $\mathbf{H}_t$ is lacking, one has to include these unknown parameters in an extended state vector. This immediately implies that the filtering problem becomes nonlinear, because the recursive estimator of a state that is thus extended now involves multiplications of the state with matrices depending on the same state. Hence the KF given by Equation 6 no longer applies. In the next section we present an extension of the Kalman filter that can be applied to arbitrary nonlinear state-space models.

The Extended Kalman Filter (EKF)

Consider the following nonlinear analogues of Equations 1 and 3:

$$\mathbf{x}(t+1) = \mathbf{f}_{t+1}[\mathbf{x}(t)] + \mathbf{w}(t+1) \qquad \mathbf{y}(t) = \mathbf{h}_t[\mathbf{x}(t)] + \mathbf{v}(t) \qquad (7)$$

where $\mathbf{f}_t[\cdot]$ and $\mathbf{h}_t[\cdot]$ are nonlinear vector-valued functions that are sufficiently smooth (cf. Sage & Melsa, 1971, p. 93, footnote, for an exact specification of the smoothness conditions), but are arbitrary otherwise. It is assumed that $\mathbf{w}(t)$ and $\mathbf{v}(t)$ are Gaussian white noise series with mean zero and covariance functions given by Equations 2 and 4, respectively. Equation 7, together with

Equations 2 and 4, constitutes the nonlinear state-space model that will be used in the following under the denotation NSSM. For an extensive discussion of the mathematical theory of NSSMs the reader is referred to the excellent monograph of Isidori (1989).

There exists a voluminous literature on recursive state estimation in NSSMs. Chen (1993) provided a recent compilation of application-oriented papers, including key references to the published literature. In what follows, we focus on a more or less straightforward adaptation of the KF given by Equation 6 to accommodate NSSMs. The EKF concerned can be derived from first principles (cf. Sage & Melsa, 1971, chapter 8), but for our present purposes a concise heuristic description suffices. The reader should be warned, however, that the simple substitution rules presented next are based on rather intricate theoretical developments.

Given the assumption that $\mathbf{f}_t[\cdot]$ and $\mathbf{h}_t[\cdot]$ in Equation 7 are smooth nonlinear functions, consider their Taylor series expansions about $\mathbf{x}(t|t)$ and $\mathbf{x}(t+1|t)$, respectively, and keep only the first-order terms:

$$\delta\mathbf{A}_{t+1} = \delta\mathbf{f}_{t+1}[\mathbf{x}(t|t)]/\delta\mathbf{x}(t|t) \quad \delta\mathbf{H}_{t+1} = \delta\mathbf{h}_{t+1}[\mathbf{x}(t+1|t)]/\delta\mathbf{x}(t+1|t) \qquad (8)$$

where $\mathbf{x}(t+1|t) = \mathbf{f}_{t+1}[\mathbf{x}(t|t)]$. Notice that $\delta\mathbf{A}_{t+1}$ and $\delta\mathbf{H}_{t+1}$ have the same dimensions as $\mathbf{A}_{t+1}$ and $\mathbf{H}_{t+1}$ in Equations 1 and 3, respectively. Substitution of $\delta\mathbf{A}_{t+1}$ for $\mathbf{A}_{t+1}$ and $\delta\mathbf{H}_{t+1}$ for $\mathbf{H}_{t+1}$ in the expressions for $\mathbf{K}(t+1|t)$, $\mathbf{X}(t+1|t)$ and $\mathbf{X}(t+1|t+1)$ of the KF given by Equation 6 then defines the analogous expressions of the EKF. The remaining expression for $\mathbf{x}(t+1|t+1)$ in the EKF reads

$$\mathbf{x}(t+1|t+1) = \mathbf{f}_{t+1}[\mathbf{x}(t|t)] + \mathbf{K}(t+1|t)\{\mathbf{y}(t+1) - \mathbf{h}_{t+1}[\mathbf{x}(t+1|t)]\} \qquad (9)$$

Implementation of the EKF

The basic recursive scheme comprising the EKF can be readily implemented. Yet it can be shown, both on theoretical grounds and in numerical (Monte Carlo) studies, that the EKF is vulnerable to instabilities and can give rise to deteriorating state estimates. There exist various options to improve the performance and stability of the EKF. In this section we present the options that have been included in our implementation.

Consider the situation at time $t+1$ when a new observation $\mathbf{y}(t+1)$ has just become available. At that moment the EKF also has in store $\mathbf{x}(t|t)$ [and its covariance matrix $\mathbf{X}(t|t)$] obtained at the preceding time t. Because $\mathbf{x}(t|t)$ is the most recent update of the state estimate, $\mathbf{f}_{t+1}[\cdot]$ and $\mathbf{h}_{t+1}[\cdot]$ are linearized about $\mathbf{x}(t|t)$ and $\mathbf{x}(t+1|t) = \mathbf{f}_{t+1}[\mathbf{x}(t|t)]$, respectively, in the construction of the EKF according to Equation 8. Application of the EKF recursive equations then yields $\mathbf{x}(t+1|t+1)$ based on $\mathbf{y}(t+1)$, $\mathbf{x}(t|t)$, and $\mathbf{x}(t+1|t)$. The

EKF, however, is based on a linearization method and hence constitutes an approximate Kalman filter. One way to improve the quality of the approximation is to improve the estimates $\mathbf{x}(t|t)$ and $\mathbf{x}(t + 1|t)$ using the new observation $\mathbf{y}(t + 1)$. This can be regarded as a special case of smoothing, which is discussed later. It results in an iteration in which $\mathbf{f}_{t+1}[\cdot]$ and $\mathbf{h}_{t+1}[\cdot]$ are relinearized about the improved estimates of $\mathbf{x}(t|t)$ and $\mathbf{x}(t+1|t)$. Within each recursion step this iteration may be repeated as many times as is desired. The resulting EKF with iteration is described in Sage and Melsa (1971, section 9.4).

According to Equation 9, $\mathbf{x}(t + 1|t + 1)$ is determined by two terms: a prediction $\mathbf{f}_{t+1}[\mathbf{x}(t|t)]$ and a correction based on the new observation $\mathbf{y}(t + 1)$, namely, $\mathbf{K}(t + 1|t)\{\mathbf{y}(t + 1) - \mathbf{h}_{t+1}[\mathbf{x}(t + 1|t)]\}$. The (q,p)-dimensional matrix $\mathbf{K}(t + 1|t)$ is called the gain and depends according to Equation 6 on $\mathbf{V}$ and $\mathbf{X}(t + 1|t)$, where $\mathbf{X}(t + 1|t)$ depends on $\mathbf{W}$ and $\mathbf{X}(t|t)$. Hence the gain is a function of the covariance functions of the innovations process, measurement noise, and the state estimate at the preceding time t. The gain determines the degree to which a new observation affects the recursive state estimate. In particular, if the gain becomes too small then the EKF becomes insensitive to new observations. In order to prevent the EKF thus becoming insensitive, the following options are available in our implementation. First, in each recursion step the condition of the covariance matrix $\mathbf{X}(t|t)$ is checked. If one or more of the eigenvalues of $\mathbf{X}(t|t)$ are too small then this is remedied by slightly perturbing $\mathbf{X}(t|t)$. Second, a specific variant of so-called covariance modification of $\mathbf{W}$ (cf. Goodwin & Sin, 1984, section 3.3) can be invoked. This can be understood as follows. Let the state include unknown parameters, in the way described in the Kalman filter subsection. More specifically, let the kth element of $\mathbf{x}(t)$, that is, $x_k(t)$, be a fixed but unknown parameter. Then it follows that the time-dependent evolution of $x_k(t)$ is simply given by $x_k(t + 1) = x_k(t)$. Hence $w_k(t)$, the kth component of the innovations process, is zero. Also, the kth diagonal element w_{kk} of $\mathbf{W}$ is zero, and this may cause insensitivity of the EKF. To counteract this insensitivity, the kth diagonal of $\mathbf{W}$ is modified and assigned a small positive value: $w_{kk} = \varepsilon^2$.

Compared with a nonrecursive batch implementation in which a complete (historic) time series $y(t)$, $t = 1, \ldots, T$ is used at once, a recursive filtering implementation of a given estimator is always suboptimal. This is because at each time $t < T$ the state estimate obtained by filtering only is based on the observed series up to time t, whereas the analogous batch estimate is based on the complete observed series. To get a recursive implementation that makes use of the same information as its batch analogue, it should yield state estimates $x(t|T)$ for all times $t = 1, \ldots, T$. Such a recursive estimator is called a smoother. Heuristically speaking, a smoother consists of a regular filtering of an observed time series up to time T, followed by a filtering backward in time from time T to time 1. In fact, this is only one version of smoothing. For alternative types of smoothers the reader is referred to, for example, Sage and Melsa (1971, sections 8.3 and 9.5).

This concludes our concise description of options aimed at improving the performance and stability of the EKF. The options concerned (iteration, covariance modification, smoothing) are available in our implementation of the EKF. In the illustrative applications discussed in the next sections, we specify which options have actually been used.

PARAMETER ESTIMATION IN A STOCHASTIC MODEL OF PHASE TRANSITIONS

In a now famous paper, Haken, Kelso, and Bunz (1985) presented a theoretical model of phase transitions in oscillatory motions of the two index fingers. Under the instruction to increase the frequency of out-of-phase, antisymmetrical motion, the finger motions shifted abruptly to an in-phase symmetrical mode. That is, the relative phase of the oscillatory finger motions shifted suddenly from π to zero if the driving frequency was increased in a continuous fashion.

Let $\phi(t)$ denote the relative phase at time t of the oscillatory finger motions. Then Haken et al. (1985) make the following *Ansatz* (i.e., conjectured phenomenological model) concerning the dynamics of $\phi(t)$:

$$\frac{d}{dt}\phi(t) = -\frac{d}{d\phi}V[\phi(t)] \qquad V[\phi(t)] = -a\cos[\phi(t)] - b\cos[2\phi(t)] \qquad (10)$$

where a and b are parameters of the potential function $V[\phi(t)]$. Hence the equation of motion of the relative phase is given by the gradient of a periodic potential. The parameters a and b are considered to be dependent upon the driving frequency Φ: $a[\Phi]$ and $b[\Phi]$. This implies that changes in the driving frequency cause changes in the values of a and b. As the changes in Φ are assumed to take place relatively slow, no equations of motion for the parameters are given (so-called adiabatic elimination) and the functional form of $a[\Phi]$ and $b[\Phi]$ is left implicit. Haken et al. (1985) proved that Equation 10 has the required properties in that continuous slow (adiabatic) variation of the parameters a and b (caused by ditto variation of the driving frequency Φ) yields a sudden shift in the equilibria of the relative phase. More specifically, they proved that the transition concerned occurs when the ratio a/b, where $a > 0$ and $b > 0$, approaches the critical value $(a/b)_{\text{crit}} = 4$ from below. If the initial value of a/b is smaller than the critical value of 4, then the equilibria of Equation 10 are $\phi_{\text{eq}} = \pm\pi$ and there is out-of-phase, antisymmetrical finger motion. Then, if the ratio a/b increases continuously (caused by adiabatic increase of the driving frequency Φ), the original equilibria $\pm\pi$ become unstable, disappear, and a new stable equilibrium $\phi_{eq} = 0$ emerges at the critical value of 4. From then on there is in-phase, symmetrical finger motion.

Haken et al. (1985) proceeded by presenting further intriguing theoretical elaborations that are not considered here but that we hope to address in a forthcoming paper. Presently, we only note the following features of their theory. The theoretical model given by Equation 10 constitutes an *Ansatz*. That is, it is conjectured to be a plausible model for the observations concerned. This conjecture is corroborated both by analytic proof that the model has the required qualitative features (phase transitions induced by continuous adiabatic variation of model parameters) and in simulation studies. No attempt was made (and may not have been intended either) to fit the model to empirical or simulated data. As to that, an important step was made by Schöner, Haken, and Kelso (1986), who introduced a stochastic analogue of the Haken et al. (1985) model.

Schöner et al. (1986) made the following *Ansatz*:

$$d\phi(t) = -\frac{d}{d\phi} V[\phi(t)] \, dt + \sigma \, d\zeta(t) \tag{11}$$

where $\phi(t)$ is again the relative phase between the two oscillating fingers and $V[\phi(t)]$ is the potential function defined for Equation 10. The parameter σ is related to the standard deviation of the so-called random innovations $\sigma \, d\zeta(t)$. The term $d\zeta(t)$ denotes the formal differential of the standard Wiener process $\zeta(t)$; it is a formal term because the Wiener process is almost nowhere differentiable (cf. Gardiner, 1990). In fact, $d\zeta(t)$ can be best conceived of as a generalized function that only exists in integrated form. Yet a powerful analysis of Equation 11 can be carried out by means of the special, so-called Ito calculus.

Schöner et al. (1986) used the Ito calculus and other tools of stochastic calculus to obtain derived statistics for the stochastic differential (Equation 11) that can be compared with their empirical analogues. In this way the stochastic version of the Haken et al. (1985) model of phase transitions in oscillatory finger motion can be corroborated empirically. In the first section of this chapter this was considered to be an indirect approach to model fitting. It constitutes an important step toward direct fitting of Equation 11 to the data. But to the best of our knowledge such a direct fit has not been carried out yet. We next show how the Schöner et al. (1986) model can be directly fitted to an observed time series of relative phase $\phi(t)$ by means of the EKF.

Simulation of the Schoener et al. Model

Our discussion of Equation 11 has been somewhat cryptic. The reason is that we use the simplest possible approach based on a discretized version of Equation 11 and therefore do not need to elaborate the technicalities involved in dealing with a Wiener process. For a thorough discussion of alternative, more sophisticated numerical methods for stochastic differential equations the reader is referred to the excellent monograph by Bouleau and Lepingle (1994).

Consider Equation 11 on the time interval $[0,T]$ and let t_k be a set of equidistant points partitioning $[0,T]$. Let $\delta t = t_{k+1} - t_k$. Then the simple Euler discretization of Equation 11 is given by:

$$\phi(t_{k+1}) = \phi(t_k) + \frac{d}{d\phi} V[\phi(t_k)] \, \delta t + \sigma \text{sqrt}(\delta t) \zeta_{k+1} \qquad (12)$$

where ζ_k is an independently identically distributed Gaussian variable with mean zero and variance equal to one. If δt is taken sufficiently small then Equation 12 constitutes an approximation of Equation 11 in some well-defined sense (cf. Bouleau & Lepingle, 1994, pp. 274–278).

Figure 12.1 shows a simulated realization of Equation 12 with the following specifications. The time interval is $[0,100]$, while $\delta t = .01$. A time series of 10^4 data points is thus generated. Notice, however, that every 10th data point is depicted in Fig. 12.1. Hence the actual time step in Fig. 12.1 is $\delta t^* = .1$, associated with a subsample of 1,000 data points. This data reduction was invoked to reduce the running time of the EKF. The parameter σ is fixed at $\sigma = .1$. The parameter a in the potential function is fixed at $a = 1.0$. In contrast, the parameter b in this potential function is time-varying according to the

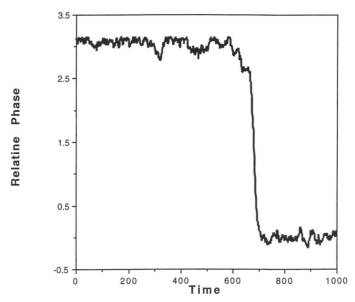

FIG. 12.1. Time series of relative phase generated by discretized Schöner et al. model (Eq. 12), time step = .1.

following scheme: $b(t_k) = b(t_0)[1.0 - (k/100) \delta t]$, where $b(t_0) = .5$. Hence the b parameter decreases linearly from the initial value of .5 to 0 across the time interval [0,100]. This implies that the ratio a/b increases from an initial value of 2 to 10^4 across [0,100]. Moreover, a/b will reach the critical value of 4 in middle of this time interval. Figure 12.1 shows, however, that the actual transition in the simulated time series occurs at a later time. Such delays in actual transitions are common in stochastic systems (cf. also the discussion of relaxation times in Schöner et al., 1986).

A Direct Fit of the Schöner et al. Model

Next Equation 12 is directly fitted by means of the EKF to the time series of relative phase depicted in Fig. 12.1. This resembles the common situation in empirical research where a given model with unknown (free) parameters has to be fitted to an observed time series. To keep the analysis as simple as possible, it is assumed that the parameter b in the potential function V is the only unknown parameter that has to be estimated recursively. Recursive estimation of all three parameters in Equation 12 simultaneously, namely, the parameters a and b in the potential and the parameter σ in the random innovation component, requires additional elaborations that would unnecessary complicate the intended illustrative application and therefore is deferred to a separate paper.

To start with, we set up the particular instance of the nonlinear state-space model given by Equation 7. Let $\mathbf{x}(t)' = [x_1(t), x_2(t)]$ be the two-dimensional extended state, where $x_1(t) = \phi(t)$ and $x_2(t) = b(t)$. Then the state evolution is described by:

$$x_1(t + 1) = x_1(t) - (\sin[x_1(t)] + 2x_2(t) \sin[2x_1(t)]) \, \delta t^* + w_1(t + 1)$$
$$x_2(t + 1) = x_2(t) + w_2(t + 1) \tag{13}$$

where $\delta t^* = .1$ (see previous subsection) and $w_1(t)$ is a Gaussian white noise process with mean zero and variance $\sigma^2 \delta t^* = .001$. Given that $b(t)$ is a deterministic time-varying parameter, $w_2(t)$ is vanishing. But in the subsection on the extended Kalman filter we argued that if elements of $\mathbf{w}(t)$ are zero, the performance of the EKF may be affected in that it becomes increasingly insensitive to the data. Hence the option of covariance modification is invoked and $w_2(t)$ is taken to be a Gaussian process with zero mean and variance equal to 10^{-4}. The measurement model is simply given by:

$$y(t) = x_1(t) + v(t) \tag{14}$$

Strictly speaking, $v(t)$ is vanishing in the present application, but again we invoke the option of covariance modification and take $v(t)$ to be a Gaussian white noise process with zero mean and variance equal to 10^{-6}.

Figure 12.2 shows the EKF estimate of $b(t)$. It is seen that after an initial transient deflection, the linearly decreasing trend of the true $b(t)$ is recovered by its filtered estimate. Figure 12.3 shows the estimated standard errors associated with the filtered $b(t)$ estimate. After an initial transient the recursively obtained standard errors stabilize at a value of about .1. Notice that the standard errors are biased upward because the covariance modification option was invoked. It was argued in the subsection on the extended Kalman filter that smoothing, involving filtering followed by filtering backward in time, makes better use of the information in the data. Hence the analysis was repeated while invoking the smoothing option. Figure 12.4 shows the smoothed estimate of $b(t)$. Now the initial transient deflection of the filtered estimate has disappeared and the linearly deceasing trend of the true $b(t)$ is rather faithfully recovered. The standard errors associated with the smoothed $b(t)$ estimate are depicted in Fig. 12.5. The latter estimates are smaller than their analogues for the filtered $b(t)$ estimate (notice the difference in scale between Figs. 12.3 and 12.5). Again, the standard errors shown in Fig. 12.5 are biased upward because the option of covariance modification was invoked.

Discussion

The time series of relative phase depicted in Fig. 12.1 has a rather simple bimodal appearance. Initially the relative phase lingers steadily about the value of π. Then a sudden transition occurs after which relative phase steadily lingers about the value of zero. Nothing in this time series seems

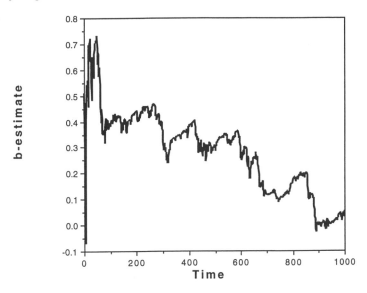

FIG. 12.2. Filtered estimate of $b(t)$ in Schöner et al. model, true $b(t) = .5 - t/1000$; $t = 0,1, \ldots , 999$, time step = .1.

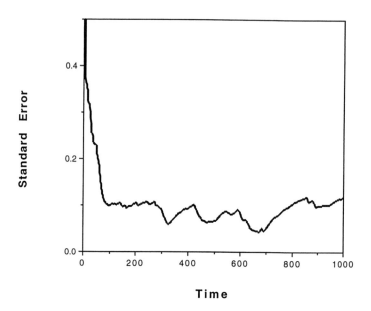

FIG. 12.3. Standard errors of filtered *b* estimate in Schöner et al. model, time step = .1.

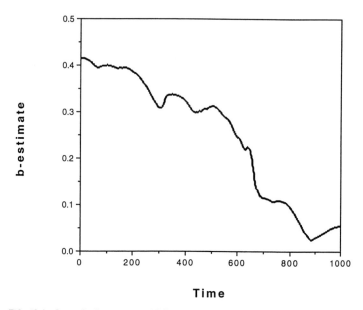

FIG. 12.4. Smoothed estimate of $b(t)$ in the Schöner et al. model. Time step is 0.1. True $b(t) = .5 - t/1000$; $t = 0,1, \ldots , 999$.

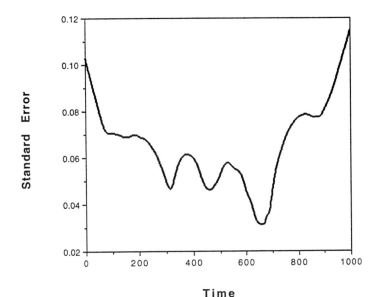

FIG. 12.5. Standard errors of smoothed *b* estimate in Schöner et al. model, time step = .1.

to indicate that it was generated by a process model (i.e., the discretized Schöner et al., 1986, model given by Equation 12) in which one of the parameters [i.e., $b(t)$] changed continuously in time according to a linear trend. Yet the EKF faithfully recovers the underlying true time course of $b(t)$. This suggests that our implementation of the EKF can yield reliable estimates of time-varying parameters in direct applications of the Schoener et al. (1986) model to nonstationary single-subject time series.

The possibility of fitting a suitably discretized version of Equation 11 directly to time-series data opens up new and powerful ways to carry out detailed tests of the validity of the theoretical model of phase transitions concerned. The rich tool kits of nonlinear time series analysis and applied systems theory can be used to assess the goodness of fit of the Schoener et al. *Ansatz* in each individual case and can indicate ways to adapt their *Ansatz* if the fit is found to be unsatisfactory. Moreover, this approach allows for principled tests of the invariance of model parameters across subjects and/or experimental conditions.

PARAMETER ESTIMATION IN A STOCHASTIC NONLINEAR GROWTH MODEL

In a number of innovative publications, Van Geert (1991, 1994, chapter 6, this volume) has developed an encompassing formal theory of growth in terms of a class of nonlinear evolution systems. The basic components of these systems can be characterized as deterministic difference equations of the logistic type (cf. Hofbauer & Sigmund, 1988), whereas the coupling between components can range from competitive and facilitating interactions of the Lotka–Volterra type (cf. Thatcher, chapter 5, this volume) to intricate conditional dynamic relationships. In a typical application a particular evolution system is defined for a given developmental process and whether the system can generate important qualitative features of the observed process is assessed by means of simulation. Hence such applications belong to the indirect approach to nonlinear dynamical modeling defined in the opening section. It is impossible within the confines of this section to do justice to Van Geert's theory, and therefore the reader is referred to the cited publications for further details. In what follows we concentrate on one of the simplest cases of the class of evolution systems considered by Van Geert.

Let $z(t)$ refer to a univariate metrical characteristic of a so-called grower (developmental process) at time t. Consider the following deterministic difference equation modeling the evolution of $z(t)$:

$$z(t + 1) = z(t) + \theta_1 z(t)^2 + \theta_2 z(t)^3 + j(t + 1) \tag{15}$$

where $j(t)$ denotes the effect of external influences. Equation 15 is referred to as the cubic growth model, and it constitutes a reparameterized version of one of Van Geert's growth models. The original version concerned is recovered by making the following substitutions: $\theta_1 = rk^{-2}$ and $\theta_2 = rk^{-3}$, where r is the rate of growth and k denotes the carrying capacity associated with the maximum level of $z(t)$ that can be sustained in a given environment (cf. Van Geert, 1991). We next consider the direct fit of the cubic growth model given by Equation 15 to a single-subject time series.

Simulation of Van Geert's Cubic Growth Model

We consider the simulation of a single realization ($N = 1$ time series) of four variants of the cubic growth model. Only the first variant is deterministic and consists of a simulation directly based on Equation 15. The remaining three variants are stochastic analogues of Equation 15, where the stochasticity is of increasing complexity.

Model I. For $t = 1, 2, \ldots, 100$, let $k = 25$, $r = 1$, and $j(t) = 1$. Notice that, to simplify the illustrative application, the external influences $j(t)$ are taken to be constant. Then the values of the parameters in Equation 15 are $\theta_1 = 1.60E - 3$, $\theta_2 = 6.40E - 5$, and $j(t) = j = 1$. The notation $cE - n$ means c times 10^{-n}. The time series $z(t)$ generated by means of Model 1 is depicted in Fig. 12.6.

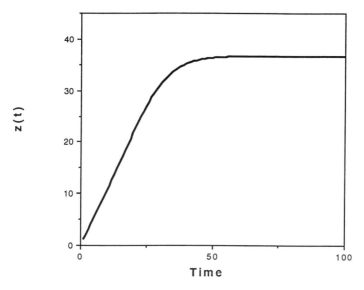

FIG. 12.6. Model 1 (Eq. 15), $\theta_1 = 1.6E - 3$, $\theta_2 = 6.4E - 5$, no stochastic influences.

Model 2. This is a stochastic variant of Equation 15 in which all parameters have the same values as in Model 1. Yet the growth process $z(t)$ is not observed directly, but instead the observations are corrupted by additive measurement error. That is, the manifest process is defined by $y(t) = z(t) + e(t)$, where $e(t)$ is taken to be a Gaussian white noise process (discussed earlier) with mean zero and variance equal to 1. Notice that the latent growth process $z(t)$ is deterministic, whereas the manifest process $y(t)$ is stochastic. The time series $y(t)$ generated by means of Model 2 is depicted in Fig. 12.7.

Model 3. This is also a stochastic variant of Equation 15 in which all parameters have the same values as in Model 1. An innovations process $a(t)$ is added to Equation 15 in the following way: $z(t + 1) = \theta_1 z(t)^2 + \theta_2 z(t)^3 + j(t + 1) + a(t + 1)$. The innovations process $a(t)$ is taken to be Gaussian white noise with mean zero and variance equal to 1. Notice that, in contrast to Models 1 and 2, $z(t)$ is now a stochastic nonlinear growth process. Notice also that $z(t)$ is a manifest process. The time series $z(t)$ generated by means of Model 3 is depicted in Fig. 12.8.

Model 4. This is combination of Models 2 and 3. Again all parameters have the same values as in Model 1. An innovations process is added to Equation 15 in exactly the same way as described for Model 3. Moreover, the stochastic growth process $z(t)$ thus defined is latent, whereas the associated manifest process $y(t)$ is obtained by adding measurement noise to

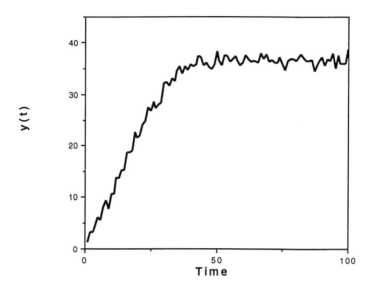

FIG. 12.7. Model 2 (Eq. 15 + measurement noise), θ parameters as in Model 1, WNV noise = 1.0.

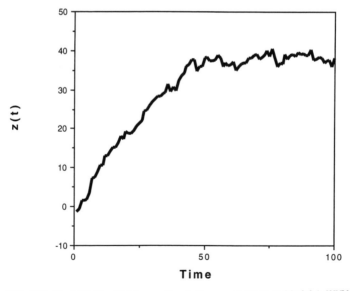

FIG. 12.8. Model 3 (Eq. 15 + innovations), θ parameters as in Model 1, WNV innovations = 1.

286

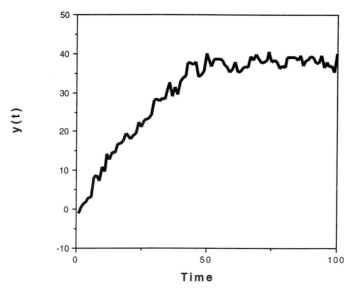

FIG. 12.9. Model 4 (Eq. 15 + measurement noise and innovations), WNV noise
= 1, WNV innovations = 1.

$z(t)$ in exactly the same way as described for Model 2. The time series $y(t)$
generated by means of Model 4 is depicted in Fig. 12.9.

Direct Fit of Van Geert's Cubic Growth Model

Equation 15 can be fitted directly by means of the EKF to the time series
depicted in Figs. 12.6–12.9. Given that the cubic growth model is univariate
and has three parameters, the extended state is four-dimensional. Hence
the state evolution is described by

$$x_1(t + 1) = x_1(t) + x_2(t)x_1(t)^2 + x_3(t)x_1(t)^3 + x_4(t) + w_1(t + 1)$$
$$x_i(t + 1) = x_i(t) + w_i(t + 1) \quad i = 2,3,4 \tag{16}$$

whereas the measurement model is given by

$$y(t) = x_1(t) + v(t) \tag{17}$$

In Models 1–4 the parameters are taken to be deterministic and constant.
Because the EKF appears to perform satisfactorily without invoking the
option of covariance modification (discussed earlier), we do not use this
option and delete $w_i(t)$, $i = 2,3,4$. Hence the second line of Equation 16 simply

reads: $x_i(t + 1) = x_i(t)$, representing the evolution of the parameters θ_1, θ_2, and j for $i = 2,3,4$, respectively.

Model 1 then is obtained by also deleting $w_1(t)$ and $v(t)$ from Equations 16 and 17. Model 2 is obtained by dropping $w_1(t)$ from Equation 16 but retaining $v(t)$ in Equation 17. Model 3 implies that $w_1(t)$ is retained in Equation 16 but $v(t)$ is deleted from Equation 17. Finally, Model 4 is obtained by keeping $w_1(t)$ and $v(t)$ in Equations 16 and 17.

The EKF estimates for Models 1–4 are presented in Table 12.1. For each model Table 12.1 presents the values of $x_i(100|100)$, $i = 2,3,4$, that is, the recursive parameter estimates at the final time point $t = 100$. Because the parameters in Equation 15 are taken to be constant, their recursive estimates obtained at the final time point are the most reliable because they are based on all available information. Estimated standard errors are given in Table 12.1. To illustrate, the evolution of the recursive EKF parameter estimates, $x_i(t|t)$, $t = 51, \ldots, 100$, $i = 2,3,4$ and the associated standard errors for Model 4 are depicted in Figs. 12.10–12.12. Only the parameter estimates at tne final 50 time points are given in order to be able to show the fine details of their convergent behavior.

The results given in Table 12.1 show that the true parameter values in the four variants of the cubic growth model are faithfully recovered by means of the EKF. This is particularly noteworthy because the length of the time series generated according to each model is short. Moreover, as soon

TABLE 12.1
EKF Parameter Estimates in the Cubic Growth Model at Final Time Point

True Value	Estimated Value	Standard Error
Model 1: No measurement noise and no innovations		
1.60E − 03	1.60E − 03	1.04E − 04
6.40E − 05	6.40E − 05	6.27E − 06
1.00	1.00	1.78E − 04
Model 2: Measurement noise and no innovations		
1.60E − 03	1.57E − 03	2.16E − 04
6.40E − 05	6.35E − 05	5.37E − 05
1.00	1.08	3.57E − 02
Model 3: Innovations and no measurement noise		
1.60E − 03	1.99E − 03	1.35E − 03
6.40E − 05	7.00E − 05	3.40E − 05
1.00	0.83	0.24
Model 4: Measurement noise and innovations		
1.60E − 03	1.93E − 03	1.52E − 03
6.40E − 05	7.14E − 05	3.66E − 05
1.00	1.11	0.33

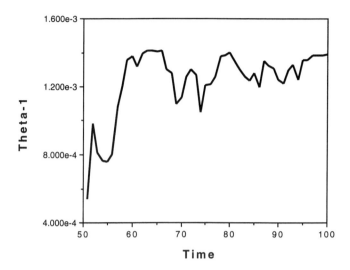

FIG. 12.10A. EKF estimation in Model 4, WNV innovations = 1, WNV noise = 1, θ_1 true = 1.6E − 3.

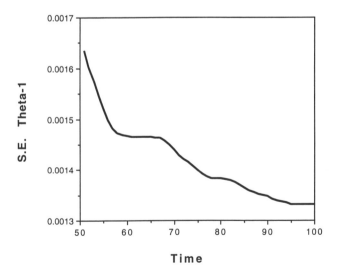

FIG. 12.10B. EKF estimation in Model 4, WNV innovations = 1, WNV noise = 1, standard error θ_1.

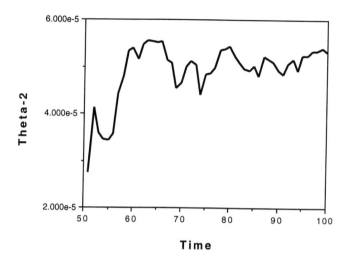

FIG. 12.11A. EKF estimation in Model 4, WNV innovations = 1, WNV noise = 1, θ_2 true = 6.4E − 5.

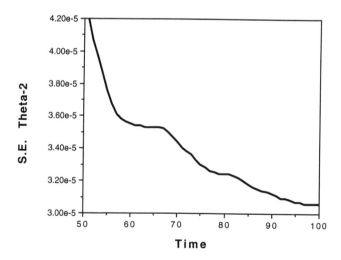

FIG. 12.11B. EKF estimation in Model 4, WNV innovations = 1, WNV noise = 1, standard error θ_2.

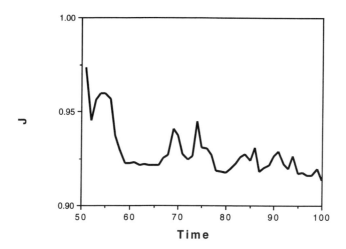

FIG. 12.12A. EKF estimation in Model 4, WNV innovations = 1, WNV noise = 1, *J* true = 1.0.

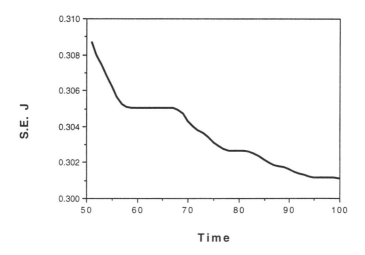

FIG. 12.12B. EKF estimation in Model 4, WNV innovations = 1, WNV noise = 1, standard error *J*.

as the mean level of a time series reaches a stable value, the information conveyed by additional observations diminishes. Only during the limited time span in which the growth process increases from zero to its asymptotic mean value are observations maximally informative regarding the underlying dynamics. This would seem to restrict even further the information content of the short time series shown in Figs. 12.6–12.9.

GENERAL DISCUSSION AND CONCLUSION

We first discuss some general points concerning the illustrative direct fits of nonlinear dynamical models presented in the two preceding sections. Then we proceed with a consideration of additional issues of increasingly general scope related to recursive estimation, including an outline of a powerful generalization of the estimation scheme. In closing we address a new challenge in the statistical analysis of stochastic nonlinear dynamical models that might set the stage for new developments.

The results of the direct model fits reported in the preceding sections appear to be quite satisfctory. The EKF is capable of yielding reliable parameter estimates under what seem to be rather difficult circumstances, at least from a statistical point of view, namely, a bimodal process undergoing an irreversible phase transition and a short, transient growth process. Moreover, each model is fitted to a singular realization of a process ($N = 1$). Hence our approach would seem to be especially appropriate for applications to the idiosyncratic noisy time series typically observed in the biological and social sciences. In case one has available an ensemble of multiple realizations of the same process ($N =$ many) a straightforwardly extended version of the EKF can be applied simultaneously to these multiple realizations. In empirical applications, however, it first has to be ascertained that the multiple observed series indeed constitute realizations of the same process. As to this, Nesselroade and Molenaar (1995) presented a convenient statistical test to identify a homogeneous subset of multiple realizations of the same linear state-space model and related the issue of homogeneity at stake to the statistical mechanical concept of ergodicity.

The EKF was applied to simulated time series that were generated at equidistant time points and did not contain missing values. Yet the EKF could have been accommodated rather easily to time series observed at irregular time points and/or having missing values. We do not elaborate these and related issues concerning applied time-series modeling, such as a posteriori model validation, but refer the reader to the existing literature (e.g, Shumway, 1988; Tong, 1990). There are a few additional points, however, that have not been addressed in our illustrative applications of the EKF but that require special mention. First, the options of covariance modification and iteration were invoked in the application of the EKF considered in the parameter estimation section, whereas these options were not used in the next section. The decision of whether or not to use these options was based on a comparison of the estimated and true parameter values. The question of when to use one or both of these options in applications to empirical data can also be answered in this operational way. That is, one carries out a pilot simulation study of the model to be applied to empirical data in order to decide whether or not to use these options. Second, attention has been restricted in the two preceding sections to recursive estimation of the focal model parameters. The covariance functions $V(u)\delta(u)$ of the measurement error (cf. Equation 4) and $W(u)\delta(u)$ of the innovations (cf. Equation 2) have been fixed at their true values (setting aside the invocation of covariance modification in the parameter estimation section). Yet in applications to real data these covariance functions will usually be unknown and hence constitute nuisance parameters that have to be estimated also. Recursive schemes for the estimation of the covariance functions concerned can be found in Chen (1993). We next outline an alternative approach in which focal and nuisance parameters can be treated on equal footing. Third, it may of course happen in empirical applications that a given model (*Ansatz*) does not yield a satisfactory fit to the data. One then faces the task of trying to modify the initial model in such a way that a satisfactory fit is obtained. Although such model modification is a relatively straightforward affair in linear state-space modeling, it can be notoriously difficult in the context of nonlinear dynamical modeling where canonical forms from which suitable modifications can be derived are lacking. Some guidelines can be found in Priestley and Heravi (1986; see also Priestley, 1988; Tong, 1990), but this is an issue that at present is mainly unresolved.

At a more general level the question of how to determine identifiability of multivariate parametric state-space models figures predominantly. That is, can the unknown parameters be uniquely determined from the observed data? In fact, this question should be answered affirmatively before a direct model fit can be sensibly carried out. For linear state-space models Molenaar (1995a) presents a practical solution that consists of (a) Fourier transformation of a given parametric model to the frequency domain, (b) rewriting the frequency-dependent complex-valued model as a real-valued analogue, and (c) applying standard software for covariance structure models (Bekker, Merckens, & Wansbeek, 1994) to the real-valued analogue. For nonlinear state-space models, however, the situation is much less clear. The only practically feasible scheme we know of has been proposed by Lecourtier, Lamnabhi-Lagarrigue, and Walter (1988). It pertains to continuous-time, deterministic, nonlinear state-space models and hence can be conceived of as a necessary criterion for the stochastic nonlinear models considered in the two preceding sections (cf. Molenaar, 1995a). At present a suitable (alphanumerical) implementation of this scheme appears to be lacking. Furthermore, what is ultimately needed is a sufficient criterion for identifiability of stochastic nonlinear systems. Clearly, this is an issue that deserves much more dedicated effort.

We already alluded to the special recursive schemes that are required to estimate the covariance functions of the innovations and the measurement noise. That is, these covariance functions cannot be simply estimated by means of the EKF along with the other model parameters. It is possible, however, to define an alternative, general estimation approach with which all unknown parameters in a state-space model can be estimated simultaneously. Basically this approach consists of the following steps:

1. Construct the likelihood function for a given time series $y(t)$, $t = 1,2,$ $\dots,T$ and a given parametric state-space model. Notice that this likelihood function involves the unknown values of the latent state $x(t)$, $t = 1,2,\dots,T$.

2. Choose plausible initial values for the unknown parameters in the state-space model.

3. Using the current parameter estimates, estimate the latent state evolution by means of the EKF.

4. Using the current estimate of the latent state process, maximize the likelihood function with respect to the parameters. This yields updated parameter estimates.

5. Go to step 3 until the value of the likelihood function no longer increases.

Together, steps 1–5 constitute an instance of the expectation–maximization (EM) algorithm in which the expectation step is obtained by means of the EKF. For a detailed description in the context of linear state-space models with constant unknown parameters, the reader is referred to, for example, Shumway (1988). An extension to linear state-space models with arbitrarily time-varying parameters is given in Molenaar (1994). For applications to nonnormally distributed time series the reader is referred to the excellent monograph by Fahrmeir and Tutz (1994). At present, applications to parameter estimation in nonlinear state-space models seem to be lacking in the published literature.

As was already indicated in the introductory section, the possibility of fitting parametric models directly to noisy time series constitutes the necessary next step in extending the new paradigm of nonlinear dynamics to the biological and social sciences. Nonlinear dynamics is especially pertinent to the study of developmental processes because it provides us with powerful causal mechanisms explaining the emergence of structural and functional organization in ways that transcend the traditional categories of genetical and environmental influences (Molenaar, 1986). Self-organization is a distinctive characteristic of nonlinear dynamical systems and typically involves the occurrence of bifurcations, that is, sudden qualitative changes in the configuration of equilibrium states regulating ongoing system behavior. In the jargon of nonlinear dynamics, each equilibrium acts as an attractor in state-space and a bifurcation concerns a sudden change in the types and number of such attractors as a result of continuous variation of system parameters. In most applications in the biological and social sciences, attention has been restricted to so-called local bifurcations like the Hopf bifurcation (a point attractor becomes unstable and is replaced by a limit cycle). Yet the variety of possible bifurcations is much larger, including global bifurctions, crises, and dynamic bifurcations (cf. Ott, 1993). We expect that the recursive estimation schemes presented here will help uncover the existence of these more intricate types of bifurcations in empirical applications. For instance, in the study of dynamic bifurcations it is required to know the detailed trajectory of time-varying system parameters. An elementary example of how this can be accomplished was given in the section on parameter estimation.

In closing we would like to indicate that the versatility of EKF-based recursive estimation schemes also pertains to the modeling of deterministic chaos. A successful application to parameter estimation in the bivariate Ikeda map, given a univariate observed time series confounded with white noise measurement error, is reported in Molenaar (1995b). In this context Casdagli et al. (1992) proved the possible breakdown of Takens's embedding theorem, according to which the latent state of a multivariate map can always be faithfully reconstructed from univariate observations. That is, they show (taking the Ikeda map as an example) that the presence of measurement error of even a very small magnitude can completely destroy the fidelity of the reconstructed latent state. This raises new and important challenges concerning the feasibility of any analysis of noisy time-series data generated by a nonlinear system displaying deterministic chaos. In particular, these challenges concern the indirect approaches that are inspired by Takens' embedding theorem. It appears, however, that for the magnitudes of measurement noise considered by Casdagli et al. (1992), parameter estimation in the Ikeda map by means of the EKF still yields reliable results (Molenaar, 1995b).

Clearly, the direct modeling of chaotic time series can succeed in situations where indirect approaches fail. In this chapter we stressed the importance of the direct fit of nonlinear dynamic models in general and presented a definite recursive estimation scheme (and some variants thereof) to accomplish this. We hope that this will further enhance application of the powerful paradigm of nonlinear dynamics in the biological and social sciences.

REFERENCES

Basar, E. (Ed.). (1990). *Chaos in brain function*. Berlin: Springer-Verlag.
Bekker, P. A., Merckens, A., & Wansbeek, T. J. (1994). *Identification, equivalent models, and computer algebra*. San Diego: Academic Press.
Bouleau, N., & Lepingle, D. (1994). *Numerical methods for stochastic processes*. New York: Wiley.
Caines, P. E. (1988). *Linear stochastic systems*. New York: Wiley.
Casdagli, M., Eubank, S., Farmer, J. D., & Gibson, J. (1992). State space reconstruction in the presence of noise. *Physica D, 51*, 52–98.
Chen, G. (Ed.). (1993). *Approximate Kalman filtering*. Singapore: World Scientific Publishing Company.
Chung, K. L. (1982). *Lectures from Markov processes to Brownian motion*. New York: Springer-Verlag.
Fahrmeir, L., & Tutz, G. (1994). *Multivariate statistical modeling based on generalized linear models*. Berlin: Springer-Verlag.
Gardiner, C. W. (1990). *Handbook of stochastic methods for physics, chemistry and the natural sciences* (2nd ed.). Berlin: Springer Verlag.
Gilmore, R. (1981). *Catastrophe theory for scientists and engineers*. New York: Wiley.
Goodwin, G. E., & Sin, K. S. (1984). *Adaptive filtering, prediction, and control*. Englewood Cliffs, NJ: Prentice Hall.
Grossberg, S. (1982). *Studies of mind and brain: Neural principles of learning, perception, development, cognition and motor control*. Dordrecht: Reidel.
Haken, H. (1983). *Advanced synergetics*. Berlin: Springer-Verlag.
Haken, H., Kelso, J. A. S., & Bunz, H. (1985). A theoretical model of phase transitions in human hand movements. *Biological Cybernetics, 51*, 347–356.
Hannan, E. J. (1970). *Multiple time series*. New York: Wiley.
Hannan, E. J., & Deistler, M. (1988). *The statistical theory of linear systems*. New York: Wiley.
Hofbauer, J., & Sigmund, K. (1988). *The theory of evolution and dynamical systems*. Cambridge: Cambridge University Press.
Isidori, A. (1989). *Nonlinear control systems* (2nd ed.). Berlin: Springer-Verlag.
Jazwinski, A. H. (1970). *Stochastic processes and filtering theory*. New York: Academic Press.
Kalman, R. E., Falb, P., & Arbib, M. (1969). *Topics in mathematical system theory*. New York: McGraw-Hill.
Koopmans, L. H. (1974). *The spectral analysis of time series*. New York: Academic Press.
Lecourtier, Y., Lamnabhi-Lagarrigue, F., & Walter, E. (1988). Volterra and generating power series approaches to identifiability testing. In E. Walter (Ed.), *Identification of parametric models* (pp. 50–66). Oxford: Pergamon Press.
Molenaar, P. C. M. (1986). On the impossibility of acquiring more powerful structures: A neglected alternative. *Human Development, 29*, 245–251.
Molenaar, P. C. M. (1994). Dynamic latent variable models in developmental psychology. In A. von Eye & C. C. Clogg (Eds.), *Analysis of latent variables in developmental research* (pp. 155–180). Newbury Park, CA: Sage.
Molenaar, P. C. M. (1995a). Dynamic factor analysis of multivariate (non-)stationary time series.
Molenaar, P. C. M. (1995b, July). *Recursive estimation in nonlinear state-space models*. Paper presented at the 9th European Meeting of the Psychometric Society, Leiden, The Netherlands.
Molenaar, P. C. M., & Hartelman, P. (1996). Catastrophe theory of stage transitions in metric and discrete stochastic systems. In A. von Eye & C. C. Clogg (Eds.), *Categorical variables in developmental research* (pp. 107–130). New York: Academic Press.
Nesselroade, J. R., & Molenaar, P. C. M. (1995). Pooling lagged covariance structures based on short, multivariate time-series for dynamic factor analysis.
Nicolis, G., & Prigogine, I. (1977). *Self-organization in nonequilibrium systems: From dissipative structures to order through fluctuations*. New York: Wiley.

Ott, E. (1993). *Chaos in dynamical systems*. Cambridge: Cambridge University Press.

Priestley, M. B. (1988). *Non-linear and non-stationary time series analysis*. London: Academic Press.

Priestley, M. B., & Heravi, S. M. (1986). Identification of non-linear systems using general state-dependent models. In J. Gani & M. B. Priestley (Eds.), Essays in time series and allied processes [Special volume]. *Journal of Applied Probability, 23A*, 257–272.

Sage, A. P., & Melsa, J. L. (1971). *Estimation theory: With applications to communications and control*. New York: McGraw-Hill.

Schöner, G., Haken, H., & Kelso, J. A. S. (1986). A stochastic theory of phase transitions in human hand movement. *Biological Cybernetics, 53*, 247–257.

Shumway, R. H. (1988). *Applied statistical time series analysis*. Englewood Cliffs, NJ: Prentice Hall.

Thom, R. (1975). *Structural stability and morphogenesis*. Reading: Benjamin.

Toda, M. (1989). *Nonlinear waves and solitons*. Dordrecht: Kluwer.

Tong, H. (1990). *Non-linear time series: A dynamical system approach*. Oxford: Oxford University Press.

Van der Maas, H. L. J., & Molenaar, P. C. M. (1992). Stagewise cognitive development: An application of catastrophe theory. *Psychological Review, 99*, 395–417.

Van Geert, P. (1991). A dynamic systems model of cognitive and language growth. *Psychological Review, 98*, 3–53.

Van Geert, P. (1994). *Dynamic systems and development: Change between complexity and chaos*. New York: Harvester-Wheatsheaf.

AUTHOR INDEX

SUBJECT INDEX